OXFAM COLL

YEATS ANNUAL NO. 6

Frontispiece: W. B. Yeats Lithograph on card, 277 × 200 mm. The sketch was done by Ivan Opffer in Copenhagen, in 1923, when Yeats travelled to Stockholm for the Nobel Prize ceremony. Private Collection, London.

YEATS ANNUAL No. 6

Edited by Warwick Gould

First published 1988

Published by
THE MACMILLAN PRESS LTD
Houndmills, Basingstoke, Hampshire RG21 2XS
and London
Companies and representatives
throughout the world

Typeset by Wessex Typesetters
(Division of The Eastern Press Ltd)
Frome, Somerset

Printed in Hong Kong

British Library Cataloguing in Publication Data
Yeats Annual—No. 6
1. Yeats, W. B.—Periodicals
821′.8   PR5907
ISBN 0–333–39072–5
ISSN 0278–7687

Contents

List of Abbreviations

The works listed below are cited in the texts by abbreviation and page number. Some individual essays use additional abbreviations, as explained in the appropriate notes.

Au   *Autobiographies* (London: Macmillan, 1955).

AV A   *A Critical Edition of Yeats's* A Vision (1925), (eds) George Mills Harper and Walter Kelly Hood (London: Macmillan 1978).

AV B   *A Vision* (London: Macmillan, 1962).

CL 1   *The Collected Letters of W. B. Yeats*, volume one 1865–95, (eds) John Kelly and Eric Domville (Oxford: Clarendon Press, 1985).

E&I   *Essays and Introductions* (London and New York: Macmillan, 1961).

Ex   *Explorations*, sel. Mrs W. B. Yeats (London: Macmillan, 1962; New York: Macmillan, 1963).

L   *The Letters of W. B. Yeats* (ed.) Allan Wade (London: Rupert Hart-Davis, 1954; New York: Macmillan, 1955).

LDW   *Letters on Poetry from W. B. Yeats to Dorothy Wellesley*, intro. Kathleen Raine (London and New York: Oxford University Press, 1964).

LMR   *Ah, Sweet Dancer: W. B. Yeats Margot Ruddock, A Correspondence* (ed.) Roger McHugh (London and New York: Macmillan, 1970).

LNI   *Letters to the New Island* (ed.) Horace Reynolds (Cambridge, Mass.: Harvard University Press, 1934).

LRB   *The Correspondence of Robert Bridges and W. B. Yeats* (ed.) Richard J. Finneran (London: Macmillan, 1977; Toronto: Macmillan of Canada, 1978).

LTSM   *W. B. Yeats and T. Sturge Moore: Their Correspondence, 1901–1937* (ed.) Ursula Bridge (London: Routledge & Kegan Paul; New York: Oxford University Press, 1953).

LTWBY   *Letters to W. B. Yeats* (eds) Richard J. Finneran, George Mills Harper and William M. Murphy (London: Macmillan, New York: Columbia University Press, 1977).

Mem	*Memoirs* (ed.) Denis Donoghue (London: Macmillan, 1972; New York: Macmillan, 1973).
Myth	*Mythologies* (London and New York: Macmillan, 1959).
OBMV	*The Oxford Book of Modern Verse, 1892–1935*. Chosen by W. B. Yeats (Oxford: Clarendon, 1936).
SB	*The Speckled Bird, With Variant Versions* (ed.) William H. O'Donnell (Toronto: McClelland and Stewart, 1976).
SS	*The Senate Speeches of W. B. Yeats* (ed.) Donald R. Pearce (London: Faber & Faber, 1961).
UP1	*Uncollected Prose by W. B. Yeats*, vol. 1 (ed.) John P. Frayne (London: Macmillan; New York: Columbia University Press, 1970).
UP2	*Uncollected Prose by W. B. Yeats*, vol. 2 (eds) John P. Frayne and Colton Johnson (London: Macmillan, 1975; New York: Columbia University Press, 1976).
VP	*The Variorum Edition of the Poems of W. B. Yeats* (eds) Peter Allt and Russell K. Alspach (New York and London: Macmillan, 1957). (To be cited from the corrected third printing [1966] or later printings.)
VPl	*The Variorum Edition of the Plays of W. B. Yeats* (ed.) Russell K. Alspach (London and New York: Macmillan, 1966). (To be cited from the corrected second printing [1966] or later printings.)
VSR	*The Secret Rose: Stories by W. B. Yeats: A Variorum Edition* (eds) Phillip L. Marcus, Warwick Gould & Michael J. Sidnell (Ithaca: Cornell University Press, 1981).
Wade	Allan Wade, *A Bibliography of the Writings of W. B. Yeats*, 3rd edn, rev. Russell K. Alspach (London: Rupert Hart-Davis, 1968).
YA	*Yeats Annual* (to be followed by number and date).
YAACTS	*Yeats: an Annual of Critical and Textual Studies* (to be followed by number and date).
YL	Edward O'Shea, *A Descriptive Catalog of W. B. Yeats's Library* (New York & London: Garland Publishing, Inc., 1985).
YO	*Yeats and The Occult* (ed.) George Mills Harper (Toronto: Macmillan of Canada, 1975; London: Macmillan, 1975).
YT	*Yeats and The Theatre* (eds) Robert O'Driscoll and Lorna Reynolds (Toronto: Macmillan of Canada, 1975; London: Macmillan, 1975).

Editorial Board

Notes on the Contributors

Pamela Bickley teaches at W. B. Yeats's old school, now The Godolphin and Latymer School, Hammersmith, and in the English Department, Royal Holloway and Bedford New College, University of London. Her own field of research is Dante Gabriel Rossetti.

Yves Bonnefoy, the distinguished poet, holds the Chaire d'Études Comparées de la Fonction Poétique at the Collège de France.

Roy J. Booth is a Lecturer in the English Department, Royal Holloway and Bedford New College, University of London. His current research interests include sixteenth and seventeenth century poetry, and the Elizabethans in Ireland.

Richard Allen Cave is Reader in Drama in the Department of Drama and Theatre Studies, Royal Holloway and Bedford New College, University of London. The editor of *Hail and Farewell* and *The Lake*, he is author of *A Study of the Novels of George Moore* and general editor of the *Theatre in Focus* series.

Wayne K. Chapman is writing a doctoral dissertation at Washington State University on Yeats and the English Renaissance.

William J. Feeney is Professor of English at De Paul University, Chicago. He is the author of *Drama in Hardwicke Street: a History of the Irish Theatre Company* which is noticed in this volume. He is the editor of a ten-volume series of reprints of early Irish dramas.

Barton R. Friedman is Professor of English and former Chairman of Department at Cleveland State University, Ohio. He is the author of *Adventures in the Deeps of the Mind: the Cuchulain Cycle of W. B. Yeats* and of *Fabricating History: Refractions of the Revolution in France*.

R. A. Gilbert is an antiquarian bookseller who specializes in Hermetica. His *The Golden Dawn, Twilight of the Magicians* and *A. E. Waite: a Bibliography* were followed by two anthologies of writings by member of The Golden Dawn, and by *The Golden Dawn Companion*. His studies

Notes on the Contributors

include a life of A. E. Waite. He is the editor (with Michael Cox) of *The Oxford Book of English Ghost Stories*.

John Harwood is Senior Lecturer in English at The Flinders University of South Australia. He is currently working on the authorised life of Olivia Shakespear for The Macmillan Press.

Richard Londraville is Professor of English at New York State University College at Potsdam. He is the author of many articles on Yeats, Jeanne Robert Foster, and on Chinese and Japanese literature and theatre.

Colin McDowell is a public servant in the Australian Bureau of Census and Statistics and associate editor of *Scripsi*. He is the author of many articles on Yeats, *A Vision*, and Ezra Pound.

Phillip L. Marcus is Professor of English at Cornell University, and one of the general editors of The Cornell Yeats Series. The author of *Yeats and the Beginning of the Irish Renaissance*, co-editor of *The Secret Rose, Stories by W. B. Yeats: a Variorum Edition*, and editor of *The Death of Cuchulain* in the Cornell Series, he is currently working on editions of the manuscripts of *Responsibilities* and of *The Celtic Twilight & The Secret Rose* for the Macmillan *Collected Edition of the Works of W. B. Yeats*.

Stephen Parrish is Goldwin Smith Professor of English at Cornell University and is general editor of The Cornell Wordsworth. He is one of the General Editors of The Cornell Yeats Series, and is editing *The Wild Swans at Coole* manuscripts for this series.

James Pethica was educated at Merton College, Oxford. He is Junior Research Fellow at Wolfson College, Oxford, and is editing Lady Gregory's diaries, 1892–1902.

Virginia Rohan is an academic administrator at Smith College, Northampton, Massachusetts. She is currently preparing an edition of the manuscripts of Yeats's *Deirdre* for the Cornell Yeats Series.

Richard Taylor is Professor of English at Universität Bayreuth and is author of *The Drama of W. B. Yeats, Irish Myth and the Japanese No*. His *A Reader's Guide to the Plays of W. B. Yeats* was published in 1984, and he is now working upon a Variorum Edition of Pound's *Cantos*.

Deirdre Toomey is the assistant editor (with David Bindman) of *The Graphic Works of William Blake* and Research Editor of *Yeats Annual*.

Hugh Witemeyer is Professor of English at the University of New Mexico and the author of *The Poetry of Ezra Pound Forms and Renewal, 1908–1920* as well as of a study of George Eliot. With George Bornstein he has prepared a new edition of *Letters to the New Island*, a volume in the Macmillan *Collected Edition of the Works of W. B. Yeats*.

Marion Wynne-Davies wrote her doctorate at Royal Holloway and Bedford New College, University of London, on Arthurian poetry in the English Renaissance. She is currently working on *Women and Arthurian Literature: the Feminine World of Romance* for The Macmillan Press, and is editing a collection of essays on the public role of women in Renaissance fiction. She lectures at the Polytechnic of North London.

Katharine Worth is Professor of Drama and Theatre Studies and Head of Department at Royal Holloway and Bedford New College, University of London. Her books include *The Irish Drama of Europe from Yeats to Beckett* and a new edition of Yeats's *Where There is Nothing* and *The Unicorn from the Stars*.

List of Plates

Frontispiece: W. B. Yeats Lithograph on card, 277 x 200 mm. The sketch was done by Ivan Opffer in Copenhagen, in 1923, when Yeats travelled to Stockholm for the Nobel Prize ceremony. Private Collection, London.

1 A page of an early manuscript draft of *Cathleen ni Houlihan*, in the hand of Lady Gregory, with her pencilled inscription "All this mine alone/A.G.". Photograph courtesy of the Berg Collection, New York Public Library (Astor, Lenox and Tilden Foundations).

2 A page of an early manuscript draft of *Cathleen ni Houlihan*, in the hand of Lady Gregory, with her pencilled inscription "This with WBY". Photograph courtesy of the Berg Collection, New York Public Library (Astor, Lenox and Tilden Foundations).

3 Olivia Shakespear, passport photograph, 1921. Photograph courtesy and © Omar Pound.

4 Olivia Shakespear and Omar Pound at Hindhead [?], c. 1935. Photograph courtesy and © Omar Pound.

5 Olivia Shakespear and Harry Tucker at Sidmouth, c. 1935. Photograph courtesy and © Omar Pound.

6 Shri Purohit Swami. From a hand-coloured photograph, sent by the Swami to Olivia Shakespear as a Christmas Card, c. 1934. Photograph courtesy and © Omar Pound.

7 Detail of drawing of W. B. Yeats in the San Francisco *Examiner* 31 January 1904. A staff artist drew him as he was being interviewed by Ashton Stevens.

8 Studio portrait photograph of W. B. Yeats, probably done in America, c. 1914. Collection Phillip L. Marcus.

9 Studio portrait photograph of W. B. Yeats by Underwood & Underwood, New York (1920). Collection Phillip L. Marcus.

10 W. B. Yeats, Edith Shackleton Heald and Edmund Dulac at The Chantry House, Steyning, the first of a sequence of photos taken possibly on Sunday, 13 June 1937, or in the summer of 1938. Photograph courtesy of The Huntington Library.

11 Nora Shackleton Heald, W. B. Yeats, Helen Beauclerk and (in front) Edith Shackleton Heald, The Chantry House, Steyning, 1937 or 1938. Photograph courtesy of The Huntington Library.

Editor's Note

In *Yeats Annual No. 6* we are very proud to publish Yves Bonnefoy's translation of "Nineteen Hundred and Nineteen": it is something of an event in the history of Yeats's reputation to be able to register his impact upon a distinguished French poet. This issue also records Yeats's impact upon America in 1904 and in 1920. On the latter occasion he inspired John Quinn's "An Evening in New York with W. B. Yeats", here printed for the first time. It has been found necessary to cut some of Quinn's own conversation, on a principle John Butler Yeats might perhaps have endorsed. Padraic Colum once recalled JBY's response to his own suggestion that Quinn talked well. "Yes," JBY replied, "but like all lawyers he exhausts the subject."

The rest of this issue is dominated by manuscript materials, presented and assessed, and more of these materials are being prepared and edited for future issues of *Yeats Annual*. But in spite of the significance of such contributions, we continue to look for the best critical writing, especially that devoted to reassessment of Yeats's poems. We are also pleased to provide space for unpublished images, even when they are not associated with any of the articles in a particular issue. Examples of these in the current issue are the frontispiece, the two studio portraits sold in the 1986 Gilvarry sale (Plates 8 and 9) and the sequence of photographs taken, mainly by Nora Shackleton Heald, at The Chantry House, Steyning, in 1937 or 1938 and sold at Christie's in 1978.

Dr Roy Foster of the Department of History, Birkbeck College, University of London, Malet Street, London WC1 is working upon the biography of W. B. Yeats for the Oxford University Press, and Professor Ann Saddlemyer, Director of the Graduate Centre for the Study of Drama, University of Toronto, 214 College Street, Toronto, Ontario M5T 2Z9 is working upon a biography of George Yeats. Dr John Harwood of the English Department, School of Humanities, The Flinders University of South Australia, Bedford Park, S.A. 5042 is working on an authorised biography of Olivia Shakespear for The Macmillan Press. All three would welcome information from readers.

Other bibliographical projects continue, and their compilers would also welcome assistance. Colin Smythe (P.O. Box 6, Gerrards Cross, Bucks, SL9 8EF) is working on a complete revision of the Wade/Alspach *Bibliography*, while K. P. S. Jochum (Lehrstuhl für Englische

Literaturwissenschaft, Universität Bamberg, Postfach 1549, D–8600 Bamberg) is revising his *Classified Bibliography* into *100 Years of Yeats Criticism.* Conrad Balliet (Department of English, Wittenberg University, Springfield, Ohio 45501) is compiling *W. B. Yeats: a Guide to the Manuscripts* for Garland, and Professor William H. O'Donnell, who now joins our Editorial Advisory Board, continues to add to his Preliminary Checklist of Portraits and Studio Portrait Photographs of W. B. Yeats, published in *Yeats Annual No. 3.* Professor O'Donnell is now Chairman of the English Department, Memphis State University, Memphis, Tennessee 38152.

Yeats Annual will publish a list of books dispersed from Yeats's library in a future issue, and I should be grateful to hear of such items from booksellers, librarians and collectors. Contributions to No. 8 should reach me by 1 May 1988 and those for No. 9 by the same date in 1989 at:

Department of English
Royal Holloway and Bedford New College, University of London
Egham Hill
Egham
Surrey   TW20 0EX
UK

to which address offprints, review copies, and other bibliographical information should be sent. Further information for contributors is available upon request.

Note

While this volume was in press, we learned with great regret of the death of Professor Richard Ellmann. Professor Ellmann, who had provided the editor with wise and kindly advice on a number of submissions to this journal, had just selected scholars and colleagues and friends to contribute to *Yeats Annual No. 7* which was to have been a volume of essays in his honour and will now be one in tribute to his pioneering work on W. B. Yeats. The essays will be edited by his colleague at Emory University, Professor Ronald Schuchard, and the volume will appear on the fiftieth anniversary of W. B. Yeats's death, in January 1989.

WARWICK GOULD

Acknowledgements

I am indebted to Miss Anne Yeats and Mr Michael B. Yeats for permission to use both published and unpublished materials by W. B. Yeats in this volume, as well as being indebted to both of them for assisting many of the contributors in making unpublished materials available to them. Other unpublished materials by Lady Gregory have been made available by Colin Smythe, on behalf of Anne de Winton and Catherine Kennedy. The unpublished writings of John Quinn have been made available through the courtesy of Dr Thomas Conroy. The cover design, adapted from Thomas Sturge Moore's designs for H. P. R. Finberg's translation of *Axël* (1925), is reproduced in this form by permission of Miss Riette Sturge Moore to whom I owe an especial debt of thanks.

For permission to reproduce the images to be found in the plates of this book, I am indebted to Mrs Betty à Beckett Opffer, Omar Pound, Professor Phillip L. Marcus, the Huntington Library, and the Berg Collection, New York Public Library (Astor, Lenox and Tilden Foundations), Raymond Yeates, the Abbey Theatre, Ms Pamela Brunger Scott of *The San Francisco Examiner*, Michael Hewson, Catherine Fahy and the staff of the National Library of Ireland, Dr Lola Szladits and Mr Donald Anderle of the Rare Books and Manuscripts Division of the New York Public Library, and the Department of Special Collections, State University of New York at Stony Brook were all very helpful.

Numerous research libraries, such as the Harry Ransome Humanities Research Center, University of Texas, Austin, the Washington State University Library, The British Library, including the Newspaper Library at Colindale and the staff of the North Library, the University of London Library were of great assistance to a number of contributors including the editor, and have been thanked separately elsewhere in this volume.

Linda Shaughnessy and Esther de Burgh Thomas of A. P. Watt & Co., Kim Scott Walwyn and Katie Ryde of the Oxford University Press, Roy Foster of Birkbeck College, University of London, and John Kelly of St John's College, Oxford, were of great assistance in respect of permissions. Frances Arnold and Tim Farmiloe of the Macmillan Press were particularly helpful during the preparation of this volume, as were a number of colleagues at Royal Holloway and Bedford New College, University of London. David Ross supplied many photographs, David Ward and Angela Carter provided much assistance in the library, and Valerie Murr and Christina See provided much-needed secretarial skills.

A host of friends and colleagues has again provided bibliographical information: most have been thanked elsewhere. Others who helped at various stages, including with the reading of many submissions, include the Editors of the Advisory Board, Professor James Lovic Allen, Harry Cockerham, Richard Allen Cave, Martin Dodsworth, Professor Richard Ellmann, R. A. Gilbert, Professor George Mills Harper, John Harwood, Professor Ruth Nevo, Roger Nyle Parisious, Professor Stephen Parrish, Professor Ann Saddlmyer, Professor Tetsuro Sano, Professor Richard Taylor, Professor Donald Torchiana. The contributors are as indebted as the editor to the alert and learned curiosity of Deirdre Toomey, who as Research Editor has again found ways of making this a better book.

WARWICK GOULD

ARTICLES

"Our Kathleen": Yeats's Collaboration with Lady Gregory in the Writing of *Cathleen ni Houlihan*

James Pethica

When explaining in the preface to his *Plays in Prose and Verse* in 1922 how often Lady Gregory had collaborated with him in playwriting, Yeats concluded that of the eleven plays in the volume only two could be considered "wholly" his work (*VPl* 1306). So extensive was the collaboration in the years between Lady Gregory's first tentative contribution of "a sentence here and there"[1] to *Diarmuid and Grania* in 1900, and the last occasion of their working together in 1927,[2] that even its full range remains uncertain. For besides contributing abundantly to each other's work – Yeats's influence, as critic, on Lady Gregory's plays being no less considerable than her more direct contribution to his – they worked together on numerous other projects: writing scenarios for Douglas Hyde, constructing an acting version of *Deirdre of the Sorrows* from the fragmented mass of manuscripts left by Synge at his death, and, throughout their time at the Abbey, acting as critics and "playdoctors" to the hundreds of scripts submitted for their consideration.[3]

Yet though both writers frequently acknowledged the collaborative nature of their partnership, little attempt has been made to clarify either the degree or dynamics of their work together. In part this may be accounted for by the persistence of a stereotypical view of Lady Gregory as merely Yeats's patron, Abbey Theatre factotum, and accessory to genius, rather than as an artist whose assistance and counsel he valued and sought; and in part by a sense of unease that two such unequal talents should have been so closely involved (Lady Gregory had herself been quick to insinuate that Yeats's turbulent collaboration with George Moore over *Diarmuid and Grania* was undesirable, on the grounds that it was an alliance between "a man of genius and a man of talent"[4]). When not simply ignoring the partnership, many early critics either discounted Yeats's acknowledgements of Lady Gregory's contributions to his work as flattery and overstatement, or roundly deplored such collaborative

3

influence as they were prepared to admit. Forrest Reid, for example, dismissed the "new note" her involvement sounded in Yeats's prose plays as being not in even "superficial harmony with that of Mr Yeats's genius", and specifically denounced the Kiltartan idiom she introduced to the revised edition of *Stories of Red Hanrahan* as "monotonous, facile . . . charmless" and "distinctly boring".[5] More recently, with a "mountainous record of the relationship"[6] available in the form of correspondence, drafts of plays and other manuscript material, the extent of the collaboration has been more readily acknowledged; yet the impression prevails that assessments of the creative partnership are bound to remain controversial and inconclusive. As Richard Finneran has remarked:

> Given the nature of their collaboration, as well as the state of the surviving manuscripts (a manuscript in Lady Gregory's hand, for instance, could have been dictated by Yeats), it seems essentially impossible to assign a particular passage to one or the other.[7]

While this supposition holds true for most of the manuscripts, a number of them do provide either direct evidence of authorial responsibility, or compelling general indications of the respective contributions made by each writer. Moreover, the manuscripts also provide a wealth of other evidence valuable towards characterising the nature of the collaboration. Such a characterisation is indeed of greater value than the simple apportionment where possible of passages or sections to either writer, since at its most intense the partnership involved a genuine creative interdependence far removed from piecemeal connection of individual efforts. As Lady Gregory remarked of *The Rising of the Moon* in a letter of 1903: "Yeats helped me, as I helped him in *Cathleen* and the *Pot of Broth*. It is wonderful in playwriting how one mind seems to supplement another."[8]

The most striking example of such direct evidence occurs in an early manuscript draft of *Cathleen ni Houlihan*, now held by the Berg Collection. Providing considerable insight into the process of composition of the play, the draft resolves much of the controversy which has surrounded Lady Gregory's part in the work. For although it was an "open secret"[9] in Dublin that *Cathleen ni Houlihan* had been jointly written, and Yeats's own notes freely acknowledged Lady Gregory's assistance, no consensus has been reached as to the extent of her share in the play. Advocates of Lady Gregory have argued variously for the predominance of her hand in the work. On the basis primarily of an entry in her Journal for 1922, in which Lady Gregory recalled having written "all but all of" *Cathleen ni Houlihan*, Daniel Murphy for instance concluded that she had written the play "in its entirety".[10] Drawing on stylistic evidence and the recollections of the Gregory family, Elizabeth Coxhead likewise judged

Lady Gregory's share in the actual writing of the play to have been predominant, although, mindful of Yeats's assertion that the idea for *Cathleen ni Houlihan* had come to him in a "dream almost as distinct as a vision" (*VPl* 232), she conceded that the conceptual responsibility for the work had been his:

> Short of being actually in the library at Coole with them, one cannot put one's finger on what is his and what is hers. The naturalness and life of the peasant family (even though they do not yet speak with the richness of mature 'Kiltartan') suggest that everything is hers except the symbolic speeches of Kathleen; in a word, that he thought of it and she wrote it; and this is the assertion made to me by the Gregory family, who had many times heard it from her own lips.[11]

By contrast, Yeats's advocates have generally viewed Lady Gregory's share in the play as restricted solely to recasting the dialogue in the idiomatic Kiltartan style he so often praised in her own work. Judging the nature of the collaboration to be most accurately reflected by Yeats's remark in a lecture given shortly after Lady Gregory's death, that she "rewrote [the play] in dialect" for him, Antony Coleman concluded that to "urge a more substantial obligation . . . [would be] to misread the language of courteous gratitude" Yeats had adopted in his notes to the play.[12]

But even without the manuscript evidence itself, the accounts both Yeats and Lady Gregory gave of their partnership in playwriting make clear that their collaboration on *Cathleen ni Houlihan* must have involved a greater degree of mutuality than such broadly partisan assessments would suggest. In their autobiographical writings each recalled that Lady Gregory's involvement in Yeats's work during the first years of their friendship had been largely limited to a role as amanuensis and folklore gatherer. In numerous writings from this period, such as the series of six folklore articles begun in 1897 with "The Tribes of Danu", Yeats made extensive verbatim use of materials she had collected and recorded. But though sufficiently conscious of the extent of his debt to have felt the need by 1898 to invite her formally to assist him in work on a "big book of folk lore" (*L* 305) – a project completed more than two decades later as *Visions and Beliefs in the West of Ireland* – he evidently regarded these folklore materials more as the product of mere practical effort in collecting than as a genuine creative subsidy. Even in letters to Lady Gregory herself he referred proprietorially to the first articles compiled from her gatherings as if his alone,[13] and in his letter inviting collaboration he stressed that the "actual shaping and writing" of the projected book – in effect the creative aspect of the work – would remain solely his preserve. (Given that her materials had formed the bulk of these articles, it is unsurprising that Lady Gregory should have

harboured a grudge against Yeats for his somewhat dismissive attitude
to the "peasant talk" he had appropriated (*L* 305). Venting her
irritation in a conversation with John Quinn in 1913, she would assert,
proprietorial in her own turn, that "The Prisoners of the Gods" had in
fact been "written by her".[14])

In the course of 1901, however, the partnership entered a new phase.
As Lady Gregory recalled:

> [Yeats] was slow in coming to believe I had any gift for writing, and he
> would not encourage me to it, thinking he made better use of my
> folk-lore gatherings than I could do. It was only when I had read him
> one day in London my chapter the "Death of Cuchulain" that he came
> to look on me as a fellow writer.[15]

This first reading in February 1901 of her work towards *Cuchulain of
Muirthemne* made Yeats belatedly aware of the scope of Lady Gregory's
ability, and, establishing her as a creator in his eyes, heralded a more
intimate mode of collaboration between them, with Lady Gregory
contributing directly and abundantly to his plays. Dedicating *Where
There is Nothing* to her in 1902, he wrote elatedly of the creative
compatibility they had soon discovered:

> . . . I never did anything that went so easily and quickly, for when I
> hesitated, you had the right thought ready, and it was always you who
> gave the right turn to the phrase and gave it the ring of daily life. We
> finished several plays, of which this is the longest, in so few weeks, that
> if I were to say how few, I do not think anybody would believe me. (*VPl*
> 1292)

Nor was this phase of intense collaboration simply a matter of Lady
Gregory helping Yeats to realise projects he had already planned. Her
description in *Our Irish Theatre* of the genesis of *The Travelling Man* attests
to a complex interchange of creative impetus, and to the volatile mix of
collaborative and independent effort their partnership involved:

> *The Travelling Man* was first my idea and then we wrote it together.
> Then Mr. Yeats wrote a variant of it as a Pagan play, *The Black Horse*.
> . . . It did not please him however, and then I worked it out in my own
> way.[16]

So too, even in cases where Yeats's ideas for a play seem to have been
well developed, Lady Gregory's part in the actual process of writing
necessarily resulted in a changed conception or treatment of the work.
Notably, when seeking her help towards the revision of *Where There is
Nothing* in 1907, Yeats found that "her knowledge of the stage and her

mastery of dialogue had so increased that [his] imagination could not go neck to neck with hers" (*VPl* 712), and he eventually made over his scheme of revision for her to work out in her own way.

Cathleen ni Houlihan, written during Yeats's summer stay at Coole in 1901, was the first fruit of the new creative partnership. Work on the play was probably begun in early September, for one of the pages of the manuscript includes part of an abandoned letter from Yeats to F. R. Benson – written on Coole Park stationery, but addressed from Dublin – which almost certainly dates from late August. Yeats must have started the letter during the brief visit to the Pan-Celtic Congress which punctuated his summer in Galway, and taken it with him unfinished when returning to Coole on 29 August.[17] With typical frugality, Lady Gregory must have subsequently appropriated the discarded sheet, along with other odd scraps of stationery, for use in the draft. More certain is that the play was completed before Yeats's return to London in November. On the 24th of that month, Lady Gregory reported in a letter to Yeats from Dublin that Edward Martyn, "only just come up" from Galway, had suggested that the new work be produced by the Irish Literary Theatre the following year.[18]

The Berg Collection draft, in Lady Gregory's hand throughout, comprises 26 manuscript pages loosely contained in a penny notebook of the kind she generally used for folklore writings and drafts of plays. Inscribed on the outer cover of the notebook is the working title for the play – "The Poor Old Woman" – while on the inside cover, above the initials "A.G.", is an apparently later addition, "First sketch for Cathleen ni Houlihan". The manuscript pages, numbered here in the order in which they appear in the notebook, fall into three distinct sections, distinguished by both paper type and compositional sequence. Pages 1–10, on coarse ruled paper apparently from the notebook, and pages 11–20, on slightly larger plain sheets, together constitute a complete draft of the play, the two sections connecting at a point just after the Old Woman enters the Gillane cottage. Pages 21–6, written on miscellaneous scraps of stationery, consist of draft fragments of dialogue later incorporated between pages 11 and 18, and sectionally cancelled, presumably in the process: pages 21–3 are on small light blue Coole Park stationery (pages 22–3 comprising the outer leaves of a doublesheet, with Yeats's abandoned letter-fragment and the deleted Coole letterhead within); page 24 is on a white sheet of the same size; page 25 is on a slightly larger white sheet; and page 26 is on a single sheet of unheaded Coole letterpaper. Since these six pages consist of unconnected passages of dialogue, and appear to have been sketched solely for the second section of the main draft – their having been numbered 1–6 suggests that they are not a fragment of a complete earlier draft of the play – they are transcribed here following the main draft. Page 20 is likewise transcribed in the position it appears in the Berg notebook (even though this puts it

out of narrative sequence) to reflect that it was written at a later stage
of composition, replacing material physically cut from the bottom of
page 9.

*   *   *

The most immediately revealing features in the draft are Lady Gregory's
two pencil annotations: "All this mine alone", at the end of the first
section of ten pages, and "This with W.B.Y." at the head of the second
section. While there is no specific evidence to indicate when she added
these annotations to the manuscript, it seems unlikely that they date
from so long after the completion of the play as to be of doubtful accuracy
or candour. The satisfied tone apparent in "All this mine alone" is
particularly suggestive of recent accomplishment, and Lady Gregory
would have been less likely to note her personal share in the work so
self-consciously once close collaboration with Yeats had become
relatively routine for her.

The first annotation confirms what might have been inferred from
Yeats's own notes to the play: that the cottage scene which leads up to
the entrance of the Old Woman was entirely Lady Gregory's work. As he
recalled:

> One night I had a dream almost as distinct as a vision, of a cottage
> where there was well-being and firelight and talk of a marriage, and
> into the midst of that cottage there came an old woman in a long cloak
> . . . I thought if I could write this out as a little play I could make
> others see my dream as I had seen it, but I could not get down out of
> that high window of dramatic verse, and in spite of all you had done for
> me I had not the country speech. One has to live among the people,
> like you . . . before one can think [their] thoughts . . . and speak with
> their tongue. (*VPl* 232)

In affirming that Lady Gregory's ability to reproduce the "country
speech" needed for the play was only possible because of her intimate
knowledge of the country people and her ability to "think" like them, the
passage effectively acknowledges her responsibility not only for the
idiom of the peasant dialogue, but also for its internal logic. Yeats, in
other words, had conceived of the cottage setting in general terms – as a
place of "well-being" to be disrupted by Cathleen ni Houlihan's call –
but the realization of the scene was dependent on Lady Gregory's greater
sympathy for and dramatic sense of peasant life. In his 1908 preface to
The Unicorn from the Stars he acknowledged this more specifically, writing
that her skill in representing "the country mind and country speech"
had been essential in *Cathleen ni Houlihan* to counter his own tendency to
"symbolise rather than to represent life" (*VPl* 1295–6).

But while Yeats's notes are vague as to the practical nature of Lady Gregory's help, the manuscript draft makes clear that she worked independently in developing the opening section of the play. The manner in which the first section ends just after the arrival of the Old Woman suggests that after discussing Yeats's scenario the writers agreed that she alone should draft the cottage scene – individuating the peasant family and establishing a context for the dramatic climax – and that only then would Yeats become directly involved, introducing and taking responsibility for the central symbolic character of Cathleen. (The probability of such a sequence is strengthened by Willie Fay's report to William Boyle that Lady Gregory had written all the play "except the part of 'Cathleen'".[19] Fay almost certainly derived so specific an account direct from Yeats, who privately acknowledged Lady Gregory's share in the work on a number of occasions.[20]) Pages 1–10 of the surviving manuscript may even represent Lady Gregory's first attempt at writing the scene, for although they include few revisions or deletions, the preliminary nature of the work is clear from the hasty manner in which Michael's account of the "bargain" has been left completely undeveloped and much other dialogue has been left in indirect speech. Confusion between "Bridget" and "Winifred" as the mother's name likewise suggests an early stage of composition.

But even in its rudimentary form this section of the draft approximates closely to the final text of the play. Much of the dialogue was retained with little or no change in the published version, with the sequence of action reorganized rather than radically modified. Lady Gregory may well have resisted substantial revision of the scene, for she certainly did so when the play was finally produced in April 1902. When Yeats wrote to her shortly after the first production, suggesting that an element of foreboding should be introduced early in the action to help prepare for the sudden change of intensity and mood following Cathleen's entrance, her response was firmly discouraging: "I hope you won't alter Kathaleen – I am sure the simple enjoyment of a comfortable life, without any shadow of what is to happen, is the best opening."[21] Having observed, however, that the first audience had taken "some little while to realize the tragic meaning of Kathleen's part" (*L* 368) Yeats was convinced of the need for revision, and effected the changes notwithstanding her reluctance.

The second section of the draft, in contrast to pages 1–10, evidently involved a close and continuous collaboration between the writers; but here Lady Gregory's annotation, "This with W.B.Y.", offers no elucidation of their respective shares. Since the peasant realism of the opening section had been entirely Lady Gregory's work, she presumably retained primary responsibility for the characters she had established; her hand is distinctively present in the domestic detail of Peter's covetousness and Bridget's bustling solicitude in the second section. And given Yeats's primary interest in the central figure of Cathleen, it is likewise almost certain that the most rhetorically charged of her speeches were his work. In his preface to *The Unicorn from the Stars* Yeats indeed implied just such a division between their respective contributions to *Cathleen ni Houlihan*, differentiating pointedly between the peasant realism Lady Gregory had supplied and the "high life" of his own poetic symbolism:

> I could not get away, no matter how closely I watched the country life, from images and dreams which had all too royal blood, for they were descended like the thought of every poet from all the conquering dreams of Europe, and I wished to make that high life mix into some rough contemporary life without ceasing to be itself. . . and to do this I added another knowledge to my own. (*VPl* 1295)

Yet this emphatic distinction between the sovereignty of his own "high" poetic themes and the "rough" low-life nature of Lady Gregory's work not only marginalizes her contribution, but also crucially ignores or evades the practical question of how such professedly divergent styles came to be so successfully integrated in *Cathleen ni Houlihan*. Yeats's confident recollection of having "added" Lady Gregory's knowledge to his own implies that (like Harold Bloom's prototypical "strong poet"[22]) he simply absorbed and appropriated her talent for peasant realism as if it were a passively available raw material. But it was precisely in the fusion of realistic and supernatural or symbolic elements that Yeats failed most conspicuously in his early plays. From the awkward on-stage appearance of the angels in *The Countess Cathleen* to the burning harp and off-stage birds of *The Shadowy Waters*, his earliest attempts to dramatise the meeting of "man and phantom" or to represent supernatural effects were, as he came to recognise, at best but partial successes, in which the "reverie" could be destroyed by the slightest error of emphasis or presentation: "even if an electric lamp that should have cast but a reflected light from sky or sea, shows from behind the post of a door, I discover at once the proud fragility of dreams" (*VPl* 1299). In *Cathleen ni Houlihan*, by contrast, symbolic and naturalistic levels of meaning complement and intensify one another, achieving the "mix" Yeats had sought in which poetic is integrated with realistic "without ceasing to be itsself".

The manuscript draft gives some indication of how much the success of this fusion owed to Lady Gregory's influence. First, by establishing realism as the dominant mode in the opening section, she must have significantly circumscribed Yeats's scope for treating the role of Cathleen in the remainder of the play. As his notes show, he had conceived of the cottage setting only as a background to his central vision of her sudden appearance and mysterious power. But the "piece of human life"[23] Lady

Gregory provided as framework necessarily precluded too direct a movement towards overt supernatural suggestion, and ensured a continuing focus on the peasant roles; as he acknowledged, only the "burden of knowledge [of the country mind]" that she provided had kept the play from "the clouds" of symbolism (*VPl* 1296). That Yeats needed to make revisions in 1902, to signal more effectively the contrasting gravity of Cathleen's part, reflects how fully his original conception of her role became subject in the course of composition to the realistic mode Lady Gregory established. Even in the final form of the play Cathleen's otherworldliness is never overtly confirmed during her appearance on stage. Although an audience is soon made aware of her symbolic significance – most directly when she reveals her name, but also by the patriotic associations of phrases such as "my four beautiful green fields" – the Gillane family fail to recognise her supernatural nature fully until her off-stage transformation is reported in the closing lines. Not only does this gap between the audience's knowledge and that of the peasant characters generate the main dramatic tension of the play, but the maintenance of realism on-stage also removes the potential for awkwardness or absurdity that the overt introduction of supernatural figures occasioned elsewhere in Yeats's early drama.

Lady Gregory's direct share in the second section of the play also appears to have been considerable. The dialogue fragments on pages 21–6 of the draft, consisting primarily of exchanges between Cathleen and members of the peasant family, suggest that the writers recognised the possibility of difficulties at these points of interaction, and felt the need for preparatory notes before completing the draft. But almost all the exchanges take a question and answer form, with the Old Woman responding to simple questions directed by the Gillanes. They ask her if she would like food or drink, enquire about her land and how she lost it, and ask who it was that put her "astray". In the completed second section the pattern is even more pronounced, with all of Cathleen's speeches, save those after she gets up to leave, coming in response either to direct questions, the confidence-inviting "You look as if you had your share of trouble", or Peter's silent offer of money. The impetus of the dialogue is hence predominantly determined by the peasant characters, and by the naturalistic course of their efforts to "place" their enigmatic visitor relative to the world of their own experience. Only with Cathleen's climactic concluding speeches is this pattern broken, the semblance of conversation ending in the intensity of her call to action. In the published text the change is particularly emphatic, for whereas Cathleen's penultimate speech in the draft is nominally directed to Peter – "You wonder there were songs made about me" – in the final version her words become eerily distanced – "They are wondering that there were songs made about me." In his fascination, Michael likewise becomes oblivious to his surroundings, and the mechanical emptiness of

his response to his mother's efforts to distract him – "What wedding are
you talking of? What clothes will I be wearing tomorrow?" – emphasises
how fully his contact with the questioning objectivity of his family has
been severed.

This subordination of supernatural to peasant realism until the
closing lines of the play reflects not merely Lady Gregory's success in
developing the realistic background Yeats had envisaged, but more
significantly points to the influence of her experience as a folklore
gatherer in determining the final form of the play. Whereas Yeats's
primary interest in folklore was always the possibility of finding
confirmation of "actual experience of the supernatural" (*Au* 400), Lady
Gregory's interest was primarily anthropological, focussing on the
manner in which peasants explained supernatural experiences and
integrated them into their view of the world. Her folklore researches thus
gave her not only that knowledge of "the country mind and the country
speech" for which Yeats sought her help with the play, but also provided
her with a model for the meeting of natural and supernatural which
answered directly to his aspiration of fusing realism and symbolism.
Rather than focussing on the political idealism behind Michael's
response to Cathleen – his fascination is complete even before Patrick
brings the news that the French have landed, confirming that her call is
that of country – the play nominally follows the course of a peasant tale of
enchantment: the Old Woman's enigmatic answers quickly make the
Gillanes suspicious that she may be a "woman from the north" –
whether vagrant, witch or faery, certainly a person of dangerous power –
and as Michael begins to respond to her appeal, Bridget becomes openly
alarmed that he "has the look of a man that has got the touch". While
Yeats had explored this theme before, notably in *The Land Of Heart's
Desire* – Delia's effort to distract Michael directly recapitulating Shawn
Bruin's attempt to protect Mary from enchantment in the earlier play by
holding her in his arms – both the ambiguity of Cathleen's identity and
the primary focus on the peasants' reaction to the unknown (rather than
on the supernatural world itself) seem distinctive of Lady Gregory's
folkloric perspective. Yeats's almost exclusive characterisation of the
play in political terms, as concerning "the perpetual struggle of the cause
of Ireland and every other ideal cause against private hopes and
dreams" (*VPl* 234), likewise suggests that the association of Cathleen's
call with the lure of "the others", and the Gillane's uncertainty as to her
identity, were not part of his original conception of the work.

Lady Gregory's influence on the second section of the play might be
traced further, for her own preoccupation with the idea of self-sacrifice
for Ireland's sake accorded closely with Yeats's central theme in *Cathleen
ni Houlihan*. In "The Felons of Our Land" for instance, a highly
Nationalist article published in 1900, she had surveyed the ballads and
poems written about "the moving failure of Irish rebels", celebrating in

particular the heroism of those who had given their lives in "a battle that was already lost".[24] The sustained force of her personal identification with the idea of sacrifice for the "rebel" cause is attested to most powerfully by an entry in her journal for 1921, written when negotiations between de Valera and Lloyd George briefly offered hope of peace:

> Just now . . . I seem possessed with the passion for Ireland, for my country. . . . If this truce should come to an end, the bitter war begin again, I wish to put myself on the side of the people, I wish to go to prison, I think even to execution (tho' I will not take a life – yet one may attain to this by "comforting the King's enemies").[25]

Given this emotive identification with the patriotic theme of the work, it is unsurprising that Lady Gregory should have made a distinctive imaginative contribution to Cathleen's part. As Richard Finneran has noted, the Old Woman's song "I will go cry with the woman", which Yeats acknowledged had been suggested "by some old Gaelic folk-song", was almost certainly based on Lady Gregory's translation of the lament "Fair-haired Donagh", included in her article "West Irish Folk Ballads" in *The Monthly Review* for October 1902.[26] The link is confirmed by her note "2 verses (Fair Haired Donagh)" on page 12 of the manuscript draft, Yeats's scenario for the play having doubtless quickly called the ballad to her mind as apposite to Michael's fate: commemorating "some Connachtman" hanged in Galway for an unspecified political crime against "the Gall", the ballad ends with a lament that the "marriage portion coming home for Donagh" will not be "cattle nor sheep nor horses" but "tobacco and pipes and white candles" for use at his wake.[27] A further contribution is suggested by an obituary of Lady Gregory published in *An Phoblacht* in 1932, which specifically ascribed to her the Old Woman's closing lines "They shall be remembered for ever".[28] While this attribution is not supported by other evidence, the only manuscript of the lines being a fair copy in Yeats's hand,[29] Lady Gregory's enduring interest in ballads praising Irish political martyrs – both as collector and composer – suggests that even if not written by her the lines may have owed something to her inspiration.[30]

The evidence of the manuscript draft makes clear how extensive Lady Gregory's collaborative share in *Cathleen ni Houlihan* became. While Yeats had initially sought her help specifically to "create peasant dialogue", the realism of the setting and characters she developed independently in the opening section of the play tempered his tendency "to symbolise rather than to represent life" and grounded the development of the play within a realistic framework. Her emphasis on the emotional ties and "hopes and dreams" of the peasant family also invested Yeats's political allegory with tragic force, by vividly realising

the well-being that Cathleen's call destroys. Most importantly, Yeats's
scenario directly engaged the imaginative concern Lady Gregory shared
with him for both Irish Nationalism and folklore, such that she was able
to complement and catalyse the work conceptually, rather than simply
putting his ideas "into speech" (*VPl* 232).

The success of *Cathleen ni Houlihan* was immediate, with crowds being
turned away and "continual applause" greeting the work by the time the
first production run closed on 4 April 1902 (*L* 368). Mary Walker was to
recall, with only slight exaggeration, that "Even the smuggest and most
patronising critic could find no fault"[31] with the play. Only the title
remained a matter of uncertainty, with the writers debating the
respective merits of "Hoolihaun's Daughter", "They shall be
remembered for ever", "The Daughter of Hoolihan" and "The Poor Old
Woman" even after printing of the work was begun in May.[32] The final
choice was presumably made by Yeats, for Lady Gregory had cautioned
that "Kathaleen ni Houlihan . . . will always be mixed up with the
Countess Cathleen by people of fuzzy minds, and I think they are on the
increase".[33] Despite the acclaim the play received, however, Yeats
appears to have made no public acknowledgement of Lady Gregory's
part in the work prior to dedicating *Plays For An Irish Theatre* to her in
February 1903 (*VPl* 232). In the excitement of the success he indeed
repeatedly referred to the play in unequivocal terms as his own, writing
to Henry Newbolt on 5th April about the success of "my *Kathleen ny
Hoolihan*" (*L* 369), and stating with disingenuous specificity in his letter
to *The United Irishman* published the same day "I have written the whole
play in the English of the West of Ireland, the English of people who
think in Irish" (*VPl* 235).[34] But even after acknowledging Lady
Gregory's help, Yeats evidently remained uneasy as to her collaborative
share in the work, and though he wrote in his dedication "We turned my
dream into the little play *Cathleen ni Houlihan*", by October 1903, in the
essay "An Irish National Theatre" he had become distinctly less candid:
"I had a very vivid dream one night, and I made *Cathleen ni Houlihan* out
of this dream" (*Ex* 116). As would be the pattern with most of their
collaborative work, Yeats thereafter alternated between acknowledging
and neglecting Lady Gregory's share in the play, crediting her on several
occasions in notes and prefaces to the various editions in which *Cathleen
ni Houlihan* appeared, but in other contexts generally making no mention
of her help.

This variable acknowledgement may have stemmed in part from
equivocation on Yeats's part as to the extent of Lady Gregory's
contribution to the play. As in the case of the folklore articles he had
compiled from her gatherings in 1897 and 1898, his sense of dominant
creative responsibility – together with the fact that the original
conception of the play was his alone – must have encouraged a
proprietorial attitude and obscured how fully her collaborative influence

modified the work. But given that Yeats confided privately to Lennox Robinson "more than once" that Lady Gregory's share in *Cathleen ni Houlihan* was so great that "the authorship of the play should be ascribed to her",[35] it seems probable that his inconsistency reflected instead an unconscious process of revisionism. For the tendency of "strong poets" to clear imaginative space for themselves by misreading or emphasising the limitations of their creative precursors is paralleled in particularly acute form by the underlying tensions inherent in collaborative partnerships. In jointly-written work the bounds of creative responsibility (and thus obligation) are at their most uncertain, while the very act of seeking assistance in some sense signals a creative lack; yet the impulse to overcome anxieties of influence or indebtedness is inhibited by both the direct personal contact involved and, at the time of writing at least, by the practical need to suppress artistic egotism if the work is to be successfully completed.

With their assertion of exclusive authorial responsibility, Yeats's most celebrated references to *Cathleen ni Houlihan* – "Did that play of mine send out / Certain men the English shot?" (*VP* 632) and "The author of *Kathleen ni Houlihan* addresses you"[36] – may be read as signalling a correspondent anxiety about his creative debt. (A similar anxiety is suggested by his cold response to Lady Gregory's assumption of the role of Cathleen – the part of the play most his own – for three nights at the Abbey in 1919.)[37] But Lady Gregory, too, appears to have latterly developed a proprietorial attitude towards the work. Like her journal claim to have written "all but all" of *Cathleen ni Houlihan*, her nominally magnanimous refusal to insist on full recognition as co-author hints at a private and condescending conviction that the success of the play had depended primarily on her contribution. As Elizabeth Coxhead noted:

> when her family . . . urged her to stake her claim, she always refused with a smile, saying that she could not take from [Yeats] any part of what had proved, after all, his one real popular success.[38]

Yet however significant the underlying creative tensions may have been in the relationship, the remarkable durability of Yeats's collaborative partnership with Lady Gregory attests to their success in avoiding or defusing overt strains and disagreements. Sustained by high personal regard, the friendship was rarely other than generous and mutually complimentary, with both writers conscious of the many strengths of their collaboration. Their personal exchanges regarding *Cathleen ni Houlihan* were characteristic of this reciprocity and concord. Inscribing Lady Gregory's copy of the second volume of *Plays For An Irish Theatre* in March 1904, Yeats unstintingly acknowledged her part not just in *Cathleen ni Houlihan*, but *The Hour Glass* and *The Pot of Broth* as well: "Lady Gregory from her friend the writer of something of this book".[39]

The opening of the Abbey later that year provided Lady Gregory with an appropriate occasion to respond in kind. When news of the first night reached her at Coole she wrote simply to Yeats, expressing her greatest pleasure not in the enthusiastic reception of her own new play, *Spreading the News*, but in the success of the work they had written together: "So many thanks for your telegram – I have seen paper and I like to feel all have gone well – *especially our* Kathleen".[40]

NOTES

1. Lady Gregory, *Our Irish Theatre* (London: Putnam, 1913) p. 80.
2. Yeats and Lady Gregory doubtless continued to comment on one another's work up until her death in 1932, but their revisions together of dialogue for his version of *Sophocles' King Oedipus* appears to have been their last formal collaboration. See David R. Clark and James B. McGuire, "The Writing of *Sophocles' King Oedipus*", *YAACTS 2*, 1984, 30–74.
3. Scenarios for Hyde, see *Our Irish Theatre*, p. 83 and *Seventy Years: Being the Autobiography of Lady Gregory*, ed. Colin Smythe (New York: Macmillan, 1976) pp. 379–80: work on *Deirdre, Our Irish Theatre*, p. 138; criticism of Abbey plays – "one of our heaviest tasks" – *Our Irish Theatre*, pp. 99–103.
4. George Moore, *Ave* (London: Heinemann, 1911) p. 273.
5. *W. B. Yeats: a Critical Study* (New York: Dodd, Mead, 1915) pp. 187, 194.
6. William M. Murphy, *Prodigal Father: the Life of John Butler Yeats 1839–1922* (Ithaca: Cornell University Press, 1978) p. 201.
7. *Editing Yeats's Poems* (New York: St. Martin's Press, 1983) p. 108.
8. TLS to Wilfrid Scawen Blunt, 26 July 1903 (Berg Collection MS 65b3466#1).
9. George Moore, *Vale* (London: Heinemann, 1914) p. 204.
10. "Lady Gregory, Co-Author and Sometimes Author of the Plays of W. B. Yeats", *Modern Irish Literature: Essays in Honor of William York Tindall* eds Raymond J. Porter and James D. Brophy (New York: Iona College Press, 1972) p. 47.
11. *Lady Gregory: a Literary Portrait* (London: Macmillan, 1961) p. 68. Coxhead follows Lady Gregory's usual spelling "Kathleen"; all such variants – "Kathaleen", "Hoolihan" etc. – are left unregularized in this article.
12. "A Calendar for the Production and Reception of *Cathleen ni Houlihan*" *Modern Drama*, XVIII, no. 2 (June 1975) 136.
13. See letters of 24 Dec. 1897 (*L* 292–3), and 11 Jan. 1898 (Berg Coll.).
14. "Statement by L.G. to J.Q." (Manuscript Division, New York Public Library). See also *Prodigal Father*, pp. 196, 404–5, 622.
15. *Seventy Years*, p. 390. Lady Gregory recorded the occasion in her diary entry for 11 Feb. 1901: "I read Yeats my translation of Sons of Usnach and of Cuchulain's Death – and he was enthusiastic, says I must go on, and that it will be a great book" (Holograph diary, vol. 15, Berg Collection).
16. *Our Irish Theatre*, p. 105.
17. Unpublished letter to Lady Gregory, 27 Aug. 1901. (Coll. MBY.)
18. ALS to Yeats, 24 Nov. 1901 (Berg Collection MS 65b3817).
19. *Joseph Holloway's Abbey Theatre: A Selection from His Unpublished Journal 'Impressions of a Dublin Playgoer'*, eds Robert Hogan and Michael J. O'Neill (Carbondale: Southern Illinois University Press, 1967), p. 105.
20. See below, p. 15.
21. ALS to Yeats, 10 Apr. 1902 (Berg Collection MS 65b3571).

22. *Yeats* (New York: Oxford University Press, 1970) and *The Anxiety of Influence* (New York: Oxford University Press, 1973) *passim*.
23. Richard Ellmann, *The Identity of Yeats* (New York: Oxford University Press, 1954) p. 295, quoting Yeats's notes "for Horace Plunkett's use during the inquiry of 1904 into the Abbey theatre's patent".
24. Quoted in Donald Torchiana *W. B. Yeats and Georgian Ireland* (Evanston, Illinois: Northwestern University Press, 1966) p. 79.
25. Entry for 20 July 1921, Holograph Journal vol. 8, Berg Collection.
26. *Editing Yeats's Poems*, p. 130.
27. Lady Gregory, *Poets and Dreamers* (London: John Murray, 1903) pp. 49–51.
28. *W. B. Yeats and Georgian Ireland*, pp. 78–9.
29. Yeats papers, Robert R. Woodruff Library, Emory University.
30. Her poem "The Old Woman Remembers" for instance, written between 1921 and 1923, was intended as a "rosary of praise" to "tell out [the] names" of Ireland's dead in the struggle for independence; see *Collected Plays 2: The Tragedies and Tragic-Comedies* ed. Ann Saddlemyer (Gerrards Cross, Buckinghamshire: Colin Smythe, 1970) pp. viii, 357–61.
31. Maire Nic Shiubhlaigh *The Splendid Years: Recollections of Maire Nic Shiubhlaigh as told to Edward Kenny* (Dublin: James Duffy, 1955) p. 20.
32. Lady Gregory to Yeats, 25 May and 29 May 1902 (Berg Collection MSS 65b4470 and 65b3568). Yeats to Lady Gregory, 23 May and 27 May 1902 (Berg Collection and MBY Collection, respectively).
33. ALS to Yeats, 25 May 1902 (Berg Coll.).
34. Yeats had used an almost identical phrase, in the preface to *Cuchulain of Muirthemne* which he had completed some two or three weeks earlier, praising Lady Gregory's discovery of "a living speech . . . [the] speech of those who think in Irish" (*Ex* 4). Ironically, Lady Gregory herself had recommended the phrase, writing to Yeats on 31 Dec. 1901: "Would you like to be paid for the [*Cuchulain*] preface in advance? . . . There is a phrase we may use in that newscutting you send, 'the ~~English~~ talk of people ~~used to thinking~~ who think in Irish.'" (Berg Collection MS 65b3441).
35. Robinson, unpublished biography of Lady Gregory (Berg Collection).
36. Mary Colum, *Life and the Dream* (Garden City, New York: Doubleday, 1947) p. 139.
37. Lady Gregory recorded that after her second appearance in the role, Yeats "came up to the gallery . . . and said coldly it was 'very nice, but if I had rehearsed you it would have been much better'". He may have had specific grounds for coldness if she had openly expressed her opinion that all the part needed was "a hag and a voice". See *Lady Gregory's Journals 1*, ed. Daniel J. Murphy (Gerrards Cross, Buckinghamshire: Colin Smythe, 1978) pp. 55, 58.
38. *Lady Gregory: a Literary Portrait*, p. 68.
39. "Modern Literature from the library of James Gilvarry" (New York: Christie's Cat., 7 Feb., 1986) p. 187 (Lot 487).
40. ALS to Yeats, 28 Dec. 1904 (Berg Collection MS 65b3598).

Note: Typographical conventions used in the transcript follow those adopted in Phillip Marcus's edition of the drafts of *The Death of Cuchulain*, save that illegible words or conjectural readings are given in angled brackets, to distinguish them from editorial additions, given in square brackets.

[1]

Michael Gillane, going to be married
Peter Gillane, his father
Bridget Gillane, his mother
Patrick Gillane, his brother –

–

Scene, inside a cottage –
Bridget standing at a table
undoing a parcel – Boy sitting
by fire – Peter the other side of
the fire –
Peter – What is that cheering
about? (Patrick gets up & goes
over to window) Is it a
hurling match they are having
today?" –
Patrick – No there's no hurling
today – Its down in the town
the cheering is – (P remains at open window
Bridget – I suppose the lads
are having some sport – Come

[2]

hither Peter, & look at Michaels
wedding clothes –
Peter shifts his chair to the table –
~~Winif~~ Bridget says "You had no
clothes like that the day you
married me, & no coat to put
on of a Sunday more than
you had any other day"
Peter says, Well we never
thought in those days a son of
our own would be buying grand
clothes like that for his own
wedding, or that he would have
so good a place to bring a wife to
Patrick, Here's Michael coming back

father –
Peter – hopes he has brought
back the wife's fortune safe, &
that her people didn't break
the bargain at the end,

[3]   3

after all the trouble he had
making it (He describes the
making of the match) Michael
comes in, & puts a bag of
    ∧ the mother says he is late he says ‹??›
"Have you got the fortune, Michael?"
Michael says, here it is safe –
(Bridget has all this time
been examining the clothes
pulling the seams, examining linings
& pockets etc – Now she
puts them over on the dresser.
Peter rises & takes up the
bag in his hands. Then he sits
down & empties it on the table
& counts & handles the money
excitedly – Peter – Yes, I made
the bargain well for you, ‹?young›
Michael (He tells how he
made the bargain, every
now & then stopping to count, &

[4]   4

& telling how Bartley made
such an offer, & says I etc etc
& says he etc etc" –
    Win He had never thought
to see so much money within his
four walls
Bridget says "You seem well
pleased to be handling the money
Peter" –
Peter says he had never thought
to see so he wishes he had
had the luck to get £100 or

£20 itself with his wife – Bridget
says, well if she didn't bring
much, she didn't get much –
What had he the day she
married him but a flock of
hens & he feeding them, & a
few lambs & he driving them
to the market at Killala

[5]   5

If she brought no fortune she
worked it out in her bones
(She is indignant, & bangs down
a jug that she has in her
hand on the dresser) Laying
the baby, Michael that is
standing there now, in a stook of
of straw while she dug the potatoes,
& never asking big dresses, or
anything but to be working –
****
Peter says * she was the best woman
****
in Ireland – Patrick turns * round
****
"They are cheering again father
~~I think~~ "May be they're landing
horses from Enniscrone over the
strand – They do be cheering
when the horses take well to the
water,
                           leaning
Michael who has been standing
on wall
  by the fire, goes over to the

This page has been torn in two along the line marked ***.

[6]   6

~~window & looks out~~ –
~~Peter goes on that~~ but that
money is good too – He never
thought to see so much money

within his 4 walls – They can do
gr things with it, they can
take the ten acres of land
they have a chance of since
Jamsie Dempsey died, & stock
it, & they will go to the May?
fair at Ballina to buy the
stock –

[7]   7

window – ~~He tells Patrick~~ He
says it cant be horses, & tells
Patrick to go down & see what it
is about – He ~~call~~ takes his
place at window – Patrick goes
but turns at door saying "Dont
let Delia forget the greyhound
pup she promised to bring me,
                    comes
when she ~~is coming~~ to the house" –
He goes out –
Peter says "It will be Patricks
turn next to be looking for a
fortune, but it wont be so easy
for him to get it, & he with
no place of his own" – Bridget
says, now ~~they are~~ things are
going so well with them, &
the Regans such a good
back to them in the district
& Delias own uncle a

[8]   8

priest, she does be thinking ~~<??>~~
they might make Patrick himself
a priest some day & he
so good at his books –
They will be able to give him
learning, & not to be sending
him tramping the country like
a poor scholar –
   ~~I think~~ Michael at the
window says I think I see some

old woman coming up the
               Bridget
hill father" – Peter says it will
be one of the neighbours coming to
see the wedding clothes" Peter
says "We'll put the money
out of sight, it[s] no good
to ‹?have› all the neighbours
handling it" he gets up
& puts it in a box.
Turning back he says "did

[9]   9

      Peter
~~Winifred~~ asks did the girl, Delia,
ask to keep any of the money
for her own use – Michael says
          she did not
she did not ^seem to take much
notice of it or to look at it at
all – Winifred says that is no
wonder, why would she look at
it when she had himself to
look at, a fine strong young man.
~~She~~ It is proud she must be
to get him – a good strong boy
that would use the money well
& would not run through it
for drink" – ~~Peter thinks it is~~
~~Michael has a right to be proud~~

The remainder of this page has been cut off.

[10]

Michael opens door – stays by it
Old Woman enters,
           Peter turns for box –
"God save all here"
All "God save you kindly" –
K – You're well sheltered in
       ~~the w~~ outside the weathers wild & theres
here, but theres a ~~sharp~~ wind

coming up
blowing from the sea –
Bridget Sit down there by
the fire & welcome – (She comes to it
~~Peter Have you travelled far today)~~
                    door
Michael still at the window watching
with growing ⎰ ity
her   curious ⎱ ly – Peter, coming
over from box to table –
"Have you travelled far today –

> **All this mine alone**
> **A.G.**

[11]

This with W.B.Y.

She has sat down – They ask her has
she come far – She makes mysterious answer
She has come very far, who has come so
far as she has – She is always on the
roads Everybody knows she has never
 since she has been astray Sometimes they think
any rest   ~~They ask her~~
I am quiet but I'm not quiet in my
heart – They think if they dont see me
in the daytime I am quiet, but they
don't know that I am walking through
the night –
P   What was it put you astray
K   Too many strangers in the house –
B   Indeed you look as if you had your
share of trouble –
K   I have my share of trouble indeed –
B   What was it put that trouble on you
K   My land that they took from [me] –
         Was it much
P   ~~Had you much~~ land they took from you

[12]   2

K Four beautiful green fields –
B ~~What is the name you have~~
K ~~My fathers name is Hoolihan~~
P (to Bridget) Do you think could she
be the widow Casey that was turned out
of her holding at Augh‹???›
B She is not, I saw the widow Casey
       one
~~not long~~ time in Ballina, a stout fresh
       cheering heard   noise
woman – ^Peter says Did you hear any ‹?cheers›
She sings to herself, her voice getting
louder – The young man comes over
              v faint
from the window & says "What are you
         2 verses
singing, maam –   (Fair haired Donagh)
K – ~~I'm singing a~~ singing I was
about a man that I knew – The
song says how – – –
    It
~~He~~ was a man that loved me,
& that died for love of me –
Many a one has died for love

[13]   3

of me –
M – ~~What Was that long ago – When was~~
~~that~~
       ago ~~that happened~~
M – Is it long ~~you have been remembering~~
~~that song?~~
        But there were
K Not long, not long – Some other
died for love of me a long time ago –
~~There was a man of the O~~
Where they neighbours of your own?
K "Come here beside me and I'll tell
you about them – There was a red
man of the Neill's from the North,
was one of them, & a man of the
O'Sullivans from the South, & there was
one Brian that lost his life on

the strand at Clontarf, & there were
a great many in the West – some that
died yesterday & some that died a
hundred years ago & there are some
that will die tomorrow – Come nearer
nearer to me –

[14]   4

Bridget (uneasily) Is she right, or is
she a woman from the North –
Peter – It must be her trouble that sent
her wits astray –
B – The poor thing, we should treat her
well –
        offer
Peter – Give her a drink of milk & a bit
of the oaten cake –
B – Maybe we ought to give her something
to bring her on her way, a few pence,
or a shilling itself, & we with so
much money in the house.
P – Indeed I wd not begrudge it to her
if we had it to spare, but if we go
running through what we have, we'll have
to break the hundred pounds & that wd be
a pity –
B Shame on you Peter – Give her the shilling
& yr blessing with it, or our own luck will
go from us –
Peter goes to box & brings out shilling.

[15]   5

   ridget offers her milk – Will you have
B – ~~There will be no blessing on the~~
        drink of milk maam
~~marriage if we forget the poor~~
~~Peter comes & offers her the shilling – Bridget~~
K – This is not my time for eating & drinking
P – Comes with shilling & offers it – (She motions
it back) K – That is not what I want – It
is not silver I want –
Peter – What is it you are asking –

K – Whoever gives me anything must give
me himself, must give me all –
(Peter goes back to table, staring at shilling
in his hand, & shows it to his wife –
                              man
Michael – Have you no ~~husband~~ of
your own maam –
K I have not – With all the lovers that
brought me their love, I never set out
the bed for any –
M Are you lonely on the roads maam –
K I have ~~my thoughts~~ & I have my hopes –
M What hope have you to hold to maam

[16]   6

K The hope of getting my beautiful fields
back again, & of putting the strangers
out of my house –
M – How will you do that, maam –
K – I have good friends that will help
me – They are gathering to help mc
now – I am not afraid – If they are put
down today, they will get the upper hand
tomorrow – I must be going now to meet
my friends – She gets up & goes
towards door – Michael Let me go
with you & help you – (he starts up –
his mother puts her hand on his arm –
                              trying fitting
~~Ha~~ You have a right to be ~~trying~~ on
yr wedding clothes, Michael –
K It is not the help of a man
going to his wedding that can ~~help me~~
          me   land
~~to~~ get back my own –

[17]   7

~~Peter~~ Tell us yr name before you go maam –
K Some call me the daughter of Hoolihan –
P – I think I knew some one of that name
Who was it? It must have been somebody
I knew when I was young – No I remember

I heard it in a song –
K And you wonder there were songs
made about me – My name is in many
& many a song – Songs about me & about
those that are going to die for love of
me – I heard a song on the wind
this morning
                    2 lines of song –
Yes yes, many that are now red cheeked
will be pale cheeked – Many that have been
free to walk over the hills & the bogs &
the rushes will be sent to walk in hard
streets in far countries – Many a good

[18]   8

plan shall be broken – Many that have
gathered money shall not stay to spend it,
many a wedding shall be broken because
the bridegroom is not there to meet the
bride – Many that were red cheeked
shall be pale faced for my sake – & yet
think
that they were well paid for all their
trouble – goes out singing ‹?joyously› –
            listening –
Michael makes a step to follow her –
Bridget seizes his arms – "The
wedding clothes Michael, they must be
fitted on, you must be ready for
the wedding tomorrow –
Michael – What are you talking about –
Whose wedding is to be tomorrow? –
            cheering outside
the neighbours come rushing in –

[19]   9

Patrick & Delia with them –
Pat – The French have landed at Killala –
Peter takes his hat off & his pipe from
his mouth & stands still –
Delia goes & lays her hand on Michael
he does not notice her – Bridget

calls her to her – & says "Did you
see an old woman going down
the hill –
Delia – No, but I saw a young
girl, & she had the walk of
a queen

Song in distance –

[20]

~~9   Delia asks~~ $\frac{11}{10}$

Bridget says its likely Michael is
not thinking of the money either but of
what sort she is to look at
M – says Well, ‹??› would like a
nice, comely girl to be beside you
& to go walking with you – The
fortune only lasts for a while, but
the woman will be there for ever –
A knock at the door, Michael
says that ~~hes~~ must be the old
woman he saw coming up the hill

He opens door –

[21]   1

take
Will you have a drink of
milk ~~& a bit~~ & a ~~bowl~~ bit
of the soup – ?

The time is not come
for eating & drinking –

─────

~~Had~~ Is it much land
you had?

Four beautiful green fields

──

~~A~~ were they neighbours
of your own? –

There was a man of
the O'Neill's from the

The text on this page is in pencil. Each of the three sections of dialogue has been cancelled
with a vertical ink stroke, and the entire page has been further cancelled in orange crayon.

[22]   2

North, & a man of the
O'Sullivans/from the
South and one Brian
that died ~~by in the~~
                at Clontarf
~~east~~ by the sea –
        { a
and { ~~in the~~ great many
in the West – This is
a song I/made for
one of them –   + + +
_____

The poor thing, we should
treat her well – I will
give her one of the
oaten cakes I made

[23]   3

yesterday, & a bit of
fresh butter – Take this
with you, maam, you'll
be glad of it before
night –
        That is not enough
to give me, I will not
take it –
B – Do you hear that
Peter? ~~It is~~ I suppose
it is money she is
                        spare
wanting – We might ~~give~~
her a few pence, or

Text in pencil, cancellations in ink (on both pages above).

Pages 22 and 23 are on the outer leaves of a doublesheet of Coole stationery that has been
turned inside out so as to hide the letterhead. Beneath the letterhead, which he has deleted,
is an abandoned letter in WBY's hand:

                8 Cavendish Row
                        Dublin
        Dear Mr Benson: Mr
        Moore told me last night

[24]   4

a shilling itself, now there
is so much money come
into the house –
Peter – Indeed I would
not begrudge it if we
had it to spare, but
if we go running through
what we have, we'll
have to break into the
hundred pounds & that
wd be a pity –
B Shame on you Peter!
give it & yr blessing
with it or yr own luck
will go from you –
(Peter offers the shilling)

[25]   5

K – It is not enough –
P – ~~What~~ If silver is not
enough for you, what is it
you are asking –
K – Those who give to
me must keep nothing
back – They must give me
all –
B – Do you think is she
a right woman? or is
she a woman from the
North?

                  —

What was is put you astray
Too many strangers in the house

Text in pencil, cancellation in ink (on both pages above).

[26] 6

B You have a right, Michael,
to fit on your wedding
clothes – ~~If you wait~~
M – Time enough, time enough
B – If you wait till
morning there might be
something wrong with them,
You might be kept late
for the wedding –
M – ~~No matter~~ Leave
me alone, they'll do
well enough –

Text in pencil, cancellation in orange crayon.

Yeats and *Deirdre*: from Story to Fable

Virginia Rohan

I have a story right, my wanderers,
That has so mixed with fable in our songs
That all seemed fabulous.

(*Deirdre*, 11. 1–3)

The manuscripts of *Deirdre*, a thousand pages of holograph and typescript that in the end were sculpted into a 759-line one-act play, bear the marks of Yeats's lifelong struggle to fuse personal utterance and public theme, self and subject. Yeats began work on his play by acquiring a welter of historico-legendary information from the many retellings of the story that had preceded him. In itself, this was not inimical to the process of playwriting; in fact, it may even have been his preferred starting point. Curtis Bradford, describing the writing of the austere and symbolical play *The King of the Great Clock Tower* some three decades after *Deirdre*, implies this was a common practice for Yeats:

> The drafts of *The King of the Great Clock Tower*, out of which *A Full Moon in March* grew, proliferate in many directions. In early drafts the King is the half-legendary Irish chief, O'Rourke of Breffany, whose great-grandfather had married Dervorgilla, and whose "body has inherited a passion/For women worthy death." As Yeats refined the telling of his fable, this Irishizing almost disappeared, and King, Queen, and Stroller, divested of personality, emerge as emblems of certain eternal aspects of human character. Then the King went, and essential man and essential woman play out an essential drama.[1]

The Irish colouring of *Deirdre* never disappears: the process of writing moves, however, in similar fashion, from immersion in the given story to the creation of fable.

Yeats's needs and goals – if not his practice – clearly differed at the time of the writing of the two plays. He never aspired to reduce Deirdre to "essential woman", but rather to enlarge her to "heroic woman". In the late Spring of 1904, when Yeats began work on his own *Deirdre*, or *The House of Usnach* as it was originally titled, he aspired to the creation of a body of literature for Ireland that was the peer of the better known continental literatures. He was particularly eager, in the months before the Abbey Theatre would open on 27 December, to provide the new theatre with verse plays which would bring the heroic figures of Irish legend before a national audience. In the process of his work he was to strip this tale of its historical details only to enhance it in ways that would emphasize its relation to the great literary traditions of the romance. He moved from the particular story to a representation of the archetypal search for love, as it is expressed in the age-old contest of men for a woman who is at once the source of turbulence and of beauty and rest, linking Deirdre with Helen, Guinevere, and Isolde. He ended by reshaping the legend into a fable, suppressing or removing even the features of the romance which had helped him to define his themes, replacing them with matter drawn from Irish materials entirely new to the received Deirdre story.

Among Yeats's aspirations for Ireland was included the creation of its *Mabinogion*, its *Nibelungenlied*, its *Morte d'Arthur*. Most frequently he is writing about Augusta Gregory's work when he voices these aspirations. In "A General Introduction for My Work", he writes:

> It was another member of that order [of the Irish land-owning aristocracy], Lady Gregory, who was to do for the heroic legends in *Gods and Fighting Men* and in *Cuchulain of Muirthemne* what Lady Charlotte Guest's *Mabinogion* had done with less beauty and style for those of Wales. (*E&I* 513)

Much earlier, in a letter written from Coole to Robert Bridges, he had directly compared the collection of Irish stories to the *Mabinogion* and the *Morte d'Arthur*:

> Her book, which she is about two thirds through, will I think take its place between the *Morte d'Arthur* and the *Mabinogion*.[2]

And in the preface to *Cuchulain of Muirthemne*, dated March 1902, he had extended the range of his comparison:

> When she had added her translations from other cycles, she will have given Ireland its *Mabinogion*, its *Morte d'Arthur*, its *Nibelungenlied*.[3]

Perhaps the most interesting remarks in the preface relate to another Irish heroine, Emer, whom he sees as joining the company of heroic women to which Deirdre already belongs:

. . . [Y]et I think it may be proud Emer, Cuchulain's fitting wife, who will linger longest in the memory. What a pure flame burns in her always, whether she is the newly married wife fighting for precedence . . . or the woman whom sorrow has sent with Helen and Iseult and Brunnhilda and Deirdre, to share their immortality in the rosary of the poets.[4]

At a critical moment in the writing of *Deirdre*, I believe that Yeats saw the possibility of fitting his own work into the tradition to which he had said Augusta Gregory's work belonged. On more than one occasion he suggested to others important work that needed doing which he then undertook himself (some say by "eminent domain"). The evidence of the manuscripts clearly supports such an hypothesis.

Since Yeats came to use the *Mabinogion*, the *Nibelungenlied*, and the *Morte d'Arthur* as interchangeable terms, implying a national or cultural expression of an heroic ideal, the critic cannot point to detailed borrowings. Certain features which created a background of associations for the work, however, can be indicated. In the journal, kept from 1908 to 1914, there is a passage which can help define these associations:

. . . When I was twenty-five or twenty-six I dreamed of writing a sort of *Légende des Siècles* of Ireland, setting out with my *Wanderings of Oisin* and having something of every age. Johnson's work and, later, Lady Gregory's work carried on the dream in a different form; and it was only when Synge began to write that I saw our movement would have to give up the deliberate creation of a kind of Holy City in the imagination, a Holy Sepulchre, as it were, or Holy Grail for the Irish mind, and saw that we must be content to express the individual. (*Mem* 184)

With the models of medieval romance in mind, he had intended to make the motive in the early drafts of *Deirdre* the chivalric trust between men bonded as were those who fought together to win the Holy Sepulchre from the Turks or to find the Holy Grail. On still another occasion it is his description of the difficulties encountered in finding the proper voice for the individual who would speak through the heroic romantic tradition that provides a key to the definition of his personal and public goals. In the Preface to *Plays for an Irish Theatre* in 1911, Yeats writes first of the "reverie", the "intensity of trance", to which tragic art moves the spectator, and of the images called up before his own mind when he saw his *Deirdre* on the stage – "a wild bird in a cage", in contrast to the "sea-born woman", whose "unshaken eyelids . . . had but the sea's cold blood" – and then continues:

But alas! it is often my own words that break the dream. Then I take

the play from the stage and write it over again, perhaps many times.
At first I always believed it must be something in the management of
events, in all that is the same in prose or verse, that was wrong, but
after I had reconstructed a scene with the messenger in *Deirdre* in
many ways, I discovered that my language must keep at all times a
certain even richness. I had used 'traitor', 'sword', 'suborned', words
of a too traditional usage, without plunging them into personal thought
and metaphor, and I had forgotten in a moment of melodrama that . . .
tragic drama must be carved out of speech as a statue is out of stone.
(*VPl* 1299)

As the manuscripts amply demonstrate, Yeats's attempt to plunge
traditional usage into personal expression provided the creative tension
at the centre of the writing and the rewriting of *Deirdre*.

Before the play was first performed, on 24 November 1906, Yeats had
found it necessary to plan three substantially different versions in order
to bring into happy co-existence his heroic national ideal and his
personal aesthetic. He began work on his own play enmeshed in the
various renderings of the traditional legend, particularly those of
Ferguson, Joyce, Todhunter, Hyde, Russell and Gregory.[5] Although
retaining the cast of characters found in the much longer preceding
literary treatments of the tale, Yeats chose from the outset to limit the
scope of the action to the last hour before the deaths of Deirdre and the
sons of Usna. Classically simple and intense, the earliest prose scenarios
project a play focused on the conflict between the trust established
among men by the codes of society and the passionate love of man and
woman which does not honour these codes.

Yeats turned to another variant of the tale for the second version. The
events of this new plot, as projected by a scenario dated 5 October 1904,
are causally linked to a sequence of dreams and prophecies, and the
downfall of the sons of Usna is to be the result of a spell cast over them.
The bulk of the work on the first two versions was probably done during
the summer and autumn of 1904 at Coole. Yeats may have spent as long
as two years, from the summer of 1904 until the end of spring, 1906,
however, intermittently working on the two versions that he called *The
House of Usnach*, but had substantially completed no more than the verse
draft of the opening scene of the second version before he abandoned it
and returned to work on the prose scenario. Work on the third version
did not apparently begin before June of 1906.

This third version marks Yeats's most significant departure from the
inherited subject-matter, giving to Fergus an unorthodox and dominant
role in the newly structured plot, rejecting all subsidiary
characterization. Using new characterization to underscore the conflicts
between the emotive or extra-rational sources of knowledge and the
knowledge derived from the rational structures of conventional society,

Yeats develops his visual and verbal figures in celebration of passionate love and high imagination. The final text of the third version may represent the state of the play as it was first performed at the Abbey Theatre. The texts of what I call the fourth version are in fact all known to be post-production revisions.

It is particularly in the early texts of the play's third version that Yeats's interest in relating Deirdre to the heroic, romantic tradition of the continental literatures can be seen most clearly. These texts are transitional, forming a bridge between the more derivative prose drafts of *The House of Usnach*, and the work for *Deirdre* with its small cast and newly defined conflict. In these transitional texts Yeats has abandoned the strict "historical" treatment of the legend in order to develop its relationship with a wider literary tradition.

This article uses some thirty illustrations from the manuscripts catalogued in the collection of the National Library of Ireland as MS 8760. The majority of these are drawn from the work on the play done in the late spring and early autumn of 1906. The texts from this period include reworkings of the prose scenario, some preliminary verse drafts developing the matter introduced into the redefined plot, redesigning the opening scene of the play, and exploring the clarified thematic structure, and the first complete verse draft of the new play. This verse draft is written in some 175 pages of three school exercise books – the largest single text in any version of the play. It was clearly produced in a single, continuous outpouring. The pages are heavily overwritten, often illegibly, as Yeats rushes to embody the results of two years of incubation.

Yeats inscribes the cover of one of the notebooks "Mss for John Quinn", indicating his own sense that the draft represents something close to a finished play, or at least, a whole play. I have indicated below which of the lines cited are from these "Quinn" notebooks. Other lines are keyed to the National Library of Ireland folder in which the manuscript pages on which they occur can be located. (The Quinn notebooks are themselves in Folder 2.)

As the references to the Holy Sepulchre and the Holy Grail in the passage quoted above show that Yeats seems to have wanted to create a background of medieval, romantic associations for his work, so in these transitional drafts a new emphasis on Deirdre's noble origins creates a similar effect. She is referred to as Queen Deirdre throughout these texts which emphasize the elaborate leisurely courtly life, with its horses and harps, palaces and needle-women, dragon stones and unicorn horns (in earlier texts narwhal tusks), and musicians who are no longer (if they ever were) the "choruses drawn from the common people" but musicians trained in the art of praising love. In a world rich with jewels, Conchubar's jewelled bed-curtains are hung with luminous carbuncles which have magical powers to banish the memories of old lovers, and in

several of these texts it is Deirdre herself who is the precious stone lacking
the proper setting of the courtly life.[6]

The jewels which Conchubar has had sewn into the curtains of the
bridal bed have the power to uproot the memories of old lovers, to make
the hostile, or at least the indifferent, passionate, to cause the old to
appear handsome. These seem Yeats's own addition to the hoard of
medieval lore he has added to the Irish substratum. The stones in
Yeats's play are said to be dragon stones, as, for example, in the speech of
the musicians which follows:

Many have told ~~you~~-me

. . . .
That Conhur loved you as a miser loves
. . . .
The dragon stone that he has hid away
Among the cobwebs of the attics, & . . . .
. . .   that his love
Burned in his face till it was like white ashes[7]

(Quinn)

Earlier in the text from which the above passage is quoted, Yeats notes:

try in this place some
old Irish story as
in Whitley Stokes
******* [translations?]
stone from dragon heart
here

(Quinn)

If Yeats's memory is correct, and at best it is typically only approximate
when making such citations, there is probably located among Stokes's
translations of the old Irish manuscripts some tale which would
illuminate the references to these dragon stones, from the brain or heart
of dragons in the gardens of the East, perhaps Libya (also the country of
origin for Conchubar's dark-skinned mercenaries), where wounds drip
not with "blood but wine" and there's "no speech but singing".[8]
Perhaps a connection, however tenuous, exists between the dragon
stones and Deirdre's sea origins in the texts of the play's earlier, second
version. Both are found linked in a story in Alfred Nutt and Kuno
Meyer's *Voyage of Bran*, where it is foretold of Mongan, the son of
Manannan (Deirdre's foster-father in those texts), that he will have the
power of shape-shifting, and be killed by a dragon stone from the sea.[9]

There is a single instance in which Yeats's reduction of the story to fable, "so that all seem fabulous", seems clearly intended to remind his audience of the resemblance of the Deirdre story to that of Tristan and Isolde. To help provide some reasonable explanation for the preparation of a bridal chamber, reported by the musicians, and for the presence of foreign soldiers in the woods about the Red Branch House, Fergus introduces the suggestion that a bride for Conchubar is being brought from overseas. Yeats uses this material in part to motivate Fergus's continuing trust in Conchubar in the face of evidence that his trust is misplaced and, it seems likely, to enhance the parallels between the Deirdre story and Isolde's journey from Ireland as the future bride of King Mark. The common paradigm for the two stories has led folklorists to believe the Tristan and Isolde legend to be derived from the much older Deirdre story.[10] Whether Yeats had any knowledge of these speculations, it would have been obvious to him that the two stories of old kings whose intended young brides were taken from them by their own knights had already many basic similarities.[11] In one of the verse drafts in preparation for the Quinn text, the possibility of a bride for Conchubar is mentioned first of all by the musicians, before Fergus has made his entrance and before they are aware that Deirdre is coming. They have been told by beggars that there is a wedding planned:

> . . . [B]ut what bride
> We have not heard in any court of the world
> Of a king's daughter to wed Conochar
> To bring her country an immediate peace
> Or strengthen war . . .

> (Folder 8)

Such, of course, were the political reasons for Iseult's marriage to Mark; they have no relevance to Deirdre's once planned marriage to Conchubar in the traditional story. The continuous insistence of the musicians that they find it incredible that the old king should forgive the young lovers might also be read as an importation from the continental romance as could Fergus's initial satisfaction at being told that Conchubar is taking a bride, saying he has "urged" him to do so, as Mark's counsellors had also urged him. This is not to be read as an attempt to reproduce for the Irish legend the details of the other story, but rather as intended to enrich the fable by making its links with the world of the heroic romance more evident. In fact, Yeats makes a somewhat ironic allusion to the Isolde story by referring to the bride from overseas, for, unlike Isolde, Deirdre is unaware of Conchubar's intentions and discovers in terror that she is to be the bride for whom the chamber has been arrayed. It eventually became clear to Yeats, however, that her terror would lose none of its impact if he removed the earlier theorising by Fergus that Conchubar was marrying a bride brought by foreign bodyguards. This material is excised very late in the play's development, apparently just before the first performance, and the result is that the parallel to the particular feature of the Isolde legend becomes less explicit in the final version.[12]

The possibility that the prominent position Yeats gives his two sets of chess partners is due to his interest in enhancing the network of associations with the continental romance, which provides several examples of the use of chess games in such key moments, is equally intriguing though less susceptible to fruitful analysis. As he reworks the scenario for the third time, Yeats introduces Deirdre's desire to play chess as the focus of the "central scene":

> In central love scene Deirdre wishes to play
> chess, that all may know that she is as calm
> as the sea mew. She then asks ~~Fergus~~ Na[ise]
> what is the other life. Is it much like this
> as many say – Naisi knows but this life
> and how to hold the sword

> (Folder 18)

And then in the major drafts of that new version he jots the following note:

> Perhaps Redstripe & seamew
> should have sat play[ing] chess
> under exactly same circumstances
> with Deirdre & Naise. This
> would prepare for the central scene of play –

> (Quinn)

Such notes would seem strongly suggestive of Yeats's interest in establishing links to the continental romance when one learns that in some variants of the medieval tales Lancelot woos Guinevere over the chessboard, while Tristan and Isolde drink the fatal potion during an absorbing game of chess.[13] There is no evidence that Yeats came into contact with these versions, however, and there is certainly no need to look beyond the Irish sources for the mere presence of the chess game in the story of Deirdre. Theophilus O'Flanagan, in the commentary on his translation of one of two versions of the Deirdre tale in *Transactions of the Gaelic Society of Dublin* notes at the first mention of chess (Naoise and Deirdre are playing chess in their place of exile when they hear the call of Fergus who has been sent to bring them back to Ireland):

In time of repose from the feats of war, the handy amusements of the
ancients of Erin were hunting and hurling . . . , a manly game peculiar
to the Irish, which shall be described in the story of Cuchullan
hereafter. Their recreative amusement was the noble game of chess.[14]

Later in the same version Naoise and Deirdre play chess in the House of
the Red Branch on Conor's board, "the thing which Conor thinks worst
of having been taken from him except Deirdri alone . . .", and Naoise, in
one of those brutally memorable moments from the Irish tales, expertly
throws a chess piece from the board, putting out the eye of Conor's spy.[15]
There is no game, however, in the older, shorter version of the story
O'Flanagan sets by its side.

Of the literary treatments of the Deirdre story that Yeats wrote about
before he began to work on his own, those of Samuel Ferguson, R. D.
Joyce, and AE (George Russell) all have chess games, but none with the
importance or the significance Yeats gives his. Yeats is struck by the fact
that in Ferguson's play (a closet monodrama), ". . . Naisi, the simple
soldier, sits calmly playing chess even when they are surrounded" (*UP1*
93). But Naisi is not playing with Deirdre here, and the play's central
conflict has to do with the failure of men's trust in man-made codes of
honour. Joyce ascribes his attachment of an ominous value to the game
Naise and Deirdre play, direct using the matter from the version quoted
from O'Flanagan above, to the fact that they are playing on the King's
board which he prized most "of all things that he had lost, / Save
Deirdre's love . . .".[16] Russell may be alone in his insight into the wider
possibilities the game offered. And Balachandra Rajan in his study,
"Yeats, Synge, and the Tragic Understanding", sees Russell as a
possible source for the metaphorical potential of the chess game Naoise
and Deirdre play before their deaths.

> AE [George Russell] makes more of the chess game and it is possible
> that Yeats took his cue from him. At a crucial stage in the disclosure of
> Conchubar's treachery Naoise is described as "inattentive" and as
> "curiously examining the chessboard." He suggests to Deirdre that
> they "finish" the game. The rather naive double entendre continues
> with remarks that Deirdre's "king is threatened" and that Naoise's
> "queen will be taken" unless he plays less wildly. Yeats uses the
> symbol more evocatively. The game itself suggests the battle of wits
> which must be waged by the lovers, while the two who once sat at the
> chessboard provide the present with a model for dying.[17]

Since there is no clear means of determining that Yeats had access to the
variants of the continental romance in which the presence of the chess
game is prelude to the lovers' deaths, it may be that the seeds of

inspiration do lie in AE's treatment. The strong parallelism with the stories of those other lovers remains simply suggestive.

In the end, it is Yeats's thematic structure that provides the clearest link between the Irish legend and heroic romance. Passionate love, its energies – destructive and creative, its conflict with the settled conventions, becomes the focus of the Deirdre story in Yeats's play, particularly in these manuscripts from the play's third version. This was not true of Yeats's Irish sources, the focus of which was the fate of the children of Usna, a focus which Yeats's earlier versions retained to some extent.[18] The newly central love of Deirdre and Naoise is given a sensual quality in Yeats's treatment linking it with the passionate liaisons of the romance, especially as they were reinterpreted in the nineteenth century by Wagner, Tennyson, Swinburne, and Laurence Binyon. In his *Memoirs* Yeats mentioned Swinburne's *Tristam of Lyonesse* (*Mem* 41), and in his essay on "Modern Poetry" in 1936 he links Binyon's *Tristam and Isoult* with his own Deirdre and Cuchulain as subjects for poetry such "as men had always written" (*E&I* 499). Yeats, who believes that the role of the artist is to shatter and recreate the mores of society, would appear to be responding much more directly to Tennyson's sin-conscious *Idylls*, however. Yeats casts no stones at his lovers: on the contrary they are depicted as more sinned against than sinning. There is an important distinction to be made, of course: unlike Isolde or Guinevere, Deirdre was never married to King Conchubar, but only "destined" for him. Nevertheless, Yeats's lovers have no flaw but an abundance of energy, more than their society could tolerate, a formula for tragedy Yeats used earlier in *On Baile's Strand*. If he has a moral model perhaps it is Wagner's *Tristan und Isolde*, the opera in which the lovers reached such heights of passion on stage that European audiences were shocked. In Yeats's play this passionate love is seen as an outpouring of the instinctual, energetic, natural life, a product of the "wild will" as opposed to the "settled will". It becomes a metaphor for the heightened reality of the imaginative life, as the lovers proclaim their belief in a love beyond death, unattainable in this life, perhaps attainable only in the art which will commemorate them.

Since all the early texts of this third version – both the preliminary verse drafts and the Quinn text – are primarily occupied with establishing Fergus's new role in the structure of the play, and with clarifying the contraries Yeats was beginning to develop, much of the imagery related to passionate love in these pages is strongly negative. Passionate love is a destructive force: it has destroyed Naoise who is described as "once the foremost of all men / But now her lover only". Fergus would rather see Naoise's name live because he had driven the invader out, or made just laws; it has "put an enmity" between Naoise and all mankind:

                    Nor would you doubt
           If passion had ~~had~~ not put an enmity,
           Between mankind & & you – it came to you
           . . . .
           That need[ed] but few years of settled will
           To have sailed into the great life of the world
           Blew high blew low unsettled everything

                                        (Folder 18)

It will destroy the country:

           [FERGUS]
           I can respect a moderate desire
           I ~~understand~~
           And such affection, as leaves room for life,
           But not this passion that burns house & kin

                                        (Quinn)

              They
           ~~That~~-blow into a flame the unnatur[al] heat
           Born out [of] the meloncy [=melancholy] & virginity
           Of ignorant youth. If you have men not boys
           Among your listeners praise, ~~praise good~~ fellow
           The loyalties that knit the world together
           Not   has well
           ~~And~~ passion that ~~well~~-nigh wrecked the world
           And this state[?] more than any.

                                        (Quinn)

Love of this kind "burns down" or "breaks down / All that this
parsimony of time . . . has built / For bodily pleasure is from the hearts
pride". Yeats indicates that this love will destroy custom, household law,
old wisdom – all the hoard of "Parsimonious & niggard time". These
references to the destructive energy of passionate love are accompanied
by others found elsewhere in connection with the Deirdre story,
references to the "face" which brought "ruin on many countries" and to
the wars and treachery stirred up by that fair face (Folder 8). All of these
references to the downfall of a state, country, or house, of course, remind
us of Helen of Troy and Guinevere, whose sin with Lancelot helped to
destroy the unity of the Round Table Knights. So in Deirdre's story, love
is "the animal fire that brings ruin and death / The upsetting of old ties
and loyalties" (Folder 8).

What the *Deirdre* manuscripts show is Yeats in the process of plucking from history the essential outlines of fable, developing a pattern that he will use again in later plays. In *At the Hawk's Well*, for example, Bradford sees Yeats developing a fable from several mythological backgrounds, stretching from the Greeks, through the Middle Ages (the search for the elixir), to the present day, where the search for immortality is presented against a contrast of domestic repose.[19] This, with a few changes, could be applied to the growth of *Deirdre*, where Yeats creates his fabulous heroine, linking the Irish materials to continental romance and, in the process, finds for a time his own theme, an elemental struggle between the forces of nature – that is, the instinctual love relationship of man and woman – on the one hand, and the forces of society on the other.

In Yeats's manuscripts the stress is on passionate love as an elemental power, and Fergus sees it as one of the destructive forces in nature. For example, when the musicians claim that they sing only of love and have no other theme, Fergus expostulates:

> It were better to have praised the thunderstorm,
> A flood in harvest, or a hawk on the pounce,
> Or anything that's dangerous and sudden.

> (Folder 11)

In one of the preliminary verse drafts his reply is phrased:

> A wild theme
> You might as well praise the waterspout
> Or thunderstorm or flood in harvest time

> (Folder 8)

The musicians do not deny that this is true, but claim that though love is dangerous this is what all people like to hear about:

> We earn our living by this trade, and know
> Of nothing that's delightful to all ears
> But an immoderate passion that buoys up
> Two lovers, and before ebb tide has come,
> Smothers them wretchedly.

> (Folder 11)

This evocation of the destructive energy of passionate love in terms of death by drowning is carried over in a single instance to the major verse draft of the play, where Deirdre, in questioning the musicians, speaks of Conchubar's frustrated love:

You mean that when a love is like that
And after crossed, it drowns [in] its own ~~flod~~-flood
    drowned
And that love ~~drowned~~ & floating is but hate

           (Quinn)

In these texts, water is used as well as fire as an image of the destructive energy of passionate love, altering the references in the earlier manuscripts, which are chiefly to fire. In the earliest prose drafts of *The House of Usnach*, Deirdre and Naoise are presented as living in harmony with nature, befriended by the creatures of the natural world, and subject to the same elemental forces. In this Yeats is following the tradition of the ancient Irish manuscripts and many of the literary interpretations derived from them. There are two examples from these early versions, the first being as follows:

> DEIRDRE (Clasping him again) Do you remember that
> first night Naoise when we were left alone in the
> woods on the edge of the sea. Towards dawn an otter
> splashed into the stream, and then we heard a bird
> cry out upon the marsh, and then I slept and the wind
> came from the sea and stirred my hair, and I awoke,
> and saw not the stars but the leaves between our-
> selves and the sky . . . .
>   (Folder 15)

The second example occurs in Deirdre's farewell speech to Ardan and Ainnle as they leave the Red Branch House to join the fight:

> DEIRDRE That is it, that is the trouble, you have
> not tasted life, you do not know what you have lost!
> You have but seen love in a mirror, and now your life
> is done! Poor blossoming branches torn from their
> own tree and swept into the waste ~~aur~~-places of the
> hills! Poor birds of the eaves in the thatch when
> it blazes up at the touch of sudden lightning! Poor
> fish of the river shallows swept away to the harsh
> sea by a spring flood!
>   (Folder 15)

In this context, fire is only one of many destructive forces. Indeed, the use of natural imagery is not consistent in these texts, as, for example, when Naoise describes the betrayal of the sons of Usna as disordering nature:

[NAOISE] Deirdre, give me helmet and sword. You
are truly a wise woman. The High King turned traitor, the Red Branch broken, the leaves on the trees
have withered, the fish have died in the rivers, the
swan has turned its colour to be nine times blacker
than the raven, the songs in the woods have turned
to harshne[ss]
. . .
. . . Why should we go on living! There is no world to
live in! The earth is mixing and changing under us
as the sea moves and changes! The air and the skies
are thick and murky like the earth! . . . The stars
have fallen into the sea, into the saltness of the
waters . . . I can hear the drowning cry of the moon . . .

(Folder 15)

Similarly, the use of fire imagery in the early texts is not consistent,
ranging from fire as a destructive element in nature, to its specific use in
the physical destruction of Deirdre and Naoise (the dark men are coming
"to fire the thatch" in one text from the earliest prose draft), to the
figurative use of the hearth-fire for the instinctual knowledge of
the musicians, to the torches, lighted by Lavarcam, as a sign of the
passionate love of Deirdre and Naoise in the second version texts, and
finally to the smouldering embers of Conchubar's passion. Some of this
fire imagery will remain in the final text, more, indeed, than of the
newly-introduced water imagery. In the transitional texts, fire comes
clearly to stand for the instinctive energy of Deirdre and Naoise's love,
and is presented alongside the violent images of death and drowning.
The use of fire and water as interchangeable images of destruction forces
Yeats to forego one of his favourite oppositions, but in fusing the two he
may have had in mind what he claimed Blake would have called the
"watery flame" which swirls around Paola and Francesca in Blake's
engraving for Dante's *Inferno*, a copy of which hung in Yeats's rooms in
Woburn Buildings.[20]
    At this juncture in the work on *Deirdre*, Yeats is more interested in
developing a different opposition, and the suggestions contained in
images of the natural, elemental, instinctual energies are all on one side
of the equation. This becomes more obvious in the Quinn text. The
images relating Deirdre to the wild creatures of nature – she is called the
"wild bird of the sea" and "wild Deirdre"; her passion is the product of a
"wild will," and she calls on the "wild creatures of the woods" to help
spoil her beauty – are augmented. The lovers' exile has been passed in
the "wilderness", and Deirdre's speech is called "wild". On one
occasion, not in the manuscripts, Yeats said that he would like Deirdre to

seem like "a wild bird in a cage" (*VPl* 1299). The word is useful because
it sums up all the natural imagery which Yeats has been using. What is at
the heart of Yeats's play is this clash between the ceremonious, the
reasonable, and the restraining forces of society, represented in the life of
the court, and the untamed energies of the passionate life.

In his efforts to bring the story of Deirdre into the line of traditional
romance, Yeats followed the path cleared by Shelley and Wagner, who
exalted the rights of the emotional life. Yeats's *Deirdre* is not a balanced
presentation of the differing rights of opposing systems. Although Fergus
will make a feeble case for Conchubar's generosity in forgiving Naoise
and Deirdre for having broken the law and will praise the ceremonious
life at court, and Conchubar himself makes a case for his right to claim
his intended bride, nevertheless all the treachery is still clearly on the
side of the king, all the error on the side of the "good willed" man,
Fergus. As the manuscripts make evident, Yeats wrote a play in praise of
the heroic woman, of "wild will", of passionate love and the powerful
and joyous shattering of common codes and lives, a theme Yeats would
rework with increasing bitterness and intensity for many years.

Once it becomes clear that Conchubar is malevolent and that escape
from him is impossible, Fergus is removed from the stage, and the
remainder of the action becomes the drive towards a "good ending".
Fergus's view can now be seen as limited: he has not understood the
passion nor realised that it is an outpouring of the whole person. All the
images of passionate love now carry positive values. Deirdre's sacrifice of
life is her triumph: she chooses to die rather than compromise the ideals
of love.

Such a reading of the manuscripts seems supported by some
consideration of the expression Yeats used in "A General Introduction
for My Work" where he describes Deirdre and the other figures of
Ireland's heroic age, as still being in the "whale's belly":

> When I wrote in blank verse I was dissatisfied; my vaguely mediaeval
> *Countess Cathleen* fitted the measure, but our Heroic Age went better, or
> so I fancied, in the ballad metre of *The Green Helmet*. There was
> something in what I felt about Deirdre, about Cuchulain, that rejected
> the Renaissance and its characteristic metres, and this was a principal
> reason why I created in dance plays the form that varies blank verse
> with lyric metres. When I speak blank verse and analyse my feelings, I
> stand at a moment of history when instinct, its traditional songs and
> dances, its general agreement, is of the past. I have been cast up out of
> the whale's belly though I still remember the sound and sway that
> came from beyond its ribs, and, like the Queen in Paul Fort's ballad, I
> smell of the fish of the sea . . . .
>   The Countess Cathleen could speak a blank verse which I had
> loosened, almost put out of joint, for her need, because I thought of her

as mediaeval and thereby connected her with the general European movement. For Deirdre and Cuchulain and all the other figures of Irish legend are still in the whale's belly. (*E&I* 523–5)

The metaphorical placing of the heroine in "the whale's belly" seems to elucidate what Yeats is saying in the Quinn notebooks, where passion and the wild will are seen as the outpouring of the whole person, and the emphasis is on the creative possibility of forming an artistic unity from different facets of the same life, especially the unity achieved when death and life form a single image. The emphasis is on the calculated but lavish expenditure of immoderate passion in the service of immoderate thought, of high imagination. All other motivation but the need to be "all love" is stripped away. It may be that the manuscripts provide a view, not available in the final text, of Yeats's attempt to place Deirdre in a world where a union of will and feeling, an outpouring of the instinctual life can still exist. It is above all in the attempts Yeats makes in the manuscripts to focus the meaning of the deaths of Deirdre and Naoise that the core of his play becomes accessible.[21]

There are three versions of what Yeats calls the "scene in preparation for death" in the pages of the Quinn notebooks. They show his struggle to clarify the search for a good ending that has become the lovers' goal – an ending befitting their lives as lovers, a death that would give meaning to their lives. None of the versions is decisive: one has been almost completely cancelled; neither one of the second or third versions seems intended to displace the other entirely. The page numbers, obviously inserted to assist the typist in the preparation of the manuscripts, indicate that selections have been made from each of the versions. No one but Yeats could follow the ordering in these pages, and it is only in the typescripts which derive from the holograph texts that we can learn his final choice. All of them show Yeats attempting to solve the same problem: how to motivate the unresisting mode in which Naoise and Deirdre die. In each version Deirdre urges Naoise to fight and he rejects her urging. He will not choose the way others have "[t]hat made the end more than their lives".

> The followers of Lugh of the Long Hand
> Or that Nuadh whose right arm was of Silver,
>   but
> That were commended for it & why should I
> Need   ~~no such~~ so much ostentation at my setting
> Being all love.
>
>   Deir.   us
>   They have reproached ~~you~~ for it.
> ~~But out & leave a good~~

> enough
> And said its not ~~enough~~ to be all love

When Deirdre assures him that he need not think she will remain alive after his death.

> For I will climb up upon the wind & meet you
> And [put] my arms about you when you rise –
> From that red death bed there

he rejects even more emphatically "any players trick" that would make their deaths memorable and reiterates his desire to be known only as a lover:

> Though I had a hundred years
> I would not lose a moment of that face
> And for that ~~reason~~ only I would be remembered.

He then urges her to play chess, as is their custom, so that they will be remembered as lovers who knew that love's customary face is justification enough. Deirdre at last agrees:

> O singing women set it down in a book
> That love is all we[ve] need of – Even though it ~~were~~ = is
> But the last drops we gather up like this.
> Those that have made themselves one thing
> And that alone – benevolence, bravery
> Music, or any good thing that you will
> . . .
> They seem to coming times as they were gods
> And had their images . . . .

She then compares their lives to the writing of a poem:

> . . . When you make up
> ~~Music, or story~~
> ~~Music,~~
> a poem to be spoken to the strings   & so
> You leave out all thats not the theme of it
> ~~We leave all out~~
> We ve left our every the[= thing] thing[= that] is not love

There is no reason to fear death, or for the musicians to sing sorrowfully:

for whats in that – what is it but putting [off]
~~What lovers in all times have found~~
What all true lovers have cried out upon.
~~Because it~~ The too soon wearied body
~~Because it came between the barrier~~
~~Because they come between them~~ barriers barriers
That are un broken when lip touches lip,
And all those changes that the moon stirs up
~~For parting love~~
Or some worse star, for parting lip from lip
A whole day long. ~~never from this day out~~
                    – I d have you laugh with me
I am no more afraid of losing love
        Through
        ~~Through~~ growing old, for temporal change is finished
And what I have I keep from this day out.

These lines, all cancelled here, are reminiscent of the *Shadowy Waters*
where the nature of the hero's desire for a perfect union of man and
woman is such that it could never be realized on earth. They are also
similar to lines enclosed in a letter to Florence Farr, dated September 30
[1906], the most precise evidence for the dating of the Quinn notebooks
(*L* 480–1). The lines are revised slightly in one of the two revisions of this
scene, and then disappear from the text.

The revisions of this scene show Yeats continuing his attempt to devise
an appropriate death for the lovers, a death unostentatious, but out of
common reach, as Naoise desires, and a death for which no one can
reproach their memory. Deirdre at first thinks this will mean Naoise
dying as heroic defender, but she comes to understand that their deaths
must form a single image with their lives. The story of Lugaidh Redstripe
and his love, which had been present in earlier texts only as an ominous
signpost of the death which awaited Deirdre and Naoise, for the first time
is woven into the development of this scene. The story presents an
imaginative ideal for a love that can meet death while contemplating the
memory that the lovers will leave behind them. The lines responding to
Naoise's plea for calm are altered slightly so as to incorporate a reference
to the sea-mew wife and to Deirdre's agreement to join Naoise at the
chess board, but they still express the wish to see life as symbolical of one
thing and forming one image with her death:

I have heard that those whove made themselves one thing
                    any thing you will
Love, music, courage ~~any you will~~
And that alone, appear for generations to ********
That never saw them, as if they have been gods
And had their images.

Yeats notes several pages later in the same notebook:

> This whole business must be so managed to lead up
> to chess playing – Naoise is heroic endurance in
> Loves pursuit & he looks to his *endurance* rather
> than to love for the respect of men – Deirdre is
> *love*.

In the second revision of this scene, Yeats seems to be concerned with making even clearer the different ways in which the lovers express a single passion, perhaps with the intention of making their union a noble and fitting image of their death. Naoise states "that there's nothing more in life / . . . / But choosing how to end it", and urges Deirdre not to waste their last few moments on the "wild ending" she proposes. He rejects the violent death of so many of the Irish heroes:

> For many have died so that Leinster king
> And Maeves first husband that she had no mind for
> And many a fabled man the followers[?]
> Of Lergery or Lugh of the Long hand
> Or that Nuadh whose right arm was of silver
> And been commended for it –

He repeats the longing he expressed in the first revision to imitate the death of Lugaidh Redstripe and his wife. Deirdre's first response, immediately cancelled by Yeats, is:

> You make our deaths an image of our lives
> For these seven years we have been shut away
> Being wi[th] one another

It seems obvious that making their deaths an image of their lives as lovers is indeed Yeats's intention. When Deirdre is persuaded to accept Naoise's argument that their lives are justified by their love, Yeats at first rephrases and then cancels entirely the passage in which Deirdre seeks to be remembered as a woman who made her life "one thing". These texts with their references to constructing a life around a single theme, as though it were a poem or a song, seems to have clarified for Yeats the tragic statement which he wishes to make in *Deirdre*. All explicit references to this are removed by the time he finishes his work on the Quinn text, and they are gradually replaced by the growing development of the parallel story of the death of Lugaidh Redstripe and his love. Yeats's images subsume the overt explanations and give significance to the newly-tightened play.

The manner in which Yeats has modified the tale of Lugaidh

Redstripe and his seamew is a miniature of Yeats's handling of the
materials of the Deirdre story. The tale itself has no connection
whatsoever with the story of the exile and death of the sons of Usna,
except that it is drawn from the tales that relate to Cuchulain, and may
be seen as material prefatory to the *Táin bó Cuailgne*. What Yeats knew of
Lugaidh Redstripe and his wife was most probably derived from Lady
Gregory's mention of them in *Cuchulain of Muirthemne*, although the
translations of the stories in which they figure and upon which Lady
Gregory based her retelling would also have been available to Yeats. In
Lady Gregory's chapter, "The Courting of Emer", the story of Lugaid
and Devorgill (her name is never used by Yeats) is told to display
Cuchulain's prowess at arms and his refusal to take any other bride but
Emer. Cuchulain has saved Devorgill, daughter of the King of
Rechrainn, from capture by the three Fomorians who have come to take
her in lieu of the taxes her father is unable to pay. He is offered Devorgill
as his bride but refuses her and returns to Ireland to seek out Emer. Lady
Gregory's text continues:

> It was one day at that time he went down to the shore of Lough Cuan
> with Laeg, his chariot-driver, and with Lugaid. And when they were
> there, they saw two birds coming over the sea. Cuchulain put a stone
> in his sling, and made a cast at the birds, and hit one of them. And
> when they came to where the birds were, they found in their place two
> women, and one of them the most beautiful in the world, and they
> were Devorgill, daughter of the king of Rechrainn, that had come from
> her own country to find Cuchulain, and her serving maid along with
> her; and it was Devorgill that Cuchulain had hit with the stone. "It is
> a bad thing you have done, Cuchulain," she said, "for it was to find
> you I came, and now you have wounded me." Then Cuchulain put his
> mouth to the wound and sucked out the stone and the blood along with
> it. And he said, "You cannot be my wife, for I have drunk your blood.
> But I will give you to my comrade," he said, "to Lugaid of the Red
> Stripes." And so it was done, and Lugaid gave her his love all through
> his life, and when she died he died of the grief that was on him after
> her.[22]

Kuno Meyer's translation of "The Wooing of Emer" in the first volume
of the *Archaeological Review* (1888) served as Lady Gregory's source for all
the details of her retelling, except for the manner of Lugaid's death which
is not mentioned in Meyer.[23] Grief for the loss of his wife is the usual
cause of death in all the sources I have been able to locate. Of the sources
cited by Lady Gregory, only Eugene O'Curry's *Lectures on the MS.
Materials of Ancient Irish History* (Dublin, 1861; 1878) ascribes the death to
another cause. In a note to a poem, translated from the Irish, which tells
of the death of Lugaidh, Conaire, and Conall at the hands of the three

Red-heads of Leinster, O'Curry says that this poem is the only source he has ever encountered in which Lugaidh fell by "the three Red-heads".[24] (An Irish footnote to the name of Lugiadh reading "riabnderg" is translated "i.e. [Lugaidh] the redstreaked" by O'Curry.) There is, however, an entry in the *Annals of Tigernach*, not cited by Lady Gregory, which brings together the two ways in which Lugaidh meets his death. As translated by Whitley Stokes in the *Revue Celtique*, this reads:

> A. D. 72 Lugaid Réoderg was slain by the 3 Rúadchenna [Redheads] Or it may be that he betook himself to (his own) sword & died of grief for his wife, Derbforgaill, who had gone.[25]

The tale of the deaths of Lugaid and Derbforgaill, translated by Carl Marstrander and published in *Eriu* in 1911, was obviously not available to Lady Gregory or to Yeats.[26] The only previous translation to which Marstrander refers is a German one, published in 1888.[27] The grisly tale in Marstrander's translation explains the reluctance to make the tale known. There Derbforgaill is mutilated and left dying by the other women after a contest to see who has the largest bladder (a sign of sexual prowess) which Derbforgaill has won. Cuchulain and Lugaid find her dying in her cottage. "This is what they say, that her soul was no longer in her when they came into the house. They also relate that Lugaid died forthwith on beholding her."[28] The nineteenth century taboos which sometimes prohibited translators from passing on to their readers accounts of the incestuous origins of their Irish forebears apparently also interfered with the account of the death of Devorgill, stressing the grief of Lugaid at her loss, but never mentioning the cause of her death.[29] By 1911 this sensitivity concerning the excesses of the ancient Irish had apparently lessened.

When Yeats decided to deepen the import of his *Deirdre* by setting up for it an aesthetic model drawn from Irish myth, he first considered the story of the love of Aengus and Edain, once in a problematic prologue written for the play in 1904, which was never used, and in the song for Deirdre's entrance, which was retained and remains the only finished work on the play preserved from the two early versions. In the many stories relating to Edain she is said to have an earthly and a fairy husband. Her adventures include a flight from her fairy husband with the help of Aengus who enables her to change shape and with whom she stays for a time; her later marriage to an earthly husband from whom her disguised fairy husband wins her back by means of a chess game; and finally her escape with her fairy husband in the shape of a swan. It seems apparent that, although this story offered some features that could be used as a parallel for the story of the love of Deirdre and Naoise, there were not enough to make the characters models for others who were to be "all love". The legends surrounding Lugaidh Redstripe and his wife, about whom little was known, were more conducive to the treatment that Yeats had in mind: Lugaidh was an heroic personage who nevertheless had not died fighting and who was remembered for his love of his wife. The form of the sea-bird assumed by Devorgill preferred an additional but almost serendipitous parallel to the imagery that Yeats was developing around his "wild bird", Deirdre. As for the chess game they played while waiting for their end, as was mentioned earlier, it is clearly Yeats's own addition.

In 1904 in an essay, "First Principles", published in *Samhain*, Yeats seemed to be working to free himself from bondage to the legendary materials. The following passage could be read as an explanation for the non-traditional development of the character of Fergus, as well as an aid to understanding what happened to Lugaidh Redstripe and Devorgill. Yeats writes:

> He [a dramatic writer] must know enough of the life of his country, or of history, to create this illusion [that the events of his play really did happen], but no matter how much he knows, he will fail if his audience is not ready to give up something of the dead letter. If his mind is full of energy he will not be satisfied with little knowledge, but he will be far more likely to alter incidents and characters, willfully even as it may seem, than to become a literal historian.[30]

From story to fable is the direction in which Yeats moved. The manuscripts show him removing extraneous character and plot, stripping the play to a simple central core. Much of the figurative language which evokes the fabulous atmosphere of the play in manuscript is removed either immediately before or after production. What remains is a body of rather elliptical references, effectively removing the action from its historical context and the world of elemental conflict from which it is seen to be derived in manuscript. Deirdre has no past beyond her unexplained appearance in the hills, where nobody can say "if she were human, / Or of the gods, or anything at all / Of who she was or why she was hidden there . . ." (*VPl* 346). There is no reference to the wars which will ensue. The position of the story as one of the tales prefatory to the *Táin bó Cuailgne* is not obvious. Apart from this, much of the language comparing passionate love to the elemental powers – particularly the forces of fire and water – has been removed. Yeats's greater interest is in expressing in an intense and compressed manner the thematic substance of the poetic play called *Deirdre*. Explicit references to history, or to the meanings of particular metaphorical images, both of which are common in the prose drafts, become extraneous to the verse play.

In the end, the properties of fire, for instance, which have been assigned through all the versions to Deirdre and Naoise's love for each

other, as well as to the way of knowing which Deirdre shares with the
musicians, come to be expressed less through the language than through
the visual symbols of brazier and torch. As the play opens, the musicians
are crouched around the brazier and later use the fire from the brazier to
light the torches which illuminate the chess table as Deirdre and Naoise
play their last game. The manuscripts show Yeats systematically
removing such language.[31] He similarly removed the explicit references
to the lovers' becoming "one thing", making their lives and deaths
express a single image, and replaced these passages not with a visual
symbol but a poetic one – the story of the death of Lugaidh Redstripe and
his wife, this process occurring during the development of the Quinn
text, with its several rewritings of the chess scene.

Several insights gained during the apparently abortive work on the
second version were more than likely responsible for this new shaping of
the matter. The effectiveness of a single character, there Lavarcam,
Deirdre's nurse and confidante, whose dialogue with the musicians
would open the play, had been demonstrated, as had been the need of
some figure opposed to the musicians and Deirdre. By the time he began
work on the third version, Yeats had a firm sense of the structure and
imagery of the play, its tensions, and the conflicting statements he
wanted Fergus to make on the one hand and Deirdre and the musicians
on the other. The dialogue of Fergus and the musicians at the opening of
the play counterpoints fear and reassurance, intuitive knowledge and the
rational knowledge based on the conventions of society. The play which
develops from this point in the manuscripts celebrates passionate love
and high imagination. It embodies tragically the destruction of the "wild
will" by the forces of constraint – represented in the "good willed" but
unaware Fergus and the "just" but vengeful Conchubar.

The close perusal of the play in progress shows us Yeats in the act of
transforming story into fable at least in part by deliberately modelling
his heroic drama after the great continental romances, for a time the
story of Tristan and Isolde in particular. In so doing, he has re-formed
the traditional tale, giving it a meaning new in the Celtic context but
venerable in the annals of European literature, and altering it in such
crucial ways that it is difficult, if not impossible, for the modern reader to
see the story of Deirdre as it existed in pre-Yeats form. In the end, he has
accomplished this transformation by reshaping still other matter from
the Irish mythological cycles to his own end, altering both that tale and
Deirdre's so that all might seem traditional.

Vivian Mercier ascribes the choices many of the late 19th and early
20th century authors of "Deirdres" made in retelling the tale in its
various ancient and more modern versions to a socio-moral discomfort
with handling such sensitive issues as suicide, sexuality, and bodily
functions of all sorts, including pregnancy.[32] Certainly the highly
selective renderings of the Lugaidh Redstripe story available to Yeats

sufficiently demonstrate that such censorship played a powerful role in the transmission of features of that tale. Still, such a reading can account for only some of the variables factored into the selection process for each particular writer. As the changing texts of Yeats's *Deirdre* manuscripts reveal, the handling of Irish myth varies as the author's attitude toward it alters. Does the tale need enhancement to make it more heroic, more romantic, to meet standards perceived in other literatures? From what materials will this "enhancement" be drawn, on what models? What features will be minimized or glossed over in order to make the fit with the chosen model closer, even more visible to the reader?

Yeats in the process of shaping his drama has brought forward only carefully selected elements of another Irish tale which he uses almost as play within play, or mirror image, of his central characters, to achieve his goal, to create a Deirdre who achieved her own unity of self and subject, aesthetic and heroic aims.

NOTES

1. Curtis Bradford, *Yeats at Work* (Carbondale: Southern Illinois University Press, 1965) p. 291.
2. Published in the foreword to *Cuchulain of Muirthemne* (Gerrards Cross: Colin Smythe; New York: Oxford University Press, 1970) pp. 9–10.
3. Ibid., p. 11; *Ex* 4.
4. Ibid., p. 16; *Ex* 11–12.
5. A detailed analysis distinguishing Yeats's treatment from earlier literary treatment of the legend can be found in the chapter entitled "The Irish Beginnings" in my edition of the *Deirdre* manuscripts, *The Writing of W. B. Yeats' Deirdre: a Study of the Manuscripts* (University of Massachusetts Ph.D. dissertation, 1974).
6. Yeats's *Deirdre* reflects the culmination of a tendency apparent in most of the previous literary treatments of the materials to model the figures of Irish legend on heroic lines. The degree to which an Hellenic parallel is present in Yeats's own heroic formulation is difficult to say. Frayne sees Yeats's Deirdre as "a mixture of Electra, Ariadne, and Antigone" (*UPl* 48). And Yeats himself uses Greek counterparts to explain the dynamics of the relationships between the leading figures in the drama: "Deirdre was the Irish Helen, and Naisi her Paris, and Concobar her Menelaus . . ." (*VPl* 389). The manuscripts do not seem to reveal the influence of Greeks models on Deirdre, however. When Yeats writes in later years of his early effort to follow Greek models, he is not concerned with character, but with the broadly structural influences of Greek drama on his own work:

    [W]hen Lady Gregory wrote her "Folk History Plays" and I my plays in verse, we thought them like Greek plays; the simple fable, the logically constructed plot, the chorus of the people, their words full of vague suggestion, a preoccupation with what is unchanging and therefore without topical or practical interest. (*VPl* 572)

7. The transcription of the manuscripts in this article reflects the actual contents of each page within the limits imposed by the legibility of Yeats's script and the accuracy of the editor. Yeats's spelling is preserved where it is clear; his idiosyncratic shorthand symbols have been expanded. The following symbols have been used throughout:

*	unintelligible symbol;
---------	word or line cancelled;
--- --- ---	[with breaks in the cancel] a single word or phrase has been cancelled and then the whole line;
. . . .	cancelled line or lines removed in quotation;
[ ]	editorial interpolation;
[=]	alternate reading proposed;
|	in margin to left of work – entire passage cancelled;
|	cancellation continued to passage on next page;
|	cancellation continued from passage on previous page.

8. My own searches through the volumes of the *Revue Celtique* and the *Irische Texte* series where Whitley Stokes's translations are published have not borne fruit. It may be that Yeats simply means that he wants an old Irish story like the ones Stokes translates without having any specific tale in mind. This is apparently a very rare, and possibly unique, acknowledgement by Yeats that he is aware of Stokes's work.

There is a reference to the be-carbuncled magnificence of Conchubar's bed in Kuno Meyer's translation of "The Wooing of Emer" (*Archaeological Review* [1888]):

> The bed of Conchobar was in the front of the house [i.e. The Red Branch here the king's house at Emhain], with boards of silver, with pillars of bronze, with the glitter of gold on their head-pieces, and carbuncles in them, so that day and night were equally light in it, with its silver board above the king to the highest part of the royal house. (p. 69)

Laura Hibbard Loomis in her "Observations on the 'Pelerinage Charlemagne'", however, states that the luminous carbuncle is a commonplace in medieval diction (*Modern Philology*, 25 (1927–28).

> [T]he tradition concerning the marvelous, sunlike carbuncle is a constant one from the oldest Irish texts through the medieval French, German and Middle English romances which have elements springing from Celtic sources. (p. 341)

Yeats's use of the carbuncle then does not provide any particular evidence by itself of his interest in linking his Deirdre with the medieval romance.

There is a remote but interesting citation from the Spanish medieval tradition, of relevance here because it links the "dragon stone" to the carbuncle. Jorge Luis Borges in *The Book of Imaginary Beings*, translated by Norman Thomas di Giovanni (New York: Avon Books, 1970), quotes the conquistador Gonzalo Fernandez de Oviedo who associated the carbuncle with the precious stone that dragons were thought to have hidden in their brain. The conquistador himself, Borges says, took his knowledge from Isidore of Seville, who wrote in his *Etymologies*: "[I]t is taken from the dragon's brain but does not harden into a gem unless the head is cut from the living beast . . ." (p. 51).

For the aphrodisiacal qualities attributed to the dragon stones, however, it may be necessary to look at sources contemporary to Yeats. In the late 1890s a Dutch scientist, Eugène Dubois, hoping to find "the missing link" went prospecting for fossil remains of early humans in Sumatra. As reported by Donald Johanson and Maitland Edey in *Lucy, The Beginnings of Humankind* (New York: 1981), the Dutch government became interested in his work and gave him convict labour to help him dig.

> The trouble with that work force was that its members stole fossils almost as fast as they found them and sold them to Chinese traders, who ground those "dragon bones" into powder for shipment to China, where they brought high prices as medicines and aphrodisiacs. (pp. 31–2)

9. Nutt, Alfred, and Meyer, Kuno, *Voyage of Bran*, II (London: David Nutt, 1897) p. 3.
10. Myles Dillon in *Early Irish Literature* (University of Chicago Press, 1948) cites the works of three scholars in support of his statement that "The legend of Tristan and Isolt derives from Irish originals" (p. 1, cf. pp. 13, 42, 43). Dillon is referring to the multiple versions of the story in the Irish tradition: the story of Deirdre; its variant, the story of Grainne; and the saga of Cano, son of Gartnan, which Thurneyesen sees as presenting yet another parallel to the Tristan and Isolt story. Dillon cites: Gertrude Schoepperle, *Tristan and Isolt* (London, 1913); Gaston Paris, "Tristan et Iseult", *Revue de Paris*, Apr. 1894, p. 138; Rudolf Thurneyesen, *ZRP*, XLIII, 385.
11. Katharine Worth has explored different but striking similarities between the situations of the lovers in *Shadowy Waters* and Wagner's *Tristan and Isolde* in *The Irish Drama of Europe from Yeats to Beckett* (London: Athlone; New Jersey: Humanities Press Inc., 1978) pp. 20 ff.
12. The "new bride" was also mentioned in the first version of the *House of Usnach*, but since Fergus was not present in these texts, this feature lacks the prominence which Yeats gives it in the newly structured third version. All the texts of the new version continue to develop this material until several retypings incorporating further work, one initialled by Yeats, have been completed. The new work on this scene, specifically excluding the "new bride" and replacing that piece of plotting with Deirdre's attempt to arouse Naoise's jealousy, is found in a 10-page typescript among the *Deirdre* manuscripts in the Berg Collection of the New York Public Library.
13. I am indebted to Colleen Taylor Sen, whose article "Women and Chess", in *Ms.* (Dec. 1972) drew my attention to H. J. R. Murray's *A History of Chess* (Oxford, 1913) who cites hundreds of instances of chess games from the medieval romances (p. 89). The sources cited by Murray would probably have been accessible to Yeats only in German texts. (A 1533 edition of *Lancelot* treated in F. Strohmeyer's *Das Schachspiel im Altfranzösischen*, in *Abhandlungen Herrn Prof. Dr. A. Tobler* [Halle, 1895] [Murray, p. 434]; Gottfried von Strassburg's *Tristan* [c. 1210], 11. 2217–25 [Murray, p. 739]).
14. (Dublin: John Barlow, 1808) p. 34.
15. Ibid., pp. 75–7 and 87.
16. R. D. Joyce, *Deirdre*, No name series (Boston: 1876) p. 222.
17. *Yeats Studies*, No. 2 (Bealtaine 1972) p. 71.
18. Vivian Mercier distinguishes between the most ancient form of the story which tells us "however unromantically, of a woman's love that is stronger than death" and the more modern versions "that present the romantic Deirdre who has become so familiar to us from Lady Gregory's narrative and the plays of "A.E." (George Russell), Yeats, and Synge ("The Morals of Deirdre", *YA* 5, 226). While not disputing the existence of a tradition in which the tale is a tragic love story, I suggest there remains a consistent emphasis throughout the treatments preceding Yeats on the trouble the woman has caused, that is, the breaking of the bonds between men, an emphasis that is finally absent entirely from Yeats's *Deirdre*.
19. *Yeats at Work*, op. cit., p. 303.
20. David Clark has used Blake's picture as an aid to interpreting three of Yeats's plays in *Yeats and the Theatre of Desolate Reality* (Chester Springs, Pa.: Dufour Editions, Inc. 1965), pp. 21–5. See frontispiece to *YA* 5 (1987).
21. Balachandra Rajan in "Yeats, Synge, and the Tragic Understanding," (*Yeats Studies*, Bealtaine 1972), calls Deirdre's death "in the grand style" a luxury, "an ornate digression from the stern line of Yeats's advance . . . [which] illuminates what will soon become impossible and what the tragic understanding will be forced to leave behind" (p. 69). Rajan sees *Deirdre* as part of a growing and changing statement of the tragic in Yeats's work which will eventually encompass both creative defiance and self-born mockery, nobility and absurdity, as Yeats extends the boundaries of the tragic for the twentieth century. At the time when Yeats was working on *Deirdre*, however, death was still "the hero's culminating announcement of himself" in the Elizabethan sense, as Rajan sees it:

Deirdre's death cannot set aside the cage, the trap and the net in which the energy of life is contained and rendered impotent. She cannot hope and does not seek to modify a world of contrivance that is hostile to her nature. What she can do is to extract from that scheme a superior work of art, a poem capable of passing into myth (p. 69).

22. *Cuchulain of Muirthemne*, op. cit., p. 48.
23. *Archaeological Review* (1888) pp. 68–75, 150–5, 231, 235, 298–307.
24. O'Curry (Dublin 1861) p. 483.
25. "The Annals of Tigernach", *Revue Celtique*, 16 (1895) p. 414. I am indebted to Maria Tymoczko for the discovery of the article cited here as well as for the Marstrander translation of the tale of the death of Lugaid and Derbforgaill cited below.
26. Carl Marstrander, "The Deaths of Lugaid and Derbforgaill", *Eriu* (1911) pp. 201–18.
27. R. I. Best's *Bibliography of Irish Philology and of Printed Irish Literature* gives the following reference for the translation to which Marstrander refers: Heinrich Zimmer, "Keltische Beitrage", *Zeitschrift für Deutscher Alternum*, XXXII (1888) pp. 196–334. Curiously enough, although the Tragedy of Dervorgilla is listed by Eleanor Hull as a tale "personal to Cuchullin", she lists no published translation. ("Appendix I: Chart of the Conachar-Cuchullin Saga" in Eleanor Hull, *The Cuchullin Saga in Irish Literature* (London, 1898).
28. Marstrander, p. 215.
29. The derivation of Lugaid Redstripe's name is a case in point. Lugaid Redstripe was apparently the product of his mother's liaison with her three brothers according to Whitley Stoke's translation of "Cóir Anmann" (Fitness of Names) in *Irische Texte* (Dritte Serie, 2 Heft (Leipzig, 1897):

> Two red stripes were over him, to wit, a circle round his throat and a circle over his waist. His head resembled Nár's, his breast that of Bres, from the belt downwards he was like Lothar [Nár, Bres, Lothar being his three fathers]. (p. 333)

Several accounts of Lugaid Redstripe omit any explanation of his name, saying that the explanations they have been given are repulsive, obscene, or have been proven to be untrue.
30. *Plays and Controversies* (London: Macmillan, 1923) p. 92; *Ex* 145.
31. In the first post-performance revisions Yeats reintroduces the "blazing house" from the earliest drafts:

> Fergus
> Men blamed you that you have stirred a quarrel up
> That has brought death to many. ~~Now at last~~ I have poured
> Water upon the fire, but if you fly
> A second time the house is in a blaze
> And all the screaming household can but blame
> The savage heart of beauty for it all
> And Naoise that but helped to tar the wisp
> Be but a hunted outlaw all his days.

The first three lines will be retained, the fourth altered, in the final text. New matter, no longer developing the image, replaces the remaining lines of the speech.
32. Mercier, Vivian, "The Morals of Deirdre", *YA* 5 (1987) 224–31.

Olivia Shakespear: Letters to W. B. Yeats

Edited by John Harwood

INTRODUCTION

The thirty-seven letters printed below seem to be all that survive from Olivia Shakespear's side of a correspondence spanning the years 1894 to 1938. Allan Wade printed 121 letters from Yeats to Olivia Shakespear: only about ten further letters to her survive, and most of these are very short. Wade was, however, forced to make significant cuts in some of the letters he did print. Commenting on the letters which did not survive, he remarked: "After Mrs Shakespear's death in October 1938, her son-in-law, Ezra Pound, sent back to Yeats all the letters from him which she had kept, and these unfortunately reached him while he was staying away from home, and some of them he destroyed, apparently at random" (*L* 12).

There is good reason to believe that Yeats's destruction of these letters was rather more systematic than Wade believed. The five surviving letters from Yeats to Olivia Shakespear for the years 1894–97 are only a fragment of a much larger correspondence: none of them, in the absence of *Memoirs*, would give any real clue to the existence of their affair during those years. Even assuming that there were no letters during the years of their estrangement (1897–1900), they were clearly in regular correspondence again by 1904, and probably as early as 1901, since Yeats contributed "The Fool of Faery" to *The Kensington* (vol. I, no. 4, June 1901, pp. 124–6), for which Olivia Shakespear was a regular reviewer. There are a number of references to their frequent correspondence during the years 1910–14 in Dorothy Shakespear's letters to Ezra Pound. Yet again, only five letters from Yeats to Olivia Shakespear survive for the years 1901–16.

These are years in which their affair may well have been resumed; in which Yeats would undoubtedly have written of the difficulties of his personal life, of his courtship of George Hyde-Lees and of Olivia Shakespear's anxieties about Dorothy Shakespear and Ezra Pound. It seems probably that the five remaining Yeats letters are accidental survivors of what was intended to be the complete destruction of the correspondence for these years.

After two letters written in 1917, there is another gap in the surviving

59

correspondence until 14 March 1920. It may well be that Yeats wrote few letters to Olivia Shakespear during the first years of his marriage; it is just as probable, however, that Yeats decided that these letters were again too personal, though for different reasons, and destroyed them.

The bulk of Yeats's surviving correspondence with Olivia Shakespear falls into the period covered by her surviving letters: late 1923 to mid-1935. Wade printed some ninety letters for this period. But, for the thirty-seven surviving letters by Olivia Shakespear, only half the corresponding Yeats letters have survived. Every indication suggest that there were two hundred or more letters on each side for these years alone.

Thus, the one hundred and thirty-odd surviving letters from Yeats to Olivia Shakespear are themselves only a fragment of a correspondence which must, on a conservative estimate, have amounted to some five hundred letters on each side. It is not clear why these thirty-seven letters from Oliva Shakespear have survived.

The letters are reproduced as written: the editorial "*sic*" has not been used except to indicate misspelling of proper names where this is not covered by the notes. Olivia Shakespear punctuated extensively with dashes, which presents certain problems for transcription, since her most characteristic mode of punctuation is to use dashes varying in length from an elongated full stop to a slash across the page, depending on the degree of emphasis required. The distinction between an elongated full stop and a shortened dash is in many cases a matter on which no two editors would agree. But I have found no case in which the sense is affected by the decision. Some contractions contain underlining of individual letters. These have not been reproduced.

Olivia Shakespear normally used letterhead paper; until 1926 she was still using up Brunswick Gardens stationery; thereafter she used paper headed "34 Abingdon Court/ Kensington W8" when writing from home. I have abbreviated this to "34 Abingdon Court" in the text, but have given all other addresses as written.

In annotating I have focused on matters of significance to Olivia Shakespear and/or Yeats. Bibliographical details of all books referred to have been given where possible, but further comment is offered only if the book in question has been discussed in the correspondence or reflects something of interest about the correspondents. Editorial silence on family matters (e.g. the state of health of Olivia Shakespear's brother Harry Tucker) indicates that the letter itself is currently the only available source of information on the subject. Because of the frequent references to Shri Purohit Swami and "Mrs Foden", and the intrinsic interest of the Swami's London career and its aftermath, I have added an appendix on the subject.

I am grateful to Omar Pound for permission to publish these letters. John Kelly kindly allowed me to consult unpublished letters by Yeats, George Yeats, Shri Purohit Swami and Mrs Foden; I am grateful to John Kelly, Oxford University Press, and the Trustees of the Yeats Estate for permission to use excerpts from unpublished letters by Yeats. I owe thanks to the Department of

Special Collections, State University of New York Library at Stony Brook, New York, for granting me access to copies of Olivia Shakespear's letters from which I made initial transcriptions. I am especially indebted to Deirdre Toomey for help with many points in the annotation.

The following abbreviations have been adopted in the notes: "OS" for Olivia Shakespear, and *"EPDSL"* for Omar Pound and A. Walton Litz (eds), *Ezra Pound and Dorothy Shakespear: Their Letters 1909–1914* (London: Faber & Faber, 1985).

Text of Olivia Shakespear's letters © Omar S. Pound.

[Letter 1]

12 Brunswick Gardens W.8
16.11.23.

My Dear Willy,

I send you 7,500 congratulations on having got the Nobel prize. It was quite a shock to us when we saw it in the Times, & we wondered if you had the same shock, or if you had heard of it before. It really is a very nice little sum of money to get unexpectedly.[1]

Thank you for your last letter.[2] I have been a long time answering it, partly because Dorothy and I have been very busy flat hunting, & partly because my plans are so uncertain, I didn't know what to say about your George's "kind invitation" – I am still uncertain! We have not found a flat. If I *don't* get one before Xmas, which seems improbable now, I may go out to Rapallo with the Pounds for a month, early in January, in which case I am afraid I shouldn't be able to get away again in Feby. But if I *do* get a flat, I shall not go abroad, & shall move in January, & might then go to you in Febry, as you suggest, when Rummel goes over. Will you tell George all this, & also that I am extremely sorry to hear she has had jaundice. It is a detestable thing – like incessant sea-sickness.

Do you remember a musician called Foulds?[3] I *think* he arranged the music for one of your Irish plays? He is now making a great splash – has written a great Requiem, which some friends dragged me to hear on Armistice Day, at the Albert Hall. Choir of 1000 voices – very big & unwieldly – we did not think the music very good – too ambitious – words mostly from the Bible. One of my friends was told that he thinks he is a re-incarnation of Pergolesi – & he gets his music through the medium of spiritistic seances (very *suspect*, from a musical point of view). Rummel is doing well here now. He had a splendid reception at Queen's Hall on Sunday when he played with orchestra (tell George).[4] I am so looking forward to your philosophical work.[5] Not that I believe you've found the answer to the universe riddle – but I want to see it all put into definite form. I have sent nearly 400 books to the War Library, & got rid of accumulations of every kind, so as to be ready to move when I want to. The cold is simply awful. D. goes back to Paris the end of the month, alas! She has been invaluable.

I wonder how your sister is going on?

Did you see the notice of the sale of Quinn's MSS, in the Times?[6] The Conrads fetched thousands. Its remarkable, seeing he is still alive.

I have been reading the three Trevelyan Garibaldi books: it's a romantic & thrilling story.[7]

With love to you both

Yrs ever
O.S.

I am feeling anxious about our elections here – If the Labour people get in there will be a capital levy & I shall be *furious*.[8]

NOTES

1. *The Times* (15 Nov. 1923, p. 12) reported the value of the award as "about £7500". See also *L* 701. The actual sum was 114935 Swedish Crowns, 20 *öre* (MS.MBY).

2. This letter has not survived. Hope Shakespear died on 5 July 1923; hence OS's decision to leave 12 Brunswick Gardens (a substantial three-storey house in South Kensington). She moved into a six-roomed flat at 34 Abingdon Court, Kensington W8, in 1924, and this remained her home until her death in 1938.

3. For an account of the life and work of John Foulds (1880–1939), English composer and cellist, see Malcom Macdonald, *John Foulds: his life in music* (Triad Press Bibliographical series no. 3: Rickmansworth, 1975). In 1915 Foulds married Maud MacCarthy (1884–1967), an Irish violinist and singer who had visited India with Mrs Annie Besant to study Indian music. It was Maud MacCarthy (then Maud Mann) who composed the music for the first performance of *At the Hawk's Well*, given in Lady Cunard's drawing room in 1916. She and Foulds were also among the musicians.

   According to MacDonald, Maud MacCarthy cultivated in Foulds "the faculty he called 'clairaudience': the ability to hear, and take down as if from dictation, music apparently emanating directly from the world of nature or of the spirit" (p. 22). Foulds appears to have drawn on this method for *Mood Pictures* (1917), settings of a number of prose poems by "Fiona Macleod".

   Foulds developed his theories of composition in his *Music To-Day* (London: Ivor Nicholson & Watson Ltd., 1934), in which he remarked that he and W. B. Yeats discussed the question of musical accompaniment for poems "more than once, some years ago, and I sympathised quite sincerely with the poet's conclusion that no musician of all those who had made the attempt had been able to enhance his poems; but that in every case (so I understood him) the effect of the songs was appreciably less than would have been the case had the poems been beautifully declaimed without music" (p. 69).

   A World Requiem, to which OS refers, was a joint Foulds/MacCarthy composition which involved a good deal of "clairaudience". OS attended the world premiére, which received a laudatory review in *The Times* (12 Nov. 1923, p. 12). It was, according to MacDonald, a great popular success ("the ovation at the end for Foulds lasted 10 minutes") but "its failure with the critics was almost total" (pp. 29–30). It had three more annual performances, in aid of the British Legion, and has never been performed since.

   I have not discovered any other reference to Foulds' identification of himself with the Italian composer G. B. Pergolesi (1710–36).

4. Little is yet known of the life of Walter Morse Rummel (1887–1953), pianist and composer and one of the foremost interpreters of Debussy (1862–1918) from about 1910 until well into the 1930s. See, however, *EPDSL* pp. 354–5. Rummel was a frequent visitor at the Shakespears' during the years 1910–14, and gave several recitals in OS's drawing room. HD (Hilda Doolittle), in *End to Torment* (Manchester: Carcanet Press, 1980) says that it was Rummel who told her that there was "an understanding" between Ezra Pound and Dorothy Shakespear. (HD arrived in London early in October 1910, believing that she herself was still informally engaged to Pound.) She also says, of Rummel: "Mrs Shakespear was very fond of him at one time" (p. 18).
   The concert mentioned by OS took place at 3.30 p.m. on Sunday 11 November. The conductor was Sir Henry Wood.
5. Yeats had undoubtedly been describing the progress of *A Vision* to OS for some time before this. See *L* 690f.
6. The sale of John Quinn's collection of the MSS and printed books of Joseph Conrad took place at Anderson's Galleries in New York on Tuesday 13 Nov. 1923 (*The Times*, 15 Nov. 1923, p. 8). The thirty lots realised a total of $110 000. One collector paid $8100 for the original MS of *Victory*.
7. G. M. Trevelyan, *Garibaldi's Defence of the Roman Republic* (London: Longmans, 1907); *Garibaldi and the Thousand* (Longmans, 1909); *Garibaldi and the Making of Italy* (Longmans, 1911).
8. The day of the forthcoming general election had just been set for 6 December. OS's income was derived entirely from invested capital; hence her opposition to the capital levy proposed by Labour. None of the parties gained an outright majority; Labour formed an uneasy alliance with the Liberals which lasted for less than a year.

[Letter 2]

n.a.
21.6.25

My dear Willy,
   I was deeply interested in the speech[1] – which I think is very good. It seems a preposterous thing to try to bring in such a bill, at this time of day – sheer tyranny. I never can make out parliamentary procedure, but I hope you'll have done something to prevent it. I have asked yr friend McGreevy[2] in one evening this week, & if he comes he may be able to tell me something about it, though perhaps as an RC he may be on the other side? He is an amusing person – I've asked Herbert Reade[3] to meet him.
   I went to see The Cherry Orchard by Tchekov the other day.[4] Its an odd mixture of satire, comedy & tragedy, & wd be rather unintelligible if one didnt know a little of Russian psychology. Its a fashion here now – I mean the play – which it seems to me must be an affectation – its badly acted – O'Donovan takes a prominent part & is not so bad. I suppose he is *your* O'D?[5] Pirandello has come over & they are doing his plays – but as I can't follow Italian on the stage, I shall not go. I've been to two Wagner operas – in German by a German company – so brotherly love is progressing! Covent Gn crammed every night. Wagner wears wonderfully well & I enjoyed it.[6]
   Ezra's Canto on the Malatestas has been translated into Italian & put among the archives of the family in the Cesena library! A lot of people have been in to read it, & there was a grand article in the Rimini paper

about him.[7] Mrs Pound senior sent me a photo of him in a USA paper as a baby – very *firm* & *bad*, tell George. I am delighted to hear that you are better. *Keep so*, if you can, in all this political excitement. I go to Dartmoor for August.[8]

With love yrs O.S.

I am reading an awfully interesting book "Travel Diary of a Philosopher" by Count Keyserling – all about different religions in their own countries.[9] He is deeply impressed by Indian philosophy but goes for the Adyar theosophists[10] & says they don't understand Indian philosophy at all! which I always suspected.

NOTES

1. WBY's speech at the Irish State debate on divorce, 11 June 1925. WBY had had his speech typed out beforehand, and may have sent OS a copy. See *SS* 89–102.
2. Thomas MacGreevy (1893–1967), was born in Tarbert, Co. Kerry, served with the Royal Artillery during WWI, and graduated from TCD in 1920 in history and political science. He was appointed English Reader at the University of Paris in 1926, but returned to London in the 1930s, where he became chief art critic for *The Studio*, and lectured on the history of art at the National Gallery. He settled in Dublin in 1941 and was appointed director of the National Gallery, Dublin, in 1950. His works include *Jack B Yeats: An Appreciation and an Interpretation* (Dublin, 1945); translations of Maillart, de Montherlant and Valéry, and studies of T. S. Eliot and Richard Aldington.
   In his *Richard Aldington: An Englishman* (London: Chatto & Windus, 1931), MacGreevy remarked how wonderful it had been, in the pre-war years, "to be able to go to Woburn Buildings on Monday evenings and hear Mr Yeats talking dark wisdom as if he had just had it straight from the mouth of the oracle at Delphi, and brighter wisdom as if he had just heard it on the lips of a char-woman, and occasionally reading a poem aloud" (p. 11).
   MacGreevy became a great admirer of OS: "To him you are always a symbol of elegance, a kind of gold and ivory image, and I approve" (WBY to OS, 2[?] Oct. 1927, *L* 729). Three letters from OS to MacGreevy are in TCD.
3. Herbert V. Reade, a friend of OS's, a mountaineer with literary interests, to judge from his *Some Oberland Climbs in 1907* (London: Spottiswood & Co., 1908).
4. *The Cherry Orchard* opened at the Lyric Theatre, Hammersmith on 1 June 1925.
5. Fred O'Donovan (1889–1952) made his debut at the Abbey Theatre in February 1908, and his London debut on 7 June 1909 as Christy Mahon in *The Playboy of the Western World*; he played Lopakhin in this production of *The Cherry Orchard*.
6. A Pirandello season opened at the New Oxford Theatre on Monday 15 June 1925. Pirandello brought his own theatre company from Rome to perform four of his plays. The Wagner season, which ran during the first two weeks of June, included *Die Meistersinger, Der Fleigende Holländer*, and *Die Walküre*.
7. Pound wrote to William Bird on 24 Aug. 1925 to say that a copy of *A Draft of XVI Cantos* (Paris: Three Mountains Press, 1925) had been placed in the Malatestiana at Cesena "by my own honourable hands with fitting inscription" (*The Letters of Ezra Pound 1907–1941*, ed. D. D. Paige, [London: Faber and Faber, 1951] p. 273). See also Peter D'Epiro, *A Touch of Rhetoric: Ezra Pound's Malatesta Cantos* (Michigan: UMI Research Press, 1983, pp. 6–7). I have not traced the article in the Rimini paper.

8. Presumably to visit friends or relatives, so far untraced.
9. Count Hermann Keyserling (1880–1946), *The Travel Diary of a Philosopher*, tr. J. Holroyd Reece, 2 vols. (London: Jonathan Cape Ltd., 1925).
10. Adyar, India, was (and is) the headquarters of the Theosophical movement.

[Letter 3]

34 Abingdon Court
3.1.26

My dear Willy

Many thanks for the interesting Abbey 21st birthday book. My only objection to it is the *awful* picture of you![1]

I have been so sorry to hear about Anne – such a worry & anxiety, & I fear George will be worn out with it. I do hope you & she will come over, & give her a little change, when the child is well enough to be left. I have said nothing about it in writing to Sidmouth, as I never *do* say anything, but I suppose they know, about Anne's illness.[2]

George will have told you, no doubt, about Dorothy's Flight into Eygpt![3] She is so enterprizing now – whereas Ezra says he is "settling down". I am very glad Aunt Chapman is dead.[4] I hope it means something substantial for G. which will at any rate set you free from money anxieties – & they are really the worst, I always think. As one grows older one wants more & more to be free of them. It's no use worrying about Age – of course it is an intolerable nuisance, but it has at any rate the merit of being inevitable – one doesn't feel its one's own fault! You are a little morbid about it, you know! I look forward, all the same, to your indictment of it.

You owe me 12/6 for the Ever Hot – so glad George likes it.[5]

I do *hope* Anne is going on well, as yr postscript indicated. Best wishes for 1926. I am deep in Dostoievsky – but he is dreadfully Christian.

yrs ever O.S.

NOTES

1. *Abbey Theatre, Dublin, Twenty-first Birthday Anniversary Performance, 27th December 1925 at 8.15* (Dublin: Corrigan & Wilson [1925], 12pp.). The "awful picture" (by Charles Shannon in 1908) appears opposite p. [5].
2. The corresponding WBY letter has not survived. OS's brother Harry Tucker (1866–1943) married George Yeats's mother, Edith Ellen Hyde Lees (1868–1941) in Feb. 1911. The Tuckers moved to Alkerton Cottage, Sidmouth, Devon, in 1924, and this remained their home until 1939, when Harry Tucker, who suffered intermittently from serious mental illness from mid-1932 onwards, had to be moved permanently to a nursing home. "Nelly" Tucker, as she was known to OS and the Yeats family, was clearly "difficult", and OS seems to have put up with her for the sake of her brother, to whom she remained very close throughout her life.

3. OS's Biblical allusion refers to a holiday visit by Dorothy Pound to Egypt early in 1926.
4. untraced.
5. possibly a thermos flask.

[Letter 4]

34 Abingdon Court W8
22.1.26

My dear Willy

The book arrived safely & I have read a good deal of it – privately I think your comments on it are very just: it is an interesting human document, but that divorce between sex & life *is*, some how, repelling. It is a pity AE destroyed vol I! What the devil am I to do with the book?[1] I don't want it to be found after I'm dead. I didn't think of this difficulty – perhaps the best way wd be to send it anonymously to some second hand book seller! & let him reap the profits.

I wonder when Vision will turn up – I hope it will be soon.

No news here – we have been very dull, owing to awful weather & Harry being kept in with a chill. I have been reading a book of Chesterton's "The Everlasting Man"[2] – a sort of defence of Christianity – really rather clever, but irritating. Somehow I never believe any of his facts are true! CHARS think he is too fat to be reliable.[3]

Harry has read Irvine's Life of Parnell[4] – & didn't care much for it. I wish P. had had a different fate – I might have tackled the book but it puts me off.

I have no scandals to pass on, or anything interesting to say, so will end.

yrs affectely O.S.

Wyndham Lewis has written a book about Shakespear called "The Lion and the Fox" which will be out shortly. He assures me it is very interesting! I think he deals with the sonnet question & takes my view of it.[5]

NOTES

1. "The book" was the second volume of Frank Harris's *My Life and Loves*, published by the author in Paris late in 1924. Vol. I was published in 1922. (See Phillipa Pullar, *Frank Harris*, London: Hamish Hamilton 1975, pp. 360–2.) The corresponding WBY letter has not survived; how the volumes came into AE's hands is not known. Harris probably sent them to AE himself. AE and Harris were in correspondence in the early 1920s; Harris greatly admired AE's writings on Irish political questions, and published an article by AE in *Pearson's Magazine* (NY, 1921). (See Henry Summerfield, *That Myriad-Minded Man: a biography of George William Russell "A.E." 1867–1935.* [Gerrards Cross: Colin Smythe Ltd, 1975] p. 203). AE would surely have wanted to destroy *My*

Life and Loves; somehow Yeats managed to rescue the second volume. In a letter to
Harris dated "Dec 23" (probably 1926), WBY said, "I thank you for this book of yours
[*My Live and Loves* Vol II], which I had already read in a borrowed copy . . .
2. G. K. Chesteron, *The Everlasting Man* (London: Hodder & Stoughton) 1925.
3. CHARS were feline household gods of the Shakespear family. CHARS say what others
think but dare not utter. See note in *EPDSL*, p. 342.
4. St. John Ervine, *Parnell*, London: Ernest Benn Ltd., 1925.
5. In *The Lion and the Fox* (London: Grant Richards Ltd., 1927), Lewis asserts that
Shakespeare was homosexual and that this is "proved by the Sonnets", no further
argument being offered. See pp. 153–4.
   Lewis was probably introduced to OS by Pound in 1912. OS was still addressing
Lewis as "Dear Mr Wyndham Lewis" in her letters to him in the early 1920s; he
painted her portrait in June 1923, for a fee of £20. By 1928 he was "Dear Wyndham,"
and they remained on friendly terms until her death.

[Letter 5. (*LTWBY* 465–66)]

34 Abingdon Court
2.2.26

My dear Willy –

I kept your parcel done up for 2 days because I thought it was a
tiresome MS. some one said she was sending registered. When I made up
my mind to open it yesty imagine my pleasant surprize when I found it
was your book![1]

It is really very noble of you to send it to me & I thank you very much.
I have looked at it with interest & terror & read the introduction & shall
slowly find out how much I can understand. It does not astonish me that
you should have made yourself ill over it! I do hope you are still better &
are writing poetry – (I don't agree with Violet Hunt on the subject).
Anne, I suppose, is going on well & I hope George is recovering from her
fatigues.[2]

Harry is still here & leaves on Monday. When he goes, I shall be in the
dentist's hands, & heaven knows what will happen.

I think Harris is a beast. It's strange how that sort of thing is always a
repetition – "Always the same thing with a different woman" – (Perhaps
you don't remember that some French woman said that marriage was
"always the same thing with the same man"). I am reading Berman's
new book about ductless glands and am much inclined to take a
chemical–mechanical view of the cosmos – which is what I've always
wanted to take.[3] Harry says he can't metaphysically accept such a view.
My difficulty is that I can't really accept *any* view. I am a true Agnostic,
& probably belong to No. 13.[4]

With love & heartfelt thanks.

Yours ever O.S.

NOTES

1. *AV [A]*.
2. The corresponding WBY letter has not survived.
3. Louis Berman, M.D., *The Personal Equation* (NY and London: Century Co., 1925). Berman, an American, explains human behaviour via a determinist theory of glandular influences. Ezra Pound reviewed Berman's *The Glands Regulating Personality* in *The New Age* in 1922; OS may have originally recommended Berman's work to him. She told Pound, in an unpublished letter dated 17 Jan. 1926, that she was looking for a copy of *The Personal Equation*.
4. Phase Thirteen: "the only phase where entire sensuality is possible" (*AV [A]* 64). Despite this opening, the tone of Yeats's commentary is sombre. His examples are Baudelaire, Beardsley and Dowson. OS's remark that she is "a true Agnostic" is her response to Yeats's assertion that the influence of Phase Thirteen upon certain writers "has caused them in their literary criticism to exalt intellectual sincerity to the place in literature, which is held by sanctity in theology" (*AV [A]* 65). This is an excellent description of OS's own attitudes, both as novelist and as critic.

[Letter 6 (*LTWBY* 467–68)]

34 Abingdon Court
14.2.26

My dear Willy –

I have been struggling with your book & find a good deal of it quite intelligible & interesting! But it wd take weeks of study to make out the system as a whole & I am afraid I shall never accomplish it. I read the Dove part as you told me to. I shall be very curious to hear what the reviewers (poor devils!) make of it: probably nothing.

I think it is rather terrible – all so unending & no rest or peace till one attains an unattainable goal. I am really thankful not to find anything about Love in it. (I don't mean sexual love) I believe men are so made that they naturally hate one another & all their talk about Love is Bunkum.

For heaven's sake don't send me any more Harris! I shall get rid of him somehow, as I shouldn't like Harry to discover him after my death.[1]

I see you had a row at the Abbey when Casey's play was produced.[2] I shall go to see it when it is over here. "Juno" is really *two* plays – a comedy and a tragedy, & they are not welded into a whole.

I wonder if you have finished your poems. I should *very* much like to see them, as you suggest. I can hardly ever read contemporary poetry – the great Eliot leaves me cold – only yours & occasionally Ezra's.

I am going to put myself into the dentist's hands this week, & goodness knows when I shall be out of them. Such a terrible nuisance. What I hate about growing old is the infirmities of age – sans eyes sans *teeth* etc. & full of rheumatics.

I hope *you* are pretty well – (As Dizzy[3] said "nobody is ever *quite* well") With love to you both yrs O.S.

I read Geley some time ago – very interesting but I think he carries his
theories too far & explains too much.[4]

NOTES

1. See WBY's reply, dated 4 Mar. (*L* 712). Harry Tucker was OS's nearest surviving
   relative in England. Her elder sister Florence (b. 1858) never married, and in 1913
   moved permanently to California, where she became a devotee of various quasi-
   Buddhist or Hindu sects. She was still alive in 1941; no date of death has yet been
   established.
2. See below, OS 28.2.1926, note 2, p. 70.
3. I.e. [Benjamin] Disraeli.
4. Geley: WBY had a copy of Gustave Geley's *From the Unconscious to the Conscious* (tr.
   Stanley de Brath, London: William Collins, 1921) in his library (*YL* 104); this is almost
   certainly the work in question.

[Letter 7 (Postcard to 82 Merrion Square)]

16.2.1926

Would you kindly tell me if "The Tarot of the Bohemians" by Papus[1] is a
good & trustworthy work? Who *is* Papus? I know it is a nom de plume.

Yrs O.S.

NOTES

1. "Papus" was the pseudonym of Gérard Encausse (1865–1916), author of various occult
   works including *Absolute Key to Occult Science: The Tarot of the Bohemians; The Most Ancient
   Book in the World; For the Use of Initiates*, tr. A. P. Morton, (London: William Rider & Son,
   1892; 2nd edn 1910, with preface by A. E. Waite). Yeats had a copy of the 1892 edition
   in his library (*YA4* 287).
   OS was enquiring on Ezra Pound's behalf. In an unpublished letter dated 17 Feb.
   1926 she wrote to Pound:
   > Re Papus. He is really Gerard Encausse – head of Martinism in Paris & member of
   > modern Rose Croix. I wonder what you are doing dans cette galère? He thinks the
   > Tarot is of Egyptian origin but Waite thinks the evidence is insufficient –
   > THE YOD
   > The YOD, (not God, CHARS say) shaped like a comma or a dot, represents the
   > principle or origin of all things. That's the kind of thing – rather like your God, who is
   > a mathematical point.
   > I shall never read it all. It tells you how to do divination . . . very complicated. I
   > expect *you* could do it with great results – judging by the cards.

[Letter 8 ("answered" in (?) George Yeats's hand across top r.h. corner)]
34 Abingdon Court
28.2.26

My dear Willy,

Thanks for 12/6 – what a funny little cheque – Also for information about Tarot book.

Your story about the old clergyman is very odd & interesting: he needn't have been so rude![1] It is rather shocking to think of a spirit bothering about *baths* – What a next world – you don't seem to feel the pettiness & horror of it. I have no news: I have been swinging between dentist & doctor (X rays) & surgeon tomorrow, as I have to have several teeth out & a cyst taken out of my lower jaw. This means a nursing home & a regular surgical operation – probably this week. Such a terrible nuisance. You needn't be afraid of seeing me minus my jaw when next we meet as it will all be inside.

I shall be in the home 10 days or so, I think. I hope you were not very over-excited & exhausted after the Abbey row. I read about it in Times & Observer – its a great advt for the play.[2]

Love to you both
yrs ever O.S.

I hope Anne is really well again.

NOTES

1. WBY's letter about the spirit of the old clergyman (named Carmichael; see his reply, *L* 713) has not survived.
2. *The Times* (12 Feb. 1926, p. 10) described the events of 11 February as follows: "There were disorderly scenes in the Abbey Theatre to-night during the performance of *The Plough and the Stars*, by Sean O'Casey, dealing with the Sinn Fein Rebellion of Easter, 1916. Reference is made in the second act to the name P. H. Pearse, who was the leader of the rebellion, and this apparently annoyed a section of the audience.
   The chief cause of the disturbance was the introduction of a Sinn Fein flag on the stage, and certain disparaging remarks which were made by one of the characters in regard to the 1916 rebellion. The stage was rushed at the beginning of the third act, and two actresses were assaulted by the demonstrators, a free fight taking place on the stage. Little material damage was done, and the arrival of the police restored order. Mr W. B. Yeats, director of the Abbey Theatre, addressed the demonstrators from the stage."
   WBY described the riot in a letter to H. J. C. Grierson (21 Feb. [1926], *L* 711).

[Letter 9]

34 Abingdon Court
21.3.26

My dear Willy

Thanks for your letter.[1] I didn't have GASS (usually spelt gas) but an anaesthetic – I don't believe it was invented in Southey's time – ?[2] It has

been a beastly job altogether, & I stayed in the home a fortnight – am still
pretty good for nothing, & stupid beyond words. I shall go away as soon
as the dentist can trust me from under his eye.

I don't feel up to grappling with more of your book at present, but will
do so later on.[3] I don't know why I'm writing as I've nothing to say &
couldn't say it if I had. By the way, I can lisp now in the most engaging
manner –

God be with you,
yrs O.S.

NOTES

1. dated 4 March, (*L*, 711–12).
2. WBY: "One of the things I dread most is gas – 'laughing gas' is I believe its lying name
   and that liar Southey called it 'a brave gas'" (*L* 711). Humphrey Davy tested the effects
   of nitrous oxide on himself in 1800; it was first used for dental purposes in 1844.
3. WBY: "When you are well again I want you to read the part of my book called 'The
   Gates of Pluto'" (*L* 711).

[Letter 10 (*LTWBY* 495)]

34 Abingdon Court
14.4.29

My dear Willy –
Your lullaby, though very beautiful, is extremely unsuitable for the
young! Leda seems to have a peculiar charm for you – personally I'm so
terrified of swans, that the idea horrifies me – a feminine point of view. I
am glad to hear you've been writing so much – the peace of Rapallo
seems to suit you. Yes: the activities of life are very barren when one gets
older. I think you probably write more easily & happily now because
you've no outside distractions warring with the inner man. I shouldn't
trouble about what yr friends or critics think – both always want you to
write something like what you've done before, & have to get used to new
work.[1]

I have been staying with Lionel's sister.[2] The 90s seem infinitely
remote & shadowy – She has an "Anthology of the 90's" with a cover like
the Yellow Book – it is all verse.[3] A great deal of Alfred Douglas – not
good or worth reprinting – And *you* are included, which I think is absurd,
because you don't belong to that set. (A sacred thing, apart, CHARS
say). But I daresay you've seen the book. We've had the most damnable
weather with snow. Omar is well & jolly. I can't make out yet what he is
really like – He certainly has a strong mechanical turn, & at times I fear
he is musical! He reminds me oddly of *Hope* in many ways – I read
somewhere that a grandson is often a re-incarnation of the grandfather!
Do you think there can be anything in this? My own impression (*now dont*

repeat this) is that he is the child I didn't have, because of a miscarriage –
That child was re-incarnated in a Cat – which I really *loved*, & it loved me
– and now Omar is another try at reincarnation of the same soul –
Needless to say these theories have not been imparted to the Pounds![4]

Wyndham has sent me the new "Enemy" – I wish he were a little
lighter – he trips up over the heaps of ideas he has.[5] I've been ill so long, &
away, I haven't seen him, or many people – & can give you no news of the
outer world – I don't seem to belong to it now.

When does the new "Vision" come out, & the new Poems?[6]

With love yrs ever O.S.

NOTES

1. OS's first paragraph replies to WBY's letter of 29 Mar. (*L* 760–1). WBY and GY were in
   Rapallo from Nov. 1928 until early in May 1929.
2. Isabella Johnson (1862–1955), who lived at Box End, Ottershaw, Surrey, throughout
   the 1920s. She and OS had known each other since childhood.
3. *An Anthology of 'Nineties Verse*, compiled and edited by A. J. A. Symons, (London: Elkin
   Matthews & Marrot Ltd., 1928) contains seven poems by WBY, including "He
   Remembers Forgotten Beauty" (1895), one of a group of poems from *The Wind Among the
   Reeds* thematically and iconographically related to those written to OS (see *Mem* 86).
4. Omar Pound was brought up in England in OS's care. OS's play with the idea of
   reincarnation here echoes some of the underlying concerns of her last novel, *Uncle Hilary*
   (1910). In so far as OS was prepared to ally herself with any school of thought, she
   described herself as a Buddhist – as did Lionel Johnson in his youth.
5. *The Enemy: A Review of Art and Literature* was published by The Arthur Press in Feb. 1927.
   Lewis's "The Revolutionary Simpleton" occupied 165 of the 195 pages. No. 2 appeared
   in Sept. 1927; Lewis's editorial material, together with "Paleface", took up 114 of the
   139 pages. No. 3, to which OS refers here, appeared in 1929; Yeats had a copy in his
   library (*YL* 191).
6. "Words For Music Perhaps", described as *Words For Music* by WBY at this point (*L*
   760).

[Letter 11]

34 Abingdon Court
Saty Oct 19th [1930]

My dear Willy –

Could you dine with me here on Friday 25th 7.30? & *don't dress*. I am
engaged before that – such a lot to do, as I have been hung[?] up with
Lionel's sister here & then another cousin. We will then decide whether
we'll go to the zoo! I think you would find it too tiring. My cousin & I saw
Mrs Pat in "The Matriarch"[1] – she is an elderly Jewish lady & is really
superb & her accent just like [indecipherable]'s sisters! (Hungarian) –

All news when we meet
yrs affecty O.S.

NOTES

1. *The Matriarch* opened at the Royalty Theatre on 8 May 1930. See Margot Peters, *Mrs Pat: the Life of Mrs Patrick Campbell* (London: Bodley Head, 1984) pp. 402–4.

[Letter 12]

34 Abingdon Court
6.3.31

My dear Willy –
I hope you are comfortably settled in by the sea-side now, & that the children have got over their measles. Thanks for yr letter.[1] I have just come back from a visit to Sidmouth – Harry has had bronchial catarrh & been in bed, but he is better. I am going to Rapallo on 25th inst – such a pity you won't be there. D & I go on to Rome for a week, & then back here via Rap & Paris, & we shall be here about end of April. I am glad to hear you've at last finished "A Vision". I wonder if you are right in reading into Shelley's Poems "more than they contain"! I like yr Doctor who escapes from life to sit in front of his Buddha – (you will realize I am reading yr letter again). No news in particular. I see a good deal of Wyndham, who is a perennial source of amusement to me. He gave me an awful account of Berlin – all sexual perverts – the men dressed as women say "we are not liked in Paris" – odd?
I read McGreevy's study of T. S. Eliot[2] – I think it is good & it's certainly interesting – but I do wish he wouldn't have long parentheses – quite unnecessary – & I was always told parenthesis was a sign of weakness – But perhaps it is a new fashion!
What is McGreevy doing? I have been hobnobbing at Sidmouth with 2 retired Indian army Colonels.[3] Both very interested in Africa, & what Harry calls my "beastly savages – " It's odd how many people I meet who like African things. Love to you both – are you likely to be in London?

yrs ever O.S.

NOTES

1. This refers in part to WBY's letter postmarked 9 February 1931 (*L* 781), but there was probably a subsequent letter from WBY which has not survived. *L* 781 explains the following references to *AV [B]*, Shelley's poems, and the "learned doctor". Lionel Johnson, writing to J. H. Bradley on 15 June 1884, asked where he could find a portrait of Shelley to give to "a cousin who almost prays to Shelley, having lost all her other gods" (*Some Winchester Letters to Lionel Johnson*, London: Allen & Unwin, 1919, p. 111). The "learned doctor" was Frank Pearce Sturm (1879–1942). There is a photograph of Sturm contemplating his Buddha in Richard Taylor's *Frank Pearce Sturm: His Life, Letters, and Collected Work* (Urbana, Chicago and London: University of Illinois Press, 1969),

facing p. 57. OS owned a small statue of the Buddha which she called "Uncle Hilary" (*EPDSL*, p. 16).
2. *T. S. Eliot: a Study* (London: Chatto & Windus, 1931).
3. One of the colonels was probably Lieut. Col. John Shakespear (1861–1942), a cousin of Hope Shakespear, and author of *John Shakespear of Shadwell and His Descendants 1619–1931* (Newcastle-Upon-Tyne: Northumberland Press Ltd., 1931).

[Letter 13]

34 Abingdon Court
23.6.31

My dear Willy –

The book came from Hatchard's last night.[1] *Very* many thanks. I shall read it with interest, & understand parts of it, I *hope*!

I trust you've not been bothered to death with affairs since you got back.[2] It is much better to be an only child, like D. & E. & O. I don't think what they say about Wyndham can be true. I got a card from him a few days ago from Atlas Mountains in Morocco; & he says he will write – (he hasn't done so yet).[3]

Nothing of interest has happened since you went away. I have had a cousin here, & we went to quite a good play – a psychological study of a murderer[4] – I always find I like the theatre *when* it is good – but that is so seldom.

I had a talk yesty with a friend who was the librarian at the Quest, and knows Eisler.[5] She thinks he turns & twist things to suit his own theories in his book, & is not reliable. But she mayn't know!

I meant to ask you what you really thought of the book – I can't be bothered with Josephus & Jesus & Paul – so I shall not read it. Do you know anything about *human radiations*? I am reading a French book on the subject by Lakowsky – interesting – It isn't auras, but radio-electrical.[6]

With love yrs O.S.

NOTES

1. Probably *Berkeley's Commonplace Book*, ed. G. A. Johnston, (London: Faber & Faber, 1930) Yeats himself left two copies in his library (*YL* 24).
2. I.e., to Dublin from London, where WBY probably dined with OS on Sat. 23 May before taking his Honorary D. Litt. at Oxford on Tues. 26 May, returning to London on the 27 May. OS is referring to WBY's intervention to save the financially troubled Cuala Press.
3. The corresponding WBY letter has not survived; I am unable to explain this reference. Lewis went to Morocco in May 1931 and appears to have stayed there for some months (see Jeffrey Myers, *The Enemy: a Biography of Wyndham Lewis*, [London: Routledge & Kegan Paul, 1980] p. 193).
4. Not identified: there were several plays running at the time which could fit this description.

5. The Quest Society was founded in 1909 by G. R. S. Mead (1863–1933) "to promote investigation and comparative study of religion, philosophy, and science, on the basis of experience" (*EPDSL*, p. 351). Olivia and Dorothy Shakespear attended meetings of the Society (which had its headquarters in Kensington) during the pre-war years. The librarian was a Miss E. Worthington; she is listed in an address book which OS began in 1910 and kept for many years; five different London addresses for Miss Worthington have been recorded and deleted, but nothing further is known about her. See also OS's letter of 9 June 1932 (p. 85) below.

6. Robert Eisler, *The Messiah Jesus and John the Baptist, according to Flavius Josephus' recently discovered "Capture of Jerusalem" and other Jewish and Christian sources* . . . (Heidelberg, 1928; London: Methuen & Co., 1931). Eisler (1882–1949), Austrian economist and historian, wrote on subjects ranging from monetary reform to lycanthropy. His *Stable Money: the remedy for the economic world crisis etc.* (London: Search Publishing Co., 1932) aroused some interest during the 1930s.

7. Georges Lakhovsky (1870–?) was a vigorous exponent of unorthodox forms of radiotheraphy in the treatment of cancer. He also wrote a number of philosophical works on the rôle of radiation in human life at large. OS is probably referred to *Le Secret de la Vie: Les Ondes Cosmiques et la Radiation Vitale* (Paris: Gauthier–Villars, 1925).

[Letter 14 (*LTWBY* 518)]

34 Abingdon Court
8.7.31

My dear Willy –

I am sending back Berkeley with many thanks for the loan. I've read it nearly all – except the Vision, which is quite beyond me. I feel sure there are lots of fallacies, which I'm not clever enough to detect – Does Croce? Could you tell me the name of his book, which I suppose is translated, as you read it?[1]

I think the arguments for the existence of a God are really childish. But then I'm no metaphysician, as you know.

I hope things are not going badly with you – I've been reading Rothenstein's memoirs – all *our* period, & therefore rather interesting – a portrait of you, with a curl of hair standing up like a question mark.[2]

Nobody I've met seems to like yr John portrait – I've concluded that I definitely dislike it, & think it is badly painted.[3]

I have read The Land of Youth,[4] & quite see why it wasn't appreciated – of course it is beautifully written, but there's too much Irish mythology & lists of genealogies – which don't interest most English people – But I wonder it didn't do better in Ireland.

I am busy with a host of pottering things – along to Lionel's sister next week,[5] but not away permanently till Augt 5th & shall be back here in the middle of Septr –

With love, yrs, O.S.

NOTES

1. The preceding WBY letter has not survived. See his reply, dated 2 Aug. (*L* 782), in relation to this paragraph.
2. William Rothenstein, *Men and Memories: The Recollections of William Rothenstein 1872–1900* (London: Faber, 1931). The 1898 portrait of WBY appears facing p. 335.
3. The 1930 portrait, which was exhibited at the Royal Academy during the summer of 1931. It was bought by the Glasgow Art Gallery, and is reproduced as the frontispiece to *Explorations* (1962) and in *YA3*, (1985): as plate 9, following p. 68.
4. James Stephens, *In the Land of Youth* (London: Macmillan, 1924). See *L* 780.
5. Isabella Johnson, in Surrey.

[Letter 15 (*LTWBY* 519–20)]

2 Fortfield Terrace
Sidmouth
24.8.31

My dear Willy –

I can't refrain from the tiresomeness of answering your letter[1] by return, which makes you my debtor in so short a time –

I was much puzzled by Ede's book.[2] How did he get hold of Sophie's Diary, & is it genuine? Ede, I hear, is a precentor[3] or something, at the Tate Gallery.

Now I knew Sophie, & she was a little middle-aged, withered, plain person, & to all of us, quite uninteresting. I never believed it possible that she could be Gaudier's mistress – or that he could have wanted her. I am inclined to think the whole story is made up. If so, it is very clear. I forget if the book says that she died in a lunatic asylum – poor devil. I don't doubt that some of Gaudier's remarks about Art were what he really said.

I own the book irritated me – it was not the Gaudier I knew. I don't think as highly of his love letters as you do. I myself, have received far, far better ones! (from various people, my dear). All destroyed – Your poem[4] is beautiful – thank you for sending it. When does the Crazy Jane series come out?

I don't know what is to be done about your "further material"[5] – the whole situation "tickles me to death," as your American ladies[6] wd say.

We'll leave it at that.

Yours affectly O.S.

NOTES

1. Not WBY's letter of 2 Aug. [1931] (*L* 782), but another, probably written between 18 and 22 Aug., which has not survived. See note 4 below.
2. H. S. Ede, *Savage Messiah*, (London: Heinemann, 1931). See also the following OS letter and *L* 782–3. The Gaudier-Brzeska literature began with Ezra Pound's *Gaudier-Brzeska:*

A Memoir (London: Allen Lane, 1916; Laidlaw and Laidlaw, n.d. [1916?]). Most of this book is in fact about Pound and Vorticism, but it helps to explain OS's proprietary interest in Gaudier-Brzeska. Six of his letters to her, written shortly before his death in action on 5 June 1915, are quoted by Pound (pp. 73–9). It is clear that OS was fond of Gaudier-Brzeska, whom she and Pound first met at a London Salon exhibition on 27 June 1913, according to Pound's recollection as interpreted by Roger Cole (*Burning to Speak: The Life and Art of Henri Gaudier Brzeska*, [Oxford: Phaidon, 1978] p. 30). (Cole misidentifies Pound's "OS" as Osbert Sitwell). There are frequent references to Gaudier-Brzeska in *EPDSL*: OS bought a white marble torso by Gaudier-Brzeska for £10 in Dec. 1913; he visited Brunswick Gardens on several occasions (including one of Rummel's recitals); Harry Tucker also bought some of his work.

All of this helps to account for the feeling behind OS's letters: that Ede is an outsider invading family territory. Ede's book (which consists largely of quotations from Gaudier-Brzeska's letters to Sophie Brzeska, together with material based on her diary), makes clear that the relation between Gaudier-Brzeska and Sophie was both platonic and pathological. Sophie Brzeska was born in Cracow in 1871 or 1872; she met Henri Gaudier (1891–1915) in Paris early in 1910; they combined their surnames and often presented themselves as brother and sister. Sophie Brzeska was never mentally stable, and her condition worsened rapidly after Gaudier-Brzeska's death in 1915. She was certified insane in November 1922 and confined in a Gloucestershire asylum, where she died of pneumonia in March 1925. Roger Secrétain quotes an interview with H. S. Ede, in which Ede describes the difficulties he faced in trying to rescue Gaudier-Brzeska's work and Sophie Brzeska's papers from the Court of Lunacy (*Un sculpteur "maudit": Gaudier-Brzeska 1891–1915*, [Paris: Le Temps, 1979], pp. 305–6).

Later biographers have not questioned the authenticity of either the diary or the letters: these materials are now in the University of Essex Library. But, even allowing for the distorting effect of Ede's commentary, Yeats's judgement of Sophie Brzeska seems rather naive.

OS was clearly upset by the devastating impression left by Gaudier-Brzeska's letters to Sophie Brzeska, which are those of a half-crazed child to a hysterical mother-substitute. His letters to OS in 1915 are mature, intelligent, and level-headed; they do indeed read like the work of another person altogether.

3. A disparaging joke about Ede's rank of curator, a precentor being a minor canon or chaplain in the Anglican church.
4. "The Results of Thought" (*VP* 504–5). WBY's first fair copy of the poem is dated "August 18" [1931]. See Jon Stallworthy, *Between the Lines: Yeats's Poetry in the Making* (Oxford: Clarendon Press, 1963, pp. 212–16).
5. The "Crazy Jane" poems first appeared as a series in *Words for Music Perhaps and Other Poems* (Dublin: Cuala Press, 1932), with the exception of "Crazy Jane Talks With The Bishop", which was first published in *The Winding Stair and Other Poems* (London: Macmillan, 1933).
6. I am unable to explain this reference.

[Letter 16 (*LTWBY* 520–1)]

34 Abingdon Court
27.9.31

My dear Willy –

We are in a nice mess here, & now there is the threat of a general election – I wonder how it all affects you? It is very difficult to understand all these financial mysteries, & I don't know anybody who really knows the inside of things.[1] Dorothy is with me. We had rather a good time with Omar at Sidmouth, & returned a fortnight ago.

Dorothy has read the Gaudier book, & dislikes it as much as I do – so does Wyndham.[2] They think it was a commercial business between Ede, who wanted to sell Gaudier things, & the publisher – or Middleton Murray[sic]. Apparently when Sophie died, all her things went into the hands of some official receiver, Ede might have come upon the Diary like that . . . known the receiver or something. D. thinks, as I did, that the letters are very unlike the Gaudier we knew, & wd like to see them in MSS. Wyndham says that such biographies are a threat to all artists & ought to be pilloried! By the way, have you seen a book by an American, Louise Morgan, called "Writers at Work" in which she gives an interview with you in a coffee shop, & presents you in a sublime light – *such gush* –[3]

What an incurable romantic you are! To go back to Sophie – I think she was merely a very tiresome, hysterical woman, always half mad – & pity more often breeds contempt than anything else. (I'm re-reading your letter).

All the private part of yr letter re affairs at Coole interested me much, but I daren't comment on it.[4] I don't know how far letters are safe?

By the time I reach my 70th year I shall be quite senile. In the mean time I am

yrs affectly O.S.

Valentine Fox left me 4 lovely old carved Chinese amber necklaces – & earrings to match – the latter are little carved Buddhas, & ought to induce a peaceful state of mind.[5]

NOTES

1. See note 3, next letter (16.10.1931).
2. See note 2, previous letter (24.8.31).
3. Louise Morgan, *Writers at Work* (London: Chatto & Windus, 1931); the interview with WBY is reprinted in *W.B. Yeats: Interviews and Recollections*, vol. II, ed. E. H. Mikhail (London: Macmillan, 1977), pp. 199–204.
4. An additional page, not printed by Wade, survives from WBY's letter dated 30 Aug. (*L* 783), while more of it is still missing. The deleted passage describes an argument between Mrs Margaret Gregory Gough and various doctors about the nature of Lady Gregory's final illness, and also refers to Margaret Gough's "hysterical desire" to gain possession of the Coole library after Lady Gregory's death.
5. Elizabeth Valentine Fox (1861–1931), née Ogilvy, m. Thomas Hamilton Fox in 1889. During the 1890s she lived at Hollydale, Keston, Kent. OS used Hollydale as the setting for her second novel, *The Journey of High Honour* (London: Osgood & MacIlvaine, 1895), which describes a house (sketched by Hope Shakespear in Aug. 1896) "in the beautiful

Elizabethan style, its tender greys and reds giving intense colour to the group of tall, scarlet and blue and white flowers standing along the walks . . ." (pp. 9–10).

Valentine Fox was OS's "sponsor" in the affair between OS and WBY. Her marriage, like OS's, was unhappy; her only daughter, Ruth (1890–1966) was born nine months and five days after the wedding, as was Dorothy Shakespear. Ruth Fox married Hugh Dalton (1887–1962), a Labour politician who became Chancellor of the Exchequer in the post-war Attlee government. In or around 1901, Valentine Fox fell deeply in love with Arthur Petersen (1859–1922), a wealthy barrister who later became a Chancery judge. To avoid a scandal, Petersen took the entire Fox family to live with him in a series of ever more luxurious houses. Hamilton Fox (1852–1923), a brewer from Kent, took to drink in his humiliation, but nevertheless outlived Petersen by some eighteen months. Petersen left Valentine Fox £1700 a year for life; the income went to Ruth after Valentine's death in 1931. See Ben Pimlott, *Hugh Dalton* (London: Jonathan Cape, 1985), pp. 122–4, 197–8.

OS and Valentine Fox had met by 1890 at the latest, and remained close friends until Valentine's death.

[Letter 17]

34 Abingdon Court
16.10.31

My dear Willy

I *did* write to you from Sidmouth about your broadcasting[1] – we went to the Tuckers to hear it, & it came through very well & naturally – you can't have got my letter.

You may have heard that Ezra's Villon opera is to be BBCd on 26 & 27[2] – but we greatly fear it may be squeezed out by the election news on the 27th – We are in a nice mess here, & I suppose it will all re-percuss on to you.

I can't think what the awful results may be if a Lab. Govt comes in. The financial side is very difficult to understand, & everyone says something different about it.[3]

I am so glad to hear you are writing poetry.

Did you see a very odd verdict given by a coroner & jury on a wicked clergyman the other day? i.e. that he had been "possessed by an evil spirit"? They're coming on![4]

Also there is the affair near Helsingfors – black magic suspected – & they've called in Scotland Yard to help![5]

I hope you are keeping well – & are not too much bothered by the general situation. I *never* believed in the League of Nations, & now Japan is defying it, & it can't do anything.[6] I've no scandal to tell you. Dorothy is here & returns to Rap early next month.

With love yrs ever O.S.

NOTES

1. "your broadcasting": probably the Irish National Programme from Belfast on 8 Sept. 1931, in which WBY read some of his poems. See *L* 786n.
2. *The Testament of François Villon, A Melodrama by Ezra Pound, words by François Villon, Music by Ezra Pound* (first performed in Paris on 29 June 1926) was broadcast on the BBC National Programme on 26 Oct., and repeated on the 27 Oct. on London regional stations. WBY, in an unpublished letter to George Yeats (from Coole Park, dated 17 Nov. 1931), refers to a missing OS letter describing the poor quality of the broadcast. See also Noel Stock, *The life of Ezra Pound* (London: Routledge & Kegan Paul, 1970) pp. 297–8.
3. "Election news": 16 Oct. was nomination day for the 1931 general election; polling day was the 27 Oct. OS need not have worried; the result was a landslide victory for the Liberal/Conservative alliance which gained over 100 seats from Labour.
4. *The Times* (15 Oct. 1931, p. 11); "VICAR 'POSSESSED OF AN EVIL SPIRIT'". The Rev F. W. C. Woollett gassed himself in his vicarage at Leesfield, Oldham, after having among other things confined his children in bed for days at a time, feeding them on dry bread and water. He laid a curse on his 19-year-old daughter when she sought employment. The Coroner, who concurred with the jury's verdict, described the deceased clergyman's letters to his wife as "diabolically venomous", and also stated "that while Mr Woollett was a lay reader a doctor prepared papers for him to be certified. Instead of being certified he was ordained".
5. OS in referring to a macabre incident which occurred near Helsingfors, in Finland, and received extensive press coverage in England. The caretaker of a pauper cemetery near Helsingfors was arrested for the ritual mutilation of over 40 bodies awaiting burial. "In his lodgings the police found incriminating correspondence and literature on necromancy and black magic. His neighbours informed the police that mysterious nocturnal meetings have occurred at the mortuary for nearly two years. It is believed that participants in those meetings belong to an international society" (*The Times*, 7 Oct. 1931).

   "The arrested caretaker, by name Saarenheimo, previously served in the Red Army. In custody he is continuously singing psalm melodies with cabalistic words. In his possession were found an English treatise on black magic, an old Swedish 'Black Bible,' various mysterious electrical appliances, and a saw, knife and grindstone."

   "Evidence has been given by neighbours that last New Year's Eve the mortuary for several hours showed red, yellow, blue and green lights in rapid succession, but when police inquired the reason, Saarenheimo explained that he was mending his electric wiring" (*The Times*, 9.10.1931).

   Further investigations revealed that similar mutilations had occurred in other parish mortuaries. Numerous families demanded exhumations, fearing that their dead had been molested. The *Daily Express* reported on 12 Oct. that Scotland Yard had been called in, possibly to check for any connection between the events at Helsingfors and the desecration of a number of graves in an Essex churchyard ("Ghoulish Work in the Night," *Daily Express*, 9.10.31). The final *Times* report appeared on 14 October under the heading, "BLACK MAGIC IN FINLAND: SEVERED LIMBS KEPT IN A REFRIGERATOR".
6. OS is referring to the events surrounding the outbreak of hostilities between Japan and China in Manchuria. There was a sombre *Times* leader on the subject on Monday 12 Oct. 1931.

[Letter 18]

34 Abingdon Court
Wedy [27.4.1932]

My dear Willy –

The Swami never came yesty & I've heard nothing so can't report on his singing.[1]

It was very good of you to remember the Balzac, & I thank you much.[2] It is *most* amusing – The name I couldn't recollect was Brantôme – 17th centy – Have you never read him? Perhaps he hasn't been translated.[3] He is much in the style of the Balzac Contes. Nothing of interest has happened since you left, except that I've bought of a new Hat – very becoming. Have you read "The Sweepstake Murders" Connington? Rather good, but complicated.[4]

I hope you are not worn out with the Academy business. I enjoyed your visit here & hope you will be over again in the autumn.[5]

yrs affectly O.S.

NOTES

1. See appendix.
2. There is no reference to a Balzac book in WBY's letter of 22 Apr. (*L* 794). WBY may have sent a volume by separate post, possibly the *Contes Drolatiques*. OS read Balzac in French.
3. Pierre de Bourdeille, Abbé de Brantôme (c. 1540–1616), author of *Vies des dames galantes*, which went through innumerable editions and had certainly been translated by 1899 at the latest.
4. J. J. Connington (pseud. of Alfred Walter Stewart), *The Sweepstake Murders* (London: Hodder & Stoughton, 1931). Stylistically unremarkable, but built around an apparently unbreakable false alibi which involves many ingenious technical devices.
5. WBY had been in London for most of Apr., and probably returned to Dublin on the 21 Apr. See *L* 794–803, especially 801–3, for details of WBY's involvement with the prospective Irish Academy of Letters. WBY from here on began to bombard OS with the works of various Irish authors to get her opinion on whether they should be included.

[Letter 19]

34 Abingdon Court
29.4.32

My dear Willy –

The Swami had never got my letter – I can't think why. He came on Wedy, when I was out, but Louisa[1] fixed up with him to come yesty. He brought his songs – It is very difficult to give an opinion about them – they struck me as being rather charming & simple but, to Western ears, a little monotonous; almost like intoning. He has no voice to speak of. They seemed to me to be different in *scale* to ours, & two were in the minor key, & *sad*. He read me the translations; one, from Urdu & Hindu is really a fine piece of work, I think. He sang me 3 – Sanskrit, Urdu-Hindu & [indecipherable]. I feel I am not enough of a technical musician to give you an opinion worth having about them. You think I am more learned in the matter of music than I am!

He stayed till 9.30 & had another meal of milk, toast & grapes whilst I had my dinner. We had a lot of talk – he is very interesting & has a certain almost child-like simplicity which is attractive – He talked a lot about India, & said what I have heard English people say, i.e. that an inferior type of Englishman goes out now – "an Englishman used to be a gentleman" he says – & the people I know about who were in India 30 years ago, were very different to those who go out now. We are agreed in a pessimistic view of the world! – He finished by giving me a vivid account of the Sturge Moore affair – Really SM. is a villain & has behaved shockingly.[2] I'm afraid I'm let in for Mrs Fode – I can't get her name – but that can't be helped. She will find out I'm not worth cultivating socially.

I wonder if the Swami has ever read Molinos, the Spanish mystic who was the first "Quietist"[3] – there is much in him which is like Eastern philosophy. I must ask him. He evidently has a great liking for you – & says he owes you a deep debt of gratitude – which is true. I wonder how you are getting on – I hope you are not worn out.

yrs affectly O.S.

I'm afraid I've been rather indefinite about the songs – but I feel sure they are good in a simple charming way – & the matter, in the case of the Urdu Hindu one, wd appeal to the Western as well as to the Eastern mind.

NOTES

1. Louisa Crook, OS's parlourmaid.
2. See appendix for an outline of the quarrel between Sturge Moore and the Swami.
3. Miguel de Molinos, *The Spiritual Guide which Disentangles the Soul* . . . (first English transition 1688). WBY's library contains two copies of the 1911 Methuen translation; one of these copies is inscribed "George Hyde-Lees 1913" (*YL* 176–7).

[Letter 20]

34 Abingdon Court
14.5.32

My dear Willy

The Cunard scandal has only reached me through the papers![1] But yesty I saw Wyndham, & I retail what he said, though you probably know it all. Apparently N.C. treated the negro "Henry" very badly, used to knock him about & made a fool of him generally, & was unfaithful with other negroes. Henry, who has a wife & children in U.S.A., left her for good. She went to U.S.A. with a well-known sexual pervert called Banting, who hails from Putney! You know about her being turned out of a negro hotel – too much commotion – & nobody seems to know where she is now. She has given up the Paris Press – it didn't pay – Wyndham says she is merely out for advertisment. I think the white woman & negro combination is *disgusting*.

I didn't know she had written a pamphlet against her mother.

I will get the "Bright Temptation".[2]

I went last week to lunch with Mrs Foden[3] & the Swami! I don't much like her, though she was affability itself & says she is going to "drop in" here. She is what I call "twittery" & an egoist; & talks too much about herself. The Swami is a Pet – & so engagingly simple – outwardly, not at all the professional saint. How badly you do write! I can't make out the word at the end of the sentence "What you wrote me about the Swami is most—?" I only hope it is "valuable" but don't suppose it is. I shan't make up by mind definitely about him till I've seen his book. Of course they suggest my going out to the proposed ashram in India – so likely![4] They don't seem to realize that I am a sheer Agnostic & don't believe in anything – though of course I think anything is possible. I listen to everybody, & wonder how you can all believe the things you do! And all different things –

I am told Rothenstein's Vol II is interesting – I found Vol I rather dull.[5] You don't say how you found Lady G?

I gather you are now in Dublin, so address there. I met T.S. Eliot & *wife* at tea the other day.[6] I've been avoiding her for years, but was finally driven into saying I'd go & see her – She was so interested in seeing "Dorothy's mother" etc – Eliot has aged & rather coarsened in looks – I'd not seen him for 5 or 6 years – but charming as ever – a little too much so.

Love- yrs O.S.

Just remembered W.L. said N.C. used to make Henry bash in doors with his head to show how strong he is, & Henry didn't like it, because it hurt!

NOTES

1. WBY's account of the "the Cunard scandal" appears in his letter to OS of 9 May, but for obvious reasons was deleted by Wade (*L* 794–5). Yeats, who had been told by Edith Sitwell that Nancy Cunard was living in a Negro hotel in Harlem, remarked: "I am not particularly shocked, though I was by the pamphlet attacking her mother. The rich should be above fear & therefore audacious as the aristocracy were in the eighteenth century – if you like negro lovers why not say so. She is typical of her cruel generation & it is always something to be typical."

   The incident in question was first publicised on 2 May 1932 by the New York *Daily Mirror*, which announced that Nancy Cunard had arrived in New York in pursuit of the singer Paul Robeson, and was staying in the same Harlem hotel. Nancy Cunard called a press conference the following day in order to deny the story. For a full account, see Anne Chisholm's authoritative biography, *Nancy Cunard* (London: Sidgwick & Jackson, 1979) pp. 193ff. The "pamphlet attacking her mother" was *Black Man and White Ladyship*, privately printed in 1931. (*At the Hawk's Well* was first performed in Lady "Emerald" Cunard's drawing room in Apr. 1916). Wyndham Lewis and Nancy Cunard had a brief affair in Venice in 1922 (see Chisholm, pp. 88–9). "Henry" was Henry Crowder, a black jazz pianist who had a long and troubled affair with Nancy Cunard.
2. Austin Clark, *The Bright Temptation: A Romance* (London: Allen & Unwin, 1932). See OS, 9.6.1932, note 5, p. 86 below.
3. Mrs Foden: see appendix.
4. WBY (and possibly OS) believed at this stage that Mrs Foden was a wealthy woman; the Swami's London disciples must also have believed the story that she was going to endow the ashram and to be guided by the Swami's master, Bhagwan Shri Hamsa.
5. The second volume of *Men and Memories* (covering 1900–22) was published by Faber in May 1932.
6. OS presumably visited the Eliots at their flat at 68 Clarence Gate Gardens NW1. Eliot left for his American lecture tour in Sept. 1932; this marked the end of his marriage to Vivien.

[Letter 21]

> 34 Abingdon Court
> May 24th [1932]

My dear Willy

I see Lady Gregory has passed away.[1] I do hope her end was quiet & peaceful. You will feel the loss of such an old & wonderful friend very much; though you expected it, death always comes as a shock.

I will not write more, as you will be overwhelmed with letters

> Yrs
> O.S.

NOTE

1. A half-column obituary for Lady Gregory, who died on 22 May, appeared in *The Times*, 24 May 1932, p. 19.

[Letter 21]

34 Abingdon Court
9.6.32

My dear Willy –

I was glad to get your letter[1] – I wrote to you at Coole when I saw the notice about Lady Gregory. I am sure you will regret Coole very much – & the ending of a chapter of one's life is always sad.

I hope you will like your summer house – it sounds charming.[2]

I went last night to the Swami's lecture – Mrs Foden's drawing room was quite full – mostly women, of course. A friend of mine met me there – a Miss Worthington – She was librarian at the Quest.[3] He lectures very well, but I am rather sorry his lectures are all about yogis – as I am more interested in his philosophy. He came to tea the other day & met my cousin Colonel Shakespear[4] at the latter's especial request as he knows all Swami's country & is much interested in Indian religions, history etc. – he is a charming man, & they got on very well. The Swami is a dear thing! I am delighted to hear his contract is signed. He knows what he owes to you.

There was a perfectly loathesome Indian at the lecture, who *lisped* & asked questions; but the others were all Europeans. It is odd what an instant antagonisms I feel towards all the other people at lectures! Why is it? I could never do anything in a mass.

You asked me to read "The Bright Temptation" – I am not a fit judge of it, because the subject bores me, & the mediaevilism (I can't spell it ever) – but of course the occasional flashes of irony are good, & it is well written.[5] It wd be, of course, more appealing to Irish people. Are you putting Clarke into yr Academy? Have you come across a book called "Naked Fakir" by Bernays – It's Ghandi – & the book is all about latter & the Irwin conversations at Delhi – & Bernays met Ghandi & Mrs Naidu often.[6] Of course I've only heard very severe strictures on Irwin – this man admired him very much – *also* Ghandi, with reservations.

Swami seems to be giving lectures at other places, so I hope he will do well. I know you like to hear about him, so have no compunction in writing about him at length.

Omar is acting (in pantomime) in *Greek myths* adapted for the children, at the Norland Nurseries! They will probably make great nonsense of them.

I hear Ezra's lecture at Florence was a success, & they were treated as honoured guests, & his expenses paid![7] Very gratifying.

I wonder what will be the upshot of these political meetings – the world jaws & nothing happens.[8]

With love yrs O.S.

I am going away for a week on Monday.

NOTES

1. dated 31 May (*L* 795–96).
2. Riversdale, Rathfarnham.
3. See OS, 23.6.1931, note 5, p. 75 above.
4. Lieut-Col. John Shakespear (1861–1942), author of *John Shakespear of Shadwell and His Descendants* (Newcastle-Upon-Tyne: Northumberland Press Ltd., 1931). "Colonel John", as he was known to OS, lived in Chelsea during the 1930s.
5. Austin Clarke, *The Bright Temptation: A Romance* (Allen & Unwin, 1932). Clarke (1896–1974), poet, novelist and dramatist, was a foundation member of the Irish Academy of Letters and became its president in 1952. *The Bright Temptation* follows the fortunes of a young Irish monk who is thrown from the wall of his monastery at night, apparently by an earthquake, falls into a river, loses his clothes, and goes through a series of adventures which culminate in his living in a cave with a beautiful young girl of quasi-supernatural origin. The book was banned in Ireland from first publication until 1954.
6. Robert Bernays, "*Naked Fakir*" (London: Gollancz, 1931). An account of Bernays's tour of India in 1930–31. Lord Irwin was then Viceroy of India; he agreed to release Gandhi from jail in January 1931. Sarojini Chattopadhyay Naidu (1879–1949), Indian poet and nationalist. She came to England in 1895 and became a close friend of Arthur Symons. She was also a friend of Yeats's and came to Woburn Buildings in the late 'nineties. In 1925 she became President of the Indian National Congress, and remained active in Indian politics until her death. See *Mem* 175.
7. See Noel Stock, *The Life of Ezra Pound* (London: Routledge & Kegan Paul, 1970) p. 301.
8. The disarmament talks at Geneva.

[Letter 23]

34 Abingdon Court
17.7.32

My dear Willy –

Your new home sounds charming.

I was bored to death with "Orlando" – & don't think it is well done.[1]

I saw the interview with you in the Express![2] You were fairly discreet except some nonsense about the French Republic & the LCC having no oath of allegiance – the comparison isn't valid. I am glad to hear your sister has designs that will give her work for some time, but I do wish you wd spell *crucifix* properly – not crusafix – its from the Latin crucib – a cross! I remember years ago telling you the same thing.[3]

You don't say George is going to USA so I conclude she is not? You mustn't come back for 70th as far as I'm concerned.[4] I've been attending Swami's lectures, but am getting tired of Yogis & unbelievable miracles. Swami says he's seen ditto "with his own eyes" but it is well-known that one's eyes are exceedingly unreliable.

I don't like Mrs Foden – I think she's *silly* & very egotistical & rather a poseuse. I feel sure she is disappointed in me, as I'm *no use* & not an enthusiast – the Swami continues to be delightful – He ends his prayer always with "Let peace, & peace, & peace, be everywhere" – I have been paying a visit to Bath – it is always a pleasure being there – such lovely 18th centy terraces & crescents, & a curious remote atmosphere –

"Murder in a Public School" by Wodethorpe, is quite good.[5]
I am going away on Aug 2nd till Sept 7th. Dorothy comes over & will
be with me till Novr.

Love yrs O.S.

NOTES

1. OS is replying to WBY's letters dated 30 June and 8 July (*L* 797–9).
2. Eric Burton Dancy, "A Great Poet speaks for Ireland", *The Daily Express* (11 July 1932)
   8. This interview (hitherto unrecorded) took place at Yeats's flat in Fitzwilliam Square,
   at a time when he acted as unofficial go-between in a controversy over the oath of
   allegiance (*CL* 1, xxiii). Yeats told Dancy that he thought the oath "should go", and
   said "After all, neither the French Republic nor the London County Council has an
   oath of allegiance of any kind. Our association must be natural. If the British
   Commonwealth of Nations is not a natural economic unit it should not hold together,
   and if it is we are not such fools as to want to vote ourselves out." Yeats felt that the oath
   of allegiance to the British Crown would provide a focus for "Communists and all kinds
   of extremists" who would be "running riot in the country" rather than resolving
   differences in Parliament because "an Irish Communist, strange to say, is a pious man,
   and objects to anything savouring of perjury".
      Yeats approved of loyalty to "the British Commonwealth of Nations and not to a
   royal house which has no organic relation to our history". He "certainly d[id] not want
   to see Ireland a republic outside the British Commonwealth". The interview focused on
   Yeats's reading of Hermann Schneider's *The History of World Civilization* tr. Margaret M.
   Green, (London: Routledge, 1931, 2v; see also *YL* 241–2). Yeats interpreted to Dancy
   the three epochs of modern Irish history in the light of Schneider's theories concerning
   the results of racial union throughout long periods of history.
3. See *L* 797–8. WBY's spelling of "crucifix" was corrected by Wade.
4. WBY travelled alone to the USA on 21 Oct. and returned at the end of Jan. 1933. OS's
   birthday was 17 Mar.
5. R. C. Woodthorpe, *The Public School Murder* (London: Ivor Nicholson & Watson, 1932).
   WBY's taste for detective fiction is recalled by Clifford Bax: "he challenged his host
   (and me) to name any detective story he had not read" (*Some I knew Well* [London:
   Phoenix House Ltd, 1951] p. 98).

[Letter 24]

Letterhead: Orchard Cottage,
Kinlet,
Bewdley.
Aug 6*th* [1932]

My dear Willy –
   I am glad to hear that you are comfortable & like your new home. I
hope it may be a house of inspiration![1]
   Just before I left London on Tuesday I got O'Connor's "Saint &
Kate"[2] – it is very clever, & I should think an excellent picture of that
type of "Saint" – (By the way, have you written the Introduction to the
Swami's book? He seems to me, to be a little anxious about it, but for

heaven's sake *don't tell him* I said so). O'Connor's book is a trifle heavy in places. I will get Francis Stuart's when I am at Sidmouth.[3] [?] was the idiot of the family,[4] & indeed, looked so, when I met him as an elderly man. I am in Shropshire & enjoying the lovely country – we have had long motor drives & tea with these "county" families. They always amuse me. I am staying with a cousin of Hope's, who has this cottage on the family estate, which is a beautiful place.[5] I suppose it will all break up & have to be sold, in time. I go next week back to town, where I meet Dorothy, & we take Omar down to Sidmouth – Letters home will be forwarded.

I don't like O'Connor as much as O'Flaherty – so far.[6] You seem to have a lot of promising Irish authors. Why are there never any Irish *musicians*?

My cousin here is an automatic writing medium, & there are 2 books here about Spiritism – one "On the Edge of the Etheric" by Findlay[7] another by a Swede – can't remember the name & the book's in the drawingrm, where a tiresome visitor is lurking. I am sure the first one is full of scientific fallacies about the Cosmos & Ether – I only *hope* their horrible next world isn't true – same conditions (only no money worries)! – same people – same self – all perfectly intolerable. And they think that's "the spiritual life"! Imagine meeting all the people one has got rid of in this life – all as affectionate as ever. *NO.* How tiresome it is of you never to tell me if you're going alone to USA.[8]

I wish you would write to me about politics – but I suppose you can't – & I am afraid of the subject – & will only say you are "heading for the abyss"[9] – If I could blow up the whole world by touching a button in the wall, I'd do so without a moment's hesitation – & hope the RC's are right when they say one can't resurrect properly without burial – though why the component parts of a body can't be re-integrated when blown up or cremated, just as well as when merely decayed, I can't see – enough nonsense –

yrs ever O.S.

NOTES

1. See *L* 799.
2. "Frank O'Connor" (Michael O'Donovan, 1903–66): *The Saint and Mary Kate* (London: Macmillan, 1932) was his first novel. In *My Father's Son* (London: Macmillan, 1968), he says that at the time of writing *The Saint and Mary Kate* "I still considered myself a poet, and had little notion of how to write a story and none at all of how to write a novel, so they were produced in hysterical fits of enthusiasm, followed by similar fits of despondency, good passages alternating with bad, till I can no longer read them" (p. 78). Yeats had a copy of the novel in his library (*YL* 194).
3. Francis Stuart (b. 1902) married Iseult Gonne in 1920. He is the author of *Racing for*

Pleasure and Profit in Ireland and Elsewhere (Dublin: Talbot Press, 1937), together with a number of novels including the autobiographical *Blacklist Section H* (Carbondale and Edwardsville: Southern Illinois University Press, 1971). In *The Coloured Dome* (London: Victor Gollancz, 1932) the last four lines of "To a Friend Whose Work Has Come to Nothing" are quoted on p. 127. See *L* 799–800.

4. One of the few places where OS's hand is illegible. A name of five or six letters beginning with "L". OS, thinking over WBY's remarks about Francis Stuart (*L* 800) may have gone to recall an example of apparent idiocy from her own circle.

5. Augusta Harriet Childe-Pemberton (1850–1942) eldest daughter of Augusta Mary Shakespear (1820–1918), Hope Shakespear's aunt. Kinlet, an estate of some 1200 acres, belonged to Roland Ivo Lacon Childe, Augusta Childe-Pemberton's nephew.

6. Liam O'Flaherty (b. 1896), Irish novelist. WBY had recommended a number of his works to OS over the years; it is not clear which of them OS had read.

7. J. Arthur Findlay, *On the Edge of the Etheric* (London: Rider & Co., 1931).

8. OS is commenting on WBY's failure to reply to her question on the subject (OS, 17.7.32).

9. WBY: "When you read these unpolitical books I will write to you about politics" (*L* 800).

[Letter 25]

34 Abingdon Court
24.5.33

My dear Willy

We are going away on the *14th* June. Dorothy came about ten days ago.

I read T. E. Hulme's book years ago. It is very good – such a pity he was killed in the war. I remember he came to tea once at Brunswick Gdns – & we heard him lecture on Bergson. I don't agree with you about "Lady Chatterley" – If you have the expurgated edition, I can't imagine what is left! It is the same thing over & over & bored me considerably. There are good passages, of course.[1]

I hope you signed Joyce's copy of yr Poems & returned it!

Frank Harris was a beast & a cad. I never met a more unpleasant personality, when I heard him lecture –

I couldn't go to Swami's 1st lecture, as I had a d– –d earache. He came to tea to meet Omar, at his own request; & they got along splendidly. I didn't think he was looking very well.

I hope you will not be greatly bored taking your degree at Cambridge.[2] I suppose it is much the same as at Oxford – Latin speeches etc. Such a storm here last night – I still feel addled –

Yours ever O.S.

NOTES

1. OS is replying to WBY's letter dated 22 May (*L* 809–10): "My two sensations at the moment are Hulme's *Speculations* and *Lady Chatterley's Lover*. . . . Frank Harris's *Memoirs*

are vulgar and immoral . . but *Lady Chatterley* is noble" (*L* 810). Hulme's lectures on
Bergson were delivered at "a private house in Kensington" (possibly Lady Low's, at 23
De Vere Gardens) "in November/December 1911" (*EPDSL*, p. 79).
2. WBY received his honorary doctorate at Cambridge in the week beginning Monday 5
June (*L* 810).

[Letter 26]

8.10.33

34 Abingdon Court
8.10.33

My dear Willy

I am very glad to have your new poems, to add to my valuable
collection.[1] Ezra once told me the most valuable possession I have is
those autographed first editions of your poems. I said "you can sell them
when I'm dead", & he took it quite seriously, & was very indignant!

I like "Crazy Jane" – but not quite as much as some of the "To be set
to music – perhaps" poems.[2] I don't believe any of them are suitable for
setting – they've too much music in themselves. I particularly like
"Three Things" – But – to go back in the book – since when has the moon
taken to child-bearing?[3] She used to be the chaste Diana? I am glad
you've put the notes – I seem to remember somewhere a picture of the
Virgin Mary conceiving through the ear[4] the point certainly requires
explanation.

There is no doubt you are a very fine poet, my dear, & I think there is
some of your best work in this book.

The scandalous part of your letter[5] – as far as I can read it – is very
amusing. I've heard no scandal for ages, & it is quite refreshing.

Omar has gone to live with the retired matron of the Norland,[6] near
Bognor, in a lovely cottage – & is going to a good day-school. He knows
people there & will be quite happy. But perhaps you won't "approve" of
this! Such an impertinent remark – as though you were a better judge than
Dorothy & myself. Tell George about Bognor – it may interest her.

The news of Harry is good at present – Nelly is very tiresome, as usual,
but I am sorry for her.

With love yrs O.S.

NOTES

1. *The Winding Stair* (London: Macmillan, 1933). See *L* 814.
2. OS is replying to WBY's letter dated 20 Sept. (*L* 814–15).
3. "The Crazed Moon" (*VP* 487–8).
4. See "The Mother of God" (*VP* 499 & n., 832). While Yeats recalled "Byzantine mosaic
pictures of the Annunciation" in the note to the poem, OS is probably thinking of the

Crivelli *Annunciation* in the National Gallery, London. The memory may be a significant one: WBY and OS spent time there during their courtship (*Mem* 86) and Yeats was to employ a Crivelli painting of the Virgin (though not of the *Annunciation*) in "Rosa Alchemica" (*VSR* 127). OS similarly employed a Crivelli in *Rupert Armstrong*. See Deirdre Toomey, "An Afterword on *Rupert Armstrong*" (*YA* 4, 101). Yeats apparently inserted a reproduction of this picture into a volume in his library (*YL* 109).

5. WBY's paragraph on "our political comedy" (*L* 815).
6. A Mrs Dickie; see OS, 19.11.1933, p. 92 below.

[Letter 27]

34 Abingdon Court
28.10.33

My dear Willy

Who by, & when? The picture[1] is exactly like what you used to be 30 years ago! Many thanks for it – It is now staring at me from the mantelpiece & reminds me of lost youth! Frustrated, futile youth.

Swami is giving a lot of lectures. Some are at a new friend's, Mrs Mitchell – a rich woman, nice & unaffected & simple. We have a Russian Prince married to an Englishwoman. They look as though they had been through unspeakable things, & Mr Bristowe says they have. She never speaks.[2]

The other lectures are at Mrs Bristowe's – Eva[3] asked me to take her, & strangely enough, she was much taken with the lecture & is coming again. I feel I may be sailing under false colours with all these people, because I am *not* a convert, tho' very much interested – if I may use such a grand term. But one can't go about explaining oneself in an egotistical way! I *think* Mrs Foden is now rather in the background. She is very cold to me!! Mrs Reade[4] was here yesterday – & tells me AE is living in London. Which seems odd. Do you remember you brought him to tea one day in Porchester Sq. & he said the room was full of yellow devils![5] I've never forgotten it – I wonder what they were; & why they were there.

With again thanks for the picture

yrs affectly O.S.

NOTES

1. The 1907 portrait by Augustus John, frontispiece to *Collected Poems* (1933). See *L* 818.
2. See appendix for the Bristowes. I have not been able to identify "Mrs Mitchell" or the "Russian Prince married to an Englishwoman".
3. Eva Ducat (1878–1975), a friend of OS's. WBY appointed Eva Ducat as his musical advisor in 1919 (WBY to Harold Watt, 16 Nov. [1919], Macmillan archive, BL Add.Ms.54898 f.49). Her *Another Way of Music* (London: Chapman & Hall, 1928) deals largely with her association with the singer William Shakespeare and his daughter.
4. Unidentified.
5. AE moved to London in August 1933, and took lodgings at 41 Sussex Gardens W2

(Summerfield, op. cit., p. 270). His only documented trip to London during the first
phase of OS's relationship with WBY was during the Easter of 1896. AE was working 6
days a weeks at Pim's in Dublin during these years and would have had little
opportunity to travel. He came to London late on Thursday 2 Apr. 1896, bringing some
of WBY's possessions with him (WBY had just moved into Woburn Buildings), and
must have returned to Dublin on Monday 6 Apr. He returned to London for an equally
brief visit on 31 Mar. 1898, but OS and WBY were estranged at this time. The
Shakespears left Porchester Square in 1899 and moved to a flat in Moscow Road,
Bayswater. I am grateful to Deirdre Toomey for information about AE's movements.

[Letter 28]

34 Abingdon Court
19.11.33

My dear Willy –
I believe I understand the 2 verses you sent me! I hope the various
ideas will be more or less elucidated in the rest.[1] It is lovely, any way, but
I do think you rather tend to obscurity nowadays. Perhaps you don't
care, but remember your thoughts & knowledge are a closed book to
many quite intelligent people. (I don't necessarily include myself in that
category, as I think I am growing very old & dull)
The Swami is pining for your advent. His eyes are very bad & I don't
know if he will go to his oculist again. I am sorry about George's not
coming & to hear of Michael's feet. I do hope she'll come after Xmas?[2]
I have been staying in the country & spent my time motoring & raving
about autumn colouring, which was simply *gorgeous*. I then spent a
weekend with Mrs Dickie & Omar. The latter very well & perfectly
happy, & *likes* school! He is coming here for a week in his holidays, when
the maids & I will have our hands full: rather a responsibility.
Wyndham Lewis has brought out a long poem in rhyme – a satire, I
gather from the reviews.[3] He told me of it some months ago, & made me
swear not to tell Ezra! I feel sure it is horrid.
Eva & Marjorie Oliver have written a child's book called "The Ponies
of Bunts"[4] – it is going, I believe, to be a huge success, as Country Life
who publish it, are booming it, ditto Harrod's, which seems to be
important. I do hope they'll make some money. Marjorie breaks in
ponies, & teaches children to ride.
You never told me about your vision – it is curious – of course
diamonds generally mean money – Perhaps you'll have a fortune or a
new love-affair (hearts).[5] Any occult meaning I don't, of course, know. I
believe at about 70–5 men often fall in love – two have done it with me –
both dead now: one I deeply regret, & one *not*.[6] Do you know Swami
believes we may re-incarnate in animal form? It rather shocks me, but
personally I hope to be a large, grey Persian Cat. He knows how deeply
indebted he is to you for this Introduction to his master's book.[7] You
must have *your name* put on the outside, for commercial purposes. I

wonder what the Finn & the Frenchman will have to say about you. I shall be able to read the latter, & perhaps the Finn will be translated?[8]

Miss Plarr has written a book about Dowson, in which she quotes Innisfree àpropos of the Rhymer's Club! It isn't a good book, but it rather amused me – about people one knew. It's called "Cynara".[9] Eva said she thought your picture was by John, but I was not sure –[10] She took me the other day to the Private View of the Portrait Painters – such rubbish & one felt one had seen it all many times before. I must end this frivolous screed. Let me know as soon as your plans are fixed.

yrs affectly O.S.

The news of Harry is *good*. He seems to be leading a normal life now.

NOTES

1. This in reply to WBY's letter dated 11 Nov (*L* 816–18), which includes draft lines intended for the opening of *The King of the Great Clock Tower* (*L* 817).
2. See *L* 816–17; also WBY's reply dated 30 Nov. (*L* 818).
3. A collection of satirical poems by Lewis, containing "Engine Fight-Talk", "The Song of the Militant Romance", "If So the Man You Are", "One-Way Song", and "Envoi", was published as *One-Way Song* in a limited edition by Faber in Sept. or Oct. 1933. OS's premonition was justified.
4. Eva Ducat and Marjorie Oliver, *The Ponies of Bunts, and the adventures of the children who owned them* (*Country Life*, 1933).
5. *L* 817.
6. The two men referred to by OS have not been identified. One possible candidate is Luke Ionides (1837–1924), whose *Memories* (Paris: Herbert Clarke, 1925) were recorded by OS in the early 1920s.
7. Bhagwan Shri Hamsi, *The Holy Mountain* (London: Faber, 1934); intro. by WBY.
8. See WBY, 11 Nov. (*L* 818).
9. Marion Plarr, *Cynara: the Story of Ernest and Adelaide* (London: Grant Richards, 1933), a bowdlerised and sentimental account of Dowson's life.
10. See OS, 28.10.33, note p. 91 above "Eva": Eva Ducat.

[Letter 29]

34 Abingdon Court
4.2.34

My dear Willy

I am much amused at your account of the Heretic's meeting.[1] I knew Nancy Campbell very well when she was girl – She was at school with Dorothy – an interesting creature, but rather a fanatic. She came here to see D. about 2 years ago: quite unchanged. I remember Joseph Campbell read us a play – which I believe you didn't accept – ages ago.

I am glad the Guru's book is about to come out.[2] It will be dry in parts, & the rest incredible! Swami had seen Eliot, & found the latter knew some Sanscrit – Who gets the proceeds of the book? I think Swami ought to, as I gather he translated it. He goes on with lectures, very interesting, but his audiences have dwindled sadly. As far as I can make out, he has made little, if any, impression here – I think the Theosophists are all against him –

I am interested to hear you are going to Rapallo – (I've not mentioned it, by the way).[3] Poor old Pound is failing, I think – heart & general debility.[4] I can't imagine what Isabel will do when he dies. At any rate she won't live with the Ezras!

I don't know what Nelly has told George, but you must have heard Harry is very unwell again – his "heart gone wrong" & he is leading an invalid life & not allowed to walk only drive – If George doesn't know all this don't let on I told you – one never knows what Nelly says. I may be going to Sidth in March to an hotel close by – am worried about Harry. He has those horrid voices in his head again, but the Dr says its all lack of proper circulation – & not his brain.

I suppose one does cease to have personal experience after a certain age, & one has to draw upon past experience. (This in relation to what you say about the new lyrics). I'm glad to hear Vision is finished at last.[5]

You ask what I've been doing – the answer is Nothing but reading, trying to keep warm, & seeing a few people. & attending Swami's lectures! I am sure he thinks I'm a convert, which I am *not* – though I am prepared to admit his philosophy *may* all be true. But so much is incredible – to a Western mind, at any rate.

I had Omar here for a week in Jany – Pantomime & children's play, both of which he loved. He is so active & intelligent it is rather tiring – but I enjoyed having him!

The Dryad ie Hilda Aldington, has turned up – very unchanged – charming & foolish & clever.[6]

With love yrs O.S.

NOTES

1. OS is replying to some comments deleted by Wade from WBY's letter dated 27 January (*L* 819). The deleted passage is as follows: "The secretary of our Academy says 'We had a society called "The Heretics". Francis Stuart gave a lecture on poetry. His elocution was not good. Shemus O'Sullivan was drunk. He had been chosen to propose the vote of thanks & said "I did not hear a word. I won't propose thanks." Then Mrs Joseph Cambell stood up. She was very angry & she became incoherent & then she beat upon her breast with her two fists. It was all so unpleasant that we have never met again.' " Nancy Campbell (née Maude, 1886?–1974) married the Irish playwright Joseph Campbell around 1909. See *EPDSL* 351. OS wrote "*spelt CAMPBELL*" across the top right-hand corner of her reply.
2. *The Holy Mountain.*

3. "I've not mentioned it": i.e. to Nelly Tucker.
4. Homer Pound in fact lived on until 1942.
5. See *L* 819.
6. HD (Hilda Doolittle, 1886–1961) seems to have come to London early in 1934 (exactly when she arrived is not clear) to dispose of a flat at 169 Sloane St. which she had leased for some ten years, and take another at 49 Lowndes Square SW1, though she spent very little time in London during the 1930's. See Barbara Guest, *Herself Defined: the Poet HD and Her World* (London: Collins, 1985) p. 222.

[Letter 30]

34 Abingdon Court
3.3.34

My dear Willy

I was glad to get yr letter. You will be absorbed in Lady G's Life now, for months.[1] It must be a tremendous undertaking but will be very interesting when done.

The poor Swami has been laid up with bronchitis & is still kept in. I enclose Mrs Bristowe's appeal – (he doesn't know I am sending it). I don't suppose you will be able to help. I am giving what I can, but have outside expenses, & can only afford 4£ – I sent the Swami a small sum not long ago, as I thought he must be in financial difficulties.[2] He does not seem to have made much impression here – the philosophy is too hard & relentless & logical for the pack of silly women who attend the lectures (very irregularly). He *ought* to have gone back to India.

Your story about the dogs & the Hen is amusing, but also horrid. The woman who half drowned a dog & then tied a can to its tail, ought to be flogged – so dreadfully cruel – But you were wise to eliminate the Hen at once![3]

No news here – one's great interest is the weather & the threatened drought. However, we've had some rain & snow. I am going to Sidmouth on the 14th. Harry has made a wonderful rally, but I am worried about Nelly, who is always on the verge of a breakdown – according to her own account –*

Have you seen T. S. Eliot's "After Strange Gods"?[4] There is a lot about you & EP in it – it is the Harvard lectures – the trail of the Anglo-Catholic serpent is over it all – but it amused me a good deal –

I will try & write a decent letter later on!

yrs affectly O.S.

*one doesn't know what is play-acting or what is true –

NOTES

1. See *L* 820.
2. The appeal was probably directed towards the foundation of the London Institute of

Indian Mysticism (see appendix), but it may have been simply to raise funds for the Swami – effectively the same object.
3. See *L* 820–1.
4. *After Strange Gods: a Primer of Modern Heresy* was published by Faber and Faber in February 1934.

[Letter 31]

34 Abingdon Court
Friday
[6 April 1934]

My dear Willy

I am sorry to hear about this operation:[1] it is always an unpleasant business, & I do hope all is going well this morning.

I will go to see you on *Monday* about 3 ock – I have an engagement near at 4.30 – I will tell nobody – The Swami is coming to tea tomorrow & is sure to make enquiries about you, but I'll lie to him!

Omar comes up on Thursday for dentist & oculist, & I shall be entirely engaged with him all the rest of the week.

Best wishes,
yrs O.S.

NOTE

1. This letter almost certainly refers to the Steinach operation, and I have dated it accordingly. So far as I know, WBY had no other operation in London between mid-1923 and late 1935. WBY's desire for secrecy further reinforces the inference. Other correspondence indicates that WBY arrived in London Thursday 5 April for the operation; as it was relatively minor it seems unlikely that he would have waited a week.

[Letter 32]

Warnford Cottage,
Warnford,
Southhamptom
3.5.34

My dear Willy –

I expect you've been too busy to write. I do hope all is going well with you & that you did not go back to your activities too soon.[1] I have been staying with Omar, who is flourishing & doing very well at school – am now with Hope's cousins (great friends of mine)[2] & am going on to some others of my own on Saty – Country looking lovely etc etc – & I really find it is good for the soul to gather primroses & listen to birds shouting all round one. I found someone had given Mrs Dickie (Omar's hostess) Vol II of the Holiday stories book by Moore.[3] She hadn't read it! I suppose Vol II would be of no value? I can't remember the proper name of the book.

I heard from Swami today. He is evidently better & has been able to translate more Upanishads. He came to tea, oh, I told you. My cousin here, saw a private view of the Aran film, the other day, & said it was beautiful – such scenery & wonderful photography.[4] Some fool in the Mirror has mixed it up with *Arran* in Scotland, in an article! I wonder if people have found out you were in London? *I* haven't said a word to a living soul. (Why "living" –? one wouldn't communicate with a discarnate soul on such a subject)

yrs O.S.

NOTES

1. I.e. after the Steinach operation.
2. Warnford Cottage was the home of Mrs E. M. ("Edie") Wood, an old friend of OS's. See *EPDSL* 121.
3. Probably *A Story-Teller's Holiday* (first published 1918); OS would seem to be referring to the two-volume set published in 1928 as part of Heinemann's Uniform Edition.
4. *Man of Aran* (1934), directed by Robert J. Flaherty. The film was a great commercial success and won first prize at the 1934 Venice film festival. See Liz-Anne Bawden (ed.), *The Oxford Companion to Film* (Oxford: OUP, 1976) p. 445.

[Letter 33]

34 Abingdon Court
25.11.34

My dear Willy

Your plays have come from Macmillan – *very* many thanks.[1] I think I like "the Resurrection" the best, but they are all good. I hope you are progressing with your theatrical schemes, your renewed activities are most interesting – I should not perhaps say "renewed" but "accelerated" – Don't you feel rather as though you had been wound up again?[2]

I have been staying with Lionel's sister – the difference between the two always amuses me – of course Lionel re-acted violently against his family & was always unjust to them – *She* is an Anglo-Catholic & has just had the new house she has built, *blessed*.[3] It is a charming house, but I feel there is something odd about it.

I haven't seen the Swami, as I've been away for a fortnight; but am going to his private sort-of meeting today. I can't make out that he is making any real progress with his proselytizing, – & am rather worried about him.

You must write my name in the book when you come again, as I am not satisfied with printed "author's compliments" –[4]

yours ever affectly O.S.

NOTES

1. *The Collected Plays* of W. B. Yeats (London: Macmillan, 1934).
2. The corresponding WBY letter has not survived.
3. Isabella Johnson had just moved into her house, Cranbourne, Woodham Way, Woking, Surrey, and this remained her address until her death in 1955.
4. WBY's longstanding practice was to write to Macmillan and ask them to send a few copies to close friends just before the release of the book in question: hence the printed "author's compliments".

[Letter 34]

34 Abingdon Court
Feby 7th [1935]

My dear Willy

I am greatly distressed to hear you have been so ill.[1] I rather wondered why you didn't write, but concluded you were busy re-organising the theatre or something & didn't bother you with a letter. It is most unfortunate for you. I do hope you won't get about & do too much – What an anxiety for George – I hope she isn't worn out. I suppose you had a nurse.

The fact is you ought not to be in London in the winter. Fred Manning has been very ill in a nursing home – much the same sort of thing – only he has asthma added.[2]

Swami has, I believe, been staying with the Bristowes in Wales. I am going to a Committee meeting tomorrow, so shall see him. Its all such nonsense – there's nothing for the Committee to do.[3] I have been seeing a good deal of Mrs Press, & like her very much.

I am going to Sidmouth 25th inst. & shall be away most of March. H.T. is wonderfully well.

I won't write any more, as I expect you ought not even to read letters. With deep condolences

Yrs affly O.S.

NOTES

1. See WBY, dated 5 February (*L* 830–1), telling OS of his severe attack of congestion of the lungs. GY then wrote to OS on 13 Feb. to say that WBY was steadily improving.

2. Frederic Manning (1882–1935) died on 24 Feb. He received a respectful obituary in *The Times* (26 Feb.), from William Rothenstein (see *Men and Memories*, vol. III, Faber 1939, p. 264). Manning, an Australian, came to London with Arthur Galton (1852–1921) in 1897. OS probably met Manning not long after that, since Galton had known Lionel Johnson in the 1880s. A section of Manning's *Scenes and Portraits* (London: John Murray, 1909), is dedicated to OS. See *EPDSL* 349–50. He and OS remained on affectionate terms throughout his life. His most renowned book is *The Middle Part of Fortune: Somme and Ancre* by "Private 19022" (London: Peter Davies, 1929) which E. M. Forster called "the best of our war novels". It was later reissued in abridged form by the same publisher in 1930 under the title *Her Privates We* by "Private 19022".
3. See appendix. Professor Ann Saddlemyer kindly suggests that this is Anita Press, a member of the Swami's circle, "who seems to have taken over the Swami after the Foden incident" (unpub. letter, 1-9-86).

[Letter 35]

34 Abingdon Court
14.6.35

My dear Willy

My tardy but sincere congrats on your having attained your 70th year. I hope the banquet was a success & that the Maharajah was not there![1] Nothing has happened here since I saw you, except that I have been reading Ezra's new Cantos, & *can't* – they are too full of American people & of financial affairs –[2]

I have seen the Swami who seems to be rather relieved by the elimination of the Bristowes – (but they were very good to him, all the same).[3] By the way, I am amused to find that Mrs Foden can't have been Lady Gweneth – Lord Gerard is a Baron, & sons & daughters are only Honourables – & grand-daughters have no title at all. She couldn't possibly have had a "courtesy title" of Lady G.[4] My authority is a cousin of Hope's, who knows Burke's peerage from A. to Z!

I am expecting Dorothy to arrive tomorrow – a horrid gale still blowing.

I see T. S. Eliot is producing a play called "Murder in the Cathedral", at some Canterbury performances – What *is* he coming to![5] Do let me know as soon as things are settled about your Mercury Theatre plays.[6]

Keep well –
yours affectly O.S.

NOTES

1. The corresponding WBY letter has not survived. On the banquet, see Letter 37 n. 1, p. 101 below.
2. *A Draft of Cantos XXXI–XLI* (London: Faber, 1935).
3. Judge Bristowe was "eliminated" by his death on 5 Apr. 1935 at the age of 77.

4. As "Mrs Foden" was not even Mrs Foden, it is hardly surprising that she was not related to the Gerard family. See appendix.
5. *Murder in the Cathedral* opened on 15 June at the Festival of Music and Drama organised by the Friends of Canterbury Cathedral.
6. See *L* 835.

[Letter 36]

34 Abingdon Court
Sunday [23 June 1935]

My dear Willy –

I was very pleased to get the Irish Times, & read it all with much interest.[1] I hope it won't turn your head! By the way, you might have brushed your hair before that photo was taken! Your one in the Radio Times with your hair perfectly flat, which I can't say is becoming – it goes too far the other way.[2]

Dorothy is here – at least she is at this moment staying with Omar. It has turned fearfully hot: & I've dropped my winter clothes.

I can't make out if the new "Vision" is coming out by itself, or whether it is one of a complete edition of your works? I wonder if your Indian trip has got any forrader.[3] I haven't seen Swami since I last wrote.

I am addled with the sudden heat,[4] so forgive a stupid but grateful letter –

yrs ever O.S.

NOTES

1. See *L* 835. WBY sent OS the *Irish Times* for 13 June 1935 ("William Butler Yeats: Aetat 70", pp. 6–7).
2. *Radio Times*, 7 June 1935, p. 53: programme notes for birthday broadcast on National Programme, 13 June, at 10.40 p.m. The photograph matches OS's description precisely, as does that in the *Irish Times*.
3. WBY may have mentioned plans for a trip to India, in an earlier letter which has not survived; by this point he was already planning his disastrous voyage to Majorca the following Nov.
4. The maximum temperature in London on Saturday 22 June was 85°F.

[Letter 37]

34 Abingdon Court
18.7.35

My dear Willy

You wrote to me just before the banquet – I hadn't expected a letter, as I knew you must be overwhelmed with correspondence.[1] We shall be away all Augt, at Hindhead, where we take Omar with us. I hope Anne will enjoy her entry into the world – rather fun taking her![2]

I am dying to see the anthology – I expect it is "old-fashioned" but *I* shall not quarrel with that.[3] Swami seems it is delighted with the Majorca prospect – it will be an odd trio![4] I believe it is a good climate – not too variable. There is a funny little American there called Chamberlain, who has been making excavations.[5] He wrote a book about Queen Elizabeth some years ago – we all knew him.

Re the 2nd time – It would have been the *3rd* – but I assure you you have missed nothing.[6]

I am glad to hear you are keeping well – I find this awful heat very addling & we are busy with people etc – but luckily *I* have nothing to do with "Social Credit" activities.[7]

Are your Noh plays etc ever going to be given at the Mercury?

I am not, of course, saying anything to Nelly about Marjorca,[8] – in fact, I hardly ever mention you & George – I shall be going to them at the end of September, after D. has gone.

yrs O.S.

NOTES

1. "the banquet": probably the P.E.N. Club dinner in Yeats's honour in Dublin on 27 June. Photographs of Yeats at the banquet accompanied a report of it in *The Irish Times*, 28 June 1935, 9.
2. See WBY to Dorothy Wellesley, 26 July 1935 (*L* 838). WBY's letter to OS on the subject has not survived.
3. *The Oxford Book of Modern Verse*.
4. See appendix.
5. Frederick Chamberlin, author of *Chamberlin's Guide to Majorca* (Barcelona: Augusta, 1925).
6. I am unable to explain this reference.
7. Presumably Dorothy Pound was engaged in some London campaign on Ezra Pound's behalf.
8. Precisely why WBY was anxious to keep the Majorca trip from Nelly Tucker's knowledge is not clear. There are two possible reasons: first, to judge from Nelly Tucker's unpublished letters concerning Florence Tucker's estate, she was hostile to Indian religions and hence possibly to the Swami; second, the fact that Mrs Foden was a member of the party and George Yeats was not could have led to protest from Nelly Tucker, even though George Yeats herself seems to have been relatively content with the arrangement.

APPENDIX: YEATS, SHRI PUROHIT SWAMI, AND MRS FODEN

The story of Yeats's involvement with Shri Purohit Swami (1882–?) and "Gwyneth Foden" (1882–1965) would appear somewhat confusing if broken up into a series of long footnotes; I have therefore provided an overview in this appendix. Most of what follows is based on unpublished correspondence, supplemented by material from public records etc. My principal sources are the Sturge Moore/Swami papers in the British Library (BL Add Ms 45732), the Sturge Moore papers in the University of London Library at Senate House, and unpublished letters of Yeats, George Yeats, Shri Purohit Swami and Mrs Foden, which John Kelly kindly allowed me to consult.

Shri Purohit Swami, according to his own account, was born in Badnera in the Central Provinces on 12 October 1882, "of a religious and wealthy family" (*An Indian Monk: His Life and Adventures*, [London: Macmillan 1932] p. 1). He arrived in London early in 1931, and according to Shankar Mokashi-Punekar met T. Sturge Moore on 15 April 1931 (*The Later Phase in the Development of W. B. Yeats*: [Karuatak University: Dharwar, 1966] p. 254). Sturge Moore began his ill-starred collaboration with the Swami by correcting the more spectacular errors of idiom in the Swami's *The Song of Silence* (Poona, 1931), and his translation of the "Bhagwad Geeta". This work was well advanced by the time Yeats met the Swami at Sturge Moore's house on Saturday 6 June 1931. It seems to have been Yeats's encouragement that prompted the Swami to begin work on *An Indian Monk*, a task he pursued with such vigour that by 23 October he had completed 39 chapters.

Sturge Moore's enthusiasm declined as the pile of manuscript grew, and in mid-October he wrote to Yeats at Coole Park, asking him to take over the editing and partial rewriting of the book. Yeats replied on 22 October, declining on the ground of overwork; he then tried to enlist AE, who in turn wrote to Sturge Moore on 2 November to decline. By early December Yeats was suggesting that Sturge Moore consult Middleton Murry in order to locate some young man desperate for publication at any price. The Swami was planning an American lecture tour; Sturge Moore, in an effort to speed up the work, hired two collaborators, both of whom turned out to be unsatisfactory.

Yeats's attitude changed abruptly when he read the first installment of the manuscript; on 8 February he wrote to Sturge Moore, praising the work and agreeing to contribute a preface. By 10 March he was speaking of *An Indian Monk* as one of the world's great books in letters to Sturge Moore and George Yeats. From this point on he was in regular correspondence with the Swami.

On 29 February, however, the quarrel between the Swami and Sturge Moore broke out. The Swami, having received a gift of £20 from an Indian friend, sent £10 of this to Sturge Moore as payment for his labours, and offered him the remaining £10 on condition that he revise the Swami's five books of poems. Sturge Moore was furious; he replied that the proper offer was a share of the royalties, and more or less demanded a percentage, whereupon the Swami became somewhat evasive. Sir Francis Younghusband tried unsuccessfully to intervene on the Swami's behalf. In the last week of March the Swami sent "Miss Foden", as he then called her, to collect the manuscript from Sturge Moore.

Yeats arrived in London in the first week of April, and lunched with the Swami and Mrs Foden on 7 April at the latter's apartment at 19 Lancaster Gate Terrace W2; the Swami at this stage was living at 7 Lancaster Gate Terrace. On 12 April, Yeats met Sturge Moore for lunch, having persuaded him that he might as well help with the final corrections since everyone knew he had worked on the book; on 14 April Yeats delivered the corrected manuscript (though not the preface, which was not completed until 5 October) to Macmillan on the Swami's behalf. He took the Swami's side in the continued altercation with Sturge Moore (the correspondence on the subject continued for another six months), and went to some trouble to pay off one of the hired collaborators, a Mr Bosworth Goldsmith, who seems to have been threatening legal action.

Yeats and the Swami collaborated on a series of books over the next five years; the literary aspects of this collaboration are well-known. They corresponded extensively, and met whenever Yeats was in London. During 1932–35, an organisation devoted to the promulgation of the Swami's philosophy developed in Lancaster Gate; at one stage the area seems to have been packed with Swami enthusiasts. One of these was Leonard Syer Bristowe (1857–1935), a retired judge of the South African Supreme Court, who with his wife Hilda moved from Hertfordshire to 46 Lancaster Gate, late in 1932. Aided by Sir Francis Younghusband (1863–1942), he arranged a series of lectures by the Swami, to which OS refers in several of her letters, and early in 1934 began collecting subscriptions to found the London Institute of Indian Mysticism, whose sole purpose seems to have been to provide a platform for the Swami. Its headquarters may have been at the "Fellowship Club" at 51 Lancaster Gate, which the Swami used as a business address.

Yeats was offered the presidency of the Institute in May 1934, but declined; Judge Bristowe then took office. The membership included Sir Francis Younghusband, Lady Elizabeth Pelham, Margot Collis, and possibly Edmund Dulac, together with Mrs Foden, who was supposedly going to endow an ashram in India, to be guided by the Swami's Indian master, Bhagwan Shri Hamsa. The devotees were planning to emigrate to this establishment, there to take up a life of enlightened contemplation.

Even before the foundation of the Institute, however, the Swami's audiences had begun to dwindle, possibly as a result of the lectures themselves, possibly owing to the attacks of rival theosophical groups who resented the Swami. The Institute suffered from the usual internal tensions; Margot Collis became hysterical at committee meetings; the Bristowes fell from power early in 1935, and Judge Bristowe died on 5 April. The Swami's health was undermined by the English winters; his eyesight was failing.

All of these obstacles might have been surmounted, had it not been for the Swami's association with Mrs Foden. The scattered references in *Letters to W. B. Yeats* do not add up to a very coherent picture; they tend to reinforce Lady Elizabeth Pelham's remark to Yeats that the whole story was "quite beyond the unravelling of any human being" (30 July 1936; *LTWBY* 584). The editors say that the Swami had "an illicit love affair with Mrs Foden (her Christian name is never mentioned) who followed him to India" (*LTWBY* 582). Mrs Foden herself claimed that she had had a child by the Swami (*LTWBY* 584; unpublished letters to Marie Sturge Moore, February 1937).

There is good reason to hesitate before accepting these claims. Every statement of Mrs Foden's concerning Yeats or the Swami that I have been able to check is false. The list would occupy several pages. To take a more general and striking instance: her name was not Gwyneth Foden. She was born Gertrude Hilda Woolcott, at 19 Woodstock Street W1, on 28 October 1882. Her father, Henry George Woolcott, is described as a tailor on the birth certificate, though by the time of her marriage he had changed his occupation to "artist". Her mother Emily's maiden name was Eaton. On 6 June 1901, at the age of 18, she married Henry Charles Riddell (1871–1956) at the registry office at St George's Hanover Square. Riddell is described on the marriage certificate as a bachelor of private means. All the surviving documentary evidence indicates that they were never divorced. When they separated is not known. Mrs Foden (as I will call her to avoid confusion) had assumed the name Gwyneth Foden by 1926; she published a novel under that name with A. H. Stockwell in October 1926 (2nd impression December 1926). Stockwell were not a fastidious firm; *A Wife's Secret*, though well within the bounds of middle-class decorum, is essentially genteel pornography.

The Swami, in his acknowledgements in *An Indian Monk*, described Mrs Foden as "novelist and journalist". The only other book published under the name Gwyneth Foden was *My Little Russian Journey* (London: A. H. Stockwell, 1935, 40pp.). In an unpublished letter to Yeats (17 November 1936), the Swami says fearfully that Stockwell will publish anything Mrs Foden writes (by this stage her output consisted largely of poison pen letters denouncing the Swami). To judge from her unpublished correspondence, the bill for proof correction would have been massive.

It is possible that Gertrude Riddell took up with a Mr Foden at some point before 1926; she may well have decided that "Gwyneth" sounded more "artistic" than "Gertrude". As Mrs (sometimes Miss) Foden, she had met the Swami by June 1931; they lived a few doors away from one another in Lancaster Gate Terrace for the next four years. It is not at all clear who was exploiting whom. Mrs Foden seems to have been slavishly devoted to the Swami; on the other hand, Yeats was convinced that she had collected several hundred pounds from the Swami's friends "to pay for an alleged illness' (unpublished letter to

Dorothy Wellesley, 9 June 1936). She maintained (and the Swami certainly believed) that she was suffering from cancer throughout these years. But the progress of the disease was somewhat peculiar. In late 1933 her condition was supposedly serious; on 2 April 1934 the Swami told Yeats that the cancer was now "inoperable" and that radium treatment was the only hope. In March 1935 she was "completely cured"; in February 1937 she claimed that she was about to undergo major cancer surgery; she died of heart failure in October 1965 at the age of 82.

There is every reason to believe that the "cancer" followed the ups and downs of her association with the Swami. I am likewise sceptical about the possibility that the 50-year-old Mrs Foden could have had a child by the Swami – a child no one ever saw – and whose existence was mentioned only in connection with attempts to blacken the Swami's character.

Yeats met Mrs Foden in April 1932, and despite OS's warnings became mildly infatuated with her. But he was under no illusions about her complete lack of taste and sensibility. (If Mrs Foden had had her way, *The Holy Mountain* would have been called *Love's Pilgrimage*; Yeats kindly but firmly insisted on the former). Nor, on all the available evidence, was there ever any sexual relation between them.

The ill-fated voyage to Majorca was planned as early as June 1935; Yeats corresponded frequently with Mrs Foden on the subject from then onwards. The idea was that Mrs Foden would look after Yeats and the Swami (neither of whom could withstand another London or Dublin winter); she was so eager to assume this role that she offered to pay Yeats's expenses. Yeats believed that she was a wealthy woman, though the supposed wealth (apart from that collected from the Swami's admirers) almost certainly did not exist. Yeats, fortunately, declined the offer.

After many delays, Yeats, the Swami and Mrs Foden sailed for Majorca on 29 November 1935. Mrs Foden spent the voyage quarrelling with the stewards, and at one point appeared in the dress of an Indian temple dancer, to the astonishment of the Hindu seamen. The Swami was sea-sick. By Christmas, both Yeats and the Swami were beginning to wilt under Mrs Foden's care; they held anxious consultations about ways of diverting her energies; Yeats, under the influence of a powerful cocktail served by Commander Alan Hillgarth, the British Consul in Majorca, told Mrs Hillgarth that Mrs Foden's book on Russia had no literary merit. Mrs Foden overheard, and shut herself in a darkened room for two days. Yeats described these and many similar incidents in his letters to George Yeats.

His health had been uncertain since their arrival; on or around 20 January 1936 he became seriously ill. George Yeats arrived on 2 February to nurse him; he was suffering from kidney trouble, breathing difficulties, and heart disease, and he remained very ill throughout February and March. Mrs Foden later claimed that she had nursed him single-handed for months; a Spanish doctor had in fact been in constant attendance during the days before George Yeats's arrival.

While Yeats was out of action, Mrs Foden and the Swami quarrelled irrevocably. Mrs Foden returned to London in mid-February, and began an intensive campaign against the Swami (and to a lesser extent Yeats) which lasted until mid-1937 at least. Yeats first mentioned the quarrel in a letter to OS on 10 April 1936. Wade (*L* 851–2) was forced to delete the passage, as Mrs Foden was still alive, and in December 1952 had refused him permission to print any of Yeats's letters to her; Wade, understandably nervous, omitted the few references to Mrs Foden in the published letters from his index. Yeats warned OS that she would probably receive "mad, threatening letters", and described the whole business as "a witches cauldron".

Those in Majorca were distracted by the bizarre events following Margot Collis's appearance in mid-May (though the two crises soon became interrelated). The hapless Swami sailed for India on 13 May 1936; he found the heat in Bombay unbearable; Mrs Foden's communications pursued him everywhere, even in the pages of the *Bombay Chronicle*; she allied herself with his estranged daughter, who joined in the campaign. By the end of July 1936, Mrs Foden had written denouncing the Swami to George Yeats, T. S. Eliot, Lady Elizabeth Pelham, Edmund Dulac and Commander Hillgarth. She visited the Faber offices to tell Richard De La Mare that the Swami was not a Swami and knew no Sanskrit; she told Eliot that the Swami was about to become the centre of a homosexual scandal (hoping to frighten Faber away from publishing the Swami's translation of the *Upanishads*); she told Dulac and Hillgarth that the Swami was wanted by the CID. She found another ally in Margot Collis's husband, and attempted to prove that the Swami had extracted £100 from Margot Collis by "undue influence"; Margot Collis's solicitors responded by threatening her with legal action. Commander Hillgarth (who must have wondered what had hit Majorca) joined forces with Lady Elizabeth Pelham to quash the rumours flying about London.

Mrs Foden seems to have spent the latter part of 1936 composing a "memoir" of Yeats and the Swami; she offered this work to George Yeats as a contribution to the biography which, she claimed, George Yeats was writing. When this offer was declined with majestic politeness in January 1937, Mrs Foden made the same offer to Sturge Moore via his wife. Sturge Moore agreed on condition that he retained the right to destroy the entire manuscript, whereupon Mrs Foden changed her tune, saying that she already had a publisher in view. It is clear from Mrs Foden's letters that no sane publisher would have touched the manuscript, and that what she was hoping was that some distinguished friend of Yeats would rewrite this libellous document into connected sentences and see it through the press. Mrs Sturge Moore then consulted George Yeats, who warned her not to have anything more to do with the matter.

Mrs Foden, on her own account, then deposited the manuscript with her lawyers and went off to have a major operation for cancer on 9 February 1937 (having spent the previous day composing several pages of typed abuse of the Swami to Mrs Sturge Moore). The operation must have been successful. On 12 December 1952 Mrs Foden wrote to Allan Wade, refusing him permission to print Yeats's letters to her, and telling him that her lawyers were holding sealed packages of letters from famous people she had met; some to be destroyed on her death, and some to be returned to the relatives. There are indications that Mrs Foden may have engaged in amateurish attempts at blackmail at some point in her career. Yeats's letters, however, were bought by a Mr Farmer some time before Wade wrote to her, as part of sale to benefit the Nightingale Hospital in London.

Henry Charles Riddell died at 6 Moreton Place, Pimlico, on 6 October 1956. His effects (valued at £111), together with the proceeds from his life insurance, were equally divided between Mrs Vera Lauderdale of 13 Portman Avenue SW14, and "Gertrude Hilda Riddell otherwise Gwyneth Foden" of 78 Balcombe St NW1 (the address to which Wade had written in 1952). Mrs Foden died on the same day of the year: 6 October 1965; the death certificate was made out in both names. Her effects (valued at £583) went to "my great-niece and her husband/Doreen Margaret Mackinnon/Alexander Fleming ditto".

The Swami seems never to have recovered. Dr Punekar says that he died in hospital after an operation (*The Later Phase*, p. 255), but gives no date. Whether he was simply a genial old fraud, or whether he believed in his spiritual mission to the West, remains in doubt. As he said himself, "I have committed many mistakes in life. . . . I am an old offender and no one can cure me. I have renounced everything . . . I have renounced my renouncement as Lord Dattatraya advised in the Awadhoota-Geeta, and as a fool I am not ashamed to confess my folly" (to WBY, 5 Aug. 1937; *LTWBY* 594). There is an Indian point of view, to which he alludes here, from which even his association with Mrs Foden can be seen as a manifestation of wisdom. However enlightened his view of the whole episode, he was evidently relieved to be able to say at last: "I think, Mrs. Foden's fire is out" (to WBY, 28 Apr. 1938; *LTWBY* 597).

Yeats, as so often combining prescience with naiveté, summed up the story proleptically in his comments on Sophie Gaudier-Brzeska to OS in Aug. 1931: "An hysterical woman has sometimes a strong fascination, she is a whirlpool – such a problem to herself that everybody within reach is soon drawn in" (*L* 783).

The Annotated *Responsibilities*: Errors in the *Variorum Edition* and a New Reading of the Genesis of Two Poems,
"On Those That Hated 'The Playboy of the Western World', 1907" and "The New Faces"

Wayne K. Chapman

I

An annotated copy of one of Yeats's collections, which has come to light at Washington State University's Holland Library, allows corrections in the standard editions of Yeats's poems and plays as well as the standard bibliography upon which these depend.[1] *Responsibilities and Other Poems* (London: Macmillan, March 1917) proves to be more than a mere "second impression" of the English edition of *Responsibilities and Other Poems* (1916; *Wade* 115). Since both the Variorum *Poems* and Variorum *Plays* have followed *Wade*, a number of the variants reported for the poems of *Responsibilities* and *The Green Helmet*, the play *The Hour-Glass*, and the notes for this collection, are errors of oversight. Now that all the materials for detecting these errors are at hand – including the annotated volumes listed in Edward O'Shea's *A Descriptive Catalog of W. B. Yeats's Library* (1985) – we can have a much clearer view of the transmission of Yeats's texts.

The 1917 "impression" of *Responsibilities* at WSU has a story to tell, however, beyond the correction of errors. As an author-annotated text, it shows that Yeats made further revisions in this volume, ostensibly for yet another reprint.[2] Although a third impression was not made, almost all of his intentions were carried out in the 1922 editions of *Later Poems* and *Plays in Prose and Verse* – both published by Macmillan – and, in the case of the holograph poem pasted over the song "The Well and the Tree", into the Cuala Press edition of *Seven Poems and a Fragment*. Virtually complete in 1912, "The New Faces" had a frustrating and extraordinary history, including a role in the first draft of a major poem, "A Prayer for my Daughter". But since the chronology is important, the story of the holograph and the annotations will follow a list of changes that had already appeared in the 1917 text.

Yeats would have had good reason to use the London reprint of 1917 for his revisions because it was the most advanced text of those poems. All of the changes marked in one of his 1916 London editions of *Responsibilities*, YL 2412, were realised in the 1917 reprint. Because he has relied too much on the authority of *Wade* and the *VP*, O'Shea is mistaken in interpreting the annotations in 2412 as "apparently made to provide a partial copytext for WADE 134, LATER POEMS, London, 1922". In fact, the annotations he transcribes constitute an almost complete list of all textual variants between *Responsibilities* 1916 and *Responsibilities* 1917. The "second impression" of 1917 differs considerably more from the original than does the 1916 American edition of *Responsibilities and Other Poems* (New York: Macmillan, 1 Nov. 1916; *Wade* 116), which agrees with the first London edition except occasionally in punctuation and spelling. As illustrated below, then, a significant stage of the revision of these poems had been completed much earlier than previously thought. The dates 10 October 1916 and March 1917 define the stage broadly. But, in fact, all textual changes, save in the notes, were made in a copytext submitted to Macmillan on 20 December 1916.[3] (The following changes in the 1917 printing, apart from the dates altered on the title page, are listed in the order of their appearance.)

1. Pages vi & vii: in Contents, "Two Years Later" has been added, after "To a Child Dancing in the Wind" (p. vi), causing a serial shift in titles from that point on; p. vii now begins with "Reconciliation" instead of "King and No King" etc.
2. Page 40: the 1916 title "THE ATTACK ON 'THE PLAYBOY / OF THE WESTERN WORLD,' / 1907" has been changed to "ON THOSE THAT HATED 'THE PLAY-/BOY OF THE WESTERN WORLD,' / 1907". (Note that the hyphenation of "Playboy" in this printing leads to the subsequent odd variant "Play-Boy" noted in the *VP*.) The Contents (p. v) still bears the 1916 title.
3. Pages 66 & 67: part II of "To a Child Dancing in the Wind" now bears the title "Two Years Later". (*VP* reports the change first in the 1921 *Selected Poems*.) "I" and "II" stand, respectively, over the two titles, and only part I appears on p. 66.
4. Page 76: l. 9 of the *English Review* (1909) version of "An Appointment" has been restored: "Nor heavy knitting of the brow". This was absent in the 1914 Dundrum and the 1916 Macmillan editions. (Change attributed to *Later Poems* by *VP*.)

5. Page 78, l. 2 of "The Dolls": "balls" (1916 edn) has been corrected to "bawls". (*VP* attributes the change to *Later Poems*.)
6. Page 80, l. 6 of "A Coat": "eye" (1916) becomes "eyes". (*VP* attributes this to *Later Poems*.)
7. Page 99, l. 6 of "The Fascination of What's Difficult": "an Olympus" (1916) becomes "Olympus". (*VP* attributes this change to *Later Poems*.)
8. Page 104: the last line of "To a Poet . . ." has been revised to "But was there ever dog that praised his fleas?". (This follows in *Later Poems* according to *VP*.)
9. Page 137, l. 214 of *The Hour-Glass*: from "I had forgotten who I spoke to," "who" is corrected to "whom". (*VPl* reports that the change was first printed in *Plays in Prose and Verse*.)
10. Page 162, l. 440 of *The Hour-Glass*: from "Said that my soul was lost unless I found out," the 1917 printing omits "out". (*VPl* attributes this change to *Plays in Prose and Verse*.)
11. Beginning p. 184 to the end: Yeats has deleted two paragraphs, or about two whole pages, from the notes, substituting the following:[4]

[I leave out two long paragraphs which have been published in earlier editions of this book. There is no need now to defend Sir Hugh Lane's pictures against Dublin newspapers. The trustees of the London National Gallery, through his leaving a codicil to his will unwitnessed, have claimed the pictures for London, and propose to build a wing to the Tate Gallery to contain them. Some that were hostile are now contrite, and doing what they can, or letting others do unhindered what they can, to persuade Parliament to such action as may restore the collection to Ireland. – Jan. 1917.]

This last, in the final gathering, is an extensive revision. Indeed, Yeats himself has used the word "edition" to distinguish this text from the London and New York editions which preceded it. At the end of the 1917 "impression", in the notes, he has introduced changes that involve taking down and completely resetting the type for individual pages. There, five pages have been taken down and reset for four. By comparing the London 1916 first edition with the 1917 "impression" (see *Wade* 115), one finds that pp. xii, 188 (1916)>pp. xii, 187 numbered ("THE END" inserted) followed by a verso blank page and by 2 leaves of which the recto of the first bears a printed list of "THE WORKS/OF/ WILLIAM BUTLER YEATS / [list of 15 works of WBY for sale, including '*Responsibilities and Other Poems*. 6s. net.'] / LONDON: MACMILLAN AND CO., LTD. [printed beneath a bar line]". A comparison of the signatures and the gatherings in the two books suggests that Yeats's publisher turned the last change to advantage. If the printer had to reset several pages of type, he presumably did not have to break down his lines. When adding the advertisement to the last gathering (the one beginning with signature N), he chose to bind the regularly numbered pages at twelve gatherings (octavo) to save the extra assembly of the 1916 edition's gatherings of eleven-and-a-piece. (After the N signature on page 177, N2 appears on page 179 [at right foot] but only in the 1916 *Responsibilities*, where N to the end of the book amounted to just six leaves.) Thus if Yeats felt compelled to cut two long paragraphs from his work, this cut was turned by his publisher into an opportunity simultaneously to advertise and simplify production. Both parties seem to have benefited by the change, and the product overall, a book thus corrected and revised throughout, was a more complete text of Yeats's poems than the first editions of 1916 had been.

II

The most dramatic changes still to be implemented in *Later Poems* are in a rewritten portion of "The Hour Before Dawn", or generally lines 16–67 of the Variorum text. However, Yeats's redrafting of that passage, found in MS.13,586(8) at the National Library of Ireland (NLI) and reflected in the annotations and paste-over fair hand insertion that he made in another copy of *Responsibilities* 1917 (on pages 53–6 of *YL* 2412a), occurred later, prior to the publication of *Later Poems* in 1922.[5] Less dramatic, but characteristic of his revisions at this early stage and at the next, as shown in the annotated *Responsibilities* at Washington State, are the examples of "To a Poet, who would have me Praise certain Bad Poets, Imitators of His and Mine", "On those that hated 'The Playboy of the Western World', 1907" – short epigrammatic poems with long titles and stinging tails – and another short lyric with an unusual history, a version of "The New Faces" in holograph.

Only the second, of the two printed, goes on to further revision, the first having reached its final form in the 1917 "impression". Both poems, as Yeats's Journal attests, are roughly contemporary – though not as nearly so as once thought.[6] And both poems went through several changes of title. The Variorum shows that most of the changes made in the title of the *Playboy* poem occurred, for a while, almost as often as the poem appeared, until *Later Poems* – although the title in fact had been corrected in the 1917 printing of *Responsibilities*. In manuscript, only one other title is known, perhaps the earliest: "On the attack on 'the Play Boy'".[7] On the other hand, "To a Poet . . ." has only two nearly identical variant titles in its first two printings and "came right" with the 1911 New York edition of *The Green Helmet and Other Poems*. Conversely, its most interesting and variant title exists at the manuscript level: "To AE, who wants me [to] praise some of his poets, imitators of my own."[8] In addition, both poems show that last lines, too, received more than a little revision – as they well might in a successful epigram, which depends on the deliberate precision and timing of the author. For example, "To a Poet . . .", which found its final form in the *Responsibilities* of 1917, would have at least seven versions of its last line, fewer than half of them in print:

1. But tell me do the wolf dogs praise their fleas. (*Journal version A*)
2. But where's the wolf dog that has praised his fleas. (*Journal version B*)
3. But tell me – does the wild dog praise his fleas? (*Journal note, Wade*)
4. But tell me does the wolf do[g] praise its fleas? (*uncorrected ts.*)
5. But where's the wild dog that has praised his fleas? (*3 printings to 1912*)
6. But have you known a dog to praise his fleas? (*Responsibilities* 1916)
7. But was there ever dog that praised his fleas? (*Responsibilities* 1917)[9]

In the case of "On Those that hated 'The Playboy' . . ." – which has been revised in the course of the 1917 printing, was subsequently corrected in variant form in the WSU copy, and finally appeared finished in *Later Poems* – there are more than last lines to report because half of the last line was invariable. Yeats always knew what he intended for the finish: "sinewy thigh", the symbol of "all creative power", as he wrote in his Journal (*Mem* 176). Similarly, his first two lines, all his rhymes, and "great Juan" poised in the centre of line 4 were all devised from the earliest draft. What he worked out in revision is the timing of the middle and penultimate lines. Since much is already known about the poem's textual evolution, transcripts of the earliest version from unpublished manuscript and the 1917 version as corrected in the WSU property are all that need to be given here.

The earliest draft must have produced the version copied out in Yeats's Journal on 5 April 1910 (*Mem* 244). Still, more about the poem's birth is told by the unpublished postscript of a letter Yeats wrote to Lady Gregory from London. The postscript, on a separate sheet of stationery, has been pasted into Lady Gregory's presentation copy of Yeats's *Collected Works* (1908), on a double sheet at the beginning of volume 7, now in the Berg Collection at the New York Public Library.[10] Undoubtedly stuck in for the new poem that it contained, the postscript places Yeats in London, early in 1910, when official business had taken him there to raise funds for the Abbey Theatre. Moreover, it shows that considerable time must be allowed after Yeats entered that now well-known note in his Journal, between entries of 3 and 4 March 1909 (*Mem* 176) and 7 March, when he wrote to Lady Gregory about it, reporting that "Griffith and his like" were like "the Eunuchs in Ricketts's picture watching Don Juan riding through Hell" (*L* 525).[11] On the occasion of his later interview with the painter, he discovered that he had mistaken the figures in the picture that he had called to mind in his Journal (see Plate 4 in *YA4* [1985] and J. G. P. Delany's article on

Yeats, Ricketts and Shannon).[12] Hence the idea became Yeats's *property* before he undertook to write the poem. The postscript, as it appears in the Berg Collection –

PS.

Ricketts told me the other day at the ~~Sicilleans~~ last night of the Sicileans (where I came in for Grassos wonderful Othello) that I had invent[e]d that picture of the ~~Eune~~ Eunecs looking at Don Juan – they were old women. On Monday finding I could claim the idea I made this poem.

"on the attack on 'the Play Boy'"

Once when midnight smote the air
Eunics ran through Hell, & met
Rou[n]d about Hells gate, t[o] stare
At Great Juan riding by;
And, like these, to rail & sweat
~~Madened~~
Madened at his sinewy thigh.

Yeats's letter to Lady Gregory, extant though unpublished, is dated "Tuesday" and was posted two days later, in London, on 7 April 1910.[13] In addition, Yeats's account in the postscript makes it clear, once compared with the schedule of theatrical engagements published in the London *Times*, that the earliest draft of the poem (not extant) was made on the day *before* it was copied into the Journal from another surviving ms.[14] Obviously, such conclusions are based substantially on references in the postscript – references to the Sicilian players of Giovanni Grassi (spelled "Grasso" by Yeats and by the press), to the last night of "Grasso's" performance in the role of Othello, and to the "Monday" on which the poem was made. Ricketts's picture, it has turned out, long credited with being the source of inspiration for the poem, may not have been its catalyst.

In "The Theatre", a lecture of 7 March 1910 – the first of three delivered that week at the Adelphi Club to raise money for the Abbey – Yeats began with a comparison which was to become the main one of his speech: a contrast between the modern intellectual "feat of skill" exemplified by Galsworthy's *Justice* and the play of primitive instinct, the "joyous spontaneity of . . . art" that he witnessed in an unspecified play from the repertory of "Grasso's" company. "Last week when I was thinking how I was to arrange my thoughts for this afternoon I saw two plays which may help me to express my meaning – the Sicilians and 'Justice'."[15] Yeats agreed with the anonymous *Times* critic who reviewed

their opening night and continued to report on them.[16] Of Grassi in
particular, the reviewer wrote, he was "a kind of human volcano,
disquieting when on the smoulder and positively terrifying in active
eruption. . . . When you come away from the theatre you cannot rid your
mind of him. He is something more than an actor; he is a physical
obsession" (*The Times*, 23 Feb. 1910, pp. 12f). Likewise, Yeats confessed
to his audience that he thought Grassi "the greatest actor in the world";
and as the postscript of his letter to Lady Gregory shows, he thought
Grassi's Othello "wonderful". Indeed, it is likely that Yeats found
Grassi's Othello at the final performance, on Saturday, 2 April, quite as
awe-inspiring as had the reviewer in *The Times* two weeks before: "It was
an Othello . . . glowing with life and passion. . . . Grasso, with all his
eruptive violence and molten heat, keeps the beauty of the part, the
majesty and the pity of it" (*The Times*, 22 Mar. 1910, pp. 12f). On
Monday, 4 April 1910, his mind toying with a picture of Don Juan in hell
and obviously still affected by the memory of Grassi's volcanic stage
presence, Yeats set down, as the postscript of his letter testifies, the first
draft of his *Playboy* epigram.

VP tells most of the rest of the story. The first published version of the
epigram on *The Playboy* appeared in *The Irish Review* in December 1911. It
appeared next in *The Green Helmet and Other Poems* (Macmillan, 1912) but
then was shifted over to *Responsibilities* in the 1914 Dundrum (Cuala
Press) edition, which was combined with *The Green Helmet* poems, in two
sections, in the 1916 Macmillan editions of *Responsibilities*. The *Playboy*
poem, revised each time, retained its position, out of chronology, in the
Responsibilities group, where it has remained ever since. The last
significant revision of the poem occurred with the publication of *Later
Poems*, though the final title change, noted incorrectly in *VP*, actually
occurred as early as the revised 1917 reprint of *Responsibilities*. Still, if *YL*
2412a shows lines 3–5 of the poem to be revised in Yeats's hand for *Later
Poems*, this change was anticipated by the annotations in another of
Yeats's books, one which never found its way back to his library. These
are the annotations in *Responsibilities* (1917) at WSU, which are
transcribed here with the printed text:

ON THOSE THAT HATED 'THE PLAY-
BOY OF THE WESTERN WORLD,'
1907

ONCE, when midnight smote the air,
Eunuchs ran through Hell and met
From thoroughfare to thoroughfare/   5/
To mob / ~~While that~~ great Juan ~~galloped~~ by;   riding/
And like these to rail and sweat
Staring upon his sinewy thigh.

Before *Later Poems* and with these corrections, the title, the first two lines and the last are completely finished. The corrections in the fourth line are in the direction of its final form; only "To mob", characteristic diction of Yeats's middle period, was not implemented at last, dropping out in favour of "Upon" as Yeats found the solution to the problem that the temporary stasis of line 3 imposed upon the poem. In content and rhythm, "From thoroughfare to thoroughfare" – a parenthesis and stalling point – contributes much less to the poem than "On every crowded street to stare / Upon. . .". Yeats's omission of the comma at the end of line 3 seems to anticipate this solution, as does his idea for the revision "To mob / ~~While that.~~" The only other changes beyond those of the correct version in the WSU text are the substitutions of "Even" for "And" in line 5 (two syllables for one to perfect the metre of a defective line) and the colon for semicolon at the end of line 4, both of which make the final turn of the epigram, from Eunuchs as metaphor to "those that hated 'The Playboy . . .'" (or "Griffith and his like", as Yeats wrote to Lady Gregory), a much more precise and devastating gesture of vengeance and art. These final touches came with Yeats's revision of the volume now numbered 2412a in *YL*.

III

The creation of most of the poems of *Responsibilities* and *The Green Helmet*, unlike the *Playboy* epigram, could be detailed without regard to the marked copy of *Responsibilities* at WSU. Yet such reconstruction would not tell the whole story – nor could it report Yeats's abortive attempt to introduce into the *Responsibilities* unit, a second poem which he was trying to fit into the canon. This poem, eventually entitled "The New Faces", finally found its place in *The Tower* (1928). Since the poem is an almost exact contemporary of "To a Wealthy Man . . .",[17] one of those poems . . . *Written in Discouragement, 1912–1913*, it might well have appeared earlier beside its sister poems "To a Friend whose Work has come to Nothing" and "To a Shade". Jeffares speculates, on a suggestion from Mrs Yeats, that Yeats withheld the poem from publication as a matter of tact and may have continued to withhold it because he did not wish to remind Lady Gregory, the person to whom it is addressed, of her nearly fatal illness of 1909.[18] While this explanation is partly sound, it requires updating because of evidence that has now come to light.

First, the relationship between the poet and his dear friend was not as delicate as Jeffares supposed. Yeats did not keep secret the new poem that he had written, and liked, a poem whose conceit for turning compliment to the woman it addresses is more than usually morbid, asserting first, unflatteringly, that she is old and then asking her to imagine that both she and the poet are dead. Not only did Yeats *not* keep this poem a secret, but the poem's very first reader was Lady Gregory, who read it in a rougher version almost as soon as it had taken shape on paper. The text in that instance was provided in a letter of 7 December 1912, now in the Berg Collection.[19] "I am crossing over to night –" Yeats writes, "I didn't start at once to day because I waited [wanted?] to write the poem that came into my head on my way to the train on Thursday night", two nights before. The body of the letter bears first this version of the then untitled poem:

>   that have grown
> If you, ~~and you are~~ old, are the first dead
>   Catalpa
> Neither ~~Catalpa~~ tree, nor scented ~~lime~~ lime
>   feet
> Should hear my living ~~tread~~, nor would ~~I trea~~
>   I tread
> Where we wraught that shall break the
>   teeth of Time.
> Let the new faces play what tricks they will –
> ~~And yet your ghost an[d] mine do what they~~
> Your ghost & mine for all they do or say
> Shall walk the stairs and garden gravel
>   still
> The living seem more shadowy than they.

When Yeats wrote to Lady Gregory on this occasion and drafted "The New Faces" – which he also copied, and partly composed, in his Journal – he was anticipating her departure to America, where she was soon to lead an Abbey touring company. He could say goodbye to a friend whom he had good reason to believe he would see again despite a premonition of misfortune that he confided in his Journal on 28 December 1912: "I am troubled over Lady Gregory's journey to America, I have a sense of ill luck about it. I wish I had her stars . . ." (*Mem* 267–8). The first draft of the poem which he was to make from such worry (in NLI MS.13,586[12]) shows the Yeats persona not as a "shade", but as a lonely man walking the empty estate of Coole:

> shou[ld] you die first ~~never sh~~
> noth[in]g ~~of me if you sho[ul]d~~ die the first
>   ~~That~~
> li[vin]g

                         be[i]ng
If you die fir[s]t as ma[y]be ~~f[or?] you[re]~~ old
~~No foot of mine[?]~~
~~Noth[in]g [ ] of me will~~ tred
~~Not[hin]g [of?] me will~~
~~I would tred t[he] paths sha[d]ed by lim[e]s~~
~~shaded by chesnut trees~~
I wou[l]d n[o]t tred t[he] paths shaded by limes
shaded by chesn[u]t trees

The absence of presence given to Lady Gregory's part in this scene,
however, soon gave way to the "companionable" ghost that we begin to
recognise emerging in the next stage of drafting – a presence, Yeats and
Lady Gregory as the "passionate dead":

~~If you being old are the first dead~~
~~If you as ma[y]be being old are the first dead~~

If you – and you are old – are t[he] first dead
Neit[her] Catalpa tree nor scented lime
~~Shall~~
~~Shall have~~
Should hear my living feet, nor would I tread
                    wraught   teeth
Where we ~~wraug[h]t~~ that shall break the ~~time~~ of time
Let th[e] new faces play what tricks th[ey] will –
A[n]d yet your ghost & mine do what th[ey] may
Shall walk the sta[i]rs & garden gravel still
The living seem more shadowy than they –

In th[e] old rooms – for all th[e]y do or say
                will   grav[e]l
Our shades ~~shall~~ walk the garden ~~grav[e]l~~
                              ∧   still
The living seem mor[e] shadowy than they –

(This stage of the early draft is preserved in NLI MS.13,589[11].) At this
point, Yeats turned to drafting his letter, revising the poem as he copied
it over and, as an afterthought, devising the alternative to its last three
lines. In fact, the postscript of Yeats's letter suggests that he was
soliciting a response from Lady Gregory, a judgment on which of two
versions was better:

Hear [sic] is an alternat[e] end t[o] this poem

Let the new faces play what tricks they will
              all
In the old rooms – for they do or say
   shades   ^
Our ~~ghosts~~ will walk the garden ~~grav~~ gravel
                         still
The living seem more shadowy than they

Yeats's own judgment is clear from the second draft. The manuscript record shows, moreover, that only at this point did he copy the poem into his Journal,[20] which did not contain, in any case, the only fair hand copy of "The New Faces" in existence up to 1922, when the poem was finally published. There were several others.

The second complication to Jeffares's account of the circumstances surrounding this poem concerns the delay in publication. Why was it delayed for ten years? And why, when the poem did appear in print, must it find its place in so different a body of poems to those Yeats had written in 1912? To the first question, Jeffares has offered this explanation: "... to publish his poem written in 1912 would have seemed to Yeats's sensitive conscience an unnecessary reopening of a subject [Lady Gregory's illness of 1909; see *Mem* 160–3] which might have troubled Lady Gregory, even though he was praising her, because he had not now the immediate theme of her illness on which to base his thoughts, and might seem to be commenting upon her age".[21] In large part, this explanation is now open to question. Furthermore, it does not address the second question, which is important because Yeats did try to have the poem published (as the WSU text shows) reinstated with its contemporaries. While the real answer to both these questions is complex – and I believe the questions are so joined – the key to understanding their common problem is perhaps recognition of Yeats's literary judgment, as well as of his effort to be tactful.

Although we may never know exactly what Lady Gregory's objection was to the poem in December, 1912, we can be sure that she took care to acknowledge Yeats's feelings. Her letter of 9 December (unpublished and in the Berg Collection, file 65B4299) shows that she fully understood the personal compliment that he intended. Yet it was *her* desire, not his, that he withhold the poem from publication. And the motive behind her request was left for her correspondent to interpret:

The lines are very touching. I have often thought our ghosts will haunt that path and our talk hang in the air – It is good to have a meeting place anyhow, in this place where so many children of our minds were born – You won't publish it just now will you? I think not.

Her response is both gracious and firm, prompting Yeats's decision to withhold publication for a time, perhaps intentionally for years. While the letter is mute on her objection to seeing the poem in print just then, it is unlikely that her somewhat enigmatic response had anything to do with her illness of 1909. More likely, she was irritated – and for a simple reason. Since she was but sixty and was in relatively good health when she received Yeats's poem, and may well not have felt as old as it makes her out to be, one guesses that she did find it personally unflattering. Perhaps hurt by the commanding tone of her silence (her "I think not"), Yeats closed one of his first letters from London on this occasion (a letter dated "Thursday [c. 15 December 1912]" by the editors Torchiana and O'Malley) with the following assurance: "You need not fear that I shall publish this poem at present . . .". But he quickly added, "– I have written [it] on a blank page of my collected edition for safety",[22] thus serving notice that he might yet publish the poem at a later time. Apparently she saw nothing objectionable in its compliment nor faulty about its artistry – or else she would have protested at seeing it in print, and she did see it in print, in 1922, 1928 and 1929.

Yeats's subsequent attempt to adapt the poem to the stanzas of "A Prayer for my Daughter" (in the version dated "April 14[?] 1919"; NLI MS.13,588[15]) perhaps imperfectly reflects his view of Lady Gregory's objection of 1912. To be sure, more than six years had passed; he was now married and a father and may not have permitted her to see the "Anne poem" – as he referred to it in an unpublished letter of 5 July 1919 – until it had been revised. Indeed, because of the natural shift in their personal and working relationship by then (Mrs Yeats, for instance, had assumed most of the secretarial duties once performed by Lady Gregory), there is no reason why he should have shown her the earliest draft. Nevertheless, his attempt to mine material from a poem that he chose not to publish over her objection is extraordinary and virtually a unique case in his poetry. Moreover, it is significant that the unpublished version of "The New Faces" exerted a recognisable influence over both the surviving and excised octaves of "A Prayer for my Daughter". The clearest evidence of this appears on the verso of leaf 7:

Nor think th[a]t being dead I cannot hear
    or   I cannot if god will
~~nor~~ that ~~god willin[g] I may not~~ ap[p]ear
                            alive
Amo[n]g those places th[a]t ~~alive~~ I lov[e]d
    motionless   at   or ~~a~~
~~Sta[n]di[n]g t[o] think by~~ lake ~~or~~ wood
        upon a
or hurry thoug[h]t driven ~~[ ] on a~~ vaporous foot

Where for some twenty year[s] or so
                    paced
My frie[n]d & I ~~walk[ed]~~ t[o] & ~~for~~ fro
Upon the gravel by the Kat[a]lpa root.

Among three stanzas that Yeats wrote about Coole, this one was revised and assigned the important final position in a version that was two stanzas longer than any printed version. Rough at best, the last working draft of stanza XII appears as follows:

nor think th[a]t being dead I cannot ~~hea~~ hear
~~For it is certa[i]n that I shall apea apper appeor~~ For it is certain
                                                                    that
~~Because it is certa[i]n that for many a~~ year   I shall appear
Standing t[o] think where I have often sto[o]d
By the lakes edge, in th[a]t blue wood   path
                              where the ~~rock~~ climbs between
~~on the short path by th[e] Katalpa root~~   a rock & root
or ~~where~~ else, where twenty year[s] or so
my frie[n]d & I paced to & ~~fro~~ fro
Hungry thought driven on a vaporous foot.

Old matter is being reshaped. The alternating rhyme of the eight-line poem has given place, as yet unsatisfactorily, to the *aabbcddc* stanza of "A Prayer . . .". But before this problem could be resolved, stanzas X–XII – stanzas about Yeats at Coole, all serving to counter the longer poem's bitter treatment of Helen/Maud Gonne – were cut, as Stallworthy points out.[23] The Catalpa tree, which is featured prominently in the three excised stanzas and, before that, vaguely anticipated by the "flourishing hidden tree" of line 41, yields to the traditional, if rather hackneyed, "spreading laurel tree" in the stanza appended to the poem in typescript. Similarly, the manuscript shows how old material was reworked in the surviving sections of the new poem until this source was concealed. Consider, for example, lines 45–8 in stanza VI: "Nor but in merriment begin a chase, / Nor but in merriment a quarrel [in ms., "On that, ~~all~~ when eyes upon a promised face / With present faces quarrel," > "For the excitement of an unknown face / With customary faces quarrel" > final version] / "O may she live like a green laurel / Rooted in one dear perpetual place."

In light of this manuscript, it seems unlikely that Lady Gregory's reaction to the early version of "The New Faces" played a great part in Yeats's decision to cut the Coole stanzas from "A Prayer for my Daughter". Those stanzas paid great compliment to Lady Gregory, certainly, as the presiding spirit of her garden (even though Yeats made himself the guardian ghost of the twelfth stanza). It is more likely Yeats made the cuts because he feared that he was repeating himself, especially repeating the gestures and imagery of "The Wild Swans at Coole" and recycling, in substance, an old poem. But even if he *was* reluctant to show her the Coole stanzas – and he did ask her opinion of "A Prayer for my Daughter" – he had already cut them from two versions of the poem that she saw,[24] perhaps deciding at last that the 1912 poem was more successful than what he had tried to make from it.

For his part, Yeats seems always to have been pleased with the older poem, so much so that when other poems of that period had undergone successive revisions (as had the *Playboy* poem, for example), "The New Faces", preserved in a number of ms. fair hand copies, changed hardly at all from the text worked out in Yeats's letter of 7 December 1912. One such copy is found in NLI MS.13,586(12), beside the earliest draft of the poem and beside a fair ms. copy of "The Mountain Tomb" (ca. August 1912). Another such fair hand copy of "The New Faces", as Yeats reported, was written at the foot of page ix of volume 1: *Poems Lyrical and Narrative*, in one of his private sets of *Collected Works in Verse and Prose* (1908), item 2325 in *YL*. A third, nearly identical fair hand version of this poem, copied neatly on the back of a sheet of personal stationery in the winter of 1920/21, was pasted onto page 49 of *Responsibilities and Other Poems* (1917), now at Washington State University. It was evidently his intention by then to put the poem before the world in very nearly its original condition and beside its contemporaries. So why didn't he follow through with his plan to publish the poem in this way if he simply had to delay publication until Lady Gregory no longer objected to the poem's assertion about her age – i.e., until such time, in eight years, when she was old? From the evidence of the WSU annotations and from the circumstance of this poem's creation, it is demonstrable that the poem, on its way to publication at last, collided with two more projects and that the uncommon destinies of the three were determined by artistic, as well as personal, judgment.

IV

Mrs Yeats may have known more than she told Jeffares, forty years ago, when she suggested that "The New Faces" was withheld for "reasons of tact".[25] If she had anything to do with the typescripts of "A Prayer for my Daughter" or, in two years, with the preparation of copytexts for *Selected Poems* (1921; *Wade* 128) and *Later Poems* (1922; *Wade* 134) – both of which figure in the marked copy of *Responsibilities* at WSU – she knew in detail how much of a problem it was for her husband to get this short lyric into print. Evidently, once Yeats felt that the poem could be printed, he had yet to create a textual environment that would suit it. Two of his objectives are plain from evidence now at hand: (1) he wished to avoid representing the poem as a new work, and (2) its introduction beside lyrics of the same period was to be accomplished simply. Neither of these objectives was realised. We have long known that Yeats made a regular practice of ordering and reordering his poems to provide large contexts for individual works and, often, to emphasise continuity. We have not known the full extent of how this was tried in *Responsibilities*. The following list of annotations in the WSU text (hereafter called "WSU *R* 1917") constitutes a veritable showcase of his methods:

1. Page i: beneath the half-title "RESPONSIBILITIES / AND OTHER POEMS," Yeats has pencilled "1903–1914".
2. Page iii: a long, nearly vertical slash has been drawn down the title page in pencil.
3. Page v: on this first page of Contents, a long vertical line has been drawn down the page in pencil, and check marks, in ink, have been made beside the page references of the following poems: "Introductory Rhymes", "The Two Kings", "Paudeen", "When Helen Lived", "Beggar to Beggar Cried", and "The Well and the Tree" (which has been cancelled by means of a pencil line and over it written the title "To a Friend").
4. Page vi: on the second page of Contents, a long diagonal line has been drawn across the page in pencil, and, in ink, check marks have been made beside the page references of "A Memory of Youth" (where a mark stands to the left of the title, too) and beside "A Coat". Then the dates "1909–1912 –" are cancelled in pencil for the group of poems "FROM THE GREEN HELMET AND OTHER POEMS, / 1909–1912 –".
5. Page vii: on the third page of Contents, a long diagonal line has been drawn down the page across the remaining Contents. At the bottom, a squiggly cancellation in pencil has been made through the following:

THE HOUR-GLASS – 1912	117
NOTES	181

6. Page ix: beneath the section title, "RESPONSIBILITIES", have been pencilled the following dates:

    ~~1914~~ [struck over violently]
    1912–1914

7. Page 40: ms. corrections have been made upon the poem "On those that hated 'The Playboy of the Western World,' 1907", as reported above.
8. Page 49, pasted over the printed text of "The Well and the Tree": a fair copy of "The New Faces" in the version of 1912. Beneath possibly its first title, the text of this ms. (given below) is copied on the back of a half-sheet of stationery, which is pasted, heading side

down, into the book. The stationery heading consists of the address "4. BROAD STREET./OXFORD". Though variant from the accepted version in *VP*, the holograph is not the corrupt text of the first printing.[26]

To a Friend

If you that have grown old were
    the first dead,
Neither Catalpa tree nor scented
    lime
Should hear my living feet, nor
    would I tread
Where we wraught that shall break
    the teeth of time.
Let the new faces play what tricks
    they will
In the old rooms; for all they do
    or say
Our shades will walk the garden
    gravel still
The living seem more shadowy
    than they.

9. Page 83: beneath the section title, which is centered on this otherwise blank page ("FROM THE GREEN HELMET / AND OTHER POEMS"), is the following inscription of dates (in ink):

    ~~1903–19012~~ 1912 ["19012" violently cancelled]
    1903 ~~1909~~ – 1912 ["1909" struck over several times]

10. Page 117: a short diagonal line (from left to right), in pencil, through the section title "THE HOUR-GLASS / NEW VERSION – 1912" and, above this, the one word "Omit–."

11. Page 119: across the first page of the play "The Hour-Glass", Yeats has drawn (from left to right) a long diagonal line in pencil.

The time must have seemed favourable for the publication of "To a Friend" (i.e., "The New Faces") in 1920. It must have begun to seem so, at the close of the preceding year, when Lady Gregory had asked Yeats for his publisher's leave to quote the notes and several poems from *Responsibilities* in her biography of Hugh Lane.[27] It would be more than a year before he could read her work and send his praise of it. But she had his commitment, on 13 December 1919, in a letter of the same day on which he wrote Macmillan for the firm's consent.[28] Both letters bear his address at 4 Broad Street, Oxford, his residence only since that October (see *CL1* xxii). Lady Gregory had been eager to remind him of this favour, which, it seems, he had promised her for some time, and he must have been no less eager to see this business concluded before he let his house, in January 1920, and left Oxford for a tour of America. To be sure, the Yeatses were back in Oxford in June, and there were visits to Coole and Ballylee in the summer. Their return to Oxford in the autumn prudently coincided with a stepped-up guerilla war in Ireland. In their absence, Lady Gregory sent news about the condition of their Irish property – a service for which they were grateful. And while she published *Hugh Lane's Life and Achievement* in the midst of this war, Yeats, who then lived in a state of uneasy retirement from Irish public life, revised his poems and planned new selected and collected editions of his work.

The eight titles marked in the Contents of *WSU R* 1917 – with the indicated substitution of "To a Friend" for "The Well and the Tree" – very probably represent Yeats's original choice of lyrics for *Selected Poems* (New York: Macmillan, 1921). There are several reasons for concluding as much, all based on textual evidence. First, *all* titles marked in *WSU R* 1917 are also marked in the Contents of *YL* 2412c, a copy of *Responsibilities* 1917 which Yeats used to record his progress with the review of these poems in late 1920, simultaneously underscoring those titles in a typescript Contents as he went along. Once he was satisfied with a poem, he wrote "complete" beside its title in the typed list NLI MS.30,044). But he made other comments, as well. Fortunately, beside *"the grey rock"*, which was not marked "complete" and hence was probably the last poem worked in this review, he noted, "as far as 'foot after foot was giving way'", precisely at which location in *YL* 2412c, at the top of page 7, he had written: "Revising from here – / Dec 1 1920". (For titles marked in *YL* 2412c and in NLI MS.30,044, see the supplementary notes in this journal, pp. 241–3, below.) In point of fact, *none* of the titles marked in *WSU R* 1917 had appeared in *A Selection from the Poetry of W. B. Yeats* (Leipzig: Bernhard Tauchnitz, 1913; *Wade* 103), a copy of which Yeats marked, likewise in its Contents, and in which he left the instruction: "add poems marked / in 'Responsibilities' & 'Wild Swans' / beginning with those in 'Responsibilities.' / WB Yeats." This was the basic copytext for *Selected Poems*, to which marked copies of *Responsibilities* and *The Wild Swans at Coole* were added. (See *YL* 2419 and the supplementary notes on p. 244.) Moreover, if the selection designated in *WSU R* 1917 was new, fitting neatly into a body of poems that Yeats thought ready for use by December 1920, it was virtually the same size as that employed in the edition of June 1921, and actually had two poems in common with it.[29] Indeed, the selections match in number except for one poem added, in the latter case, from the *Green Helmet* division. Hence, in all likelihood, Yeats first prepared this copy of *Responsibilities* as partial copytext for *Selected Poems* – in late 1920 or early 1921 – intending that it be used in the way his note in *YL* 2419 instructs.

Why should this plan miscarry just as it was on the verge of being implemented?

Lady Gregory's unfavourable reaction to "Reprisals" may have had something to do with it. After his successes with "In Memory of Major Robert Gregory", "An Irish Airman Foresees His Death", and "Shepherd and Goatherd" (all in 1918), Yeats was suddenly met with a stern rebuff after posting to her a corrected ts. carbon copy of this new poem, then entitled "To Major Robert Gregory, airman".[30] In the accompanying letter of 26 November 1920, his confidence is most apparent and was, no doubt, partly the cause of her irritation.[31] She had a number of reasons for disliking the poem and cited some of them in her Journal. But primarily, it seems, she did not think the poem "sincere" and was vexed that he would send it to a newspaper without her consent:

> Yeats writes enclosing lines he has written and has, without telling me, sent to *The Times*, I dislike them – I cannot bear the dragging of R., from his grave to make what I think a not very sincere poem – for Yeats only knows hearsay while our troubles go on – and he quoted words G. B. S., told him and did not mean him to repeat – and which will give pain – I hardly know why it gives me extraordinary pain and it seems too late to stop it . . .[32]

This was a *serious* incident which would have poisoned the climate for his plan to unobtrusively introduce "The New Faces" into a selection of long-published work. This fact must have crossed Yeats's mind. On 2 December, when Lady Gregory wrote in her Journal that she was still worried about Yeats's poem, she had by then "wired and written begging him to suppress it", citing her personal displeasure.[33] On 12 December he responded with a long defensive letter on the "feeling in England about 'Reprisals' ", by which he meant the atrocities alluded to in the poem he addressed to young Gregory's ghost.

Put in personal terms, a request from Lady Gregory was something Yeats respected. Hence she prevailed, and his new poem was suppressed. However, she couldn't have known all the consequences of this episode – not all of them were so straightforward. For example, since Yeats's selection of poems in *WSU R* 1917 seems to have had as much to do with creating an environment for his unpublished lyric of 1912 as with suggesting the poetic range of *Responsibilities*, the incident very probably caused a radical tonal shift in the affected section of *Selected Poems*. One can't be sure exactly when this shift took place. It may have been in February 1921, when he wrote to praise the Lane biography and dropped the following correction into his postscript: "The poem given on page 138 'To a friend' etc. was meant for you, not for Lane."[34] To be sure, once he *had* prudently withheld "To a Friend" (i.e., "The New

Faces"), Yeats seems to have committed himself to the safest selection
possible: one based on the poems that Lady Gregory had herself chosen
to quote in the Lane biography. So when "Introductory Rhymes", "The
Two Kings", "Beggar to Beggar Cried", "A Memory of Youth" and "A
Coat" all went with the unpublished lyric (save "Paudeen" and "When
Helen Lived"), the tone of that part of *Selected Poems* shifted in the
direction of *Poems Written in Discouragement, 1912–1913.*

   More definite are the dates associated with Yeats's later use of the
WSU text – i.e., to annotations (1) and (2), (5)–(7) and (9)–(11). The
very first of these annotations is evidence that he was then planning a
new collected edition of his work. The dates "1903–1914", which he had
newly assigned to the works of the entire *Responsibilities and Other Poems*
(omitting the play, the notes, and the song "The Well and the Tree"),
are not the actual dates of the poems themselves (1908–1914, according
to their composition) but are meant to suggest continuity with the group
of lyrics that was to have preceded them – in *Later Poems*, the fourteen
lyrics from *In the Seven Woods* (both Dun Emer and Macmillan, 1903; see
Wade 49 and 50). Annotation (1) thus necessitates annotation (4), where
"1909–1912" was struck from the Contents beside the section title
"THE GREEN HELMET AND OTHER POEMS", as a group the
oldest poems of the book. Furthermore, such dating as to suggest
continuity is behind annotations (6) and (9), as well. If annotation (9)
sets back the dates of *The Green Helmet* poems to 1903 while extending
them to 1912, annotation (6) completes the continuum by assigning the
partly new *Responsibilities* group the dates "1912–1914". (See dates
similarly entered in *YL* 2401 [*Poems: Second Series*], 2412a [*Responsibilities*
1917] and 2444a [*The Wild Swans at Coole*, 1920].) Moreover, the
cancellation of the notes to the poems and of the 1912 version of *The
Hour-Glass* in verse is strong evidence that the remainder of the volume
was not meant to stand with the poems and that those cuts were related
to another project – that of a volume of collected plays, perhaps not at
that stage *Plays in Prose and Verse* (London: Macmillan, 1922), but at
least a collection which would have provided occasion to reprint, and
revise, elsewhere the excised play and to reprint the excised song with the
play, *At the Hawk's Well*, of which it is part.[35] (See annotations (3) and
(5), confirmed by (8), (10), and (11); cf. *YL* 2412a and the Contents of
Later Poems, Wade 134.)

   The Macmillan records (Macmillan Archive, British Library) tell
how an edition of Yeats's collected work was first attempted and support
a late-1921 dating for this second phase of annotations in *WSU R* 1917.
In 1916, Yeats, Watt and Macmillan had been able to come to terms on a
proposed six-volume Collected Work and had signed the contract for
Macmillan's first edition of *Responsibilities* (B. L. Add. MS.54,897, f.
197).[36] However, by 16 November 1919, writing from Oxford and about
to embark on a lecture tour to America, Yeats notified Watt of the

impossibility of seeing through even a few of the proposed six volumes
before his departure (B. L. Add. MS.54,898, ff. 49–50). At that time and
on a later occasion, on 23 December 1920, Yeats made a proposal that
was eventually the one followed in 1922, when a two-volume edition of
his work was published by Macmillan. Yeats proposed that Bullen's
edition of *Poems: Second Series* (1908; *Wade* 83) be joined with
Responsibilities and the lyrical part of the Unwin edition of early poems,
with additional poems to appear at the end. When the proposal had been
made in 1919, Yeats had thought that Macmillan's reader could make a
text based upon revised copies of these books, which he would send.
More than a year later, back from his tour and writing on Broad Street
stationery, Yeats repeated his proposal, adding that his *Wild Swans at
Coole* should be incoporated into the contents of a volume of "Shorter
Poems" (B. L. Add. MS.55,003, ff. 64r and v, 65r and v). Difficulties
with Unwin explain why Yeats's early poems were omitted from the
two-volume edition of poems and plays published in 1922. However, the
project went forward according to his proposal: Sir Frederick Macmillan
wrote to Watt on 27 April 1921 accepting it (B. L. Add. MS.55,570,
f. 300) and negotiations began in January 1922. *YL* 2401, Yeats's library
copy of *Poems: Second Series*, is annotated and bears revisions that were
introduced in *Later Poems*. (See pp. 239–41 and 245, notes on *YL* 2401,
2412a and 2444a.)

The most revealing piece of evidence in the Macmillan letter-books is
a long fragment of a letter from Yeats to his agent (B. L. Add.
MS.54,898, ff. 54–8, misfiled) comprising the detailed plan for the
"collected uniform edition", the plan that H. Watt subsequently read to
Sir Frederick on Friday of the week of 10 January 1922 (see B. L. Add.
MS.54,898, f. 137, and MS.55,576, f. 106). In this letter, Yeats wrote:
"If Macmillan will send me two copies 'Plays for an Irish Theatre,'
'Responsibilities,' 'Wild Swans at Coole,' I will get to work with a paste
pot and let him have a couple of specimen volumes at once". Two
conclusions can be drawn from this statement: (1) Yeats needed clean
texts with which to prepare copy; and (2) preparation of actual copy for
Later Poems came later.[37] Macmillan received Yeats's copytext with a
cover-letter from Watt dated 14 March 1922 (B. L. Add. MS.54,898,
f. 150), a week before Yeats left Oxford for good (*CL1* xxii).
Consequently, the latest annotations in *WSU R* 1917 were made before
10 January 1922, and possibly before December 1921, when Yeats
conceived of the final placement of "The New Faces" among six new
poems. The corrections to the *Playboy* epigram obviously postdate the
marking of titles in that copy and are in line with those made in
February–March 1922 (in *YL* 2412a). Abandoning his thought to
introduce "The New Faces" into a Collected Edition at that time – and,
hence, the "specimen volume" he had already prepared for it – naturally
meant that he would have to call for a new set of books.

Yeats probably had not discovered, in April of 1921 – when he was engaged in "writing a series of poems on the state of things in Ireland", "a series of poems ('thoughts suggested by the present state of the world' or some such name)", as he wrote to Lady Gregory and Olivia Shakespear (*L* 668) – that his old poem had found its place. "I have written two and there may be many more", Yeats wrote to Mrs Shakespear. "They are not philosophical but simple and passionate, a lamentation over lost peace and lost hope". More confidentially, he wrote to Lady Gregory: "I do not know what degree of merit they have or whether I have now enough emotion for personal poetry. I begin to feel a difficulty in finding themes. I had this about twelve years ago and it passed over". Only a little later, in August, Yeats's letters to his friends would brighten with anecdotes about his daughter and with news of his son's birth. The obvious pride and great pleasure that he projected on this last occasion (*L* 673) were not translated into poetry until December of that year, when he remembered what he had tried to do, in 1919, in the excised last stanza of "A Prayer for my Daughter". The "strong ghost" that he bids "stand at the head / That my Michael may sleep sound" naturally developed from the guardian spirit that he had associated with himself on a similar occasion. And thus it was entirely appropriate that "The New Faces" be given a place between "A Prayer for my Son" and "Nineteen Hundred and Nineteen" (then called "Thoughts upon the Present State of the World") when his sisters went to press with *Seven Poems and a Fragment* in June 1922.

Yeats's work revising his poems for what became *Later Poems* was therefore more extensive than one would have thought and perhaps more than Yeats himself had originally planned. Surely the work of revising the poems of *Responsibilities* (London, 1916), hitherto unknown in detail, was almost the beginning of a substantial series of revisions culminating, for most of the poems, in the texts of *Later Poems*. By way of conclusion, it is useful to summarize the steps of the series as follows:

Oct. 1916 – *Responsibilities and Other Poems* (London, 1916)

Dec. 1916 – revisions represented by *YL* 2412

Mar. 1917 – *Responsibilities and Other Poems* (London, 1917)

1920/21 – *WSU R* 1917, use aborted for *Selected Poems* (1921)

1921 – *WSU R* 1917, use aborted for collected poems

(notes & poems, w/o "The Well and the Tree") revisions: *YL* 2412a (Feb.–Mar. 1922)	(*The Hour-Glass* in verse) revisions: *YL* 2412c (1920/21–Mar. 1922)	("To a Friend," i.e., "The New Faces") The new poems (Apr. 1921–Apr. 1922)

1922 – *Later Poems*	*Plays in Prose and Verse*	*Seven Poems and*
(with revisions in	(with 9 other plays of	*a Fragment*
YL 2401, 2444a	1902–22, plus the 1903	(as per *Wade* 132)
& Cuala Press	version of *Hour-Glass*)	
Michael Robartes . . .)		

When he wrote to Charles Ricketts on 5 November 1922, about the excitement when Mrs Yeats first brought up to his study the two green-cloth volumes of *Later Poems* and *Plays in Prose and Verse*, Yeats's very great pride and satisfaction are again evident in his words: "not being able to restrain her excitement I heard her cry out before she reached the door 'You have perfect books at last'. Perfect they are – serviceable and perfect" (*L* 691). *Later Poems* and *Plays in Prose and Verse* were perhaps only the best that could be done at the time. His claim in the Preface of the former, for instance, was not true. It did *not* contain "all poetry not in dramatic form that [he had] written between [his] seven-and-twentieth year and the year 1921" (*VP* 853). But it *was* almost the final stage in progress toward definitive texts for most of the poems gathered in the first Macmillan edition of *Responsibilities*.

NOTES

1. I am indebted to Michael and Anne Yeats for their permission to use unpublished materials quoted in this article, and to Anne Yeats, additionally, for her hospitality and the opportunity of studying her father's books first-hand. I wish to thank the following libraries for their permission to use materials belonging to them: Manuscripts, Archives and Special Collections, the Washington State University Libraries, Pullman, Washington; the National Library of Ireland, Dublin, Ireland; the Henry W. and Albert A. Berg Collection, New York Public Library (Astor, Lenox and Tilden Foundations); and the Harry Ransom Humanities Research Center, the University of Texas Libraries, Austin, Texas. I am grateful to John Kelly, General Editor of the *Collected Letters of W. B. Yeats*, and to the Oxford University Press for allowing me to quote certain of Yeats's unpublished letters, and to Colin Smythe for permitting the use of one by Lady Gregory. My thanks to the Department of Manuscripts, British Library, and the following persons: Virginia Hyde, Warwick Gould, Deirdre Toomey, James Pethica, Richard J. Finneran, David R. Clark, Leila Luedeking, Lola Szladits, Catherine Fahy, and Cathy Henderson. This investigation was supported in part by funds provided by Washington State University.

2. So advertised by the last owner, W. Thomas Taylor, Bookseller (Austin, Texas) in item 50 of the sale catalogue "A Christmas Miscellany", 1973. As one of a long run of Yeats items with ownership attributed to "a Gentleman", this book, as lot 600, was sold by Sotheby's to the firm of Francis Edwards on 6 July 1971. From Edwards, the book was sold in rapid succession to Bernard Quaritch Ltd, to the rare book dealer W. Thomas Taylor (1973), and finally to the WSU Libraries (also in 1973). Originally, the book may have been given to Olivia Shakespear when Yeats moved from Oxford to Dublin in March 1922. This is suggested by two books of the same run: lots 598 (*A Selection from the Poetry of W. B. Yeats*; *Wade* 103) and 614 (*Modern Poetry*; *Wade* 188), both inscribed to her by Yeats. The first was then inscribed by Ezra Pound to Ronald Duncan, a friend of the Pounds and one-time guardian of their son, in

England, with access to the family library. The second was later signed "Raymond Duncan", according to Sotheby's catalogue. Both books, as with the WSU text and a dozen others in the same run, were provided with expensive morocco-backed slip-cases, probably the addition of a collector or dealer.

3. With a letter (n.d.) received by Macmillan on 20 Dec. 1916, Yeats sent "a revised copy of 'Responsibilities' for new edition" (B.L. Add. MS.55,003, f. 39). It's likely that this copy is now *YL* 2412.

4. It is certain that copy for this revision came *after* the other changes were communicated to Macmillan. With a cover-letter dated " Jan 13 [1917]", Yeats sent the firm such copy, explaining that he had to make "another alteration" in *Responsibilities* due to a "request" made by Lady Gregory (B.L. Add. MS.55,003, f. 41). Both full and excised versions of the notes are given in *VP* 818–20. But the references are confusing since the editors do not distinguish between the London 1916 and 1917 printings.

5. I agree with O'Shea that volume 2412a in the Yeats library provided "additional copytext for WADE 134", or *Later Poems*. I do not agree, of course, that 2412 provided the rest of it. See my notes on *YL* 2401, 2412a and 2444a (pp. 239–41 and 245 below).

6. See *Mem* 176, 221–2 and 244; also see A. Norman Jeffares, *A New Commentary on the Poems of W. B. Yeats* (Stanford University Press, 1984), 92 and 115. The undated ms. of "To a Poet . . ." is in Yeats's Journal between the dated entries of 23 and 27 April 1909, when he was staying at Dunsany Castle. The standard date for the *Playboy* poem is given in Jeffares, who says: "This poem is written in Yeats's Diary with the date 5 April 1909". However, no year is affixed to the ms. in Yeats's Journal, only "April 5". Donoghue, moreover, is right in dating its entry "April 5 [1910]" and is supported by surrounding entries. Beyond this evidence is the testament of another early ms. (now in the Berg Collection) which Yeats sent to Lady Gregory when he was in London for an extended period, as he clearly was not on 5 April 1909 (see *L* 527). Even Ellmann's cautious dating of "1909", in *The Identity of Yeats* (New York: Oxford University Press, 1964), 289, misses the mark, as it turns out. By the testament of a letter of 5 April 1910 – to be quoted shortly – it is certain that the first draft of "On the attack on 'the Play Boy'", as it was then called, dates not from 5 April 1909, but from 4 April 1910. Finally, Wade (*L* 525n) has placed the occasion but mistaken the year in which Yeats recited a version of the poem to him over lunch.

7. As given in transcription from the Journal (*Mem* 244) and in ms. in the Berg Collection.

8. From the Journal, entered between 23 and 27 April 1909 (*Mem* 221), as well as from a very similar uncorrected carbon ts. at the National Library of Ireland (NLI) in MS.13,583.

9. Journal version A and Journal version B are alternative endings. (See *Mem* 221–2.) "Journal note, Wade" stands for a note that Allan Wade inserted into WBY's Journal, reporting this as a line Yeats once recited to him in a restaurant in the summer of 1909. (See *Mem* 222.) The strong similarity between the Journal ms. and the uncorrected carbon ts. in NLI MS.13,583 suggests that Yeats's Journal was itself the copytext for the first ts., which is headed "From MSS book XYZ". Still, some changes are apparent in one final line of the three that are rehearsed in the ts.

10. See New York – New York Public Library – The Research Libraries, *The Dictionary Catalog of the Henry W. and Albert A. Berg Collection of English and American Literature*, 4 (1969) 487.

11. The date of this letter, which Wade has given as "Sunday [March 8, 1909]", should in fact be "Sunday [7 Mar. 1909]". A corrected ts. of this letter (NLI MS.18,688) gives "Eunics", Yeats's misspelling.

12. For discussion of Ricketts's painting in light of Yeats's poem, see J. G. P. Delaney, "'Heirs of the Great Generation': Yeats's Friendship with Charles Ricketts and Charles Shannon", *YA* 4 (1985) 60–1.

13. This letter, in its postmarked envelope, is an uncatalogued item in the Berg Collection, which has now, through recent acquisition, most of the extant Yeats/Lady Gregory correspondence.

14. This document is now owned by the University of Texas Libraries and is part of the Yeats collection at the Harry Ransom Humanities Research Center at Austin. The HRHRC ms. is signed but not dated, and it is slightly rougher than the Berg Collection ms. in spelling ("sweat" is "swet"; "sinewy" debatably differs as "sinewey"). That they were composed in proximity to each other is confirmed by the misspelling of "Eunuchs", common to both of them, and by the same hesitation over the word "maddened". It is likely that Yeats copied the one from the other – undoubtedly the Berg Collection ms. from the HRHRC ms. The punctuation of the Berg Collection ms. is no more satisfying than that of the other, coinciding in no more than a single comma (after "Hell" in line 2); the punctuation of each makes some contribution to that finally used in the first printing. When the poem came to be copied into the Journal almost without punctuation, however, it would seem as if such formal problems were momentarily suspended in deference to the preservation of content. When the three texts agree in all but punctuation and spelling, it seems likely that the Journal entry of 5 Apr. 1910, was also copied from the HRHRC ms.

15. *YT* 17. See also Yeats's lecture of 19 Dec. 1913, delivered at another London location and published by Robert O'Driscoll in "Two Lectures on the Irish Theatre by W. B. Yeats", *Theatre and Nationalism in Twentieth-Century Ireland*, Robert O'Driscoll, ed. (University of Toronto Press, 1971), 66–88, 209–12, where another reference to Grassi's work is made in this vein (75, 210n).

16. The play on opening night (22 Feb. 1910, the night after *Justice* opened) was *Feudalismo*, possibly the play Yeats had in mind in his lecture. In the early weeks of their six-week engagement at the Lyric Theatre, the Sicilians were alternating five plays. However, only *Feudalismo*, one of the staples of their repertoire, continued for matinees, with another play introduced in later weeks, as *Othello* became a roaring success and the nightly feature in their last two weeks in London. The troop had not had a London engagement in two years, and London seems to have welcomed it back enthusiastically.

17. Dated in Mrs Yeats's copy of *Responsibilities* (*YL* 2412d), "Mss. Oct. 25, 1912 [but in the left margin] Dec. 24, 1912". NLI MS.13,586(3), "To a Wealthy Man . . .", shows the first complete draft dated "Dec 24 1912" and a revision of the ending dated "Dec 25/1912". Jeffares, following Ellmann, has dated "The New Faces" December 1912 (*A New Commentary on the Poems*, 236). But an unpublished letter in the Berg Collection suggests that 7 Dec. 1912, might be the exact date.

18. A. Norman Jeffares, " 'The New Faces: a New Explanation", *Review of English Studies*, 23 (Oct. 1947) 349–53.

19. See *Berg Collection Catalog*, 4, 486.

20. The untitled text of "The New Faces", entry 242 of Yeats's Journal (*Mem* 267), is dated generally "December 1912". But the version of the poem found there is a fair copy as revised in the letter and uses only the ending substituted in the postscript. Apart from the punctuation (which is minimal) and Donoghue's silent correction of Yeats's spelling, Yeats has revised "are" to "were" in line 1 and "rove" to "walk" in line 7. Another alternative version of the ending (with "rove") is given beneath the dated text, the only difference between these being "they" > "they'll" in line 6 and "shades will" > "shadows" in line 7. Another revision ("shades will walk" > "shadows rove") must have been added later beneath the dated version of the poem in the Journal. This revision is closer to the 1922 printed version and first appears as a correction to a bad ts. (in NLI MS.13,589[11]) apparently made for that printing. In a draft Contents for *Seven Poems and a Fragment* (NLI MS.13,589[2]), Yeats complains about that typist.

21. Jeffares, " 'The New Faces . . .'", 353.

22. Yeats's letter – published by Donald T. Torchiana and Glenn O'Malley in "Some New Letters from W. B. Yeats to Lady Gregory", *Review of English Literature*, 4.3: 11–12 – indeed closes on a theme of "indiscretion": "I don't suppose any letter you are likely to have written about Cheyne House was indiscreet – but at midnight all becomes monstrous and wild". At another point, he is the contrite bad boy serving his penance:

"– I have stayed in every evening so far trying to live a very regular life". Immediately following is the assurance not to print the offending poem. And the letter ends on a promising note of business which allied Yeats and Lady Gregory firmly: "I have a poem in my head [i.e., "To a Wealthy Man . . ."] about Lane's Gallery and Lord Ardilaun but may not be able to write it. I will try. It is not *tactless* and does not name Lord Ardilaun and might help the fund" (emphasis added). The Berg letters (from 7 to 22 Dec. 1912) show Yeats attentive, sending a gift and news about the progress of his poem "To a Wealthy Man . . .", which he thought to have published in the *Irish Times* "with editorial comment". When on 22 Dec. he wrote, "What might seem offensive in a letter or article will not do so in a poem or in a comment on it", he might have been alluding to Lady Gregory's reaction to his letter of 7 Dec. Certainly he seems more concerned about Lord Ardilaun's response to the other poem, keenly aware that Ireland's "princes" were sensitive about the way they might be praised in public.

23. Jon Stallworthy, *Between the Lines: Yeats's Poetry in the Making* (Oxford: Clarendon Press, 1963) 38–44. For a complete account of the development of "A Prayer for my Daughter", Stallworthy (26–45) is recommended. He thinks, however, that "The New Faces" was written later, noting the recurrence of the Catalpa tree in that poem of *The Tower* collection.

24. The first version of "A Prayer . . ." that she had was the corrected carbon of the ts. now in NLI MS.13,588(15). This was nine stanzas long, lacking ll. 65–72, possibly by mistake (see Stallworthy, *Between the Lines*, 43n). Yeats evidently refers to this copy (now in the Berg Collection) when he writes to her, on 5 July 1919: "I enclose a copy of Anne poem – one verse was left out in copy I showed you".

25. Jeffares, "The New Faces", 351–2.

26. The first printed version of "The New Faces", in *Seven Poems and a Fragment* (Dundrum: The Cuala Press, 1922), is in fact defective beyond what has been noted in *VP*, for "Catalpa" (line 2) appears misprinted as "Caltapa". The punctuation in line 1 of the printed version (with comma after "you" and none after "dead") is ungrammatical, not just deviant from the version of the three fair hand mss. The ts. in NLI MS.13,589 (11) – which was evidently made for Cuala Press copy – bears the misspelling "Caltapa" but not ". . . night can outbalance day", as in line 6 of the first printing and a further fair hand ms. in the NLI file. Revision of line 6 came perhaps in proof. The first printing of "The New Faces", like the final version in *VP*, gives line 6–7 as follows: "In the old rooms; night can outbalance day, / Our shadows rove the garden gravel still, / . . .".

27. Augusta Gregory, *Hugh Lane's Life and Achievement, with Some Account of the Dublin Galleries* (London: John Murray, 1921). Her letter, dated 2 Dec. 1919, is unpublished and, as with all subsequent references made to their correspondence (unless cited otherwise), is in the Berg Collection. The notes quoted in *Hugh Lane's Life* . . . (119–22) included the two paragraphs that she had asked him to cut when *Responsibilities and Other Poems* was revised in 1917.

28. B.L. Add. MS.55,003, f. 61. Macmillan, of course, approved Yeats's request but suggested that Lady Gregory mention the fact that the material came from their edition of *Responsibilities* (B. L. Add. MS.55,558, f. 913). She does cite "his book 'Responsibilities'" as the source of the "vehment note" she quotes on the controversy over the proposed Dublin gallery, but she does not cite the source of any of the poems, her main text being, in any case, *Poems Written in Discouragement, 1912–1913* (Dundrum: Cuala Press, 1913; *Wade* 107), not the *Responsibilities* editions of 1916 and 1917.

29. The poems from *Responsibilities* that *were* used with the Tauchnitz copytext and the poems chosen from *Wild Swans* . . . were "Where Helen Lived", "Paudeen", "To a Wealthy Man", "September 1913", "To a Friend whose Work has come to Nothing", "To a Shade", "Running to Paradise", "The Player Queen" and "The Mask". The first two of these were marked in *WSU R* 1917.

30. This ts., dated 23 Nov. 1920, is in the Berg Collection in an envelope upon which Lady Gregory has written: "I did not like this and asked not to have it published." Although

"Reprisals" was not published until 1948, it is well known; reprints and quotations from it are now common in scholarship. See Jeffares, *A New Commentary*, 138. For a thorough account of this affair, see Bernard G. Krimm, *W. B. Yeats and the Emergence of the Irish Free State, 1918–1939: Living in the Explosion* (Troy, NY: Whitston, 1981) pp. 47–51.

31. The offending part of the letter, now in the Berg Collection, is misquoted by Krimm (*ibid.*, pp. 50–51). Yeats said that he had "*not* asked" her leave to send the poem "at once" to *The Times* and, if rejected there, to *The Nation*.

32. Augusta Gregory, *Lady Gregory's Journals*, vol. 1: *Books One to Twenty-nine, 10 October 1916–24 February 1925*, ed. by Daniel J. Murphy (New York: Oxford University Press, 1978), 207; entry of 28 Nov. 1920.

33. Ibid., p. 208.

34. Yeats's A. L. S. to Lady Gregory (4 Broad St., Oxford), 24 Feb. [1921], now in the Berg Collection. Page ref. is to *Hugh Lane's Life and Achievement*, p. 138, where Lady Gregory introduces "To a Friend whose Work has come to Nothing", not knowing that it had been written for her.

35. Yeats, who wanted Macmillan to produce a collected edition of his work and had obtained an agreement for such on 10 July 1916 (B. L. Add. MS.54,897, f. 207), was by late 1919 especially anxious to see *Four Plays for Dancers*, among his new books, incorporated into a proposed edition of six volumes (B. L. Add. MS.54,898, ff. 49–50).

36. After postponement of a decision on the Collected Works (see correspondence of April and May 1916; B. L. Add. MS.54,897, f. 193 and MS.55,536, f. 862), a formal agreement was finally drawn up for such a project, on 27 June 1916, and sent by H. Watt to Sir Frederick Macmillan (B. L. Add. MS.54,897, f. 201; see Richard J. Finneran, *Editing Yeats's Poems* [London: Macmillan, 1983], 5–6). Macmillan's signed copy was returned on the following day (B. L. Add. MS.55,537, f. 387), and the deal was closed on 10 July 1916 (B. L. Add. MS.54,897, f. 207; – MS.55,537, f. 607, 12 July, acknowledges its receipt).

37. Yeats states in this letter that he did not wish to make such paste-up copies until he had first Macmillan's decision to do the edition.

Yeats and Arthur

Marion Wynne-Davies

> He read now many famous books of legendary stories, [but] the *Morte d'Arthur* and the *Mabinogion* kept their hold on his imagination. He had imagined all their personages so perfectly, at a time when life interested him too little to compete with their wonders, that [neither] Homer's nor Chaucer's personages, nor the personages of Norse sagas interested him as deeply. (*SB* 28)

Michael Hearne, the hero of *The Speckled Bird*, is fascinated by the mystical romance world of the Arthurian legends. Merlin and Arthur dominate the imaginative preoccupations of his childhood, the magical rites he and Maclagan devise are based on the Grail mysteries, and his relationship with Margaret is subsumed in imagery drawn from the Celtic and Medieval romances. This growing literary awareness in *The Speckled Bird* is, in Yeats's terms, an ideal one. Yeats chooses to describe Michael as reading, not the later sentimental Victorian elaborations, but the major romance and Celtic literature of the Arthurian tradition. The allegorical simplicity of *The Speckled Bird*, however, belies the complexity of response demanded by the overall use of Arthurian mythology. Moreover, the ambivalent readings suggested by Yeats's texts reach beyond his own changing perceptions and are part of the widespread transition in the concept of Arthur during this period.

Yeats's initial approaches to Arthurian material are governed by a simultaneous rejection of and yet forced reliance upon the Victorians, especially Tennyson's *Idylls of the King* (1857–88). In "The Poetry of Samuel Ferguson" (1886) Yeats writes:

> No one will deny excellence to the Idylls of the King; no one will say that Lord Tennyson's Girton girls do not look well in those old costumes of dead chivalry. No one will deny that he has thrown over everything a glamour of radiant words – that the candelabras shine brightly on the fancy ball. Yet here is that which the Idylls do not at any time contain, beauty at once feminine and heroic. (*UPI*, 95)[1]

134

The implicit condescension of "Girton girls" must be weighed with the direct indebtedness to Tennyson in "Time and the Witch Vivien" of 1889; (*VP* 720–2).[2] In Yeats's poem the enchantress is beautiful yet malignant, taunting Time with,

> ... young girls' wits are better
> Than old men's any day, as Merlin found.
> (*VP* 721)

Her sense of proud exultation exactly mirrors that of the Vivien in *Idylls* where the scene she alludes to – the enchantment of Merlin – is related.[3] The Arthurian myth itself suggested a high spiritual potential to Yeats, but, at the same time, he is dissatisfied with Tennyson's treatment of the material.

A parallel is found in Yeats's response to the romantic Victorian poets. He is able to say "I was in all things Pre-Raphaelite" and, in 1887, writes admiringly to Katharine Tynan of the "neo-romantic London poets; namely, Swinburne, Morris, Rossetti" (*Av* 114; *L* 46). Yet Yeats's poetry was clearly moving away from the abundant and ornate language of the established poets of his youth. In 1934 he recalled:

> When I was a young man poetry had become eloquent and elaborate. Swinburne was the reigning influence and he was very eloquent. A generation came that wanted to be simple, I think I wanted that more than anybody else. (*UP2* 495)

Yeats reveals an indebtedness to, and then a disillusionment with, the Arthurian works of the nineteenth century, and rejects not only the *Idylls*, but *Tristram of Lyonesse* (1882), *The Defence of Guenevere* (1858) and the romance works of the Pre-Raphaelites.[4] The Arthurian imagery in Yeats's work, however, does not create a nostalgic yearning for the golden yet distant past. Instead, it attempts to revive and install in contemporary art the more potent images of the Medieval and Celtic literatures. A passage in *Irish National Literature* (1895) illustrates perfectly this development of poetic consciousness:

> The ancients and the Elizabethans abandoned themselves to imagination as a woman abandons herself to love, and created great beings who made the people of this world seem but shadows, and great passions which made our loves and hatreds appear but ephemeral and trivial phantasies; but now it is not the great persons, or the great passions we imagine, which absorb us, for the persons and passions in our poems are mainly reflections our mirror has caught from older poems or from the life about us, but the wise comments we make upon them, the criticism of life we wring from their fortunes. Arthur and his

Court are nothing, but the many-coloured lights that play about them are as beautiful as the lights from cathedral windows; . . . It seems . . . that this age of criticism is about to pass, and an age of imagination, of emotion, of moods, of revelation, about to come in its place; for certainly belief in a supersensual world is at hand again. (*UPI* 376)

The supersensual world of the imagination transmitted through the passions and through revelation was to be restored to the Arthurian tradition. Yeats participates in the twentieth century revival of the archetypal mythology of the Grail Quest. In Arthurian legends the waste lands function as an allegory for spiritual and moral degeneracy, which must be redeemed through the search for the Holy Grail. The knights of the Round Table undertake this quest – both in a personal and public form – for a consumation with a higher religious truth. Only one perfect knight, Galahad, is destined to experience this mystical communion. Yeats internalises and personalises the quest mythology of the Holy Grail in his poetry, by pursuing a supersensual revelation. At the same time, he externalises the legend through his search for a higher spirituality to revive the Arthurian literary 'waste lands' of the Victorian age.

The renewed interest in Celtic and Medieval literature during the nineteenth century has been amply documented, the two most influential texts during this period being Lady Charlotte Guest's *Mabinogion* (1849), and Matthew Arnold's *On the Study of Celtic Literature* (1867) which Yeats owned (*YL* 8).[5] It was not, however, until the 1890s and the early twentieth century that the study of Celtic literature, with its associated Arthur and Grail legends, reached its peak. A selection of these texts gives some illustration of how prolific and influential the neo-Celtic movement became; those which Yeats owned are indicated by a '*'. On the study of Celtic myth: H. d'Arbois de Joubainville, *Introduction a l'étude de la littérature celtique* (1883)* and *Le Cycle Mythologique Irlandais* (1884)*; J. Rhys, *Lectures on the Origin and Growth of Religion as Illustrated by Celtic Heathendom* (1886)*; E. S. Hartland, *English Fairy and Other Folk Tales* (1890)* and *Mythology and Folklore* (1900); E. Renan, *The Poetry of the Celtic Races* (1896)*; I. B. John, *The Mabinogion* (1901); J. G. Frazer, *The Golden Bough* (1911); and J. L. Weston, *From Ritual to Romance* (1920). On more particularly Arthurian and Grail material: A. Nutt, *Studies on the Legend of the Holy Grail* (1888)* and *The Legends of the Holy Grail* (1902)*; J. L. Weston, *The Legends of the Wagnerian Drama* (1896); S. Evans, *In Quest of the Holy Graal* (1898)*; and J. Rhys, *Studies in the Arthurian Legend* (1891)* (*YL, passim*). Each of these studies links disparate legends within a central mythology. Hence Rhys is able to equate Aengus with Merlin, Dermot with Pwyll and Cuchulain with Kulhwch.[6] Beneath a superficial anthropological realism, the neo-Celticists were concerned with the mystical and spiritual aspects of the legends. For example, Arthur is seen by Rhys as a Celtic sun-culture divinity.[7] This religious identification is often transposed onto the literary expressions of modern sensitivities. By analogy, the introduction of the imaginative world into Yeats's romance and Celtic imagery, not only expresses an individual authorial quest but also, with more far-reaching implications, a literary quest of the Arthurian tradition for a new identity.

In *The Speckled Bird* Michael is influenced primarily by two Arthurian texts: *Morte d'Arthur* and the *Mabinogion*. Yeats's work echoes this two-fold debt and the ensuing argument will focus upon the significance of Yeats's conflation of sources. Arthurian romance constitutes an important contribution throughout Yeats's work, from the courtly tone of the early verse to the symbolic indebtedness of the later poems. In *The Island of Statues* (1885) the shepherdess Naschina breaks the enchantment of the Isle and awakens the "statues", one of whom wonders:

> Doth still the Man whom each stern rover fears,
> The austere Arthur, rule from Uther's chair?
>
> *Naschina.* He is long dead.
>
> (*VP* 678)

The suggested melancholy for the faded golden age of Arthur is common to Medieval and Renaissance romance texts, including Malory's *Morte d'Arthur* and Spenser's *The Faerie Queene*, a source, as Yeats acknowledges, for his own poem.[8] Yeats's interest in Arthurian romance persisted. In "Towards Break of Day" (1921) there is an almost obsessive return to familiar Arthurian images, such as the white stag:

> I dreamed towards break of day,
> The cold blown spray in my nostril.
> But she that beside me lay
> Had watched in bitterer sleep
> The marvellous stag of Arthur,
> That lofty white stag, leap
> From mountain steep to steep.
>
> (*VP* 399)

The later work embodies the domination of the imaginative sensitivity – the dream world – and its spiritual unity with the central mythos of Arthurian legend symbolised by the white stag.[9] For Yeats the poetic attractions of Arthur reside not in the chivalric tradition, but in the spiritual elements of the legends. Lancelot is identified with the visionary qualities of a poet in "A Bundle of Poets" (1893; *UP1* 277). Tristan becomes a great tragic persona in *The Celtic Element in Literature* (1897; *E&I*, 182) and, with "Pelanore" [Pellenore] in "Gitanjali" (1912; *E&I*, 394), an embodiment of the "mystery" of courtesy.

By focusing upon the mystical and imaginative elements of the Arthurian romance tradition, as embodied by *Morte d'Arthur*, Yeats is able to unite that material with the Celtic tales of the *Mabinogion*. The fusion is often achieved in the language of the poem by isolating in the reader's awareness a potent and visually dramatic symbol, with a possible multiplicity of interpretations. The white stag functions in this manner.

Similarly, Yeats writes of the "white deer with no horns" in "He Mourns for the Change that has come upon him" (1899) that,

> My deer and hound are properly related to the deer and hound that flicker in and out of the various tellings of the Arthurian legends, leading different knights upon adventures and to the hounds and to the hornless deer at the beginning of, I think, all tellings of Oisin's journey to the country of the young. The hound is certainly related to the Hounds of Annwvyn or of Hades. (*VP* 153)

The symbols denote several base texts and Yeats freely compounds the romance Arthurian material with the Irish (Oisin), Welsh/*Mabinogion* (Annwvyn) and Classical (Hades) mythologies.

The conflation of allusions is also Yeats's method with the white stag symbol. In "Maid Quiet" (1892; *VP* 171) the "death-pale deer" is Irish, while in "Miraculous Creatures" (1902; *Myth* 65) and in "Lullaby" (1929; *VP* 522) the same creature is mainly Arthurian:

> Sleep, beloved, such a sleep
> As did that wild Tristram know
> When, the potion's work being done,
> Stag could run and roe leap
> Under oak and beeches bough,
> Stag could leap and roe could run.

(VP 522v)

The image of the white stag conjures for the reader an array of mythological sources which suggest an absence of a precise allusion, but simultaneously imply an underlying substructure of meaning. Yeats's syncretic method indicates, but does not elucidate, a deeper interpretation. For example, in his 1897 annotation to "Maid Quiet", he suggests that

The 'pale deer' were certain deer, hunted by Cuchullain in his battle
fury, and, as I understand them, symbols of night and shadow.
(*VP* 171)[10]

This broader mythological meaning of "night and shadow" must be
considered suspect in its simplicity, for the symbolic language of the
poems continually evades a single interpretation or ascription and
retains its intense emotive individuality despite the complexity of
reference.

The other Arthurian text to exert an influence on Yeats's work is the
Mabinogion. Lady Charlotte Guest first issued her translation, with the
parallel original, of the Medieval Welsh tales in 1849, and subsequently
brought out a compilation of the English versions alone in 1877.[11] In
"The Celtic Element in Literature" (1897) Yeats reveals a detailed
knowledge of Guest's *Mabinogion*, reciting tales and incidents from the
book with assured familiarity. For example, he recounts exactly an
episode from the tale of Peredur the son of Eurawc in the *Mabinogion*:

> ... and one finds it [the ancient religion] in the not less beautiful
> passage about the burning tree, that has half its beauty from calling up
> a fancy of leaves so living and beautiful, they can be of no less living
> and beautiful a thing than flame: "They saw a tall tree by the side of
> the river, one half of which was in flames from the root to the top, and
> the other half was green and in full leaf. (*E&I* 176)[12]

In "Vacillation" (1931/2) he recalls the image of the half-flame, half-leaf
tree:

> A tree there is that from its topmost bough
> Is half all glittering flame and half all green
> Abounding foliage moistened with the dew;
> And half is half and yet is all the scene;
> And half and half consume what they renew,

> (*VP* 500)

The double-natured tree resembles the Sephirotic tree of the Kabbalah –
while at the same time suggesting the deeper symbolism of the universe
and the human mind, one half benign, the reverse malignant.[13] More
especially, to one such as Yeats, well-versed in Arthurian lore, the tale of
Peredur would have signified the Grail Quest, and the vision of the
mystical tree would have suggested the revelationary experience of the
Grail Knight when he enters the spiritual or fairy world.

In Yeats's work, as in generally the neo-Celtic revival, the legends of the *Mabinogion* and *Morte d'Arthur* do not remain within the bounds of fictional reference. In "The Celtic Element in Literature" Yeats writes:

> the legends of Arthur and his Table, and of the Holy Grail, once, it seems, the cauldron of an Irish god, changed the literature of Europe, and, it may be, changed, as it were, the very roots of man's emotions by their influence on the spirit of chivalry and on the spirit of romance ... (*E&I*, 185)[14]

This quasi-anthropological argument is expanded in an evangelical tone towards one more politically and mystically immediate:

> It [the Irish Renaissance] comes at a time when the imagination of the world is as ready as it was at the coming of the tales of Arthur and of the Grail for a new intoxication. (*E&I* 187)

The Celtic nature of the Arthurian tradition made its implication in Yeats's personal poetic nationalism inevitable.

The Arthurian symbols are no more contained by the ideologies of the neo-Celtic movement, than they are defined in terms of a single source text. For Richard Ellmann,

> The ultimate purpose of Yeats's use of nationality in his verse was, paradoxically, to enable him to transcend it.[15]

Through Arthurian symbolism Yeats lays claim to significations beyond the fictional world and, consequently, suggests a deeply rooted desire to write poetry which would "transcend" the confines of a literary and nationalistic tradition. In Arthurian terms, the possibility of transcendence was offered by the image of the Grail, and Yeats's purpose was avowedly mystical.

When Michael Hearne, as a young man, moves to London he becomes wholly immersed in the mystical cult of the Holy Grail. Yeats here draws upon his experiences with the Order of the Golden Dawn, but uses the Grail cult to camouflage and to protect his developing interest in a Celtic Mystical order (which itself did not draw upon Arthurian material). As a novelist he would have found the accessibility of the Arthurian legends very useful.[16] The choice of the Grail for the central magical symbol of *The Speckled Bird* is significant both with regard to Yeats's poetic themes, and to the spiritual aspect of contemporary opinion on Arthur.

The search for the Grail in the Arthurian legends became, for the neo-Celticists, identified with an eternal and immutable "quest" myth, which was essentially non-Christian. The imaginative force which this archetypal symbol exercised may be seen in the revival of Grail literature, such as J. L. Weston's *From Ritual to Romance* (1920), T. S.

Eliot's *The Waste Land* (1922) and J. Cowper Powys's *A Glastonbury Romance* (1932), and in the popularity of Wagner's opera, *Parsifal*.[17] The power of symbols to provoke common responses, which thereby lays claim to a universal significance for art, was promoted further by the concept of the collective unconscious.[18] Thus the Grail becomes – more so than stag or tree – an image of the mystical inspiration and transcendence of literature. As Yeats wrote in "The King's Threshold" (1904), poetry must be guarded

> . . . as the Men of Dea
> Guard their four treasures, as the Grail King guards
> His holy cup, or the pale, righteous horse
> The jewel that is underneath his horn,
> Pouring out life for it as one pours out
> Sweet heady wine . . .
>
> (*VPl* 265)

For Yeats these symbols could only be mobilised in the imagination through the operation of a mage figure. The effect of this belief is twofold: first, the magical element of the Golden Dawn is transferred to the Grail imagery, and secondly, Yeats focuses attention, not on the knight of the Grail – Perceval – but on the Arthurian magician, Merlin.

The enchantment of Merlin by Vivien is referred to as early as 1889 in "Time and the Witch Vivien" and Yeats's interest in this narrative persisted. In his essay "Swedenborg, Mediums, and the Desolate Places" (1914) he writes:

> Merlin, who in the verses of Chrétien de Troyes was laid in the one tomb with dead lovers, is very near and the saints are far away. (*Ex* 44)

The story is repeated at far greater length in *A Vision* (*A*, 197; *AV B*, 286–7). Yeats misattributes the legend of Merlin's entombment to Chrétien: it actually occurs in the *Huth Merlin*.[19] The mistake may be accounted for by the inclusion of the *Huth Merlin* narrative under the title "Niniene" in the collection *King Arthur and the Table Round. Tales chiefly after the Old French of Chrestien of Troyes* (1897), a text which Yeats undoubtedly used.[20] The entombment of Merlin as recounted in the Huth Ms. is, in Arthurian terms, one of the least known treatments of Merlin's "death". Merlin takes his love, Ninian, to a cave in the 'forest perillous' where the two lovers are buried. That night while the enchanter sleeps, Ninian weaves an enchantment over him and entombs him with the lovers. It was transcribed for the first time, in French, in 1886 and existed in English in only three synopses, two of which are undeniably obscure.[21] By far the most common version remains that of the *Vulgate Merlin* which was utilized by both Malory and Tennyson. In this tale Merlin is again enchanted by Ninian, but it is while he sleeps beneath a tree and his prison is an invisible tower not a tomb. Yeats's choice of source is clearly influenced by the two major differences between the *Huth* and *Vulgate* which, indeed, are those he draws attention to himself: a stone tomb and the two dead lovers. The tomb symbol is central to Golden Dawn Second Order Rosicrucian ritual and is recalled in "The Body of the Father Christian Rosencrux" and "The Mountain Tomb" (*E&I* 196–7; *VP* 311), while the tale of the two buried lovers would have appealed to Yeats's sense of mystical union.[22] Both tomb and lovers seem, therefore, to echo Yeats's magical and emotional concerns.

Yeats's Arthurian symbolism is personal: the Golden Dawn and Maud Gonne are transposed into the mysticism of the Grail and Merlin, and into the powerful and romantic women of the Medieval tales.[23] This material is encapsulated and explored in *The Speckled Bird* (1896–1902/3).

Malory's *Morte d'Arthur* and the *Mabinogion* are Michael's, as they are Yeats's, most important Arthurian sources:

> It was an edition of the *Mabinogion* which his father had bought [mainly] for its large margins and fine print and for those engravings of knights and ladies which have as much romance as seemed admirable to a generation that had learned from Sir Walter Scott to understand the picturesqueness, the bodily energy, the sudden transformations of the life of the Middle Ages, while too sceptical and too sectarian to understand its magic and its mysticism. (*SB* 9)

The references throughout the novel to these works, and especially to the *Mabinogion*, are numerous; and they are the two texts Michael chooses for Margaret to read (*SB* 27).[24]

The white stag symbol occurs, significantly, as part of the double-vision experienced by the lovers, which clearly foreshadows "Towards Break of Day". Margaret relates her dream to Michael:

> She saw enormous multitudes of birds and in the midst of them was one very beautiful bird wearing a crown, a bird like a great white eagle. It had lit on a great tree, the others were perching among the branches. And then she saw beasts of all kinds coming and they were following a great white deer who had a crown upon it.

and at the end of the description Michael responds, "We have been sent the same dream" (*SB* 101). Similarly, Yeats's Arthurian symbols are, as in the poetry, products of conflated sources. The bird in Margaret's dream is the Eagle of Gwern Abwy from the *Maginogion* tale of "Kulhwch

1. A page of an early manuscript draft of *Cathleen ni Houlihan*, in the hand of Lady Gregory, with her pencilled inscription "All this mine alone/A. G.". Photograph courtesy of the Berg Collection, New York Public Library (Astor, Lenox and Tilden Foundations).

3. Olivia Shakespear, passport photograph, 1921. Photograph courtesy and © Omar Pound.

4. Olivia Shakespear and Omar Pound at Hindhead [?], c. 1935. Photograph courtesy and © Omar Pound.

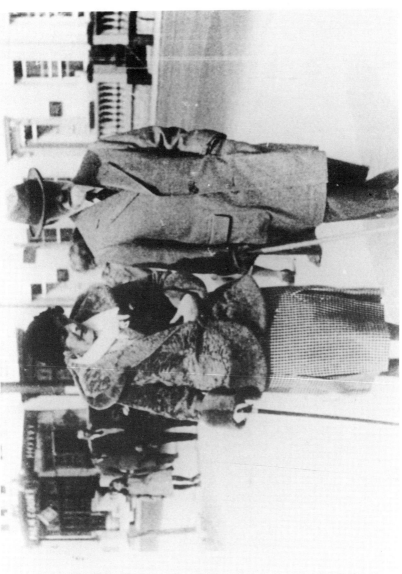

5. Olivia Shakespear and Harry Tucker at Sidmouth, c. 1935. Photograph courtesy and © Omar Pound.

6. Shri Purohit Swami. From a hand-coloured photograph, sent by the Swami to Olivia Shakespear as a Christmas Card, c. 1934. Photograph courtesy and © Omar Pound.

"The English stage is quite despicable"

7. Detail of drawing of W. B. Yeats in the San Francisco *Examiner* 31 January, 1904. A staff artist drew him as he was being interviewed by Ashton Stevens.

8. Studio portrait photograph of W. B. Yeats, probably done in America, c. 1914. Collection Phillip L. Marcus.

9. Studio portrait photograph of W. B. Yeats by Underwood & Underwood, New York (1920). Collection Phillip L. Marcus.

10. W. B. Yeats, Edith Shackleton Heald and Edmund Dulac at The Chantry House, Steyning, the first of a sequence of photos taken possibly on Sunday 13 June 1937, or in the summer of 1938. Photograph courtesy of The Huntington Library.

11. Nora Shackleton Heald, W. B. Yeats, Helen Beauclerk and (in front) Edith Shackleton Heald, The Chantry House, Steyning, 1937 or 1938. Photograph courtesy of The Huntington Library.

12. W. B. Yeats and Edmund Dulac in the orchard, The Chantry House, Steyning, 1937 or 1938. Photograph courtesy of The Huntington Library.

13. W. B. Yeats, Edmund Dulac, Edith Shackleton Heald and Helen Beauclerk in the orchard, The Chantry House, Steyning. Photograph courtesy of The Huntington Library.

14. MS draft of "Am I a fool or a wise man?", NLI MS 13, 587 (4). Photograph courtesy of The National Library of Ireland.

15. MS draft of "Portrayed before his eyes", NLI MS 30, 189. Photograph courtesy of The National Library of Ireland.

16. Christ with a perspex cross in *Calvary*, directed by Raymond Yeates at the Peacock Theatre, Dublin, September 1986. Photograph courtesy of The Abbey Theatre, Dublin.

and Olwen", yet it also parallels the titular "speckled bird", which is the owl of *Jeremiah* 12:9.[25] The conjunction of owl, eagle and vision mirrors Michael's hallucinatory experience as a boy:

> The bird was perching on what seemed the side of a hill, and over its head one or two stars [were] shining faintly. He knew at once by its ragged wings that it was the Owl of Cwn Cawlwyd, the oldest of all birds except the Eagle of Gwen Abwy, and that it had come out of Wales to speak to him. (*SB* 16)

The mythological interpretation of the "bird" compounds Welsh, Christian and Irish (the Irish Eagle is also said to be the oldest of all birds) sources.[26] The constant shifting of reference – the bird is both eagle and owl – and the eternal changing of image-patterns invites interpretation.

As Michael grows older the immediate emotive impact of the Arthurian tales weakens and he turns to the more spiritual aspect of the legends in the mysteries of the Holy Grail. The Grail becomes a symbolic focus for this section of the novel. In a letter to Margaret, Michael writes:

> We have read all we could find of the legends of the quest in old poems and stories, but we have not always followed them very closely, for we have been taught by visions and dreams . . . using any symbol that is but [?] of the Grail quest to call up visionary reverie. . . . They [great myths] never pass away, and though the books of the world and the memories of men were to perish, one would have only to fast a little to discover them in dreams and in visions. But I said all this to you long ago and you believed it. (*SB* 203)[27]

This mystical transcendence is, for Yeats, conjoined to a visionary experience which must be shared with the beloved. On the narrative level this intention is satisfied by the shared dream, but the implicit meanings of the deep mythological structure of the Grail, denies this harmonious fulfillment of the Arthurian symbolism: the emphasis is on questing.

Michael's boyhood experiences prove to him that fasting induces visions. As a boy he hallucinates:

> He ate nothing all day and when it began to get a little dark went up into the lumber-room . . . he turned round and saw clouds . . . [which] parted suddenly, as if they had been blown away of [?] a sudden, and he saw in their stead a streak of bright orange light, like sunset . . .

and when Margaret dreams she also notes that "all at once everything had got very full of light" (*SB* 16 and 101). An analogous event is related by Yeats in *Memoirs*:

> One night I heard a voice, while I lay on my back, say I would be
> shown a secret, the secret of life and of death, but I must not speak of it.
> The room seemed to brighten and as I looked towards the foot of the
> bed I saw that it was changed into precious stones. (*Mem* 127)

Yeats interprets his experience as a sexual dream. The similarity of the
descriptions, together with Michael's hallucination of a beautiful
woman and Margaret's mutual dream, affirms the erotic connotation of
the visions. Translated into the Arthurian framework the fasting or
"barrenness of the hills" (*SB* 100) becomes the waste lands, and the
sexual vision is the mystical communion from the Grail which fertilises
the sterile earth.[28]

In *The Speckled Bird*, however, the brightness of the dreams quickly
fades into cold mundane realism. Michael comes to in the lumber room,

> . . . and found that he was lying on the floor beside the mirror and that
> he had left the door open and that a wind was blowing from an open
> window in the passage. (*SB* 17)

Margaret, with Michael, finds the prosaic Harriet trying to keep warm,
and is

> . . . troubled to find it was so late. The moon was already setting and
> they were afraid they would lose their way. (*SB* 101)

Realism in prose fiction demanded, in Yeats's understanding, the
description of the incoherent and meaningless nature of daily life.[29] Thus
the form of *The Speckled Bird* undermines imagery and the spiritual nature
of its theme. According to William H. O'Donnell:

> The stories and novels do, however, help to illuminate the extreme
> importance of his debate over the merits of the supernal quest during
> the 1890s and his eventual rejection of that quest, as signalled by *The
> Speckled Bird*, in favour of an artist's necessary attention to the material
> world, even though he never lost his admiration for occult magi.[30]

Further, O'Donnell suggests that in *The Speckled Bird* form balances
theme, as the satire of the occult in Maclagan balances Michael's truly
spiritual dreams.[31] But the failure of the Grail quest and the reassertion
of the waste lands combines uneasily with the imaginative Arthurian
symbolism. In *The Speckled Bird* structure and theme work against, and
with, one another to call into question the more complex natures of
realism and romance.

Arthurian literature is indissolubly bound to romance. In the
Medieval legends of Arthur narrative content and form developed

together and incorporated, rather than confronted, the Renaissance move towards epic and the sentimentalizing and patriotism of the Romantics and the Victorians. Thus the nature of romance is, often, the essence of Arthurian fiction. By incorporating Arthur in his work Yeats inevitably considers the notion of romance and its ability to answer the demands of a changing tradition.

The "other world" of Arthurian romance is an idealized and often allegorized setting through which the hero journeys on a spiritual and/or physical quest. The interest is, not in the ending of the tale, but in the continual and diverse digressions.[32] The quest is continued and its end continually postponed: the waste land is sterile yet fertilization by the Grail is always possible. Michael's quest for spiritual enrichment and his relationship with Margaret conform to the traditional romance theme. Moreover, the imagery of animals, unreal landscapes – as when Michael confronts Margaret at Gleann-na-ma-Sidhe – magic and dreams exactly adheres to the formula of the Medieval and Celtic Arthurian texts. At the same time, Michael, Margaret and Maclagan are unmistakeably drawn from Yeats, Maud Gonne and MacGregor Mathers, and generally, the characterizations of the novel are more realistic than emblematic.

The neo-Celtic movement showed a parallel impasse: the anthropological tracings of Arthurian legends to early cultures were uneasily linked to the material's mysticism. The inherent romance of the Arthurian tales had to answer the demands of modern prose fiction for a myth capable of encompassing both contemporary realities and spiritual needs, as well as sustaining the imaginative power to confront and rise beyond the political and social upheavals of the time. The Arthurian literature of the twentieth century evolved into this new role, as may be seen from the works of John Cowper Powys, T. H. White and Charles Williams, as well as in the more popular manifestations.[33]

Yeats's Arthur is part of this evolution. He embodies the transition from the pure romance symbolism to the demands of realism for a greater answerability to contemporary concerns. For Yeats the poetic power of Arthurian imagery remains intact, but the narrative must always recede into the waste lands:

> I have no happiness in dreaming of Brycelinde,
> Nor Avalon the grass-green hollow, nor Joyous Isle,
> Where one found Lancelot crazed and hid him for a while . . .
> To dream of women whose beauty was folded in dismay,
> Even in an old story, is a burden not to be borne.

> (*VP* 209–10)

NOTES

1. A similar attitude is expressed in: *L*, 46, 219, *UP1* 277, and *The Egoist*, I (1914) 57. An examination of Yeats's critical treatment of Tennyson is made in: Richard Fallis, "Yeats and the Reinterpretation of Victorian Poetry", *Victorian Poetry*, vol. 14 no. 2 (summer 1976) 93 and George Bornstein, "Last Romantic or Last Victorian: Yeats, Tennyson, and Browning", (*YA*, I [1982] 114–32).
2. Vivien represents Yeats's first love, Laura Armstrong (*L* 118).
3. *The Poems of Tennyson*, ed. C. Ricks (London: Longmans, 1972) pp. 1593–620.
4. Swinburne, "Tristram of Lyonesse" in *Tristram of Lyonesse and Other Poems* (London: Chatto & Windus, 1882) pp. 1–169; Yeats owned Swinburne's *Poems and Ballads* (1871) and *Poems and Ballads* Second Series (1884), (*YL*, 273–4). For further references to Swinburne: see *L* 546, 608; William Morris, "The Defence of Guenevere" in *The Defence of Guenevere* (London: Bell and Daldy, 1858) pp. 1–17; Yeats owned *The Defence of Guenevere* (1904 edition) and *The Collected Works* (1910–15), (*YL* 183). A similar allusion to Morris may be seen at *Au* 141.
5. Yeats owned a copy of the 1877 English translation which was presented to him in 1898 by Lady Charlotte Guest's daughter, who was a friend of Lady Gregory's (*YL* 158); hereafter the 1877 edition of the *Mabinogion* will be cited as *Mab*. In the same year he reviewed Ernest Rhys's *Welsh Ballads and Other Poems* and made reference to *Mab* (*UP2* 92). For a more general treatment of the Arthurian literature of the nineteenth and early twentieth centuries see: Van Der Ven-Ten Bensel, *The Character of King Arthur in English Literature* (Amsterdam: H. J. Paris, 1925) 175–204 and Stephen Knight, *Arthurian Literature and Society* (London: Macmillan, 1983) pp. 187–216.
6. Rhys, op. cit. (London: Williams and Norgate, 1886), pp. 151, 191, 493.
7. Ibid., pp. 383–543. Ven-Ten Bensel, *op. cit.*, p. 206.
8. On Yeats's edition of Spenser in the series *The Golden Poets* (Edinburgh: TC and EC Jack, 1906), see G. Bornstein, "The Making of Yeats's *Spenser*", *YAACTS*, 2 (1984) 21–9. For other references to Spenser, see: *Au* 66–7, 92, 150, 313.
9. The image of parallel dreams records the actual experience of Yeats and his wife, and Mrs Yeats confirmed Malory as the source of the white stag. See: A. Norman Jeffares, *A New Commentary on the Poems of W. B. Yeats* (London: Macmillan, 1984) p. 198, hereafter cited as *NC*. Yeats's prose works reveal a continued interest in Malory, see: *UP1* 270, *E&I* 13, 42–3, 55, and *VP1* 1282–3.
10. For a similar explanation of the deer see: *VP1*, 1283. See also Richard Ellmann, *The Identity of Yeats* (London: Faber and Faber, 1963) p. 50, hereafter cited as *Ellmann*.
11. For a study of Yeats's use of *Mab* see: F. A. C. Wilson, *Yeats's Iconography* (London: Victor Gollancz, 1960) pp. 256–7.
12. *Mab*, 109. Yeats gives a similar extended account of the legend of Pwyll and Arawn in *UP2* 282 and in Lady Isabella A. Gregory's *Visions and Beliefs in the West of Ireland* (Gerrards Cross: Colin Smythe, 1970) pp. 104, 364; the tale of Pwyll and Arawn is found at *Mab* 337–59.
13. See also: *NC* 38 and *Ellmann*, 47.
14. His source for the cauldron/grail is A. Nutt, *Studies on the Legend of the Holy Grail* (London: David Nutt, 1888) p. 185. For Yeats's approach to the Irish legends see: Daniel Hoffman, *Barbarous Knowledge* (Oxford University Press, 1970) 22, and Phillip L. Marcus, *Yeats and the Beginning of the Irish Renaissance* (Ithaca: Cornell University Press, 1970).
15. *Ellmann* 15.
16. On Yeats and the Order of the Golden Dawn see: Graham Hough, *The Mystery Religion of W. B. Yeats* (Sussex: Harvester Press, 1984) p. 22 and Ellic Howe in *The Magicians of the Golden Dawn* (London: Routledge & Kegan Paul, 1972) p. 251, which offers a single reference to the Grail. One of Yeats's associates in the Order of the Golden Dawn, A. E. Waite, however, was interested in the mystical aspects of the Grail: *The Hidden*

Church of the Holy Grail (London: Redway, 1909) and *The Holy Grail Its Legends and Symbolism* (London: Rider and Co., 1933).

17. Weston, op. cit. (Cambridge University Press, 1920). Eliot, *Collected Poems* (London: Faber & Faber, 1974) pp. 61–86; Powys, op. cit. (London: The Bodley Head, 1933). For Yeats's interests in *Parsifal* see: *UP2* 91–2, 125, 485–6; *E&I* 150–1, 484–5; and *Au* 150–1.

18. Hough, op. cit., pp. 44–5. K. K. Ruthven, *Myth* (London: Methuen, 1976) pp. 22–3.

19. *Merlin. Roman en Prose Du XIII Siècle*, eds G. Paris and J. Ulrich (Paris: Librairie de Firmin Didot, 1886) II. pp. 191–8; *SB* 9.

20. Op. cit. (London: A. P. Watt & Son, 1897) II. pp. 136–9. The textual similarities are so distinct as to preclude a superior source.

21. English Versions: accepted text, Lucy A. Paton, *Studies in the Fairy Mythology of Arthurian Romance* (Boston: the Athenaeum Press, 1903) p. 219. For the two less well known synopses: (i) see footnote 20 and (ii) Edith Capper, "The Magic of Merlin" in *The Leisure Hour* (1898) 635–6. Although Yeats would have been familiar with *The Leisure Hour*, since his father was an illustrator for this periodical, his more immediate source is *King Arthur and the Table Round*.

22. *UP1* 376–7; *NC* 120–1; *Ellmann*, 63.

23. *NC* 53; *Mem* 41, 125; Hough, op. cit. 46–53.

24. For references to Malory see, *SB* 9–11, 27, 116 and for *Mab*: *SB* 10–11, 16, 27, 101, 149–51, 157, 173, 245–7.

25. Eagle of Gwern Abwy: *Mab*, 247; *SB* 226.

26. *VP1* 203; *VSR* 212.

27. For other references to the Grail see: *SB* 64, 91–2, 196–8, 202–7; and on Wagner and the Grail, *SB* 79–80, 166.

28. The sexual imagery of the double dream in "Towards Break of Day" is commented on in *NC* 198.

29. O'Donnell *A Guide to the Prose Fiction of W. B. Yeats* (Epping: Bowker Pub. Co., 1983) pp. 131–2. Marcus, op. cit., pp. 35–60. Richard J. Finneran, *The Prose Fiction of W. B. Yeats* (Dublin: The Dolmen Press, 1973) pp. 23–7.

30. O'Donnell, op. cit., p. 3.

31. Ibid., p. 134.

32. For an analysis of the genre of romance see: Northrop Frye, *Anatomy of Criticism* (Princeton University Press, 1957) 186–206 and Patricia Parker, *Inescapable Romance* (Princeton University Press, 1979) 3–15.

33. Powys, op. cit.; T. H. White, *The Sword in the Stone* (London: Collins, 1938); Charles Williams, *Taliessin Through Logres* (Oxford University Press, 1938); and *The Region of the Summer Stars* (London: The Shenual Press, 1944).

Halfway to the Stars: W. B. Yeats in California, 1904

William J. Feeney

During his first lecture tour of America,[1] from November 1903 to March 1904, William Butler Yeats travelled from the rooted cities of the Eastern Seaboard, to the Midwest heartland, and across the desolate frontier country to California. His ten-day sojourn in and near San Francisco[2] was thoroughly gratifying. The lectures attracted large audiences, press coverage was extensive, and the climate was a welcome relief from the unusually severe winter in the East and Midwest.

The American tour was planned during the summers of 1902 and 1903, when John Quinn visited Yeats in Ireland. On 1 October 1903, from his New York office, 120 Broadway, Quinn sent out brochures on Yeats's lecture programme. They emphasized Yeats's experience as a lecturer as much as his literary achievements. Topics of the lectures were "The Intellectual Revival in Ireland", "The Theatre and What It Might Be", "The Heroic Literature of Ireland", and "Poetry in the Old Time and in the New". The fee was $75 for each lecture, including travel and other expenses.

Yeats arrived in New York on 11 November, aboard the *Oceanic*. From Quinn's apartment, 1 West 87th Street, he wrote to Lady Gregory on 16 November: "I go to the Pacific Coast in January, a five days' journey, and lecture in Father Yorke's town and stay with his worst enemy" (*L* 413).

Father Peter C. Yorke, a native of Galway, had been editor of the *Monitor*, the official organ of the Archdiocese of San Francisco. In 1902 he founded an independent Catholic weekly, the *Leader*, modelled on the Dublin weekly *Leader*, edited by David P. Moran, who never had anything good to say of Yeats. A skilful but intemperate polemicist, Yorke often crossed the faint line separating legitimate moral concerns of the church and outright politicking.[3]

The "worst enemy" was James Duval Phelan, whom Quinn had asked to make arrangements for Yeats on the West Coast. The son of an Irish immigrant and pioneer Californian, Phelan had served as mayor of

San Francisco from 1897 to 1902, and was active in Democratic party politics and in local Irish affairs. A bachelor who had inherited lucrative banking and building enterprises, he lived in the fashionable Mission District and delighted in entertaining celebrities.[4]

Originally supportive of Phelan, Yorke was angered when Phelan, probably as a matter of expedience, did not repudiate public figures who were associated with the anti-Catholic American Protective Association. During a general strike in San Francisco in 1901, the priest championed the cause of labour. When the mayor assigned policemen to protect vehicles crossing picket lines, Yorke stirred up among union workers bitter feeling against Phelan.

It is unlikely that Yeats had any previous knowledge of this parochial squabble. He may have known, however, that Yorke delivered an important speech in behalf of the Gaelic League at the Antient Concert Rooms, Dublin, on 1 September 1899. (While Yeats was in San Francisco, Yorke was elected to a third term as president of the Gaelic League of California on 31 January.) Yeats also may have been aware that Yorke was a cousin on Major John MacBride. In any event, there were exciting possibilities that Yeats might be caught up in the clash between Yorke and Phelan.

Of the impending journey to California, Yeats wrote to his sister Lily, from New York, on Christmas Day: "There, I am told, I shall find a delightful climate" (*L* 417). Eight days later ten inches of snow and sleet descended on New York.[5] It was −12 degrees in Chicago on 24 January; the *Chicago Tribune* of 26 January printed a cartoon of Californians revelling in sunshine. On 24 January the temperature in St. Paul dipped to −33. When he arrived in San Francisco, Yeats wrote to Lady Gregory:

> I left St. Paul last Friday [22 January] amidst ice and snow −14 degrees below zero. . . . Here there are palm trees and pepper trees and one walks about without a coat. (*L* 428)[6]

During most of his stay in San Francisco the high temperature ranged from 58 to 64 and the skies were clear.

His visit to the West Coast had been announced as early as 19 November, when the *Daily Californian*, the University of California newspaper, reported that Yeats would speak there and at Stanford University. The weekly *Monitor* of 9 January noted the lectures to be given by "Ireland's greatest living poet and dramatist", and reprinted portions of an article on Yeats by James G. Huneker in the New York *Sun* of 27 December.[7] It touched on the similarities of the Irish and the Polish

in their despairing patriotism, their preference for the melancholy minor scale of emotion, their sudden alternations of sorrow and gaiety, defiance and despair.

For Yeats there was handsome but qualified praise. Huneker recalled, "not without a shudder", Yeats's esoteric short stories – "The Tables of the Law", "Rosa Alchemica", and "The Binding of the Hair". The plays were filled with "impalpable charm", yet were not good theatre: "Mr. Yeats and his associates must carve their creations from harder material than lovely words, lovely dreams." His poetry, like that of Keats, opened magic casements through which a land of dreams was mistily visible. Yeats was the

> bright particular star of Celtic poetry today, and in his wavering, melancholy and rebellious music I discern more than one hint of the Celt's spiritual countryman, Chopin.

Father Yorke's *Leader* of 16 January,[8] instead of acting as devil's advocate, asserted: "To William Butler Yeats the Irish race owes more than to any [other] living man." His drama had vanquished the Stage Irishman; his poetry, though sometimes steeped in mysticism, was in touch with the common man. As evidence the *Leader* reprinted "The Ballad of Father Gilligan". The article closed by designating Yeats "the most gifted and eminent Irishman that ever set foot by the Golden Gate".

Yeats arrived in San Francisco late on 26 January, aboard the elegant Overland Limited.[9] His coming was heralded on 24 January in the San Francisco *Examiner* and the *Chronicle*. The *Examiner* report, flanked by a photograph of Yeats reflectively stroking his chin, said in part:

> Lovers of poetry and the sympathizers with the people of Ireland will make the meeting a great ovation to the poet, who is by many eminent critics regarded as the greatest of his time. . . . His raising of the curtain which has shut away from modern view the wealth of imagination and poetry in ancient Ireland is one of the notable works for which he has become famous.

A vaudeville programme at the Orpheum Theatre, reviewed by Ashton Stevens in the *Examiner* of 25 January, included a musical sketch, "The Fairy of Killarney", based on Irish legend, which

> if written and acted with any touches of lightness and imagination would not be below the notice of such a fastidious Celt as William Butler Yeats.

On the morning of 27 January the *Examiner* printed an article on Yeats and a photograph of him on which was superimposed a drawing of a stack of books and an ink well with a prodigious quill pen thrust into it. If the unsigned article had been footnoted it might have found place in a scholarly journal. Yeats was "said to have modeled his art on the inspiration of William Blake, the prophet of symbolism". His own definition of symbolism was quoted:

> Whatever the passions of man have gathered about, becomes a symbol in the Great Memory, and in the hands of him who has the secret it is a worker of wonders, a caller-up of angels or of devils.[10]

Folklore, as Yeats acknowledged, was his special field:

> Folk art is, indeed, the oldest of the aristocracies of thought, and because it refuses what is passing and trivial, the merely clever and pretty, as certainly as the vulgar and insincere, and because it has gathered into itself the simplest and most unforgetable thoughts of the generations, it is the soil where all great art is rooted.[11]

The article cited Matthew Arnold's pronouncements on the "Celtic Note", to which it related, without identifying, lines spoken by the Fairy Child to Maire Bruin in Yeats's *The Land of Heart's Desire*:

> Yet I could make you ride upon the winds,
> Run on the top of the dishevelled tide,
> And dance upon the mountain like a flame.

> (*VPl* 202)

The poet himself had said that he loved to exploit "the vast and vague extravagance that lies at the bottom of the Celtic heart".[12]

Arnold's Celtic enthusiasms in fact had not delighted Yeats. He declared, in a letter in the Dublin *Leader* of 1 September 1900:

> . . . all that I have said or written about Matthew Arnold since I was a boy is an essay in "Cosmopolis",[13] in which I have argued that the characteristics he has called Celtic, mark all races just in so far as they preserve the qualities of the early races of the world. (*UP2* 241)

Readers of the *Examiner* were reminded that Yeats was not easy to understand:

> Doubtless the poet will himself assist those earnest students who have followed his work from the beginning, and therefore his presence in this city is a privilege that will be appreciated.

On the same page the *Examiner* published the following birth announcement:

Paris, January 26. Major John MacBride, who fought against the
British in the Boer War, is the happiest man in Paris. His son was born
early this morning. Mrs. MacBride, better known by her maiden
name of Maud Gonne, is likely to make a rapid recovery.

Yeats delivered his first lecture on the afternoon of 27 January at the
University of California, in Berkeley. The *Daily Californian* of that
morning contained a notice on the lecture and a critique of Yeats by
Professor Charles M. Gayley. The site had been changed from the
Students' Observatory to the larger Harmon Gymnasium. Gayley, like
other contemporary American scholars, thought of Yeats largely as a
poet of folklore. "The Lake Isle of Innisfree" and "The Ballad of Father
Gilligan" were "redolent of the simple charm of folk-composition".

Although the topic was announced as "The Intellectual Revival in
Ireland", Yeats spoke on "The Theatre and What It Might Be". He was
escorted to the platform by Phelan and Benjamin Ide Wheeler, president
of the university. Father Yorke, who had been appointed a regent of the
university in 1902, was in the audience. Attendance was estimated at
more than 1000 by the *Chronicle* of 28 January; the San Francisco *Call* of
28 January reported it in the neighbourhood of 2000, as did Yeats in a
letter to Lady Gregory (*L* 429). Introducing Yeats, Wheeler aimed an
"aside" at Phelan:

> We, who are used to being ruled by Irishmen, think that the Irishman
> is a very material personage. In fact the inhabitants of the Emerald
> Isle have among their numbers many gifted and inspired men.

The account of Yeats's lecture in the *Daily Californian* of 28 January
was headlined, "Irish Poet and Scholar Tells of Degeneration of the
Stage". Since the time of Shakespeare, Yeats asserted, the taste of
theatregoers had grown coarse, and theatre managers accelerated the
decline by relying on extravagant sets and costumes: "It is impossible to
have good acting and good scenery on the same stage." Discarding
elaborate properties was a calculated risk; audiences were accustomed to
them. But in time they would learn that the play, not the drapery, was
the thing. There were signs of a turnabout. The Greek Theatre on the
Berkeley campus marked a return to a drama of classical simplicity. The
Irish theatre was restoring "ideas such as were laid down by
Shakespeare and his contemporaries". It had made such progress that
"even clerks and people of the lower classes have banded together to
produce plays". In his closing remarks, as reported in the *Daily
Californian*, Yeats exhorted his listeners "to do all in their power to
further the ideals for which the Irish are sacrificing themselves".

Interviewed by the *Daily Californian* after the lecture, Yeats said that
California was all that it was advertised to be, and more. He had seen at

Berkeley an institution which could become one of the great universities in the world. In an exchange of compliments the *Daily Californian* declared:

> Truly it was a privilege yesterday to listen to a man with a message in which was his soul; to see a young man who gladly throws away his chances for wealth that he may forward true art for art's sake only; to hear withal, a poet.

The reporter who covered the Berkeley lecture for the *Call* of 28 January was impressed by Yeats's appearance:

> A close observation of Mr. Yeats revealed that he affects few of the stage properties of the poet. His hair is cropped short and he does not spend any time brushing it back on his forehead. His clothes might have been cut by an American tailor and he would not be suspected of poesy but for a flowing black tie that covers up his shirt front. Still Mr. Yeats would be picked out in a crowd as some kind of a genius. His features, eye-glasses, actions, all exhibit the man of refinement.

Yeats returned to San Francisco in the evening to speak at the Alhambra Theatre on "The Intellectual Revival in Ireland". General admission was fifty cents, reserved seats were seventy-five cents. The lecture was sponsored by the League of the Cross, a body of young Catholic men pledged to abstain from alcohol. It had been founded in 1886 by Father George T. Montgomery, who in 1902 became Archbishop of San Francisco. Father Yorke became its Spiritual Director in 1894.[14]

The lecturer was introduced by Father Philip O'Ryan, a friend and associate of Father Yorke. He remarked, in part:

> During the nineteenth century the Irish race may be said to have slept under arms in the field. Little wonder the voice of the poet was silent throughout the land. Mangan and Davis died prematurely. Ferguson survived but all too brief a time. But out of the West came a young man with the soul of a poet, a man steeped in the tradition and folklore of the Gael – the poet of the Celtic Revival – William Butler Yeats.

In the "chill and windy spaces" of the theatre, said the *Examiner* of 28 January, Yeats spoke for two hours to an audience estimated at 1500–2000. Many others were turned away because the house was full.

Yeats began by observing that Gaelic Irishmen (tacitly distinguished from West Britons) knew more of America than they did of England. Americans in turn were well informed of the political situation in Ireland

but not of its cultural awakening. Because American sympathy mattered
to Ireland, Yeats had come to tell the history of Ireland's intellectual
revival.

The chivalric, naively confident poetry of Young Ireland "was very
close indeed to the national movement in politics". Its foremost figure,
Thomas Davis, although not a great poet, was the first modern Irish
writer to speak to the whole people. Aristocratic Lady Wilde was
converted to nationalism when she saw the huge crowd at Davis's
funeral.

The famine, prophesied in Mangan's "The Warning Voice", was a
turning point. The comic Ireland of fiddles and dancing feet vanished:
"She had loved much, but from that hour she hated much, and out of
that movement rose passionate, violent movements", such as
Fenianism, "that had no place for song". Parnell brought temporary
political unity, but it was accompanied "by the death of individualistic
thought".

In the face of bitter political controversies the intellectual movement
gained ground slowly. Something was needed to touch the hearts of all
the people. It was found in the efforts of the Gaelic League to restore the
Irish language. Under the enthusiastic leadership of Douglas Hyde the
league became so powerful that it was able to persuade public houses in
Dublin to close during the annual St. Patrick's Day language procession.
Dublin artisans learned Irish, and even children wished to study it in the
belief that it was the official language in Heaven. Yeats, the peaceful,
retiring man of letters, was impelled to "go on platforms and tell the
people to learn Irish", though he himself could not speak it. He and his
friends best served Ireland in another way, by creating a theatre. In the
beginning they were not certain that they would have an audience for
whom drama was a passion rather than a recreation. They were
convinced by the performance of *The Countess Cathleen* in 1899. Thirty
policemen were on hand to prevent disorder when there were protests
against the alleged blasphemy of the countess selling her soul to buy food
for starving peasants. Here was proof that Irishmen took drama as
seriously as did the audiences of Shakespeare, Molière, and Calderon.
Yeats's lawyerlike presentation of the case against his own play evoked
laughter and applause. By complimenting the protesters he turned what
could have been negative publicity into an affirmation of the Irish drama
movement.

The peroration was designed to bolster his thesis that the cultural
awakening of Ireland was a grassroots activity:

Instead of the metropolis sending down traveling companies to
corrupt the intellects of the country places, the little country places
send traveling companies up to Dublin. And the country places are
where Ireland is most vital. The sods are singing to us and it may be

that Ireland is beginning this great movement which will bring with it a more serene life, a more beautiful life.[15]

Phelan, who had rented a box at the Alhambra, was host to Yeats at a supper following the lecture. The party was delayed while Ashton Stevens, of the *Examiner*, interviewed Yeats in a theatre office.

The *Examiner* devoted almost an entire page to the lectures at Berkeley and the Alhambra, an interview of Yeats by Irish-born Charles Cahill, and photographs and drawings of the poet. According to the *Chronicle*, his accent was English, his facial expressions could pass as American,

> But as the sentiments came and the fervor – none but an intensely feeling native of the Emerald Isle could have dwelt so with refined disdain for all things English and cherished such feelings about all things Irish.

A headline in the *Leader* of 30 January proclaimed, "The Famous Irish Poet and Dramatist Delights an Enthusiastic Audience with his Brilliant Utterances". Yeats wrote to Lady Gregory:

> I send you Father Yorke's paper, he is a great Moran-ite and as he is also an enemy of my host . . . I had rather expected attack. (*L* 430)

During the interview with Cahill, Yeats was at his charming best:

> He talks, in a way to inspire, on an endless variety of topics in a delightfully elusive vein that suggests and nourishes, yet knows where to stop. Something is left unsaid, nothing is run into the ground.

Because it was a luncheon interview, Cahill asked about Dublin cuisine. This gave Yeats an opportunity to tell stories of George Moore. While he was staying at the Shelbourne Hotel, Moore fussed outrageously over his meals, and when he moved to 4 Ely Place he made life miserable for a succession of cooks. Yeats had told these stories to Lady Gregory in 1901 (*L* 351). He mailed a copy of Cahill's interview to her, with the hope that it would not come to Moore's attention (*L* 429).

Much of the conversation was on literature. When Cahill complained of the vague symbolism of recent Irish poetry, Yeats pointed to Milton and Spenser, and even Gray and Tennyson, as poets who were not always understood by their contemporaries. The best artists challenged their readers.

The greatness of English literature, Yeats remarked, could be traced to England's Anglo-French heritage. While it was a dominant cultural influence, relations between England and Ireland were relatively peaceful. Only when Cromwell forced the old Saxon mentality upon the country did English literature shrivel and racial animosity between Saxon and Celt arise. Remembering from boyhood the phrase "The curse o' Crummle on ye," Cahill thought this an ingenious theory. Yeats expressed it to Lady Gregory in 1902 (*L* 387), and in 1906 in his introduction to Spenser (*E&I* 375–6).

Stevens's interview was held back until Sunday, 31 January. It occupied the whole of page 43. Copy meandered around a large drawing of a seated Yeats, wearing a long fur-collared coat, gesturing with a cigarette in his left hand (detail, Plate 7). The dialogue was not as sprightly as the conversation with Cahill. Mostly it was Yeats on the degeneracy of the modern theatre. He chose as an exemplar a triviality, *Mice and Men*, by an American playwright, Madeleine Lucette Ryley. After long runs in London and New York, it was staged at the Gaiety Theatre, Dublin, in June 1903. Yeats walked out on it, offended by the characterisation of a man who cavalierly broke off an affair with a married woman to pursue a young girl. He insisted that it was the vulgar complacency, rather than the adultery, that troubled him. What he told Stevens was a reprise, markedly similar in wording, of an article he had written in the October 1903 *Samhain* (*Ex* 111–13).

When Stevens commented that some critics thought Yeats decadent,[16] Yeats asked, "What is decadence?" It could not be exemplified by "the bearing of thought on action" that dominated his early writing, because by that definition contemplative monks and saints were decadent. But he conceded that since he began to create plays for the Irish theatre he had veered from a "mood of pure contemplation of beauty" to a "line of action, and even in what lyrics I have written lately there has been much of this activity and life".

On 29 January Yeats travelled to San Jose to lecture at two nearby institutions, Stanford University and Santa Clara College. The talk at Stanford, originally scheduled in the chapel, was moved to Assembly Hall to accommodate an audience of 800–1000. The *Chronicle* of 29 January reported that it would be "connected with the Celtic intellectual revival or with the future of the theatre". It turned out to be "The Heroic Poetry of Ancient Ireland".

This lecture, sponsored by the English Club, was the most scholarly in Yeats's repertory. Irish legends, he said, were the ancestors of European romances. The tales of Arthur and Guinevere, and some of Shakespeare's characters, could be traced to Celtic sources:

> The old Celtic poets felt for wild nature as no modern poets feel. It has been said that in Wordsworth we see the first return to nature, yet these Irish poets wrote centuries before him.

Full appreciation of their art was delayed because not until Lady Gregory took the work in hand was it properly translated.

Unlike modern culture, which was the province of coteries, ancient Irish culture was the "heritage of the plowman". Its literature shaped a national way of life. Irish men learned from it "reverence for women that became a part of their character", and because of it the poorest peasants remained gentle people. "All ancient and heroic poetry was an endeavour to create types of heroic man-hood and womanhood". After the lecture Yeats read several of his poems, praised as works of "rare skill and beauty" by the Stanford newspaper, the *Daily Palo Alto*, of 1 February.

That evening he spoke at Santa Clara. Robert Kenna, S.J., the first American-born president of the college, enhanced its prestige by bringing in prominent speakers and by conferring honorary degrees, including an award to his nephew, James D. Phelan, in 1903.[17] Before the lecture Mr Gerald Beaumont recited a poem, written by himself, "To William Butler Yeats". It has been preserved for posterity in the *San Jose Daily Mercury* of 30 January. Phelan, who introduced the speaker, commented that California was so remote that, as its famed poet Joaquin Miller had said, a man might drop dead there and God would not know it: "Yet long before the East had their universities, California had her great colleges and seats of learning". Following his talk on "The Intellectual Revival in Ireland", Yeats and Phelan toured the printing plant of the *Daily Mercury* and then settled in at the Vendome Hotel in San Jose. Next morning they returned to San Francisco.

That evening Yeats spoke again at the Alhambra, on "The Theatre and What It Might Be". The audience had dwindled to 500 true believers who rejected the Saturday night diversions of sybaritic San Francisco to listen to a poet. The *Examiner* of 31 January stated,

> The poet's mind spoke with every word that the lecturer uttered. He used a simple eloquence that gained him the hearts of his listeners.

The *Chronicle* noted that he

> spoke more easily and altogether more entertainingly than he did last Wednesday, when he made his first address in California at the close of his initial day on the western edge of the American continent.

Newspaper accounts, especially in the *Examiner*, contained material not included in reports of the lecture when it was delivered at Berkeley. Some of his fellow Irishmen, Yeats told the audience, wondered why he placed so much importance on a national theatre. They failed to understand the correlation between eras of national greatness and a flourishing drama, as in the Golden Age of Greece and in Elizabethan England. This was no mere coincidence. Theatre was a power for good, an uplifter of public morals; Victor Hugo declared, "In the theatre the mob became a people." A national theatre thus was an integral part of Ireland's quest for nationhood.

It would be a "place for beautiful language, for the description of beautiful events – a theatre of the arts". Moving against the current of an age dominated by materialism and the decay of art, this theatre would be non-commercial: "Let us restore the theatre to its penury, then we restore it to its honor". Sets and scenery would be minimal. The strength of this theatre would be its players. Yeats spoke of a project

> for the recital of narrative poems on the stage by the bard, with persons on stage taking up the chorus, thus reviving the old Greek idea.

The repertory would consist mostly of folk drama:

> The folk plays would go with the folk poems in the proposed movement toward the perpetuation of the Gaelic tongue with all the beautiful simplicity, the poetry of the ideas expressed by those who have been born and dwelt in a land that had produced more dreamers than statisticians.

At the close of the lecture he read passages from folk plays and the writings of Douglas Hyde, and some of his own poems.

The *Examiner* of 29 January said that this would be Yeats's "farewell lecture", but on 2 February he spoke at the Sacred Heart Convent, located then at Franklin and Ellis Streets. Two hundred persons, among them Archbishop Montgomery (he also attended the lecture at the Alhambra on 27 January), were present by invitation. Archives of the convent disclose that the topic was "Poetry in the Old Time and in the New". The only press coverage was a brief summary in the *Chronicle* of 3 February:

> He discussed native Irish poetry and the dramatic appreciation of the rural Irish and added to the pleasure of his lecture by reading a number of his own poems all treating of Irish subjects and filled with a quaint, weird, rhythmic power and feeling.

The *Sacramento Bee* of 29 January reported, in a story headlined "Thursday Club May Present Poet Yates [sic]", that the local organisation was negotiating with him for a lecture in Sacramento. Next day it announced that he would make an appearance, open to the public, at the Congregational Church on 3 February. A summary in the *Bee* of 4 February indicates that he spoke on "The Intellectual Revival in Ireland". He charmed the audience with his accent and a bit of stage business:

He introduced his lecture by deliberately taking the piano stand and placing it on the pulpit in front of him. The act was unaccountable until he remarked that he did it so that he would not walk straight into the audience. Mr. Yeats wears glasses and the audience was at a loss to know whether he meant his remark to be taken literally or as a figure of speech indicating his impulse to become one of the American people.

At the conclusion he read some of his poems, which were "in blank verse [sic] and expressed the traditions of which he spoke".

Presumably Yeats boarded the Overland Limited in Sacramento at 1:05 p.m. on 4 February. It was scheduled to arrive in Chicago at 9 a.m. on 7 February.

A letter from John Quinn, mailed on 6 February, suggests that Yeats required some persuasion to travel to California. There is a faint tinge of "I told you so" in the message:

> Greetings and congratulations on your success at the Coast. I am very glad that you were so well received and have a little glow of pride in the vindication of my judgment in having you go to the Coast. (*LTWBY* 134)

Quinn may have anticipated that Yeats would benefit from a change of scenery. On 28 January, Yeats dispatched from San Francisco a wistful note to Lady Gregory:

> O the weariness of another month here, it would be a little less weary if it were here in this tropical place, but ice and snow and cold and wet and the weariness of ever new faces. (*L* 429)

Dissatisfaction of another kind had surfaced in a letter to Lady Gregory from New York on 2 January. Yeats's perception of the American media, prior to his western journey, was not entirely positive:

> Yes, there are plenty of newspaper accounts. . . . there have not been many actual reports of lectures, however. The accounts are, for the most part, interviews and descriptive paragraphs. (*L* 420)

To spread the news of Ireland's cultural awakening Yeats needed press coverage as well as live audiences. Irish–American and college-town papers were generally responsive. In bustling metropolises, however, lectures on the Irish renaissance were not especially newsworthy. The *New York Times* reported only the lecture in Carnegie Hall on 3 January. Yeats's forthcoming visit to St. Louis was announced in the *St. Louis Globe-Democrat* on 3 January – three lines in a column titled "News of the Society World".

Some articles in big-city papers created the impression that the writer saw Yeats, as the Widow Quin saw Christy Mahon, as a "curiosity man". An interviewer for the *New York Daily Tribune* described Yeats in action in his room at the Plaza Hotel, where he stayed before moving into Quinn's apartment:

> The dramatist became so enthusiastic over his subject that he had half way climbed the chair on which he first rested his foot. He now sat on the brass bar of the bed, and was apparently entirely oblivious of any uncomfortableness. (15 Nov.)

In reporting Yeats's lecture on "The Heroes of Ancient Irish Poetry" to the Irish Literary Society of New Haven, Connecticut, on 18 November, the New York *Sun* of 19 November printed nothing on its content. Almost all the article was given to a question from a man in the audience: Are there any banshees left in Ireland, and if not, why continue to frighten children with stories of them? Apparently caught off guard, Yeats finally replied, "My dear man, I don't know what you are driving at."[18]

The *Chicago Tribune* of 14 January chronicled Yeats's flurried arrival. Tired and dusty, he checked in at the Auditorium Annex, only to be told that he would have to wait an hour for a room:

> "Exceedingly strange," remarked Mr. Yeats. "I do not know where my trunk is and a boy has run away with my cases," continued Mr. Yeats. "I do not know where I am to speak and I do not know what I am to talk of tomorrow morning."

If Yeats was desirous of "actual reports of lectures" he must have been pleased by the reporting of his speeches by daily and weekly papers in the Bay Area. Phelan's social and political connections undoubtedly were helpful, but there may have been another less tangible advantage. Metropolitan San Francisco had come to be a sophisticated place. Nonetheless, not very far away men and women still were coping with the harsh environment of the frontier. While Yeats was in town, the *Examiner* carried stories of dangerous encounters with wild creatures (a bear, an elk, a wolf pack). A frontier mentality persisted, an image of California loosely stitched to the populous East by railroad tracks and telegraph wires. It was evident in Phelan's chauvinistic introduction of Yeats at Santa Clara. His arrival thus was more than an item of interest to academicians and nostalgic Irish-Americans. It was a civic occasion. An artist of international fame had crossed the Great Divide to lecture, as the *Chronicle* of 31 January put it, "on the western edge of the American continent", and he was accorded the attention and courtesy due to an honoured guest.

In San Francisco, Yeats met an old man who had known his mother when she was Susan Pollexfen, and thought her the most beautiful girl in Sligo.[19] Agnes Tobin gave him a copy of her translations of Petrarch, titled *Love's Crucifix*, published in 1902 by William Heinemann, London. From Chicago, on 7 February, he wrote to her: "I have read it over and over. It is full of wise delight – a thing of tears and ecstasy".[20]

Like Phelan the offspring of an Irish immigrant who had become wealthy as a banker in San Francisco, Tobin spent much of her time in England and Italy. On 12 February 1907 she wrote to Yeats from London, to recall the "tremendous lift" his letter had given her when she received it in San Francisco exactly three years ago, and the pleasure her brother Richard experienced when he heard Yeats read poetry during a lecture in San Francisco (*LTWBY* 178). In 1906 she sat for a portrait by J. B. Yeats in his Dublin studio.[21] She dined occasionally with Yeats, and with J. M. Synge, who shared her interest in Petrarch.[22] For a while Tobin briskly, though not productively, involved herself in the business of the Abbey Theatre. There were plans, not carried out, to stage her translation of Racine's *Phèdre*. Her negotiations with the American impresario Charles Frohman to bring the Abbey company to America came to naught.

Tobin's circle of English and Irish friends included Alice Meynell, Edmund Gosse, Arthur Symons, Maud Gonne MacBride, and Joseph Conrad, who wrote of her "genius for friendship" in dedicating *Under Western Eyes* to her in 1911. Late in 1909 Gosse asked Tobin to sound out Yeats on whether he would have any qualms about accepting a civil list pension. She thought that Yeats would refuse, as a matter of principle (*L* 542–5); but he, convinced that it would not compromise his nationalism, accepted the pension when it was granted on 9 August 1910.

After 26 December 1909 there is only one reference to Tobin in Allan Wade's edition of Yeats's letters. On 16 June 1938, in reply to a query from Maud Gonne MacBride, Yeats said that he did not know if Tobin were still alive; probably she was not (*L* 910). Actually she outlived him by a few days. He died on 28 January 1939, she died in San Francisco on 20 February following a long illness.

Among local dignitaries invited to Yeats's lecture at Santa Clara was a member of the faculty at San Jose State Teachers College, Henry Meade Bland, an entomologist, poet, and historian of Western writers. Bland made Yeats an honorary member of the Pacific Short Story Club. Writing to Bland from London on 18 December 1907, Yeats regretted that he could not attend a club meeting,

which I imagine to myself somewhere under the shadow of the palm trees. I remember how the moon light fell amongst them one night in San Jose [sic].

On 2 May 1908 Yeats thanked Bland for sending him a collection of his verse, *A Song of Autumn and Other Poems*, published by the Pacific Short Story Club, San Jose, in 1907:

> Your verses are full of happiness, full of delight in the world, the joyous expression of a most full & vivid life. The criticism I was most inclined to make is that you should go to older models, you should go to the Elizabethans. Practically all modern models are dangerous. . . .

He also acknowledged receiving an article which Bland had written on his plays. I have been unable to find a copy of it. Later, because of writing commitments, Yeats had to decline a reunion with Bland in London. On 28 May 1909 he told Bland that he saw Agnes Tobin occasionally. By her "perpetual good humour and joyousness" she was helping Arthur Symons to recover from a mental breakdown. "She seems to carry your climate with her."[23]

On his return to England after the lecture tour Yeats wrote "America and the Arts" for the April 1905 *Metropolitan Magazine*. For a variety of reasons, he asserted, the arts were not flourishing in America,

> Yet here and there one could almost hear the footsteps of the Muses; in that beautiful San Francisco, for instance, under a sky of untroubled blue, by the edge of that marble Greek theater at Berkeley College [sic], or in those ornamental gardens a little southward where the policemen ride among the pepper trees and the palm trees with lassoes before them on the saddle. Perhaps it was only the enchantment of a still sea, or a winter that endured the violets, and of a lovely book of verses from Petrarch, sent me by a young writer, that made me fancy that I found there a little of that pleasure in the Arts, which brings creative art and not scholarship, because it is delight in life itself.

Predicting the time and place of the next great flowering of the arts was imaginative self-indulgence, like the make-believe of children,

> . . . but certainly should it come into these half Latin places that will be well, for the Northern voices of the world seem to be getting a little fainter and they do not, it may be, delight us as they did. (*UP2* 342)

In the visitors' book in the San Francisco Public Library it is recorded that Yeats liked Golden Gate Park. He also admired "the Western college buildings where one saw the architecture of the old Spanish Mission House adapted to new purposes" (*UP2* 339). However, his most durable recollection, noted often in writing and in speech, was the curious mixture of the exotic and the familiar he observed at Santa Clara (which he persistently called "San Jose").

Anyone accustomed to stolid bobbies or statuesque gendarmes would take note of mounted policemen armed with lassoes. Anyone accustomed to the dour winter landscape of the British Isles would be delighted to stroll through the Santa Clara quadrangle, in January, and see the tropical vegetation dramatically heightened by moon light.[24] In setting, in geography, this was far removed from Ireland. Yet many of the boys to whom Yeats spoke were of Irish ancestry, and as he talked he came to realise that they were Irish in tradition and loyalty. They knew as much of the history and poetry of Ireland as did their counterparts in Dublin and Connacht.

In 1906 he remembered them in the preface to *The Poetical Works* of *William Butler Yeats* (*VP* 851). He brought them forward as symbolic justification for a tour of America by the Abbey Theatre company in 1911. Dubliners had been complaining that the company was on the road too often. Speaking from the stage of the Abbey on 8 September, Yeats defended the tour as a cultural bridge between native Irishmen and persons of Irish ancestry, such as the boys to whom he lectured in California:

> The Irish imagination keeps certain of its qualities, and if we are to give it, as we hope, a new voice, and a new memory, we shall have to make many journeys.[25]

In November 1922 Yeats wrote a letter to be read "to the students of a Californian school" whose name he had forgotten. (I have found no evidence that it ever was read at Santa Clara.) In the prelude he told of the Jesuit Fathers treating him to dinner and to wine from their own vineyards. Thinking it the harmless kind served at afternoon teas, he drank "incautiously", and then wondered if his lecture would be coherent. The letter actually was a philosophical history of Irish drama, an account of the hard life of dramatists who tried to educate indifferent or hostile audiences. To the students Yeats directed a rhetorical question: "And you, perhaps, walking among your palm trees in that California sunlight, may well ask yourself what is it that compels a man to make his own cup bitter?"[26] Other references to the students were peripheral. Yeats advised the masters not to read the letter to boys under the age of fifteen, and not to let them read *Ulysses*.[27]

Twenty-six years after his first visit to California the evening he spent at Santa Clara still was lodged in Yeats's memory. In a diary written in 1930, he recorded these words:

> I think constantly of some Irish lads I spoke to in California many years ago, and found as familiar with "Young Ireland" as lads at home, because they gave me perhaps for the first time a sense of a race scattered and yet one. (*Ex* 297)

164 *Yeats Annual No. 6*

NOTES

1. I wish to acknowledge the generous assistance of the following archivists and librarians: William M. Roberts, University of California; Jeffrey M. Burns, Archdiocese of San Francisco; Johanna Goldschmid, San Francisco Public Library; Sr. Katherine McShane, R.S.C.J., Convent of the Sacred Heart, San Francisco; Cynthia Decker, Santa Clara University; Linda J. Long, Stanford University; D. Steven Corey, University of San Francisco; Phyllis Levine, Cupertino, California Public Library; and Jean Keleher, De Paul University. Permission to reproduce a drawing of Yeats has been granted by Pamela Brunger Scott, San Francisco *Examiner*.

   The pioneer work in this area is Karin Margaret Strand's comprehensive study, "W. B. Yeats's American Lecture Tours", doctoral dissertation, Northwestern University, 1978. My own interest in Yeats's western journey began with research on the Dublin weekly *Leader* and its counterpart the San Francisco *Leader*.
2. The New York *Sun* of 12 Nov. reported that Yeats had been invited to lecture at the University of Oregon. He did not make an appearance there.
3. For biographical information see Joseph S. Brusher, S.J., *Consecrated Thunderbolt: Father Yorke of San Francisco* (Hawthorne, N.J.: Joseph F. Wagner, 1973).
4. Evelyn Wells, *Champagne Days in San Francisco* (New York: Doubleday, 1947) p. 248.
5. The national weather bureau report for 3 Jan. stated, "The entire country except for the Pacific Coast is experiencing temperatures 15 to 30 degrees below the seasonal average."
6. According to official reports there was 0.27 inches of precipitation on 21 Jan. Next day the low temperature was 8 degrees and skies were clear. It was −12 on 23 Jan.
7. The *Monitor* did not indicate the source of the article, and attributed it to an unidentified "eminent critic". Huneker, a sometime music critic, had written *Chopin: the Man and His Music* (New York: Scribners, 1900), hence the references to the Polish composer in the article. In the *Sun* of 22 Nov., Huneker called Yeats "a doughty opponent of mercantilism in art, whether in the theatre or in literature. . . . By all means let us hear Mr. Yeats talk on the Celtic renaissance, or, better still, let some of his plays be produced under his supervision".
8. I have cited the article as reprinted in the Minneapolis *Irish Standard* of 30 Jan. From the Richard A. Gleeson Library of the University of San Francisco I have obtained copies of the *Leader* of 23 and 30 Jan., but nobody seems to have the issue of 16 Jan.
9. The train departed from Chicago at 8.00 p.m. on 23 Jan. and was scheduled to arrive in San Francisco at 6.25 p.m. on 26 Jan. I am indebted to Mr. Edward Harney, Chicago and Northwestern Transportation Company, for train schedules and other information.
10. From "Magic" in the *Monthly Review*, Sept. 1901; reprinted in *Ideas of Good and Evil*, 3rd edn (London: A. H. Bullen; Dublin: Maunsel, 1907) p. 65 (*E&I* 50).
11. From "By the Roadside," in *An Claideamh Soluis*, 13 July 1901; reprinted in *The Celtic Twilight* (London: A. H. Bullen, 1902) pp. 232–3 (*Myth* 139).
12. From "An Irish Visionary," in *The National Observer*, 3 Oct. 1891; reprinted in *The Celtic Twilight* (1902) p. 21.
13. "The Celtic Element in Literature" (June 1898).
14. Msgr. Francis J. Weber, *California Catholicity* (Hong Kong: Libra Press, 1979) pp. 179–80.
15. The press may have been given a condensed text of the lecture. Quoted passages in the *Examiner* of 28 Jan. and the *Monitor* and *Leader* of 30 Jan. are identical. The *Examiner* included some material which did not appear in the two weekly papers. The *Call* and the *Chronicle* of 28 Jan. offered paraphrases of the lecture.
16. Huneker wrote in the New York *Sun* of 27 Dec. that decadence is "an aesthetic, not a moral, mode; and in that sense Mr. Yeats belongs to the school of Decadence, as do all of his contemporaries from Wagner, Tolstoy, and Ibsen down to the latest minor

poeticule. But to call his work decadent, meaning that it is false, artificial, morbid, or immoral, is not to say the truth".

17. Gerald McKevitt, S.J., *The University of Santa Clara: a History, 1851–1977* (Stanford University Press, 1977) p. 135.

18. A letter on this incident, signed W., appeared in the *Sun* of 24 Nov. As a "city gawk", Yeats knew nothing of the little people. W. set the record straight with quick sketches of the banshee, the will of the wisp, the leprechaun, the White Lady, and the Bowsy.
When George Pollexfen died in 1910, Lily Yeats and a nurse said that they heard the banshee (*L* 552–3).

19. W. B. Yeats, *Reveries Over Childhood and Youth* (London: Macmillan, 1916) pp. 54–5.

20. The letter is reproduced in *Agnes Tobin: Letters, Translations, Poems, With Some Account of Her Life* (San Francisco: Grabhorn Press, for John Howell, 1958) p. 74. Yeats told her that earlier he had been writing some "dull and unnecessary letters". If these were what he called "bread and butter" letters, he overlooked Phelan. In 1906, when Douglas Hyde and his wife visited the West Coast, Phelan complained to Mrs Hyde that Yeats had not acknowledged his hospitality. The matter came to Quinn's attention. Knowing Yeats to be careless rather than ungrateful, Quinn wrote to him on 13 July, suggesting that he send Phelan a letter of commendation for his services as chairman of a committee engaged in relief work after the San Francisco earthquake of 1906. Alan Himber (ed.), *The Letters of John Quinn to William Butler Yeats* (Ann Arbor: UMI Research Press, 1983) pp. 79–80.

21. Joseph Hone (ed.), *J. B. Yeats, Letters to His Son W. B. Yeats and Others*, 1869–1922 (New York: Dutton, 1946) p. 90.

22. Ann Saddlemyer (ed.), *The Collected Letters of John Millington Synge*, vol. 1 (Oxford: Clarendon Press, 1983) p. 267.

23. The letter of 18 Dec. 1907 was printed in an article on the Pacific Short Story Club, in a San Francisco periodical, *The Overland Monthly*, 52 n.s. (July–Dec. 1908) 55. Passages in the other letters to Bland are printed here with permission of Dr J. S. Kelly, St. John's College, Oxford, and Mrs Kim Scott Walwyn, Oxford University Press. The letters of 18 Dec. 1907 and 28 May 1909 are in the Bancroft Library, University of California; the letter of 2 May 1908 is in the Mills College Library, Oakland, California. I am grateful to Dr Ronald Schuchard for making copies available to me.

24. There is a drawing of the Santa Clara campus, made at the end of the nineteenth century, in McKevitt, pp. 100–1.

25. *Irish Times*, 9 Sept. 1911, p. 8.

26. The letter was published in William J. Fitzgerald (ed.), *The Voice of Ireland* (Dublin: John Heywood, 1924). An amended text was printed in Robert O'Driscoll (ed.), *Theatre and Nationalism in 20th Century Ireland* (University of Toronto Press, 1971) pp. 79–88.

27. Yeats properly referred to the students as boys or lads. During its first fifty years, 1851–1901, Santa Clara was more a boarding school or preparatory school than a degree-granting college. In 1904, the year of Yeats's visit, only 6 of 311 students were awarded bachelor's degrees. McKevitt, pp. 133, 327.

John Quinn's "An Evening in New York with W. B. Yeats"

Edited by Richard Londraville

In 1966 I was researching for my thesis on W. B. Yeats and his connection with the Japanese *Noh* when I came across an interesting note in Hone's collection of letters between J. B. Yeats and W. B. Yeats which stated that J. B. was buried in the family plot of Jeanne Foster of Schenectady, NY. I remembered vaguely that a colleague of mine, John Ormsby, had once mentioned that his wife knew a Schenectady woman who had once known Yeats. I hadn't given much thought to his remark until I read Hone's note. To be honest, I had thought that John was either joking or simply mistaken. After all, Yeats had been dead for nearly thirty years, and even his younger friends would be quite old by the mid-1960s. Also, someone who "had known" Yeats would most probably turn out to be a woman who had once been introduced to him at a cocktail party.

I couldn't have been more wrong. First I checked with John to see if the woman he had told me about was the same Mrs Foster that Hone had written of. What John told me didn't exactly fit. It seemed that this Mrs Foster had worked with the Schenectady housing authority for nearly thirty years, and had been instrumental in providing essential reforms for Schenectady's neediest people. She had been politically active, and her views were oriented to liberal social reform. An interesting and productive life, to be sure, but hardly one to suggest association with figures like Yeats and his father.

At any rate, I called Mrs Foster and asked if I might see her. After first asking me the purpose of my visit, she consented to an interview. I told her that I was interested in Yeats, especially his plays. She replied that she would be glad to talk to me on that subject. I hung up the phone, more intrigued than ever; I knew that Yeats's plays did not attract the audience that his poetry did, and someone prepared to talk about them was relatively rare, even in scholarly circles. Still, it might turn out that her knowledge of the plays was limited. I decided to take a tape recorder with me to see if I might get some reminiscences of the Yeats family from someone who had known them, in whatever capacity.

I must admit that I was not too hopeful when I drove up to Mrs Foster's house. I was admitted by a petite, impeccably groomed elderly lady who immediately put me at ease with her gracious manner. I identified myself and learned that I was, indeed, speaking to Mrs Foster. At least one of my fears was dispelled; I would not have to deal with a crochety old lady. She preceded me into her living room and asked me to have a seat. Her walls were covered with paintings and photographs; I did not recognise most of what I hurriedly glanced at, but one portrait caught me eye. It was an oil of W. B. Yeats as a young man, obviously done by his father. I squinted at it; it certainly looked genuine.

"I don't believe that I've ever seen that painting of W. B. before. Is it . . .?"

"Authentic? Yes, quite. It was done by J. B. when Willie was in his early twenties."

Better and better. Mrs Foster volunteered no more information about the portrait, but was extremely helpful concerning my interest in Yeats's drama. We talked for about half an hour, and I was impressed. She then asked me into her dining room, where the table was nearly covered with large manila envelopes.

"I looked through my papers after you called to see if there might be something which would help you with your project. I found some manuscripts which I think might be useful."

I glanced at the material spread on the table, and I could tell after a cursory examination that what she had was unusual and important. There were many letters from the Yeats family, including J. B. and all of his children. There were also documents relating to the careers of the Yeats family. Among the papers was the manuscript "An Evening with W. B. Yeats" by John Quinn.

I could not thoroughly examine the papers at that meeting, so I made another appointment to see Mrs Foster and her treasures. As I continued my research, I found that Mrs Foster's connection with the Yeats family represented only a miniscule part of her collection of manuscripts and memoribilia. In her capacity of editor of *Review of Reviews* and *transatlantic review* she had known many of the major British and American writers of the early twentieth century. I discovered this information gradually, and only as it pertained to my research. She rarely volunteered information about her past, but when I would mention Ezra Pound, or James Joyce, or some other artist, she would have stories to tell about them, and often show me documents relating to their work.

During the summer of 1968 I catalogued Mrs Foster's literary collection.[1] Only then did I become aware of the extent and variety of her collection; I realised that whatever she would spread on her living room table in the course of one of my visits represented a small fraction of her holdings. She had not kept these papers because she believed that they would one day be valuable; she explained that she was a 'squirrel", and that she seldom threw anything away, especially those mementos which reminded her of her earlier life. Many of these documents either concerned Quinn or his relations with his friends, but very few were actually written by him. In 1923, about a year before his death, Quinn gave her the manuscript of *An Evening with W. B. Yeats*.[2]

Mrs Foster told me many stories about Quinn, and the more she talked of him the clearer it became that they had shared a special friendship. She was distressed that many people regarded her as Quinn's mistress, and insisted that had not been the case. She didn't deny that she had loved Quinn – still loved him – but her marriage vows kept them from a more intimate relationship.

She spoke of Quinn as a patron and benefactor of artists, one who delighted in using his legal and business skills to help his friends. She told me of how he arranged lectures and exhibitions, bought paintings and manuscripts, and frequently loaned money or gave it away. She maintained that the abrasiveness that Quinn sometimes showed to these friends was caused by their lack of understanding of the demands of his busy life. In spite of the complaints that Quinn made of the stress his artist friends caused in an already frenetic schedule, he rarely refused to help. He often found that complying with a request was more expedient than explaining why he could not.

Jeanne Foster had met Quinn through the matchmaking efforts of J. B. Yeats. She had known of Quinn and his reputation as a Don Juan for several years, and so was understandably a bit shy about meeting him. But they knew so many of the same people and had such similar interests that Yeats was certain that they would become immediate friends. He was right. Mrs Foster showed me a charming letter in which J. B. Y. not only described her to Quinn, but also included a lovely head-and-shoulders sketch of her which could scarcely fail to intrigue any man.

Mrs Foster told me that she believed that genius only resided in men, and that she felt that her own considerable talents as writer and editor were better utilised in the service of some superior man. I can only speculate as to how sincerely she held this belief (it certainly allowed her remarkable success in a man's world), but it did not strike Quinn as a poor idea. He had for some time been looking for a secretary to handle his literary and artistic business. He had very competent help to handle the affairs of his office, but there was no one to arrange the other half of his interests.

He was used to dictating to his secretaries, but when the subject was other than law, he needed someone who could take notes and understand the subject, someone who would be able to advise him as he composed. Jeanne Foster was perfect for the job. Although she was not a professional stenographer, her experience as a reporter and editor had forced her to develop her own method of rapid notation.

Of course Quinn was a frustrated author himself. Any examination of his letters gives evidence of his attention to style and substance. In several instances (for example, his correspondence with Pound), he shows the tendency to imitate the style of the person to whom he is writing. His talents did not lend themselves to creative expression, but he had a great sense of the historical and literary value of the conversations and letters of his friends. It is no wonder that his itch to write was sublimated in letters, memos, and briefs.

There were occasions though, when Quinn felt compelled to write a more formal style. There is his famous defence of Roger Casement published *N. Y. Times Magazine* of August 13, 1916 which, although "dictated in a rush with no style about the damned thing"[3], drew praise for both style and content. Indeed, his style seems to be admirably suited for dictation; the busy lawyer and business man was used to thinking on his feet. No one would argue that a great deal of his writing could not profit from judicious editing, but the force of thought and of the historical moment is there.

I do not know to what extent Jeanne Foster supplied this kind of editing, but an examination of some of Quinn's notes of conversations which he wished to preserve show that they are almost always just that – notes. When Mrs Foster was able to accompany him on his visits to his literary friends, the conversations were recorded more or less *verbatim*.

In 1920, when W. B. Yeats was in New York prepared to set out on another cross-country lecture tour, Quinn took the opportunity to visit him at the Algonquin hotel. He brought Mrs Foster along in order to preserve the occasion. Since she already knew the Yeats family, her presence as a note-taker didn't inhibit either man.

There is a story which Mrs Foster told me which serves as a fitting end to her career as Quinn's literary amanuensis. Pleased with the success of the Yeats interview, Quinn thought that he would collect several such documents and amass his own literary history of the early twentieth century. His next subject was James Joyce.

When Quinn had the opportunity to visit Joyce in Paris, he felt that his monetary, legal, and publishing support might have placed the writer under enough obligation to cause him to submit to a recorded conversation similar to Yeats's. Mrs Foster told of arriving at Joyce's apartment fortified with sharpened pencils and plenty of memo pads, for after a few delays Joyce did consent to give Quinn an interview. But the writer who had Stephen Dedalus vow "silence, exile, cunning" was not willing to talk out his talent in idle conversation. He would only discuss recipes for the preparation of asparagus. That interview does not appear in Quinn's manuscripts.

I have corrected some spelling and typographical errors in the manuscript and changed some incidentals to conform to usage (e.g. Yeats's instead of Yeats'), and I have in places summarised some of Quinn's longer speeches. I have tried not to be too intrusive with my annotation, and therefore I have been selective in my identification of people, events, and works.

I thank Dr Thomas Conroy for his permission to print this material, and more especially for his encouragement and help during the last few years.

NOTES

1. Richard Londraville, "Jeanne Robert Foster", *Eire-Ireland*, Spring, 1970, pp. 38–44. Mrs Foster's collection contained over a thousand items of literary and artistic interest, about one quarter of which dealt with Irish material. Most of her collection was willed to William Murphy of Schenectady, New York. The "Foster-Murphy" archive is now in the Berg collection of the New York Public Library.
2. Mrs Foster gave me the manuscript in 1966 and inscribed the following note: "To Richard Londraville this copy of 'An Evening with W. B. Yeats' – Algonquin Hotel [–] for which I took the notes. Jeanne R. Foster, April 26 – 1966".

3. Quoted in B. L. Reid, *The Man From New York: John Quinn and His Friends* (New York, 1968) p. 236.

An Evening in New York with W. B. Yeats

by John Quinn

SUNDAY, 22 FEBRUARY 1920

Yeats and his wife were stopping at the Algonquin Hotel, 59 West 44th Street. I had suggested to Yeats that he and I see the Editor and the Managing Editor of *The Dial*, just rejuvenated, and that we both suggest to them that they make Ezra Pound their European representative, to secure articles and to read and sift and recommend prose, and poetry, and other contributions on politics, fiction and financial subjection, putting fiction in between politics and finance. I had arranged that the two editors should dine with Yeats and me at the St. Regis Sunday evening at 7:30. About eleven o'clock Sunday morning my man Paul[1] got Yeats on the telephone at the Algonquin, and then Yeats and I talked. I told him of the arrangement and said "Bring your wife with you also." He said: "Wait a minute, Quinn; I'll see." I heard him talking to her, and then he said to me: "Ah, Quinn, my wife says she would rather not come." When I asked "Why?" he replied. "I don't know whether it is a desire to avoid editors, or mere fatigue." I said: "Tell her that with the two young and very proper *Dial* editors she will be quite safe from any improper stories by me, and she may go when the dinner is over and we can talk business afterwards." I heard him talk to her again, and then he said to me: "My wife says she would enjoy the improper stories and that what she really feared was the young men of the *Dial*, but" he added "she says she will come."

I went to the St. Regis and met the two young men – goodlooking and cultivated – Harvard, Oxford, London and Paris, the editor Thayer[2] being obviously a man of the world – at seven. We waited till seven twenty and then went into dinner. About seven thirty a page-boy summoned me to the telephone. Mrs Yeats's voice, a little anxiously, explained that "Willie is very ill – We have telephoned to Dr. Healy – and he has promised to send a physician at once." I asked what the trouble was and she said: "Willie seems to be poisoned and is in pain and is very sorry he cannot come to the dinner." I told her that I was glad that they had sent for a physician and to tell him not to worry about not coming to the dinner. I said I would settle the thing and asked her to call me again on the telephone about nine o'clock, when the doctor had been there. She reported about nine that the doctor had been there and had examined Yeats and left medicine and a morphine tablet to take later to make him sleep.

The dinner was over at nine, and young Mr Thayer drove me in his car down to the Algonquin. I got to the hotel about 9:45. Yeats was in bed, still in some pain. He was stretched out with a long, blue nightgown on, a thing that was loose like a priest's cassock, only it was light blue. It was open down the front, and when he sat up later on it opened almost to his waist, showing at times one or both of his breasts. Over his legs and feet on the bed was a heavy hair robe. Shortly after I got there his wife ordered up tea, and during the talk that followed Yeats drank large quantities of tea, four or five cups of it, and even then seemed to be thirsty and continued to drink glasses of water.³ At first he lay flat on his back, but later on when he got interested he sat up in bed. Sometimes he had pillows propped behind his head, but mostly his head lay against the upright brass rods of the bed that made the back of the bed, just far enough apart to hold his head. His wife should have propped pillows up behind him, but she didn't. He would occasionally pull the pillows up behind his head and shoulders, but when they would slip down his head would slip into the space between the two upright brass rods, an uncomfortable position but he didn't seem to mind it a bit.

I told Yeats of the satisfactory arrangement I had made of my Pound-cum *Dial* suggestion. Yeats was very pleased. I should have said that when she had reported to me about nine o'clock on the telephone she had said that "Willie asked me to say that if necessary he would see them – in his apartment at the hotel – as he was then feeling somewhat better." But I had told her that it was not necessary. So when I got to their hotel I announced: "Well, I have met the editors and they are ours."

I knew Yeats would enjoy talk, if he did not talk himself, and so I talked and kept the talk off heavy things. It worked well with Yeats and he soon responded and sat up and talked himself.

He said his illness was due to a horrible fatiguing luncheon⁴ that he had been roped into attending the day before. It lasted hours. The speeches were horribly tedious, and the ideas – if they could be called ideas – essentially vulgar. He said that old Ely – the Chairman of the League for Political Education – under whose name the horrible luncheon had been given, and who presided throughout the long boredom – had been praised by several speakers as "a most tactful chairman", and by that Yeats said "was evidently meant a chairman who succeeded in preventing every single speaker from speaking his real convictions upon any subject".

Poetry was treated as if it were a funny thing, something to make jokes about.

Yeats: "Ah, Quinn, the kind of women and men that belong to those clubs give me a faint idea of what society would be under socialism; restless women, constantly arguing, lacking in repose, always chattering and rushing about and never seeming to feel or think calmly about anything; without any real social instincts and apparently happy only when they are vehemently arguing about or asserting some very elementary economic or political platitude. Compared to these tiresome and fatiguing club-women and social workers and political leaguers, the real society woman is a person of charm and distinction. She does not pretend or aspire. There she is! Show knows her position and has a background and often has a real charm."

Quinn: . . . [Here Quinn made a long speech attacking democracy and the glorification of the "average man".]

Yeats: "The general assumption is that people think. Whereas I often think that the contrary is the more true; that people generally do not think. I often think that an artist should assume that people generally do not think, and therefore should not think of them, should disregard them entirely in his work, and that the painter should paint or a poet should write for a few – maybe not more than twenty persons – who can feel and who do think."

Quinn: If Poe was the greatest artist that this country produced in the middle of the last century, Henry James was the greatest it produced in the last quarter of the last century and the first fifteen years of this century. When James was last here he must have been hurt by the vulgarization of life in this commercial society, this plutocratically-ruled country. In his book *The American Scene* written after his last visit to this side he said: 'It is of extreme importance to be reminded at many turns . . . that it takes an endless amount of history to make even a little tradition, and an endless amount of tradition to make even a little taste, and an endless amount of taste, by the same token, to make even a little tranquility.' "[5]

Yeats: "Of course James would say that. I often wonder, Quinn, as I go about lecturing to these eager girls at their pleasant colleges, whether I am not doing them a real harm, by telling them that mere reading, the mere collection of facts, the mere desire to be correct, which is the mark of essential vulgarity, and is not culture at all – I sometimes wonder whether I am not merely driving them into these horrible clubs and societies where there is no culture but only vulgar self-assertion."

Quinn: "You can perhaps avoid doing them any wrong by urging them all to resolve to do two things: never to join a club or a poetry society and to get married as soon as possible and to have as many babies as possible as soon as possible. Tell them that when they are young they may think that poetry and art and what passes for culture are all they want and need, but when they are thirty-five or forty they will realize that those are not the vital things; that women who have done things, who have made places for themselves in the world of art and letters and in public life would, if they had the chance, throw all those things joyfully away for a real man to stand up beside and to lie down beside and for real children to lean upon and the love them."

Yeats: "All these club-women and league-men seem to think that daily journalistic excitements represent eternal ideas. Their convictions, if one can use such a word for daily improvisations, are formed anew every day, and every day they think that their convictions have eternal value."

Quinn: "It is the result of general newspaper reading. It is all illustrative of that essay of mine, the title of which is 'How Phrases Kill Thought' – the essay that I have never written, and the old illustrations for which I forget when new ones occur, and they are constantly occurring. There is the Lincoln myth. You have heard of Lincoln, no doubt? He was once a President of the United States."

Yeats: "Yes, I have heard of Lincoln. I have been told that he is one of your immortals. England has long made George Washington one of her heroes, and now it seems that England threatens to annex Lincoln and to add what you call the Lincoln myth to her national folk-lore."

Quinn: "Well, the Lincoln myth has supplemented Whitman's grandiloquent rhetoric about the average man. Lincoln said that 'God must have loved the common people, because he had made so many of them.' That has been generally taken as a sign of Lincoln's affection for the common people. I sometimes feel that Lincoln meant it ironically and meant to say that 'God could not have loved the common people, because there were so many of them.' Sometimes I think it is the manyness of the people that makes their commonness. The Lincoln myth saved from just criticism Wilson, amazingly, during the German war."[6]

Yeats: "How is that?"

Quinn: "During the war the many, the herds and their leaders, who love to sanctify one of themselves, who create their political gods not merely in their own image but out of one of themselves, and who then devoutly worship their own creations and find them to be very good and very wise and very perfect, said: 'Don't criticize Dr. Wilson on the ground that he has made a mess of everything he has personally handled during the war. In our Civil War large numbers in those days criticized Mr. Lincoln, but Mr. Lincoln won the Civil War.'

"People who talk that way forget that merely because Lincoln was, or now seems to have been, right, is no proof at all that Dr. Wilson was right. Another illustration of how phrases kill thought."

Yeats: "Do you think, Quinn, that Wilson is finished?"

Quinn: "As finished as Caillaux[7] is – except for his nuisance value; a querulous, bad-tempered man, angered beyond endurance at the realization that the world has found him out and knows him for what he is, a mere preacher, a phrase-maker, not a thinker or a statesman or a man of culture at all."

By this time Yeats had exhausted all the tea – he must have drunk four or five cups of it – and then asked his wife for a glass of water. He said he felt feverish, and before I left, about eleven thirty, he had drunk four of five glasses of water. I smoked cigars, and his wife smoked a few cigarettes, while Yeats drank tea and water. While I was answering his question about Wilson, he sat up and said:

"I am often sorry I did not finish a poem that I had begun and sketched out and partly finished upon the Sargent[8] portrait of Wilson which is now in the Dublin National Gallery, a purchase out of Sir Hugh Lane's[9] money left to the Gallery. I saw the feeble hands, the weak fingers, the tailor-made and barber-made statesmen, the fashion-plate person, the head with more jaw than skull, the dull eye, the indecision and the vanity and the lack of breeding showing in every stroke of the brush. I compared it with a portrait hanging right beside it in the National Gallery – or near it – by Strozzi,[10] a Venetian painter, not one of the great Italian masters, and the contrast was startling. The Italian's face was the face of a hawk, of a man of the world, of a statesman and a man of power. Wilson's was that of a schoolmaster who had come into money and who tried to be a man of the world. It is an illustration of what I have often heard Sargent say his belief is: that a man *is* what he seems, what he looks."

Quinn: "Why didn't you finish the poem? I am sorry you didn't."

Yeats: "I didn't finish it because I had written about that time some other rather harsh and bitter poems, and I did not want to go on with more poems of that kind because I did not want that note of bitterness to get into my style."

Quinn: "I am sorry that you did not finish that poem. You needn't fear a too bitter note in your style because you will always have so much more boyishness and so much keener a sense of humour than so many other poets that your work will not suffer by comparison, but would gain, I think, by a certain amount of cool irony and fiery scorn.

"I thought the Sargent painting as a painting was a poor thing. It seemed to me it was the work of a painter whose best work was behind him, a man who had himself been a great painter but had never been a great artist, and that it was almost a stippled painting, but that it was a cruelly truthful revelation of the man.

"Sir Hugh Lane was here when he made that bid of ten thousand pounds for a painting that Sargent had offered to paint. The offer was auctioned at Christie's. The proceeds were to go to the Red Cross fund. Lane and I worked over the cable to Christie's manager making the ten thousand pound bid. Sir Hugh Lane said that he would perhaps have Sargent paint the Princess Patricia. Lane knew her well. Or else Queen Alexandra. Sargent's war portrait would be famous. But poor Sir Hugh would have suffered if he had ever dreamt that his ten thousand pounds had been turned into an attempted glorification of a bad-tempered, ill-bred schoolmaster like Wilson. Whose choice was that? How did the trustees of the Dublin National Gallery ever go so wrong?"

Yeats: "It was the mistake of the trustees of the National Gallery. It is another illustration of an idea of a day, a name of a moment, being considered an idea or a name of eternal value. Who will be interested in Wilson in twenty years?"

Quinn: "No one . . . [Quinn continued his intense attack on Wilson.]

Yeats: "Sargent should have painted James Stephens. That would have been a more important and more interesting work. By the by, I was told the other day that Stephens is thinking of dramatizing his novel *The Charwoman's Daughter*.[11] I wonder will he do it?"

Quinn: "I don't see a play in that novel, charming as it is."

Yeats: "I have never read it. You know that the heroine is Stephen's wife don't you?"

Quinn: "No, I never heard that."

Yeats: "Oh, yes. She was the wife of a labouring man in Dublin. Stephens had met her, and had either fallen in love with her or felt sorry for her. She had a daughter. Somehow Stephens learned, or she told him – I forget which now – that her husband used to beat her. So Stephens took her in, or took her away. The husband didn't object a bit. He seemd quite cheerful about it. And I believe that he told Stephens that he had no objection whatever, only he thought Stephens was 'a bit of a fool' to take her on his shoulders."

Quinn: "Is she such an impossible person?"

Yeats: "Not precisely, but she is a great romancer; the greatest personal folk-lorist in Dublin. Madame Gonne used to say to me that when Stephens and his wife were in Paris and Madame Gonne and friends of hers and Stephens used to criticize certain England Tories, Mrs Stephens used to object on the ground that her relations were French aristocrats. Now in Dublin she says that her relations are French aristocrats, and she always calls them by their French given names."

"I am told, George," said Yeats to his wife, "that Stephens has put me in *The Charwoman's Daughter*."

Mrs. Yeats: "Oh, I didn't know that."

Quinn: "I don't recall that either."

Yeats: "Yes, I am told – I haven't read the book – that I am in it[12] as a poet or a person who always walks about the streets smiling to himself' – And then Yeats laughed to himself and looked a little thoughtful and smiled and said: "I didn't know – I didn't think – that when I walked out I smiled to myself."

Quinn: "Have Ezra Pound and Stephens made up their little literary difference yet?"

Yeats: "I think so – in a way. You know that was a case, Quinn, where

Pound didn't attack Stephens. Pound really liked Stephens. But a quarrel is such a frequent occurrence in Pound's character; he is such a veteran, that he sometimes enters a quarrel a little too carelessly, a trifle too gallantly, somewhat too cavalierly. But with Stephens, a quarrel is a very serious thing; he has had so few of them. Pound was a little careless on that occasion. Stephens went for him with deadly effect, and demolished Pound's statement, whatever it was, in a few lines. Stephens' attack on Pound, for it really was that – was like the young man told about in the Arabian tale,[13] who went into the desert and fired off a stone from a sling. The stone struck the eye of an invisible genie. The genie rose up in fury and tore the young man in four pieces and scattered them to the ends of the earth. Oh yes, a quarrel with Stephens is a very serious matter; whereas with Pound, while he is temperamental to a degree, it is all over in a few moments after.''

Quinn: I always blamed Stephens for the Sargent Wilson. The letter signed in his name announcing the reasons why Wilson had been selected for a painting by Sargent was a childish thing.''

Yeats: "Why is it, Quinn, as you said the other day, that liberals are generally such fools in the face of great historic issues? There was that Frenchman Caillaux, who was a pacifist, and Morley[14] in England, and Massingham[15] the editor of *The Nation*,[16] who week after week in *The Nation* during the last two years of the war proclaimed that the war was lost. And you say Wilson? Why is it?

Quinn: "Because they worship formulas and are generally ignorant of facts. They think that generous sounding phrases, what they think are high ideals, can take the place of facts, whereas nothing can ever change the force of facts."

Yeats: "Why was Wilson a pacifist?"

Quinn: "Because he had convinced himself that neither side could win in the war; that the war would be a draw; that therefore it would be – not a Papal peace, not a French or English peace – but a Wilson peace . . . [Quinn continued his attack on Wilson, specifically castigating the President's policies of neutrality and pacifism and the harm they had caused Prime Minister Asquith.[17]] It seems to have done as much harm to Asquith as the fire-escape did to Parnell."[18]

Yeats: "Ah yes, the fire-escape did do great harm to Parnell, especially in our virtuous Ireland."

Quinn: "I suppose that a fire-escape is regarded in Ireland as something immoral?"

Yeats: "It reminds me of the story of Launcelot. All the ladies of England loved Launcelot, and Launcelot would have loved a fire-escape. And by the way, Quinn, I have got the real career for Ezra Pound. Some wealthy American should endow Pound and bring him over here and set him up as the editor of a very richly endowed and expensively prepared magazine, advocating royalty as the best government for America. It should come out at least every two weeks, and Pound's function would be to demonstrate how the people here really love rank and royalty, that royalty is the best form of government, and that they are all really royalists at heart, even the club-women and the socialists. Pound would be very ingenious in pointing to the numberless proofs of the love in the American hea[rt] for kings and other royal persons. But he should only advocate the idea and not any particular royal person or family. At the end of about three months he should sail away to Europe with a magnificent blare of trumpets, announcing that he was sailing to Europe to select the best candidate for the American throne."

Quinn: "But it seems to me that there would be an initial objection there, because royalties and 'kinks' and 'jukes', not to speak of kaisers and others, are about as much below par these days as the coins of their former realms, and it would be about as difficult to exchange them for American dollars as it would be to exchange their marks and roubles for American dollars."

Yeats: "Oh, not at all, not at all. Pound's report would be that Europe had passed through the age of kings and had emerged to one of pure democracy. Whereas the United States was just ripe for kings, for it was a thoroughly plutocratically-ruled country, quite ripe for kingship.

"And by the way, Quinn, that reminds me that before I left London Pound very seriously urged me to advise you to retire from the law and to come to London and to England to live. Why don't you do that?"

Quinn: "I cannot afford it."

Yeats: "Remember the exchange is going down and now would be a good time to invest in pounds and francs, and besides living is cheaper there."

Quinn: "Ah, but I have had my experience with country places and one experience was enough. . . . [Quinn told a story of his problems with renovations to his country house.]

Yeats: "Ah, Quinn, I can see you going in for a country place yet. You ought to marry the youngest girl of your acquaintance and come to Oxford and take a house and live there. Today I stopped in and saw a bit of St. John's the Divine and thought it was fine so far as it had gone. I also liked the St. Thomas in Gothic by Cram[19] on Fifth Avenue. What amazes me is where they get the artisans, for all the restorations in England, starting with the time of Morris, Gothic restorations and the rest, were all failures for they lacked artisans."

Quinn: "That is perhaps because the artisans were English, but here they can get artisans who are from the continent, French or Italian workmen. And that reminds me that Washington, which was beautifully laid out, and Detroit which was also beautifully laid out, with long noble avenues, broad circles and squares, were laid out by a French surveyor and Engineer, L'Enfant,[20] and that I had a theory that the cities which had been laid out by a loosened French intellect were fine and spacious, but that the cities that had been built by the English intellect just sprawled and grew and were added unto haphazard, like Brooklyn and like Boston.''

Yeats: ''And who built New York, who is responsible for New York?''

Quinn: ''That must be charged to God, who made it an island, a long, narrow island, and set it here by the sea, for the buildings have no place else to go but up and the streets nowhere else to run but straight. Personally I don't care for these bastard architectural imitations, either Gothic or others. . . . [Quinn attacked the ''range for imitation'' in architecture, arguing that ''There is one great original architect in this country, and that is Frank Lloyd Wright of Chicago.'']

Yeats: ''Are there any examples of his work in Chicago?''

Quinn: ''A great many and when you go there you ought to ask to be shown them, some of the best. Very few people here know, I imagine, that the Pennsylvania Station is a copy of the Temple of Domitian in Rome, an exact copy in almost every detail, with the exception, of course, of the underground excavations, and only larger. The American architect copyist probably substituted underground rails for underground graves, but the architectural structure is the same. The Union Station in Washington is also an exact copy of the Baths of Caracalla in Rome, and it is not any larger, even if it is as large. It has the Roman arches, the resting places on the sides, the promenades, and is, in short, a complete copy.''

Mrs Yeats: ''I did not know of that, but now, come to think of it, the Baths of Caracalla seemed to me to be larger and the arches greater.''

By this time it had got to be 11 o'clock. I had smoked three cigars. Mrs Yeats had smoked three or four cigarettes. Yeats had drunk five or six cups of tea and four or five glasses of water and seemed to be feeling better. So I left.

Monday afternoon, February 23rd 4 o'clock

Yeats had asked me to cash a check for them because Monday, being a holiday and Pond's[21] office closed, they felt they might run short of money before they could get a cheque cashed. So I cashed a cheque for $200 and took them down the money in large bills. Yeats had been in bed all day and was taking a bath when I got there about 4 o'clock. Yeats came out of the bathroom with a long blue cassock on and his short yellow jacket, and piled into bed again while his wife was packing trunks and putting away things in boxes. Yeats said that Marsh of the Macmillan Company was coming in in a few minutes, and soon in came little Marsh. But before Marsh came Yeats said that he had just given an interview on Ulster, an interview that he thought would be helpful to De Valera.[22]

Quinn: ''What line did you take?''

Yeats: "I simply said that the Irish problem was simplicity itself. England had encouraged and financed and had actually armed Ulster. Then she allowed the rest of Ireland to arm herself, and then she turned to the world and said, 'How regrettable it is that these two cannot agree.' The rebellion in Ireland was merely Ireland returning to first principles. . . . I have also today given an opinion upon psychic things, a difficult thing to give in an interview, but I was urged, and though I declined several times I finally agreed."

Quinn: "Is it critical of Lodge's[23] ideas?"

Yeats: "Oh, not at all; on the contrary, I think Lodge is quite sincere, although he himself has no psychic powers. I have talked to Sir William Crookes,[24] who is a much greater man. Sir William Crookes told me that he concealed for years his interest in physic phenomena because of the hostility of the public and because it would have reflected upon his standing as a scientist in the scientific world. Crookes, of course, has a higher place in the scientific world than Lodge. He is a wonderful old man, a man of beautiful, measured speech, who always speaks gently and with fine gestures and all the grace of dignified old age."

Quinn: "When I was recuperating up in the mountains two years ago from an illness I read Morley's[25] two big volumes of reminiscences, and Sir Charles Dilke's[26] life, in two volumes. The Dilke book showed Dilke to be much more of a statesman than Morley. The Morley book showed him only as a man of letters, constantly thinking of the phrase and not of the thing. For example, several long chapters on Morley's term at the India office and his correspondence with Lord Minto,[27] Viceroy of India, all showed that Morley was thinking in Roman parallels and felt sure that the correspondence would some day be published. The fact is that his Indian administration was a failure. But one thing that struck me in reading his life was that, although he professed to be a stout agnostic, he quotes the words of Herbert Spencer toward the end of his life thinking wistfully of the possibilities of an afterlife. He tells in great detail of Mill's conversion to the doctrine of a belief in God and the survival of the soul, and says that Mill's disciples, Morley among them, thought that his book on theism[28] was a recantation from his earlier principles and was due to the effect of the memory of his wife.[29] And then Morley quotes Huxley's[30] statement that if he could only believe in the soul or in an afterlife, he would infinitely prefer to feel that he would spend an eternity even in hell, if he could be alive, rather than to feel that death meant annihilation, the end of all."

Then Mr Marsh came in and a new Yeats, a different Yeats, a very practical Yeats, got into action. He told of hundreds of his books that he had autographed at schools and so on, and that among them there had not been presented to him one copy of *Responsibilities*.[31]

Yeats: I have been wondering why that was and I think I know. It is probably because of one line."

Quinn: "What is the line?"

Yeats: "Oh, it is that line[32] in the poem 'Beggar to Beggar Cried,' about his 'getting a comfortable wife and house to rid me of the devil in my shoes'; and the other beggar replies: 'And the worse devil that is between my thighs.'"

Quinn: "That would not be objected to here. You might with perfect safety allude to the organ between his thighs. One can allude to an organ with perfect safety unless one describes the organ in [the] act, or the organ in action."

Yeats: "There must be some reason. Perhaps it is because the Macmillan people here do not give it to the booksellers. My wife has been in several places and has not been able to get a copy."

Quinn: I think I perhaps know a reason, and that is that some of these romantic ladies object to such a poem as 'Romantic Ireland's Dead and Gone'.[33] But they are only a romantic few."

Yeats: "That is strange. The poem was quite true when I wrote it. It was generally approved and liked in Ireland. Everyone felt then that romantic Ireland had gone. It was the Rebellion that brought back the romance."

Quinn: "I think that the reason why the book has not sold is because of the title. The word 'responsibilities' reminds one of marriage or babies or high rents, but most of all of income taxes. Couldn't you have Macmillan's change the title? It would only involve a new title page."

Yeats: "That might be done."

Quinn: "You will have to think up a new title."

Marsh: "I am afraid we could not do that very well. I am afraid we could not put out the book under a new title unless some new poems could be added to it."

Quinn: "Well, I suggest a title that will not really be a new title but only be a restoration of the correct title. Call it 'Irresponsibilities.' You can make a statement that 'Irresponsibilities' was the true title, and it is really a better title than 'Responsibilities,' but through a mistake it was printed as 'Responsibilities.' Therefore, in making the title 'Irresponsibilities' you are really restoring the poet's original intention."

Yeats did not seem to see the humour of my suggestion.

As I was leaving about 5 o'clock his wife gave me the copy of Flecker's[34] collected poems that they had borrowed of me last week, and said that if I did not mind "he would take with him the copy of *Responsibilities* that he had also borrowed of me last week."

Quinn: "You are quite welcome to keep it. I am always glad to get rid of extra responsibilities and it is only another proof of how lightly both of you take responsibilities."

Yeats did not reply to this and I left, promising to come back about a quarter past seven to see them to the train.

About a quarter past seven I returned to the Algonquin and found them both sitting downstairs in the lobby, trunks all packed and gone and bags and parcels ready. Yeats said that none of his later trips to this country had the excitement that his first trip had; that that was all a thing of romance and eager excitement. He said that Saturday night he was down to lecture at the Brooklyn Institute of Arts and Letters.[35] He had told the taxi-man to drive him to the Brooklyn Institute and the driver took him off to a great big, black, dark building somewhere in the wilderness. There was no light inside it, and he finally told a policeman to take him to a tobacco shop where he could look up a telephone directory.

Quinn: "Of course, any title these days with the word 'institute' in it is suspect. It sounds like some sort of sobering-up place."

Yeats: "That is quite true, for when I said to the taxi driver and to the policeman that I wanted to go to the Brooklyn Institute, the taxi driver and the policeman in helping me to look through the telephone book asked me whether they should hunt for it under the title 'hospitals'. We finally found that the Brooklyn Institute of Arts and Science had their lectures at the Academy of Music. And so I was motored there but got in half an hour late. I will never forget, Quinn, one lecutre that I delivered in Chicago when I first came here. The date was fixed.[36] And the place, I discovered, was in a large drawing-room. There were four middle-aged ladies present, and no one else. I came and waited, and finally I was solemnly informed that that was the entire audience. I stood up and solemnly delivered my lecture, shook their hands and solemnly left. It was not until long after that I discovered that one of them had arranged for a lecture but that the arrangements for the lecture had not come off and that they had wanted to get out of it, but that you had held them to their contract and that you had forced them to listen to my lecture and pay you the full rates."

"I also remember, Quinn, that you had some controversy with the Chicago University on my first trip.[37] They had wanted me to deliver a lecture free, or something of that sort; you had refused. You gave me positive orders under no account to go there or accept any invitation to lunch there, for you said they were bound to get a free talk or a free lecture from me. I tried to follow orders but a deputation of young ladies invited me to come to their school and in a moment of weakness I accepted, not thinking that their school was connected to the University. When I got there I found myself in a gathering of several hundred young ladies, and that it was part of the University. I was called upon to say the customary 'few words'. You heard of it in some way and expressed your indignation to me in a day or two in a long and vigorous telegram."

Quinn: "You ought to refuse these damnable invitations and Pond ought not to let you in for them. But the further you go West the fewer you will have of them. It is all an effort to get something for nothing.

They invite you to lunch or to a reception and then get you to talk or to read without paying a fee. Pond ought to know better.

Yeats: "I suppose Pond does it for the best and it is really his affair. But at these things where I am not prepared and where I am bored I do not do well and I do not do him any credit. But with my own lectures which I have prepared and on my own ground I am all right."

Quinn: "I will settle the Pound thing[38] and I think he will have 'a new spiritual home', at least for a few months, with the rejuvenated *Dial*. It is a pleasure to do things for a man like Pound, for, as you have said, Pound is a man of temperament and learning and almost genius."

Yeats: "Yes, and Pound means what he says. Pound doesn't engage in controversy merely for controversy's sake, but because he is interested in the things he writes and talks about, and he has temperament and fire and extraordinary learning. Nothing could be better than his *Noh* book[39] or greater than the perfection of his rendering of Fenollosa's translation from the Chinese. Temperament is the whole thing, and that is why George Moore with all his industry and his artistry is not a great writer. He is lacking in temperament. The other day as I was walking through one of the streets in Oxford I saw in a bookseller's shop a large, nicely printed volume. Looking down I saw the word 'Pater' on the page. I thought it was the life of Pater by that schoolmaster – I don't remember his name –"

Quinn: "Wright,[40] the man who wrote the two volumes on Pater and books on Sir Richard Burton,[41] and lately a book on John Payne."[42]

Yeats: "Yes, that is the man. The sentences were curiously bungling but as I read on I realized that I was reading from a page of Moore's *Avowals*. I was struck by the extraordinary clumsiness and slovenliness of the writing, quite lacking in distinction. Moore is always trying for the perfect phrase, for the poignant moment. But he fails because he is lacking in temperament."

Then the man came to bring them to the station and I went there with them. As we were going down the runway to the cars Yeats said: "These great stations with their lack of advertisements are very fine ones. This is all very fine and all very severe."

I said I would wait outside the car but Yeats said, "No, come in, we have a stateroom."

Quinn: "Nobody but presidents travel in staterooms these days. Pond must be treating you well."

Yeats: "But the money comes out of us."

Quinn: "After you leave Chicago I think you would be quite comfortable in a berth, your wife taking the upper berth and you the lower because she is the younger."[43]

"By the way, have you seen your father since you got back?"

Yeats: "Oh, yes, he was with us this afternoon before you came. I know, Quinn, that while he pretends to come to see me the one that he really comes to see is George. I think George has really taken Lilly's place in his affections."

Quinn, to Mrs. Yeats: "That seems to show that he approves of you and you have been a success."

Mrs. Yeats: "I hope so."

Quinn: "Well, good-bye", shaking her hands; "Good-bye, Yeats, and good luck and a pleasant trip, and let me hear from you from time to time."

Yeats: "Good-bye, Quinn, and thanks for everything."

NOTES

1. Quinn's valet.
2. Schofield Thayer, editor with Gilbert Seldes (1893–1970) of *The Dial*. See Nicholas Joost, *Schofield Thayer and "The Dial": An Illustrated History* (University of Southern Illinois Press, 1964) pp. 166–70, and B. L. Reid, p. 434.
3. See also Alan Himber, with George Mills Harper, *The Letters of John Quinn to William Butler Yeats* (Ann Arbor; UMI Research Press, 1983) p. 253.
4. Karin Margaret Strand, *W. B. Yeats's American Lecture Tours* (Diss. Northwestern University, 1978) p. 180. Strand writes that Yeats addressed the League for Political Education on 17 February 1920 at Carnegie Hall. Evidently they also invited him to their Saturday luncheon.
5. Henry James, *The American Scene* (Boston; Harper, 1907). I have not traced the passage quoted.
6. Quinn's antipathy to Wilson is well documented; see B. L. Reid p. 131.
7. Joseph Caillaux (1863–1944). French statesman. Caillaux was not as devasted politically as it seemed at the time. He recovered his political power and was again influential in French policy during in the late 1920s and early 1930s. Holger H. Herwig and Neil M. Heyman, *Biographical Dictionary of World War I* (Westport: Greenwood Press, 1982) p. 105.
8. John Singer Sargent (1856–1925). Yeats compares Sargent's portrait of President Wilson with Bernardo Strozzi's portrait of "some Venetian gentleman" in *The Trembling of the Veil*: "Whatever thought broods in the dark eyes of that Venetian gentleman has drawn its life from his whole body; it feeds upon it as the flame feeds upon the candle – and should that thought be changed, his pose would change, his very cloak would rustle, for his whole body thinks. President Wilson lives only in the eyes, which are steady and intent; the flesh about the mouth is dead, and the hands are dead, and the clothes suggest no movement of his body, nor any movement but that of the valet, who has brushed folded in mechanical routine. There all was an energy flowing outward from the nature itself; here all is the anxious study and slight deflection of external force; there man's mind and body were predominantly subjective; here all is objective, using these words not as philosophy uses them, but as we use them in conversation" (*Au* 292). Both portraits are reproduced in Edward Engelberg's *The Vast Design: Patterns in W. B. Yeats's Aesthetic* (University of Toronto Press, 1964), Plate 1, facing p. 96.
9. B. L. Reid, pp. 213–15.
10. Bernardo Strozzi (1581–1644) Genoese painter of "Portrait of a Gentleman".
11. *The Charwoman's Daughter* (London: Macmillan, 1912). The heroine is indeed based upon Cynthia Stephens. Stephens lodged in the house of Millicent Josephine Kavanagh and her husband. After the birth of her daughter, Iris, Kavanagh left and

his wife became "Cynthia Stephens". James Stephens married Cynthia in 1919. In 1913 the Stephens moved to Paris and did attend Maud Gonne's "Tuesdays". Stephens recalled being assaulted by her monkey and parrot (Richard J. Finneran, *Letters to James Stephens* [London: Macmillan; 1974] pp. xxi, xxiii, 118).

12. Yeats, Synge and AE all appear in this novel, the last as "a tall man with a sweeping brown beard". At the same point we meet "a long, thin, black man – who looked young and was always smiling secretly to himself; his lips were never still for a moment, and, [he was] . . . buzzing like a great bee. He did not stop to shake hands with anyone, and though many people saluted him he took no heed, but strode on, smiling his secret smiles and buzzing serenely" (pp. 34–5).

13. Stephens's response to Pound, which is indeed savage, was printed in *The New Age* on 18 Mar. 1915 (Finneran: op. cit., pp. 154–5). "The Tale of the Merchant and the Genie", usually the first tale told by Sharazad, on the first of the thousand and one nights. In Richard Burton's version, it is known as "The Tale of the Trader and the Jinni". See *A Plain and Literal Translation of the Arabian Nights' Entertainments, now entitled The Book of the Thousand Nights and a Night* etc., (Benares: Kamashastra Society, 1885, I) pp. 24–7.

14. John Viscount Morley (1838–1923). English statesman.

15. Henry William Massingham (1860–1924), editor of *The Nation*.

16. *The Nation*, a leading liberal British journal.

17. Herbert H. Asquith (1852–1928). First Earl of Oxford and prime minister from 1908–16.

18. Kenneth Grahame wrote a satiric anecdote in the *St. James Gazette* concerning Parnell and a fire-escape in reference to the Kitty O'Shea affair. Peter Green, *Kenneth Grahame: a Study of His Work, Life, and Times* (London: John Murray, 1959) pp. 108–10.

19. Ralph Adams Cram (1864–1943). With his partners Bertram G. Goodhue (1869–1924) and Frank Ferguson (1861–1926), the leading church architects in the United States and the foremost proponents of the eclectic Gothic style. William D. Hunt Jr., *Encyclopedia of American Architecture* (New York: McGraw Hill, 1980) pp. 126–7.

20. Pierre L'Enfant (1784–1825).

21. James B. Pond (1889–1961). Owner of the J. B. Pond Lyceum Bureau. His father, J. B. Pond Sr. (1838–1903) founded the business in 1874.

22. Edward Clark Marsh (1875–1922) vice president and head of the publication department, the Macmillan Company, 1906–20. Himber, p. 206. The interview is untraced.

23. Sir Oliver Joseph Lodge (1851–1940). English physicist. Attempted to reconcile science and religion. *Raymond, or Life and Death* (1916) contains an account of his supposed communication with his dead son Raymond.

24. Sir William Crookes (1823–1919). English physicist.

25. John, Viscount Morley, *Recollections* (1917).

26. S. L. Gwynn & Gertrude M. Tuckwell, *The Life of the Rt Hon Sir Charles W. Dilke* (London: John Murray, 1917) 2 v. The biography of the eminent M.P. (1843–1911) was begun by Gwynn and completed and edited by Gertrude M. Tuckwell.

27. Gilbert John Elliot-Murray-Kynynmond (1845–1914). Fourth Earl of Minto.

28. *Three Essays on Religion*, ed. H. Taylor (1874).

29. Mill married Mrs Harriet Taylor, widow, in 1851. She died in 1858.

30. Thomas Henry Huxley (1825–95).

31. Macmillan, (1914).

32. W. B. Yeats, "Beggar to Beggar Cried", *VP* 299–300. Lines 5–8 read

> 'And get a comfortable wife and house
> To rid me of the devil in my shoes,'
> *Beggar to beggar cried, being frenzy-struck*
> 'And the worse devil that is between my thighs.'

								(*VP* 299–300)

33. W. B. Yeats, "September, 1913", *VP* 289.
34. James Elroy Flecker (1884–1915).
35. Strand, p. 364.
36. Strand, p. 344.
37. Strand, p. 32.
38. Quinn was promoting Ezra Pound for the foreign editor of *The Dial*. Pound accepted the post on March 24, 1920. B. L. Reid, p. 434–6.
39. Fenollosa, Ernest, and Ezra Pound, *Noh, or Accomplishment* (New York: A. A. Knopf, 1917).
40. Thomas Wright (1859–1936).
41. Richard Francis Burton (1821–90). Thomas Wright, *The Life of Sir Richard Burton* (London: Everett & Co., 1906).
42. John Payne (1842–1916). English poet and translator. Thomas Wright, *The Life of John Payne* (London: T. Fisher Unwin, 1919).
43. In *A Critical Edition of Yeats's "A Vision" (1925)*. The editors George Mills Harper and Walter K. Hood note several instances of automatic writing by Mrs Yeats in New York city and on the trip west which Yeats recorded in his notebook (pp. xix–xx).

    Mrs Foster told me of a conversation which she had with Mrs Yeats concerning the unconventionality of a honeymoon spent mainly in the pursuit and study of such arcane matters.

Mille neuf cent dix-neuf

A Translation by Yves Bonnefoy

I

Que d'inventions superbes ne sont plus
Qui semblaient pur miracle à la multitude
Et à l'abri de l'influx de la lune
Qui balaie la chose ordinaire! Il y avait
Dans ce décor de pierres et de bronze
Une statue antique, d'olivier . . . Et disparus
Pareillement, les ivoires illustres
De Phidias, et toutes les abeilles et les sauterelles d'or.

Et nous aussi nous en avons eu
Beaucoup, de ces superbes jouets quand nous étions jeunes.
La loi s'était fermée au blâme, à l'éloge,
A la corruption, aux menaces. Nos habitudes
Faisaient se dissiper la vieille injustice
Comme la cire aux rayons du soleil.
Et puisque la conscience avait mûri
Depuis si longtemps maintenant, nous ne doutions pas
Que cela durerait plus que tout futur concevable.
Ah, que de belles pensées! Nous imaginions
Que les chacals et les hyènes étaient tous morts.

Tous les crocs, arrachés! Tous les sales tours d'autrefois
Désappris, et l'armée bonne seulement pour la parade!
Qu'importait si aucun canon n'était devenu encore
Le soc d'une charrue! Le Parlement, le Roi
Pensaient que si on ne brûle pas un peu de poudre
Le trompette allait exploser en trompettant
Et sans la moinde gloire. Et peut-être même
Les coursiers somnolents des gardes ne caracoleraient pas.

Or, maintenant, les jours
Sont infestés de dragons; le cauchemar
Chevauche le sommeil; des soldats ivres
Peuvent laisser la mère sur sa porte
Se traîner dans son sang, assassinée,
Et s'en tirer sans dommage; la nuit
Peut suer de terreur comme du temps
Où nous ne cousions pas nos pensées encore
En systèmes, en lois pour mener le monde:
Nous qui ne sommes que des fouines s'entredéchirant dans un trou.

Ah, qui peut lire les signes sans s'abîmer
Découragé dans le demi-mensonge de ces drogues
Que préparent les esprits creux; qui a compris
Qu'aucune oeuvre ne durera, quelles que furent
La santé que l'on dépensa, la sérénité, la richesse
Aux chefs d'oeuvre de l'art ou de l'intellect,
Et que l'honneur non plus ne laisse de trace
De ses plus hautes tours, celui-là n'aura
Qu'un réconfort: le triomphe n'aurait
Que saccagé sa sainte solitude.

Mais y a-t-il jamais rien qui réconforte?
L'homme s'éprend, et c'est de ce qui passe,
Est-il rien d'autre à dire? Dans ce pays
Qui eût osé admettre, l'eût-il pensé,
Qu'un bigot ou un incendiaire, cela se trouve
Pour brûler ce morceau de bois sur l'Acropole
Ou fracasser les célèbres ivoires
Ou trafiquer de ces sauterelles, de ces abeilles?

II

Quand les danseurs chinois de Loie Fuller
Déployaient leur ruban de gaze comme
Une écharpe flottante d'étincelles,
Il semblait qu'un dragon d'air impalpable
Fût tombé parmi les danseurs et les soulevât,
Les faisant tournoyer, les jetant loin
Des grands remous de sa route furieuse.
Ainsi l'Année Platonique
Chasse de ses remous le bien et le mal présents
Et y fait refluer ceux d'autrefois.
Tous les hommes, tous, des danseurs, dont le pas se règle
Sur le fracas du gong le plus barbare.

III

Un poète, moraliste ou mythologue,
Compare l'âme solitaire à un cygne.
Cela me plait,
Je suis content si un miroir trouble lui montre
Avant que ne s'éteigne sa lueur brève
Cette image de sa grandeur: les ailes
A demi déployées pour le proche envol,
Et le sein en avant, gonflé d'orgueil,
Que ce soit pour s'ébattre ou pour enfourcher
Ces vents qui clament la nuit qui monte.

L'homme qui a sa propre méditation
Est perdu, dans le labyrinthe qu'il a bâti
En art, en politique.
Un Platoniste affirme qu'à ce niveau
Où l'on devrait lâcher le corps, et tout,
Les vieilles habitudes collent à l'âme.
Si seulement, dit-il, nos oeuvres pouvaient
Passer avec notre souffle,
Ce serait une heureuse mort
Car le triomphe gâte la solitude.

Le cygne s'est élancé dans le ciel désert.
Cette image peut susciter la fureur, la rage
D'en finir avec tout cela, d'en finir
Avec ce que rêva ma vie laborieuse, avec même
La page mi-rêvée et mi-écrite.
Ah, nous qui rêvions d'amender
Tous les maux et nuisances qui affligent
L'humanité, nous avons appris, maintenant
Que soufflent les vents d'hiver,
Que nous n'étions que des têtes fêlées quand nous rêvions.

IV

Nous qui, il y a sept ans, ne parlions
Que de vérité et d'honneur,
Nous glapissons de joie dès que nous pouvons
Bondir ou mordre comme la fouine.

V

Allons, moquons-nous de ces grands
Qui prirent sur eux tant de tâches
Et peinérent si dur, si tard
Pour laisser bâti derrière eux
Quelque monument, sans penser
A ces vents qui nivèlent tout.

Allons, moquons-nous de ces sages
Et de tous ces calendriers
Sur lesquels ils fixaient leurs yeux
Qui vieillissaient, faisaient mal.
Ils ne virent rien des saisons,
Ils béent au soleil, maintenant.

Allons, moquons-nous de ces braves
Gens qui s'étaient figurés
Que le bien peut être joyeux,
Et malades de solitude
Allaient proclamant la fête.
Le vent siffla, – où sont-ils?

Et moquons-nous des moqueurs
Qui ne lèveraient pas un doigt
Pour aider les bons et les sages
Et les grands et garder dehors
Cette affreuse tempête. On vit
De se moquer, n'est-ce pas?

VI

Violence sur les routes: violence de chevaux.
Quelques-uns ont pourtant de beaux cavaliers
Et des guirlandes de fleurs entre les oreilles
Hypersensibles, ou dans leur crinière qui flotte.
Mais lassés de tourbillonner de toutes parts,
Les voici disparus, et le mal reprend son élan.
Les filles d'Hérodias sont de retour,
C'est un vent qui se lève dans la poussière,
Puis l'orage des pieds qui dansent, puis ce tumulte d'images
Qui est leur but dans le labyrinthe du vent.

Et quelque fou en toucherait-il une,
Toutes se récrieraient, d'amour, de colère
Au gré du vent, car toutes sont aveugles.
Mais le vent s'abat, maintenant, la poussière retombe,
Et passe en titubant, ses grands yeux vides
Dans l'ombre de ses stupides boucles blond paille,
Cet insolent démon, Robert Artisson,
Que Lady Kyteler, folle d'amour, comblait
De plumes de paon vieux bronze, de crêtes rouges de coqs.

"MASTERING WHAT IS MOST ABSTRACT": A FORUM ON *A VISION*

"The Completed Symbol": *Daimonic* Existence and the Great Wheel in *A Vision* (1937)

Colin McDowell

Some, perhaps all, of those readers I most value, those who have read me many years, will be repelled by what must seem an arbitrary, harsh, difficult symbolism. Yet such has almost always accompanied expression that unites the sleeping and waking mind. (*AV B* 23)

I

A Vision (B) was the culmination of Yeats's lifelong wish to relate the diversity of human existence back to each human soul, thereby confounding the materialists and the religious orthodoxy which chooses to relate existence to a non-human God to whom we must all surrender our identities. The well-known "Dedication" to *A Vision (A)* treats that particular book as the fulfilment of Yeats's preoccupation with the occult. Despite what other people may have sought in occultism, Yeats claims to have had a practical purpose. "I wished", he wrote, "for a system of thought that would leave my imagination free to create as it chose and yet make all that it created, or could create, part of the one history, and that the soul's" (*AV A* xi). *A Vision (A)* was not able to provide this system of thought for very long, and Yeats continued to think about the issues raised by his communicators even after the publication of *A Vision (B)*.[1] *A Vision (B)* itself includes reservations about its own comprehensiveness, such as "The End of the Cycle" (*AV B* 301–2) where Yeats confesses that he may be too old to be rewarded for all his toil, or the "Introduction" where Yeats characterizes "The Soul in Judgment" as "the most unfinished of my five books" (*AV B* 23), which suggests that all of them are unfinished to some degree. But it is still to *A Vision (B)* that one must turn for an exposition of how Yeats related all of existence to the human soul, and other sources, published and unpublished, must be seen as footnotes to that work rather than as fundamental rethinkings of the material. Book II of *A Vision (B)*, aptly named "The Completed Symbol", offers the

193

essentials of Yeats's theory in a form which is complete enough for exposition to
build on a solid basis.

II

One of Yeats's communicators informed him that the system of *A Vision* "has its
origin in human life – all religious systems have their origin in God & descend to
man – this ascends" (*AV A* Notes 7). Not much is therefore said by Yeats about
God in *A Vision*; nor does he say much about the nearest equivalent his system
offers to God, which is the gnomically-named *Thirteenth Cone*. Richard Ellmann
has written humorously, and not without insight, of Yeats's usage of this name:
"To give God so mechanical a title was to ensure that He would be discussed
only as 'it', never as a personal deity, least of all as a Christian one. God became
thereby a feature of the Yeatsian cosmogony which like other features the poet's
symbolic vocabulary might grasp and include. And the embodiment of divinity
in so unprepossessing a term as Thirteenth Cycle stood in ironic and urbane
contrast to Yeats's claim for the cycle's unlimited powers, as if one were to say,
'Ah yes, I have given Almighty God the name of "Thirteenth Cycle" in my
scheme.'"[2] Certainly Ellmann underestimates Yeats's seriousness about
ultimate matters, as James Lovic Allen has demonstrated,[3] but the *Thirteenth
Cone* does exist as a concept partly to help domesticate the untameable. On one
level, to give anything a name allows one to believe that one is half-way towards
an understanding of it; but, more importantly, the symbolism of the *Thirteenth
Cone* encodes its own epistemological theory within its naming, implying a
progressively more complete unity of knowing subject and perceived object.
Knowledge in this case is not a prize gained all at once. It is the reward for a
spiritual discipline which attempts to widen its horizons and so encompass the
totality of being. In this process the perceiving subject is turned inside out.

"The ultimate reality", Yeats explains, "because neither one nor many,
concord nor discord, is symbolised as a phaseless sphere, but as all things fall into
a series of antinomies in human experience it becomes, the moment it is thought
of, what I shall presently describe as the thirteenth cone" (*AV B* 193). The
important phrase here is "the moment it is thought of". This qualification is
related to the later statement that "The *Thirteenth Cone* is a sphere because
sufficient to itself; but as seen by man it is a cone" (*AV B* 240). By making this
cone the "*Thirteenth*" Yeats manages to distinguish it from all of the other cones in
his system, in particular from the twelve cones or cycles of "time and space"
(*AV B* 210) which constitute the "single great cone or year of some twenty-six
thousand years", which is the life-period of an individual proceeding through all
of its allotted incarnations. The sphere becomes a cone in the following manner.
Let us imagine that the ultimate reality is a sphere floating in space all by itself –
if the word "space" has any meaning in such a situation. Everything that one
may think of is encompassed by this sphere. Imagine now that there is a
particular sentient creature within this sphere. It starts to think about what it is

and where it is. It pictures itself as a subject over and against an object, the great sphere, which is its symbol of "the ultimate reality". By doing so, the sentient creature has obviously distorted what it is trying to describe: the sphere is not "over there", because the sentient being is "inside" it. The being has in a way pictured itself as situated outside the sphere; and to any outside observer, the sphere will appear to be a circle, where the circle has become the base of a cone of which the apex is the observer. Inevitably, any attempt whatsoever to think of the sphere will posit, at the same time, the existence of the non-sphere which is trying to comprehend it. This phenomenon explains various statements Yeats makes, such as "The whole system is founded upon the belief that the ultimate reality, symbolised as the Sphere, falls in human consciousness, as Nicholas of Cusa was the first to demonstrate, into a series of antinomies" (*AV B* 187).

The *Thirteenth Cone*, then, is more a symbol of the human relationship to ultimate reality than a symbol of that ultimate itself. Occasionally, too, it can function as a type of shorthand which serves to eliminate discussion, as when Yeats writes of "*Spirits* of the *Thirteenth Cone*" (*AV B* 228, 229). No matter how well one collates all of Yeats's references to "*Spirits* of the *Thirteenth Cone*", one cannot reach conclusions about what they are, and so they serve as reminders to the reader that either Yeats or his instructors were always in possession of much more than anyone else can know – "how completely master they could be down to [the system's] least detail" (*AV B* 21) of what the reader can know only incompletely and by fits and starts. One's relationship to Yeats's discussions of his *Thirteenth Cone* mirrors, in a way which is probably intentional, one's relationship to the ultimate reality itself.

To speak of the ultimate reality as it is *in itself*, one must therefore bracket off the perceiving subject, imagining that he or she does not exist, or can meaningfully give a "God's eye" view of the totality. Yeats then divides this totality into different parts, in much the same way as the neoplatonists imagined their different hypostases. Yeats's divisions are called the *Four Principles*. For all practical purposes, the *Principles* take the place of the *Thirteenth Cone*. "I only speak of the *Thirteenth Cone* as a sphere", he writes, "and yet I might say that the gyre or cone of the *Principles* is in reality a sphere, though to Man, bound to birth and death, it can never seem so, and that it is the antinomies that force us to find it a cone" (*AV B* 240). It may be thought that "Man, bound to birth and death" is the same thing as "Man, limited to the *Four Faculties*", because Yeats uses his *Four Faculties* to define the different types of incarnation one may have throughout Book I of *A Vision*, "The Great Wheel". As we shall see, however, the *Four Principles* themselves are subject to the antinomies, and have their own discords and oppositions, or at least seem to act as though they do when we come to describe them. We could not begin to describe the *Four Principles* unless we made distinctions between them, and hence it may be said that these distinctions hold the seeds of discord. Compared with the *Four Faculties*, though, the *Principles* may be said to approach the perfection of the sphere, and so Yeats can say that the *Principles* are, "when evoked from the point of view of the Faculties, a sphere" (*AV B* 89).

Yeats's use of the word "evoke" here is precise, particularly when we consider his membership of a magical order that practised evocation of spirits. The *Principles* may not be discovered by normal thought, and will remain a mystery to those who rely on the evidence of their senses. "I shall write little of the *Principles*", Yeats explains, "except when writing of the life after death. They inform the *Faculties* and it is the *Faculties* alone that are apparent and conscious in human history" (*AV B* 207). If we say that the *Four Faculties* "are what man has made in a past or present life", the *Four Principles* may be described as "what makes man" (*AV B* 71). Another way of describing the relationship between *Faculties* and *Principles* is to say that "the *Principles* are the innate ground of the *Faculties*" (*AV B* 187). We are thus able to intuit their existence. In fact, one might say that individual *Principles* give rise to their corresponding individual *Faculties*. It is therefore more important to discover what the *Principles* are than to define the *Faculties*. The *Four Principles* are *Husk*, *Passionate Body*, *Spirit* and *Celestial Body*, corresponding to *Will*, *Mask*, *Creative Mind* and *Body of Fate*, in that order, as one may deduce from Yeats's definition of the *Principles*: "*Spirit* and *Celestial Body* are mind and its object (the Divine Ideas in their unity [by which Yeats appears to mean that when *Spirit* and *Celestial Body* join, they become the Divine Ideas]), while *Husk* and *Passionate Body*, which correspond to *Will* and *Mask*, are sense . . . and the objects of sense" (*AV B* 187–8). Now, as Yeats says that the *Principles* are not "apparent and conscious in human history", it is obvious that they are only to be described as "mind and its object" and "sense . . . and the objects of sense" in an anagogic way. Yeats does describe the *Husk* as "the human body", but this is only "symbolically" (*AV B* 188), and although he does define the *Passionate Body* in one place as "the present, creation, light, the objects of sense" (*AV B* 191), we must balance this against the denial that any *Principle* can become apparent and against the description of the *Passionate Body* as "the sum of [the] *Daimons*" (*AV B* 189). Accordingly, the "nature" that we see is not the *Passionate Body*, but a drastically reduced version of that reality. We may relate this reduction to Yeats's definition of *Mask* and *Body of Fate* as "a painted picture" and a photograph respectively (*AV B* 86). In life, what we take as "reality" is merely a selection of available realities: even a camera has to be pointed in a certain direction.

As neither *Husk* nor *Passionate Body* can be separated from the other *Principles*, at least on this side of the antinomies, and as neither *Mask* nor *Body of Fate* can be separated from *Will* and *Creative Mind*, this example suggests that all *Four Faculties* are merely a selection of a totality that is more accurately symbolised by the *Four Principles*. Such a general statement is not however satisfactory for Yeats, who is only interested in metaphysics to the degree that it can be related to "a particular man, the man of Phase 13 or Phase 17 [Yeats's phase] let us say. The *Four Faculties* are not", he stresses, "the abstract categories of philosophy, being the result of the four memories of the *Daimon* or ultimate self of [a particular] man" (*AV B* 83). "Memory" for Yeats can also refer forward: "I think Plato symbolised by the word 'memory' a relation to the timeless", John Aherne says, and the point applies to Yeats also (*AV B* 54). In fact, the *Four Faculties* are created anew in each discarnate period which follows an incarnation, the karma of that previous incarnation dictating the form they will take in the following incarnation. Yeats concentrates on past incarnations in his explanation, although karma must work both backwards and forwards: "[Man's] *Body of Fate* . . . is shaped out of the *Daimon's* memory of the events of his past incarnations; his *Mask* . . . out of its memory of the moments of exaltation in his past lives; his *Will* . . . out of its memory of all the events of his present life, whether consciously remembered or not; his *Creative Mind* from its memory of ideas – or universals – displayed by actual men in past lives, or their spirits between lives" (*AV B* 83). Just as man or "the being" divides into *Four Faculties*, so the *Daimon* divides into *Four Principles*; the *Daimon* is "the innate ground" of the man, and individual *Faculties* arise out of individual *Principles* in the period between lives.[4]

But even as he strives to deny abstraction to the *Faculties*, Yeats realises that they are abstract when compared with the *Principles*. The *Four Faculties* are abstracted from their ground; they are a fragment out of the context which gives them meaning. This fact explains the otherwise odd statement that "discursive reason" may be defined as "almost our *Faculties*" (*AV B* 194), a statement which Yeats must have made with an eye on Blake's aphorism that "Reason, or the ratio of what we have already known, is not the same as it shall be when we know more".[5] Total knowledge appears to be the prerogative of the *Daimon*. *A Vision* in fact exists in order to expound Yeats's theory of *daimonic* existence. His mature ideas appear in *A Vision (B)*. According to this schema, one may talk of two forms of "soul" or *Daimon*, the permanent *Daimon* and the impermanent *Daimon*, a distinction which goes back at least as far as *Per Amica Silentia Lunae*, but which was not used consistently in *A Vision (A)*.[6] The permanent *Daimon*, or *Daimon per se*, is "the ultimate self of [a particular] man" (*AV B* 83), and it is apparent that we may think of the ultimate self as a discarnate *Daimon* stretching over vast periods of time; every so often it punctuates itself, so to speak, by choosing to become incarnate. The *Daimon*, says Yeats, meaning the permanent *Daimon*, "contains within it, co-existing in its eternal moment, all the events of our life, all that we have known of other lives [of our own], or that it can discover within itself [of the lives] of other *Daimons*" (*AV B* 192), or, alternatively, "All things are present as an eternal instant to our *Daimon*" (*AV B* 193). The *Daimon* becomes incarnate through desire, which Yeats defines as "Deception" (*AV B* 94), in common with many of the world's major religions. It is a paradox to say that one "chooses" to become deceived, but this is what is meant by the Hindu doctrine of *Lila* or divine play and by the Buddhist doctrine of ignorance of one's true nature. "Deception" occurs when the *Daimon* tries to realise its own nature by undergoing incarnation, whereas it has no real need to "realise" that nature since it has already been eternally "realised": the *Daimon* is what it has been and will be, but what it has been and will be adds nothing to what it was before time began. This does not mean however that incarnation is unnecessary: the fact that incarnation has occurred at all indicates the necessity for it. Yeats's scattered statements on the relationship of the *Daimon* to incarnation have a convincing consistency. "Behind the *Husk* (or sense)", he writes, "is the *Daimon's* hunger to make apparent to itself certain *Daimons*, and the organs of sense are that hunger made visible" (*A V B* 189), a statement which is repeated in less detail on the following page: "the *Daimon* seeks through the *Husk* that in *Passionate Body* which it needs" (*A V B* 190). In other words, the "certain *Daimons*" which our own *Daimon* wants to find appear as the *Passionate Body* through the agency of this desire: the *Daimon* becomes an incarnate *Daimon*, meaning that the human body or *Husk* is created, in order for it to be able to see these other *Daimons*, who also manifest themselves through their own *Husks*, and for the same reason. These other *Daimons* are, from the point of view of one's own *Daimon*, the impermanent *Daimons*, whether one calls an impermanent *Daimon* by the name of father, mother, or beloved. The permanent *Daimon* needs to contact other *Daimons*, Yeats suggests, for its own purposes, possibly for validation of its own existence, or else to assist the process of self-definition by contrast: "passionate love [i.e. the *Husk*'s involvement with *Passionate Body*] is from the *Daimon* which seeks by union with some other *Daimon* to reconstruct above the antinomies its own true nature" (*A V B* 238). The assumption that another *Daimon* is necessary for this purpose is itself an example of the antinomies which bind us; but any other assumption only leads to a sterile solipsism. We shall see later that Yeats believes that the *Spirit* must unite with *Passionate Body* before it can unite with *Celestial Body*; otherwise the *Celestial Body* atrophies: "the *Passionate Body* exists that it may 'save the *Celestial Body* from solitude'", as Yeats explains (*A V B* 189).

III

It is apparent from this exposition that reincarnation is at the heart of Yeats's conception of human existence: only reincarnation allows enough room for the slow working-out of the conflicting claims of "reality and justice" (*A V B* 25). The Great Wheel of "The Twenty-Eight Incarnations" (*A V B* 105) is exactly a wheel of *re*incarnations; any classificatory use it may have is only subsidiary. Of course, any wheel whatsoever may be divided into twenty-eight phases, and so may be "every completed movement of thought or life" (*AB B* 81); but the actual Great Wheel as first introduced is equivalent to the course of twenty-eight lifetimes. In fact, it includes the periods between these lives as well, but Yeats immediately postpones this complication: "the twenty-eight phases constitute a month of which each day and night constitute an incarnation and the discarnate period which follows. I am for the moment only concerned with the incarnation, symbolised by the moon at night" (*A V B* 79). The Great Wheel, as originally described, is thus part of the "eternal instant" (*A V B* 193) of the *Daimon*, the ultimate self of the particular person. It is not the whole of the "eternal instant" because twenty-eight incarnations and their corresponding discarnate periods only take "some two thousand odd years"; whereas "the life-period of the individual [*Daimon*]" covers twelve such Great Wheels, making a year of "some twenty-six thousand years" (*A V B* 202). Yeats is silent about what happens after these lives have passed, possibly because it involves "vast periods of time" and is thus "beyond our experience" (*AV B* 213), but it is probable that each person's *Daimon*, having exhausted its allotted incarnations, melts into the *Thirteenth Cone*. However one conceives of the end of the round of incarnations, Yeats is apparently investing his *Daimons* with some of the traditional attributes of God, and so the whole of every *Daimon* is to be found in each of its parts, no matter how small, rather as the whole image is present in each shattered fragment of a hologram.[7]

We come now to the geometrical symbolism. It is my contention that the geometry is a definite aid to understanding, not a hindrance, and that to omit it is to do violence to the whole conception of *A Vision*. There is evidence enough that Yeats would have done away with the geometry had he been able to. He repeatedly "misinterpreted" it (*AV B* 19) and knew that it would be repellant to his readers because it must seem "an arbitrary, harsh, difficult symbolism" (*AV B* 23). Yet it is wise for the reader of *A Vision* to approach its symbols with the same assumption that Yeats had: if they do not seem consistent, it is not because they are incoherent, but because we have not understood them and must try harder. The assumption that the geometry is irrelevant certainly makes reading *A Vision* easier, or rather it allows one to think that one is reading *A Vision*, but it is demonstrably just as much an assumption as any other. Unfortunately, it is an assumption that closes down possibilities rather than opening them up. It also allows critics of Yeats to continue to believe that they are so much more intelligent than Yeats, because they would not have bothered with all of that nonsense in the first place.

Yeats uses the Great Wheel as the basic frame for his geometry. It is perhaps best to remember that this wheel covers a period of about two thousand years. Section VI of Book II of *A Vision (B)* turns to the major symbolism of the entire book about a third of the way through its third paragraph. Yeats here addresses the question of single incarnations and their corresponding discarnate periods: "That the small wheels and vortexes that run from birth to birth may be part of the symbolism of the wheel of the twenty-eight incarnations without confusing it in the mind's eye, my instructors have preferred to give to the *Principles* of these small wheels cones that cannot be confused with that [i.e. the double cone] of the *Faculties*" (*AV B* 197). Exactly which double cone or wheel of the *Faculties* Yeats means here is not unambiguous, but we may take it that he is referring to the double cone of the *Faculties* which defines position on the Great Wheel. "The dominant thought", he continues, "is to show *Husk* starting on its journey from the centre of the wheel, the incarnate *Daimon*, and *Spirit* from the circumference as though it received its impulse from beyond the *Daimon*" (*AV B* 197–8). I interpret "the incarnate *Daimon*" to refer to *Husk*: we have already seen that the wheel includes both incarnate periods and discarnate ones, and so "the incarnate *Daimon*" is unlikely to qualify the word "wheel". As for the "*Daimon*" in "beyond the *Daimon*", it is best seen in opposition to "the incarnate *Daimon*", which means that the "*Daimon*" of "beyond the *Daimon*" is equivalent to the whole wheel of twenty-eight incarnations. We shall see shortly that the circumference of the wheel is the meeting place of *Daimon* and *Thirteenth Cone*.

The "small wheels and vortexes" of an individual lifetime and the discarnate periods which follow are drawn as cones for easier reference. Yeats's usual example for exposition is the seventeenth phase of the wheel, and this is no exception.[8] "These cones", he explains, "are drawn across the centre of the wheel from *Faculty* to *Faculty*, two with bases joined between *Creative Mind* and *Body of Fate*, and two with apexes joined between *Will* and *Mask*" (*AVB* 198). For Phase 17, *Will* is of course at Phase 17, and *Mask* is at Phase 3, so that there will be two cones with apexes joined at the centre of the wheel, their bases rising out of the positions of *Will* and *Mask*; *Creative Mind* is at Phase 13, and *Body of Fate* is at Phase 27, so that the other cones will be joined at their bases at the centre of the wheel, with their apexes pointing directly at the positions of *Creative Mind* and *Body of Fate*. It does not seem to be important how wide the actual bases are made. The diagram Yeats gives is as follows (*AVB* 199):

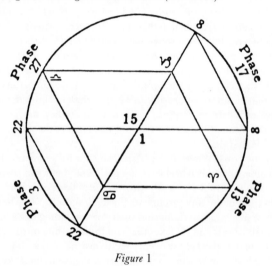

Figure 1

The verbal description is more cumbersome than the actual diagram.

Yeats next instructs the reader to divide these double cones into separate phases or sections, which are to be marked along the edges of the cones themselves so that they do not become confused with the phases of the framing wheel. Some of the names for these divisions appear in the diagram; the others are easily added. The diamond is divided into twelve, "according to the signs of the Zodiac" (*AV B* 198), and the labeling proceeds according to a solar direction, that is, "from left to right" (*AVB* 199), or clockwise. This represents the movement of *Spirit*, the active partner of *Spirit* and *Celestial Body*, during one incarnation and the discarnate period which follows it. The hour-glass is divided into twenty-eight, numbered according to the lunar convention, "from right to left" (*AV B* 199), or anticlockwise. This represents the movement of *Husk* as the active partner of *Husk* and *Passionate Body*. In terms of the "dominant thought"

(*AV B* 197), *Husk* or the incarnate *Daimon* starts on its journey from the centre of the wheel, marked "1" on the diagram, while *Spirit* begins at the circumference at Libra, as though it received its impulse from beyond the wheel. Phase 1 of the cone of *Husk* and *Passionate Body* is thus the place of birth.

Early in his exposition of the *Four Principles*, Yeats explains that "The wheel or cone of the *Faculties* may be considered to complete its movement between birth and death, that of the *Principles* to include the period between lives as well. In the period between lives, the *Spirit* and the *Celestial Body* prevail, whereas *Husk* and *Passionate Body* prevail during life" (*AV B* 188). The double cone of the *Faculties* will be discussed shortly; here, our concern is only with the two double cones of the *Principles*. Yeats postulates a type of consciousness which survives bodily death. It is this type of consciousness which provides the basis for continued existence from one incarnation to the next. "At death", he explains, "consciousness passes from *Husk* to *Spirit*; *Husk* and *Passionate Body* are said to *disappear* . . . and *Spirit* turns from *Passionate Body* and clings to *Celestial Body* until they are one and there is only *Spirit*" (*AV B* 188–9). *Husk* and *Passionate Body* disappear at death, meaning that they become subordinate to the other two *Principles*, because consciousness is no longer connected with that which sustains the human body – "*Husk*" derives its name "from the husk that is abandoned by the sprouting seed" (*AV B* 191) – or with that which sustains "the present, creation, light, the objects of sense" (*AV B* 191), that is, the *Passionate Body*. Accordingly, we are to think of consciousness as leaving the double cone of the hour-glass of *Husk* and *Passionate Body* at the moment of death, because it then enters the double cone or diamond of *Spirit* and *Celestial Body*. In traditional religious language, one leaves behind the world of the flesh, dominated by the hour-glass of time, for the world of the spirit, which is symbolised by the adamantine diamond. The dominant thought now shows *Husk* back at the centre of the wheel, at its half-way point or Phase 15, while *Spirit*, also at its half-way point, is at Aries: "Death which comes when the *Spirit* gyre is at Aries is symbolised as spring or dawn; and birth which comes when the *Spirit* gyre is at Libra, as autumn or sunset" (*AV B* 201). When the gyre of *Husk* is at its midpoint between death and rebirth, at Phase 22, the gyre of *Spirit* is at Cancer. This point is the "widest expansion" of the *Spirit*'s gyre (*AV B* 198): the opposite point, at Capricorn, is not this gyre's widest expansion because it occurs during life, when *Husk* and *Passionate Body* prevail instead. At Cancer, it may be said that *Spirit* has united with *Celestial* Body (*AV B* 198). At this stage, as the poem "Chosen" puts it, "The Zodiac is changed into a sphere" (*VP* 535), because "the diamond represents a sphere", and "at its gyre's greatest expansion *Spirit* contains the whole Wheel. Though for convenience we make the diamond narrow, like the diamond of a playing-card, its widest expansion must be considered to touch the circumference of the wheel the wheel meets the gyre of the *Thirteenth Cone*. Indeed, its gyre [i.e. the gyre of *Spirit*] touches that circumference throughout" (*AV B* 199).

Yeats appears to be choosing his language very carefully here: he is not saying that the whole wheel of twenty-eight incarnations, or the permanent *Daimon* as it has been defined earlier, is actually uniting with the *Thirteenth Cone*. He simply says that the two touch each other. The hesitation is due to the fact that what occurs at this expansion of *Spirit* is not, temporally speaking, a lasting union, although it prefigures that lasting union. Spiritually speaking, of course, the *Daimon* is timeless, and it makes no sense to predicate a before and after to it; but Yeats is writing for those of us caught in time: "Neither between death and birth", he says, "nor between birth and death can the soul find more than momentary happiness; its object is to pass rapidly round its circle and find freedom from that circle" (*AVB* 236). The circle that has been discussed so far is simply the circle of one incarnation and its corresponding discarnate period. The greatest expansion of the gyre of *Spirit* may encompass the whole diamond, which is equivalent to the whole Wheel because it touches the gyre of the *Thirteenth Cone*, but that only means that it is in contact with the twenty-eight lives of one out of its twelve wheels (*AVB* 202). All of these wheels must be exhausted before the final release. Accordingly, the union of *Spirit* with *Celestial Body* at Cancer must be thought of as "a symbol of that eternal instant where the antinomy is resolved. It is not the resolution itself" (*AVB* 214).[9] It is however a "symbol", rather than a "sign", as it partakes of the nature of what it represents: "every lesser cycle", Yeats explains, "contains within itself a sphere that is, as it were, the reflection or messenger of the final deliverance" (*AV B* 210). The *Thirteenth Cone* is itself "that cycle which may deliver us from the twelve cycles of time and space" (*AV B* 210).

The *Daimon* travels around its circle of twenty-eight lifetimes in the following manner. It is part of the definition of the cones of the *Principles* that they point to the positions of the *Faculties* delineating an individual lifetime on the Great Wheel: the two cones of *Spirit* and *Celestial Body* are drawn "with bases joined between *Creative Mind* and *Body of Fate*", while the two cones of *Husk* and *Passionate Body* are drawn "with apexes joined between *Will* and *Mask*" (*AV B* 198). The position of the *Principles* thus symbolises the fact that the *Principles* "inform" the *Faculties* defining an individual lifetime. However, it is not quite so simple. Yeats writes, with reference to diamond and hour-glass, that "The gyre of the *Husk* starts at the centre (its Phase 1), reaches its Phase 8, where the circumference can be marked *Mask*, and returns to its centre for Phase 15, passes from its centre to its Phase 22, where the circumference can be marked *Will*, and finishes at the centre" (*AV B* 198). In fact, if we trace these movements out on the two examples Yeats gives, the first of them showing "the position of diamond and hour-glass when *Will* on the wheel is passing Phase 17" (*AV B* 200), the second showing their position "when *Will* on the wheel of the twenty-eight phases is at Phase 15" (*AV B* 200), we discover that he has reversed the correspondences: Phase 8 of *Husk* in both diagrams corresponds to the actual position of *Will* defining the particular incarnation, while Phase 22 of *Husk* corresponds to the actual position of *Creative Mind*. It is possible that Yeats is trying to symbolise the opposition or reversal of man and *Daimon*; if so, he has not explained his purpose very well. But if it is assumed that he has made a simple error, not in the geometry itself, but in the labeling of that geometry, the journey of the *Daimon* in its successive lives can be explained in a direct way. To draw the cones of the *Principles* for Phase 18, for example, we position the bases of the cones of *Husk* and *Passionate Body* so that they straddle Phases 18 and 4 respectively, and point the apexes of the cones of *Spirit* and *Celestrial body* at Phases 12 and 26 respectively. To draw the cones of the *Principles* for Phase 16, we straddle the bases of the cones of *Husk* and *Passionate Body* across Phases 16 and 2 respectively, and point the apexes of the cones of *Spirit* and *Celestial Body* at Phases 14 and 28 respectively. Comparing these two figures with the figure Yeats gives for Phase 17, it can be seen that the point of Aries, which marks the birth of *Spirit*, travels in a clockwise direction, whereas the base of the hour-glass at Phase 8 travels in an anticlockwise direction. We are back at the beginning of Yeats's explanation of the movement of the *Faculties*, although it can now be seen that the *Principles* define the positions. "These pairs of opposites whirl in contrary directions", Yeats writes, "*Will* and *Mask* from right to left, *Creative Mind* and *Body of Fate* like the hands of a clock, from left to right" (*A V B* 74). In the same way, diamond and hour-glass whirl on one another in contrary directions.

The points of the *Principles* which touch the Great Wheel move in strict accordance with the movement of the internal phases as marked upon the diamond and hour-glass. "These [internal] gyres complete their movement . . . while *Will* as marked upon the circumference [of the Great Wheel] completes its phase, their *Husk* [in the hour-glass] starting at the centre when the phase begins and returning there at its end", as Yeats says (*A V B* 200). Let us assume that *Will* on the circumference is at the start of Phase 17, meaning that the *Daimon* is about to incarnate at that Phase. *Husk* will therefore set out from the centre of the Wheel, at its Phase 1, will return to the centre at its Phase 15, which is the point of death, will set out towards its Phase 22 during the after-death state, and will return once more to the centre, Phase 1, when *Will* on the circumference is at the end of Phase 17 and about to pass into Phase 18, its next incarnation. *Husk* is thus at the correct position for it to begin its journey of incarnation once more. *A Vision* (A) is helpful here: "While the Soul was passing first through the lower half [i.e. the *Husk* part] and then through the upper half [i.e. the *Passionate Body* part] of the [double] cone, the cone itself moved so that the Soul is born a phase further on than that of its previous embodiment" (*A V A* 161).

Section VII of "The Completed Symbol" explains the place of the *Four Faculties* of an individual lifetime in this scheme. Hitherto, by referring to "*Will* as marked upon the circumference" of the Great Wheel (*A V B* 200), Yeats has been concerned with the *Four Faculties* of the entire wheel, the *Faculties* which allow one to define a particular incarnation as belonging to Phase 17 or Phase 18. But there is also a wheel or double cone of the *Faculties* which represents the movement from birth, through maturity, to old age and death. "The *Four Faculties*", Yeats writes, meaning this latter set of *Faculties*, "have a movement also within the cones of the *Principles*. Their double vortex is superimposed upon the half of the cone of *Husk* and *Passionate Body* which lies between *Will* (the *Will* on the circumference of the wheel) and the centre of the wheel" (*A V B* 201). For example, if "*Will* on the circumference of the wheel" is equivalent to *Will* defining the seventeenth incarnation, we then have the following diagram, where the double cone of the *Faculties* is represented by the dotted lines:

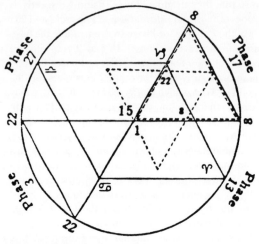

Figure 2

Yeats's exposition continues: "When *Husk* has reached [its] Phase 8 they [meaning the *Faculties* as defined by the position of *Will*] are at [their] Phase 15; when *Husk* has reached [its] Phase 15 they are at [their] Phase 1 [this in fact means the beginning of Phase 1 or the end of Phase 28]. While *Will* (*Will* on circumference) is passing through half a phase, *Husk* passing from [its] Phase 1 to [its] Phase 15, the *Faculties* complete their full movement, Phase 1 to Phase 28, and when their movement represents an incarnation [as it does here] disappear at its completion. The *Principles* thereupon take their place defining the state between death and birth" (*A V B* 201). As I understand this, Yeats is saying that the *Faculties* of an individual lifetime trace out exactly the same movement as half of the cone of *Husk*: the other half of the cone of *Husk* is said to *disappear* at death just as the *Faculties* disappear at the completion of their movement from Phase 1 to Phase 28. Accordingly, we must identify the *Four Faculties* of an individual lifetime with the gyre of *Husk*. Insofar as *Husk* is "symbolically the human body" (*A V B* 188), this is not so strange: in normal parlance we often identify ourselves with our bodies. When Yeats writes of "*Will* on circumference" as completing "half a phase" while this movement is going on, he refers back to something he wrote at the very start of his exposition of the Great Wheel: "the twenty-eight phases constitute a month of which each day and night constitute an incarnation and the discarnate period which follows" (*A V B* 79). Normally, however, as he immediately tells us, he ignores the discarnate period on the circumference of the Great Wheel, because it only adds to the confusion of the beginner, but we have now seen what he means by it. Finally, when Yeats says that the "*Principles* thereupon take their place defining the state between death and birth", he refers to the idea that "At death consciousness passes from *Husk* [or the *Four Faculties* of an individual lifetime] to *Spirit*" (*AV B* 188). The symbolism is thus completed.

IV

Those who attempt to read *A Vision* without recourse to the more difficult geometry generally remain content with a relatively simplistic dualism, such as Yeats expounded in *Per Amica Silentia Lunae*. However, an examination of the geometry of *A Vision (B)* has convinced me that Yeats's ideas are far from simple. The complexities of the "mystic geometry" (*L* 743) mirror the complexities of existence as Yeats sees them. The geometry therefore has a "braking" effect on the reader. Someone who is tempted to see in the union of *Spirit* with *Celestial Body* a final state of attainment will be deterred from drawing this premature conclusion by discovering that this union occurs once in every incarnation of the twenty-eight of the Great Wheel, and that this Great Wheel is only one Great Wheel out of the twelve that occur in the system. On the positive side, the geometry manages to depict complex relationships so that they may be taken in at a glance. Figure 2, for example, shows the relative position of the *Four Faculties* compared with the *Four Principles*: they are merely a small part of a greater totality.

A final test of the merit of *A Vision* is not in its internal consistency, although that is important, but in the parallels that can be found between its doctrines and those of a traditional symbolism.[10] The Philosophia Perennis of Ananda K. Coomaraswamy is to the point here, because it manages to unite disparate symbolisms without sacrificing intellectual rigour. In his paper "The Inverted Tree", first published in 1938, Coomaraswamy notes the various ways in which one may characterize the Brahman. "Brahman" is of course another name for what Yeats calls the "ultimate reality" (*AV B* 193). Coomaraswamy begins by explaining that the Brahman may be seen as "a single essence with two natures"; it is "in a likeness and not in any likeness", "mortal and immortal, local and pervasive", "existent and beyond", "solar and intrasolar", to quote from the *Upanishads*.[11] Yeats's equivalent for the "single essence with two natures" is ultimate reality perceived as *Principles* and *Faculties*. One may relate each of the characteristics of the Brahman to descriptions in *A Vision*. The terms "solar" and "intrasolar" may however cause some problems. By "intrasolar" Coomaraswamy alludes to the tradition which regards the sun as the gateway to what lies beyond the sun. This tradition finds expression in the *Eesha-Upanishad*. Yeats and Purohit Swami translate the relevant passage as follows: "They have put a golden stopper into the neck of the bottle. Pull it, Lord! Let out reality!"[12] When Coomaraswamy later refers to the dichotomy of "the two worlds", the "infrasolar" and the "celestial", the reader of *A Vision* is less likely to be misled: by "celestial", Coomaraswamy alludes to what Yeats calls "solar" or of the *Principles*, whereas by "infrasolar", he means Yeats's "lunar" or of the *Faculties*.[13]

There is nothing remarkable about dichotomies *per se*; most systems of thought seem to find them necessary. But as well as the twofold division of the Brahman, Coomaraswamy discusses a fourfold division which encompasses two types of three-plus-one. Yeats parallels these divisions. In *A Vision (B)* one may contrast the wheel of the *Faculties* as a whole with the wheel of the *Principles* as a whole, or one may contrast four individual *Faculties* with four individual *Principles*, or two grouped *Faculties* with two grouped *Principles*. Alternatively, one may choose to regard the *Four Faculties* as being subsumed by the *Husk*, and contrast *Husk* with the other three *Principles*. There is another type of contrast which is not stated unambiguously by Yeats, although he hints at it in Section V of "The Completed Symbol", and it is almost a precondition for the eschatology of "The Soul in Judgment", Book III. In this symbolism, *Husk*, *Passionate Body* and *Spirit* may all be regarded as parts of embodiment, each one more rarified than the preceding. *Celestial Body*, as a sphere, encompasses all the other *Principles* and the *Four Faculties*. Similar permutations occur in the *Vedas* and the *Upanishads*. According to one scheme, three parts of the Brahman correspond to earth, air and sky, and are the manifested cosmos, while the fourth part is "beyond the sky", or is a station "beyond that of sleep".[14] This last characterisation relates to the division of the soul in, say, the *Mandookya-Upanishad*, where the distinction is made between the waking condition, the dreaming condition, deep sleep and the state beyond sleep, which encompasses the three other states.[15] Yeats uses this division in "The Soul in Judgment". As I have suggested elsewhere, these states are to be equated with the *Four Principles* (*YA 4* 1986, 223). According to another scheme, the transcendent deity is composed of Three Persons, Agni, Indra-Vāyu and Āditya. "The Fourfold arrangement", writes Coomaraswamy, "is made in two different ways. The All-whole . . . is triple within the cosmos and single beyond. On the other hand, it is only with one foot or part, a fraction . . . as it were of the whole of the Divine Being, that he moves in the Three [manifested] worlds, and with three feet or parts, that is to say the major part, that he transcends these worlds. That infinite 'part' of the Divine Being which is insusceptible of manifestation includes, but also exceeds that finite 'part' which can be manifested: the Whole consisting therefore both of a known and an unknown, shown and unshown".[16] This paper has attempted to show that Yeats's dialectical manoeuvres have a similar sophistication. The nature of the subject matter, it might be said, will always force such complicated manoeuvres on all who would expound what is, in truth, beyond exposition.

NOTES

1. For the tangled history of publication and revision, one may consult Connie K. Hood, "The Remaking of *A Vision*", *YAACTS* 1 (1983) 33–67.
2. Richard Ellmann, *The Identity of Yeats* (London: Faber & Faber [paper edn] 1964) p. 159. In *A Vision*, "cone", "gyre" and "cycle" are interchangeable terms.
3. James Lovic Allen, "Belief versus Faith in the Credo of Yeats", *Journal of Modern Literature*, 4 (1975) 692–716.

4. As George Mills Harper has pointed out to me, the Automatic Script devotes considerable space to the Four Memories, which are connected to the *Four Principles* in different ways, according to whether they function during life or after death. Further information may be found in Professor Harper's forthcoming book, *The Making of Yeats's 'A Vision': a Study of the Automatic Script.*

5. *The Complete Writings of William Blake With Variant Readings*, ed. Geoffrey Keynes (London: Oxford University Press, 1966) p. 97. Shelley, as Yeats elsewhere notes, defined "mind" as "existence", meaning by "existence" "life in generation" (*E&I* 84–5). In the diagram of *Principles* and *Faculties* as Plotinian "Authentic Existants" (*AV B* 194), the *Four Faculties* appear as an emanation of *Husk*, which makes sense when we consider that *Husk* is "symbolically the human body" (*AV B* 188) as an organ of perception for beings which are bodiless. In Blakean terms, both *Faculties* and *Husk* belong to Ulro.

6. I have derived this theory from what Yeats meant by *"Passionate Body"*, taking my cue from the following passage in *Per Amica Silentia Lunae*: "The Daimon, by using his mediatorial shades, brings man again and again to the place of choice" (*Myth* 361). Needless to say, I disagree with those writers who believe that Yeats poisoned the key insights of *Per Amica* by overelaboration into *A Vision.*

7. Much remains to be written about Yeats's ideas of God. As Yeats explains in "Pages From a Diary Written in Nineteen Hundred and Thirty", he was faced with two choices when he came to conceive of ultimate matters. Reality could be thought of as "a congeries of beings", or as "a single being" (*Ex* 305). *A Vision* will talk of "the Divine Ideas in their unity" (*AV B* 187, 189). In this context it is interesting that by Gematria, the occult "science" of numbers, "the Hebrew words ACHD, *Achad*, Unity, One, and AHBH, *Ahebah*, love, each=13" (MacGregor Mathers, *The Kabbalah Unveiled* reprint, New York: Samuel Weiser, Inc., 1968, p. 7). Yeats would also have read of this in J. Abelson, "Seeing the Shekinah at Death" (*The Quest: a Quarterly Review*, ed. G. R. S. Mead, vol. V, no. 1 [Oct. 1913], 108): "The sight of the vision is an elation of unutterable joy. It is the moment of union with the Divine Presence. The root-word for 'union' is in Hebrew *ĕchăd* (which means 'one'). Among the Jews, every Hebrew letter which composes a word has its numerical value. The 3 letters which make up *ĕchăd* are *aleph*=1, *heth*=8, *dălĕth*=4, making altogether 13. Hence the sight of *13* is *union!*" Hence Yeats writes, "I substitute for God the Thirteenth Cone, the Thirteenth Cone therefore creates our perceptions – all the visible world – as held in common by our wheel" (*Ex* 320).

8. Phase 17 is of course Yeats's own phase, but Yeats's use of this particular figure is purely heuristic and implies no value judgment. Yeats simply used the figure closest to hand.

9. In context, this quotation relates to sexual union, but is applicable here because, as Yeats says, "the mystic way and sexual love use the same means" (*L* 715).

10. It might almost be said that one cannot begin to understand *A Vision* without a good grounding in occultism or mysticism. To a certain extent, this is to criticise Yeats's exposition, but so be it.

11. Ananda K. Coomaraswamy, "The Inverted Tree", reprinted in Vol. 1 of *Coomaraswamy: Selected Papers*, ed. Roger Lipsey (Princeton University Press, 1977) pp. 376–404; quotations from p. 376.

12. *The Ten Principal Upanishads*, Put into English by Shree Purohit Swāmi and W. B. Yeats (London: Faber & Faber, 1937) p. 128.

13. As this paragraph demonstrates, one should not become overly attached to the literal meaning of words. The *Upanishads* embody several different cosmological schemes, as Yeats would have discovered from R. D. Ranade's *A Constructive Survey of Upanishadic Philosophy* (1926; 2nd edn, Chowpatty, Bombay: Bharatiya Vidya Bhavan, 1968). Yeats read this book in 1937; see Naresh Guha, *W. B. Yeats: an Indian Approach* (Calcutta: Jadavpur University, 1968) p. 164. Another way of phrasing the dichotomy between what is under the sun and what is above it is that of Blake, when he denies that

he sees "a round disk of fire somewhat like a Guinea" when the sun rises, because he sees instead "an Innumerable company of the Heavenly host crying 'Holy, Holy, Holy is the Lord God Almighty'", *The Complete Writings of William Blake*, op. cit., p. 617.

14. Coomaraswamy, p. 377.
15. *The Ten Principal Upanishads*, pp. 59–61. See also *E&I* 476–7.
16. Coomaraswamy, p. 378n.

SHORTER NOTES

A New Solomon and Sheba Poem

Stephen Parrish

Am I a fool or a wise man?
And if a fool what other can
Keep clear of folly ~~when~~ if he look
Upon your devils picture book
Made up of ivory flat or slope?
King Solomon could he but hope
By wagering his wizard crown
To run his fingers up and down
As though he ran them on a board
With ivory dice or painted card
Would murmur 'now my proverbs stop
Between the rist and finger top';
And so its ~~now~~ plain I have need to prey
And yet it is not follys way
    To choose a mind for company
~~To choose for company~~
That seeks its own sincerity.
As it were a bird that is so proud
That it must leap from cloud to cloud
And after that must hurry through
A dizzier deep of blue on blue
O never did King Solomon find
A secret but in Sheba's mind.
      shall I be the better
And ~~in what way can I be~~ proved
O beauty in your labyrinth closed
A perfect scholour in the school
If I turn wise or but a fool?"

This half-rueful, half-tormented address to an enigmatic "beauty", left untitled
and unpublished, survives in a single fair copy in Yeats's hand, reproduced
above with his light revisions and idiosyncratic spellings of "wrist" and
"scholar" (readers are invited to judge whether "prey" in line 13 is a misspelling,

211

and to guess where the closing double quotes were supposed to open). The fair copy is inscribed on the two inside pages of a loose bifolium, now among drafts for poems collected in *The Wild Swans at Coole* in the National Library of Ireland: Ms. 13,587(4). At the end of the poem Yeats wrote "T.O.", apparently pointing to an early version of "The Living Beauty" on the back page of the bifolium. This version, partly obscured by an ink blot, begins:

>   To
> ~~To~~ no more ∧ suffer's but [   ]n old.
>   heart
> O ~~heart~~ let's dream that [   ] frozen the blood
> Or laid a dusky finger upon the brow,
> The beauty that is cast out of a mold . . .

Revision of line 3 on the front page of the bifolium supplies the image that ultimately open the poem:

> The wick [?burnt] out, the oil of youth all spent.

Placing "Am I a fool or a wise man" in the Yeats canon has to be a matter of balancing inferences and associations. The fair copy seems to have been written out between 1917 and 1919: the same paper was used for seven other poems, all from that range of dates. Four were gathered into the second edition of *The Wild Swans at Coole* ("Shepherd and Goatherd", "A Prayer on going into my House", "On the Death of an Irish Airman", and "Phases of the Moon"); three were published in *Michael Robartes and the Dancer* (the title poem, "To be Carved on a Stone at Thoor-Ballylee", and "The Secomd Coming"). But some version of "Am I a fool or a wise man" could well have been drafted elsewhere as early as 1914, when Solomon and Sheba first entered Yeats's verse (more probably from *The Arabian Nights* than from the bible), in "On Woman". Readers may hear an echo of the stunning image of the beauty's face as the devil's picture book in "the devil in a looking-glass" of "Beggar to Beggar Cried" (1914). Other images, like the labyrinth of the mind, can hardly be pinned down to particular dates, nor, of course, can the poem's central themes – the tension between beauty and wisdom, and the teasing affinities between wisdom and folly.

Why Yeats did not gather up "Am I a fool or a wise man" when he inserted 17 new poems into the second edition of *The Wild Swans at Coole* is impossible to say. He did include there two Solomon and Sheba poems (a third, "Solomon and the Witch", was published two years later in *Michael Robartes and the Dancer*). One of the two, "Solomon to Sheba", he had also put into *Nine Poems* of 1918, along with "To a Young Beauty", "To a Young Girl", "A Song", and "The Living Beauty", the last four, at least, thought to have been inspired by Yseult Gonne. The same five poems were arrayed together in the 1919 *Wild Swans* volume, bracketed between "Under the Round Tower" and "The Scholars", in the following order:

"Solomon to Sheba"
"The Living Beauty"
"A Song"
"To a Young Beauty"
"To a Young Girl"

After five intervening titles came the other Solomon and Sheba poem, "On Woman". Affinities of theme and tone suggest that "Am I a fool or a wise man" should belong to this group, though it seems clear that Solomon and Sheba could serve Yeats in various ways as emblematic figures. Without further evidence, all that can be said is that an exceptionally interesting poem has lain for years unread and unknown.

"Portrayed before his Eyes": an abandoned late poem

Warwick Gould

I

Port[r]ayed before his eyes [?,]
Implacably lipped,
It seemed that she moved;
It seemed that he clasped her knees
5   What man so worshipped
When Artemis roved?

II

He sat worn out & she
Kneeling seemed to him
Pitiably frail;
10   Love s anxiety
Made his eyes dim
Made his breath fail

III

There [?Then] suffered he heart ache;
Driven by Love's dread
15   Alternate will
A winding pathway took.
In Love's levelling bed
All gyres lie still.

I

The eighteen lines transcribed above (see also Plate 15) stand on a single sheet of
"loose-leaf" paper, currently catalogued as MS 30,189 in the National Library

of Ireland's recently acquired set of manuscripts formerly in the possession of Michael Butler Yeats.[1] They will certainly be familiar from Richard Ellmann's *The Identity of Yeats*[2] where they form the last section of a forty-five line "Theme for a Poem", which Ellmann dates 27 December, from a notebook used in 1934.[3]

There are some verbal and accidental differences[4] between Ellmann's version of the lines and the one above: it seems likely from these that MS. 30,189 is a fair copy or new working draft of lines 28–45 of that "theme". But, as may be seen from Plate 15, it stands on its own, bears minimal revision (to the punctuation at the end of line 1) and consists of three numbered stanzas. What precisely is the relation between "Portrayed before his Eyes" and Ellmann's "theme"?

It was never part of Ellmann's purpose in chapter VIII "The Final Form of Experience" to provide full description of mss., still less of the Rapallo Notebook in all of its frenzied complexity. Rather, he sought to show how in "some unpublished poems" – the plural is Ellmann's – "a near-sentimental theme grew hard and definite" (*IY* 209).

The problem that arises from comparison of Ellmann's 45 line theme with MS 30,189 and its 18 lines can be solved, however, without attempting to transcribe and edit all of the pages associated with the theme, and it is perhaps possible now to demonstrate the complexity of the development of a poetic idea into at least three poems. For the purpose of what follows therefore, I divide Ellmann's 45 lines into four sections, remarking before I do so that at no point in the Rapallo Notebook do all 45 lines occur consecutively. Yeats used at least twelve pages of the note book for working on these lines, and so poor is the quality of the Stony Brook microfilm print-out that there could well be more such pages. Yet I believe Ellmann was correct to associate all of these lines, though there could be some problem about their layout in his book. They undoubtedly constitute a matrix of poetic preoccupation in late 1934.

Section 1

THEME FOR A POEM

All day you flitted before me
Moving like Artemis
I longed to clasp your knees in worship
When I sat down to rest you stood beside me as a child.
5   My eyes dimmed with tears
O beloved come to me when the night thickens

That I may hope [to end] in the bed's friendship
This heart-breaking inequality.

(*IY* 209–10)

So Ellmann prints the first section, supplying an emendation in line 7. He also regularises certain spellings and the possessive in line 7, as well as supplying the hyphen in line 8. These lines stand on *SB* 2101603 (i.e. reel 21, image no 1603). Also standing on that page are lines from the last stanza of the First Attendant's song in *A Full Moon in March* (*VPl* 986, lines 145–50). It is quite clear that Yeats's title "theme for a poem" applies only to the eight lines Ellmann has transcribed and that these are indeed the theme from which the rest of Ellmann's "theme" develops.

Section 2

The ninth line that Ellmann prints stands alone in his text and is

> When old Pythagoras falls in love

The line is finally to be found in "Every loutish lad in love", the Second Attendant's song in *A Full Moon in March* (*VPl* 979, line 17). Much of the Rapallo Notebook is given over to drafts of this play, and drafts of this particular song with this particular line in it can be found on the following pages *SB* 2101630–1, alongside drafts of "He and She" (*VP* 559) and "Ribh denounces Patrick" (*VP* 556); 2101645. In its published form it becomes

> Should old Pythagoras fall in love
> Little may he boast thereof.

> (*VPl* 979)

and there Yeats traffics in mockery. But there is one further context in the Rapallo Notebook in which the line occurs and it is this one Ellmann has in mind. It deserves a new section.

Section 3

On *SB* 2101648, "When old Pythagoras falls in love" is reused as title or first line in a quite separate sequence, the reverse of mockery. Here is Ellmann's edited transcription, which runs from the ninth to the twenty-seventh line of his "theme".

> When old Pythagoras falls in love

10   Life was running out of these
      Generous eyes on men you cast
      I like other ageing men
      Sat and gazed upon a past
      In seeming all compounded of
15   Lost opportunities in love.

O how can I that interest hold!
What offer those attentive eyes?
Mind grows young, this body old
When half closed that eyelid lies
20   A sort of sudden glory shall
About my stooping shoulders fall.

An age of miracle renew
Let me be loved as though still young
Or fancy that the story's true
25   When my brief final years are gone
Then shall be time to live away
And cram those open eyes with day.

(IY 210)

The poem is immediately recognisable as "Margot", enclosed in a letter to
Margot Ruddock of 26 or 27 November, 1934. "Here is a first poem for Margot. I
wrote the first verse on Sunday but could get no further", Yeats said, detailing
the successive bouts of "utter black gloom" that interspersed his writing of the
piece, and George Yeats's attempts to avert gloom and bring the poem to birth.
The text as sent to Margot Ruddock is as follows:

MARGOT

I

All famine struck sat I, and then
Those generous eyes on mine were cast,
Sat like other agèd men
Dumfoundered,[2] gazing on a past
5   That appeared constructed of
Lost opportunities to love.

II

O how can I that interest hold?
What offer to attentive eyes?
Mind grows young and body old;
10   When half closed her eye-lid lies
A sort of hidden glory shall
About these stooping shoulders fall.

III

The Age of Miracles renew,
Let me be loved as though still young
15   Or let me fancy that it's true,
When my brief final years are gone
You shall have time to turn away
And cram those open eyes with day.

(*LMR* 33–4)

Ellmann's transcription of the lines does not fully accord with my own reading of them: I read "& then" instead of "of these" in his tenth line. This reading seems to accord better to with what the line became, viz., the first line of "Margot". It also seems that "When old Pythagoras falls in love" is intended as a working title, as Ellmann's spacing probably conveys; that "men" in Ellmann's line 11 should read "mine" as in "Margot" line 2; that Ellmann's line 16 should end with a question mark (as in "Margot" line 7) rather than an exclamation mark. The last two lines evidently gave Yeats much trouble, even in this full draft, and there is even a possibility that they have finally been added in a different hand, probably George Yeats's. The Notebook has been turned on its side, earlier efforts cancelled, and the two lines entered in a spikier hand than Yeats's. The point must remain open, again because of the quality of the Stony Brook reproductions, until inspection of the original ms is possible.

"Margot" is further worked at in other places in the Rapallo Notebook, *SB* 2101646; 2101647 (where the first line approximates to that found in the letter quoted above), and on *SB* 2101621, where an early version of stanza II shares the page with a draft of "Ribh considers Christian Love insufficient" (stanza 4, *VP* 558). From these pages I conclude that Ellmann's lines are a not quite finished, first full draft, and that they are probably subsequent to the version sent to Margot Ruddock in the 26 November [27?] letter. The evidence is the redeployment of diectics (lines 8–10) as well as the improvements to lines 5, 9, and 11, and the change to line 1.

Section 4

A fair copy of Ellmann's lines 28–45, bearing the date "Dec 27" stand on *SB* 2101677: the differences noted above (footnote 3) would support a reading of this page as being almost identical with NLI MS 30,189. The difference would be that *SB* 2101677 supplies a full stop after "knees" in the fourth line. Ellmann might be right to read "Lover anxiety" in line 10, but Yeats's control of the possessive is so slender as to allow him to use or omit the apostrophe at will within four lines of stanza 3, and the reading here is as likely to be "Loves" as "Lover".

The poem is also worked upon *SB* 2101672, along with some lines from *The*

King of the Great Clock Tower (*VPl* 995, lines 45–53); in a furious circlet of stanzas on the facing page, *SB* 2101673; and again on *SB* 2101674 and 2101675.

II

It is certainly demonstrable that "Margot" and "Portrayed before his Eyes" grow from the one matrix. In an earlier letter, of November 13, 1934, Yeats had written to Margot Ruddock from Dublin

> I have in my head two poems "for Margot" but I may not write them yet. A long toil on the play [*A Full Moon in March*] has tired me and I want the rest of practical work or of a change to prose. I must not meet you again a tired man. However the play opens with a song partly addressed to you. (*LMR* 24–5)

This comment is followed by a version of "Every loutish lad in love" (*VPl* 979). So it is plain that there are two *more* poems for Margot Ruddock, "Margot", and, surely, "Portrayed before his Eyes" awaiting composition. I suggest that by this date the eight line "theme for a poem" from *SB* 2101603 had been entered into the Rapallo Notebook and that this theme is the theme of "Portrayed before his Eyes". Already the matrix suggested two poems, rather than one, to be written, as well as the play-lyric "partly addressed" to Margot Ruddock. And Ellmann is surely right to record this association in his collection of lines which show the growth away from a "near-sentimental" poetic idea. And how clearly the whole matrix, in the context of this anxious letter, shows the connections between "[v]ersemaking and lovemaking" to which Ellmann draws attention in "W. B. Yeats's Second Puberty".[5] The later letter which accompanies "Margot", attributes the "utter black gloom" of its composition to fear of "this nervous inhibition. . . . I pictured Margot unsatisfied and lost. How could I finish the poem? How could I finish anything?" (*LMR* 31–2).

III

"Margot" as we have seen, did not come easily. "I will not know for some months whether it is good or even if it runs smoothly", Yeats apologised in his letter (*LMR* 32). One problem, perhaps allied to that process of clarification Ellmann describes in the progress from poem to poem within the overall "theme" of old Pythagoras falling in love is the paralysing closeness of self. This was solved in "Every loutish lad in love" by farce, but "Margot" relies upon self-projection. Four years later Yeats was able to re-use Pythagoras when he reconsidered the Delphic Oracle's pronouncement on the fate of Plotinus. In "News for the Delphic Oracle" Pythagoras reappears, but it is not his eyes but those of Peleus which are "blinded" rather than "dimmed" with tears, and the beloved's half-closed eyelid becomes a trope for the delicacy of Thetis' limbs.[6]

Perhaps too, line 16 (in Ellmann's version, line 7 in the *LMR* version) "O how can I that interest hold?" is rehandled in the first two lines of "Politics".

IV

And so, finally, to "Portrayed before his Eyes". The hardness and definition finally achieved in this visionary lyric rely as much upon a transumption of "Margot" as upon a return to the original eight line theme. Much of the biographical experience seems abandoned and its topos is left behind. For Ellmann the "near-sentimentality" lies at the outset (of the 8 line theme), in the "unconvincingly hyperbolical" (*IY* 211) comparison of the woman to Artemis, and in his view the comparison becomes "more indirect and casual as the poem develops". The change of narrative perspective, made possible in this poem perhaps by the completion of "Margot", is largely responsible for the superiority of this lyric over "Margot". Impersonally narrated, the vision of the woman as possibly an "[i]mplacably lipped" goddess of statuesque stillness *and* as a "[p]itiably frail", kneeling mortal, is pushed beyond question. Sentimentality and the hyperbolical disappear with the first-person narrator, modern worshipper is compared to ancient one, the goddess becomes more implacable, the beloved more human, the comparison the more marvellous. Yeats can be confident that his reader will follow the winding pathway of this visually *narrow* poem to "love's levelling bed".[7] The newly-achieved perspective is such that the poet no longer "speaks directly", he is now "part of his own phantasmagoria", he has been "reborn as an idea, something intended, complete" (*E&I* 509).

The third stanza is perhaps not quite "right", but the central image of the stilled gyres is, as Ellmann says, a "hard-bitten" image (*IY* 211), because of self-confessedly temporary one. Its momentary peace is apprehensible, if remote. "Portrayed before his Eyes" is curious among Yeats's poetical manuscripts, unsigned (but dated), unpublished and perhaps unfinished, but "complete".

NOTES

1. "Portrayed befores his Eyes" is transcribed from NLI MS 30,189 and published here for the first time by courtesy of the Yeats Estate. I am grateful to Miss Anne B. Yeats and Mr Michael B. Yeats and to Linda Shaughnessy of A. P. Watt & Co. for permission to publish them.
2. Richard Ellmann, *The Identity of Yeats* (London: Macmillan, 1954). See pp. 209–11 of the 1964 Faber and Faber edition, hereafter *IY*.
3. The notebook is numbered 351 in the collection of Michael B. Yeats. I have not seen the original, but am grateful to Peggy L. McMullen assistant archivist of the W. B. Yeats Collection of the Frank Melville Jr. Memorial Library, the State University of New York at Stony Brook, for supplying a copy of it, and to the Yeats Estate and A. P. Watt Ltd, for agreeing to its being made. This notebook is the "Rapallo" Notebook, which contains drafts of the opening of a new version of *The King of the Great Clock Tower*, the

"Supernatural Songs" etc. See Curtis Bradford, *Yeats at Work* (Carbondale and Edwardsville: Southern Illinois University Press, 1965) pp. 134, 268.

4. The differences are as follows: Ellmann reads line 1 [lacks comma]; line 3 "moved,"; line 4 "knees."; line 7 "and she"; line 10 "Lover anxiety"; line 12 "his heart fail"; line 13 "Then"; line 14 "by Love and dread"; line 16 "took,". I read however "moved;" in line 3 of the Rapallo Notebook version (described below), also "Loves anxiety" in line 10, "his breath fail" in line 12; "There suffered" in line 13; "Love s dread" in line 14; "took." in line 16; "Love's levelling" in line 17. I am most grateful to the late Professor Ellmann for discussion of the problems of this manuscript in an exchange of letters.

5. Richard Ellmann, *W. B. Yeats's Second Puberty: a Lecture delivered at the Library of Congress on April 2, 1984* (Washington: Library of Congress, 1985) p. 7. This lecture was collected in *Four Dubliners* (London: Hamish Hamilton, 1987).

6. Margot Ruddock was of "distinguished beauty of face and limb", Yeats recalled in his introduction to *The Lemon Tree* (London: J. M. Dent & Sons, 1937) p. ix. Their letters throw a certain light upon that "sudden" or "hidden glory" of "Margot" stanza II. Yeats counsels Margot Ruddock "[n]ever be swept away into anything; live in self-possession, wisdom", quoting the last three lines of "To a friend whose work has come to nothing", before proceeding to define "the way of wisdom" in a way which casts light on his use of that phrase as title of a 1900 essay. "The way of wisdom is our own way, not the way of our ancestors, who throng in our blood, not the way found by some act of submission to a church or a passion, to anybody or anything who would take from us the burden of ourselves, that burden is our *glory* . . ." (*LMR* 21, my italics).

7. The last two lines are quoted by Jon Stallworthy in *Between the Lines Yeats's Poetry in the Making* (Oxford: Clarendon Press, 1963, second imp., 1965), p. 152. Stallworthy uses the lines to explicate drafts of "Chosen", line 14 ". . . and I take/That stillness for a theme". These drafts may date from 1926–27. The sexual symbolism of the gyres and of the Thirteenth Cone is implex but by 1934 self-sufficient. Professor Ellmann kindly informed me that these lines were praised by Sir Michael Tippett on the appearance of *The Identity of Yeats*.

"Worst Part of Life": Yeats's Horoscopes for Olivia Shakespear

Deirdre Toomey

In *Yeats's Golden Dawn*, George Mills Harper quotes "a most revealing note in Yeats's hand: '1900 – from April till February 1901 "worst part of life". Both in regard to ♀ matters & other things.'" Because of his interest in the Golden Dawn troubles of 1900, Harper interprets this note as referring not to Yeats's frustrated love for Maud Gonne – "♀ [Venus] matters" – but to the Order of the Golden Dawn, "[s]ince Venus occupies a central position in the symbolism and ritual of the Golden Dawn".[1] Two things must strike the reader as odd. First, Yeats's use of quotation marks around the key phrase, and second, the apparent contradiction of *Memoirs* which suggests that for Yeats the period 1897–98 was the worst period of life (*Mem* 125). An examination of a scrap of paper in the collection of Michael Butler Yeats provides the solution.

A small bifolium of blue deckle notepaper, with the Coole Park letterhead, contains Yeats's note, and runs in full as follows.

Coole Park,
Gort.
Co. Galway.
[printed]

OS.
events for rectification

1890 June ♀ event   Little.

1897 Early June . & on for 8 months
momentous. ♀. Principle period of kind.

1900 from April till Feb 1901
     'worst part of life'. Both in regard to ♀ matter[s?] & 'other things

"nothing happened in the summer of 1905"
of slightest interest. In April went to
new house.

was there [?] illness or marriage

at ♄ ♂ MC. 23. 47

[*Note*: The astrological symbols in the above document are as follows: ♀=Venus; ♄ =Saturn; ♂=Mars. I am unable to identify Yeats's symbol ♇ in line 3. MC=medium coeli.]

That these comments refer to "events for rectification" in *Olivia Shakespear's* life, and not Yeats's is indicated by the presence of her initials at the top of the page. This manuscript is one of a body of astrological calculations and horoscopes executed by Yeats for Olivia Shakespear, mainly in the period 1910–1. Thus the comments in quotation marks are her own words, spoken or written.

This list of "events for rectification" is not a horoscope proper, but a list of biographical occasions to be used by Yeats to rectifiy her natal horoscope, first cast by George Pollexfen in 1895,[2] against the main events of her life. In this list Yeats does not note the period of his own affair with her. The most significant dates for her are 1897 and 1900–1. Her affair with Yeats ended in early 1897, if we are to accept the evidence of *Memoirs*: "My liaison lasted but a year" (*Mem* 89). Yeats recalled that it was ended by a visit from Maud Gonne, (possibly in February 1897). Yeats was subsequently unable to summon up enthusiasm; Olivia Shakespear went "weeping away". Having risked divorce and the loss of her daughter by having an affair[3] she would have suffered on finding that she had not disturbed the "image" of Maud Gonne in Yeats's heart. No doubt she did. But the evidence of the "rectification" seems clear. From early June 1897, Olivia Shakespear seems to have had the "momentous" Venus event of her life, the "[p]rincipal period of kind".

This interpretation is supposed by a second horoscope of c. Summer 1910. On ruled exercise paper, it is headed "notes on the Horoscope of OS." and it is also in the collection of Michael Yeats. Among its astrological calculations are two for June 1897, as follows:

? { rectification which brings ♀ σ MC during
97 { eight months that follow June 1897 should
{ be tried ~~with ♀ σ MC primary~~.

97 By secondary direction ☽ r was σ ♀ p about
June 1987

[*Note*: The astrological symbols are as follows: ♀=Venus; σ=in conjunction; MC=medium coeli; ☽ =Moon; r=radical; p=progressed.]

This 1897 "♀[Venus] event" need not have been consummated for it to have been "momentous", but the cancelled reference to "your other lover"[4] in the draft of "After Long Silence" can be read in this way.

As for the "'worst part of life'". it is not difficult to see the reasons: "'other things'" no doubt included the death of Olivia Shakespear's mother on 14 May 1900. A very moving letter of condolence from Yeats survives, in which he refers to the fact that "you cared for nobody else as you cared for your mother",[5] a remarkable statement. About this time too, there was a financial disaster in the Shakespear household and they sold their large house in Porchester Square and moved to a mansion flat.[6] As for unhappiness in "Venus matters", the renewed contact with Yeats could have coincided with the end of the second affair.

Richard Ellmann stated, presumably on George Yeats's authority, that Yeats and Olivia Shakespear had another affair c. 1903[7] but this date is not mentioned in any of the horoscopes. The second document seems to substantiate the affair, however, while suggesting a different date. In it, Yeats compares his own planetary configurations and those of Olivia Shakespear at two periods in their lives.

> 95–6 During Dec Jan –95 –96 her $\leftmoon$ p was
> σ my $\venus$ r (June 1910 $\sigma\!\!\!\!-$ my $\venus$ r).

[Note: $\leftmoon$ =Moon; p=progressed; σ =in conjunction; $\venus$ =Venus; r=radical; $\sigma\!\!\!\!-$ =opposition]

From the comparison and its implicit concern with $\venus$ [Venus] I assume that Yeats and Olivia Shakespear in June 1910 either had a second affair or became very close emotionally in a way that paralleled the involvement of late 1895 and early 1896. The note continues with an elaborate analysis of Olivia Shakespear's horoscope for the autumn of 1910 with some anticipations up to February 1911. As the future tense is used for October 1910 and the past tense for June, I assume that these calculations were done at Coole Park.[8] These calculations are in some cases detailed and would require further astrological investigation, but their biographical drift is clear.

When Yeats wrote his very moving account of his first affair with Olivia Shakespear in *Memoirs*, begun in 1915, he wrote with full knowledge of her subsequent sexual history. Yet he gave no indication of their later relationship, beyond cancelling "it was the end of our liaison" (MS.MBY) and susbtituting "it was the breaking between us for many years" (*Mem* 89).

In "Friends", composed during January, 1911, Yeats recalls three women Lady Gregory, Olivia Shakespear, and Maud Gonne. A crux[9] in the reading of this poem turns on the reiterated emphasis in lines 4–9 on an absolutely uninterrupted serene friendship during fifteen "[m]any-times-troubled years". A. Norman Jeffares was apparently told by Maud Gonne MacBride that this passage referred to the friendship with Olivia Shakespear, and that the friend of lines 10–16 was Lady Gregory.

This second ascription is apparently confirmed by an unpublished letter to Lady Gregory of 2 January 1911, in which Yeats quotes a draft of these lines and identifies Lady Gregory as the friend. The draft employs the images of hand and unbinding but it has no "dreamy load". Instead it refers to a very different thing, "Youth's bitter burden". It was this "bitterness" compounded of poverty, insecurity and social humiliation that Yeats described to Lady Gregory in his first confessional conversation with her in July 1897, and which she recorded in her diary. She even records the word.

Indeed, Lady Gregory did free Yeats from this burden. But in the poem itself – as distinct from the draft – a process of phantasmagorical shifting has taken place. The process is eminently familiar from studies such as Jon Stallworthy's *Between the Lines*. The "bitter burden" is displaced by the "dreamy load", a powerfully explicit image for an incapacitating virginity.

The really problematical[10] lines remain lines 4–9, for those who would choose to read lines 10–16 as relating to Lady Gregory. It is of course easy to ascribe those fifteen years of uninterrupted friendship to Lady Gregory, whom Yeats had indeed known for such a period of continuous friendship since 1896. But if we ascribe the lines to Olivia Shakespear, we have to accept that Yeats is lying about his own life and hers in a hurtful and unnecessary way. He had known Olivia Shakespear for seventeen years at the time of writing the poem, a period which included an estrangement lasting at least three years. Given the quadruple emphasis of the lines upon continuity

> One because no thought,
> Nor those unpassing cares,
> No, not in these fifteen
> Many-times-troubled years,
> Could ever come between
> Mind and delighted mind;

> (*VP* 315)

the ascription to Olivia Shakespear involves an assumption of some crassness on the part of the poet. The recent emotional rapprochement of June 1910 and possibly afterwards must have reminded Yeats of how much he owed in terms of sexual development – "what none can have and thrive" – to Olivia Shakespear. Lines 10–16 are the appropriate expression of a great debt.

NOTES

1. Yeats's Golden Dawn (London: Macmillan, 1974) pp. 27–9.
2. George Pollexfen's long horoscope for Olivia Shakespear was cast c. Oct. 1895 and is in his horoscope ledger, now in the collection of Michael Butler Yeats. Pollexfen is not particularly accurate on personal appearance, but he is remarkably accurate in some details of her character. He saw the native as having a "very good intellect", a "deeply creative and imaginative poetic genius"; he detected "a fondness for strange paths or curious subjects . . . plenty of courage . . . sometimes rashness". He saw an interest in

the occult and a "comprehensive" mind. He was sure that success and personal development would come through "Books or publications". He did not realise that she was married and predicted "the man [she will marry] most likely would be a Dark Saturnian man very eccentric & wayward not an ordinary person & not much happiness would result". Pollexfen thought that she should avoid marriage. He foresaw a moderately happy life but anticipated that her father would die shortly. In fact he died during the following August. I am most grateful to Mr Yeats for allowing me access to his collection and to the Yeats Estate and Dr Roy Foster for permitting the publication of unpublished materials.

3. John Harwood, "Olivia Shakespear and W. B. Yeats", *YA* 4, pp. 86–7, and note 25.
4. See the transcription in David R. Clark, *Yeats at Songs and Choruses* (Gerrards Cross: Colin Smythe, 1983) p. 78 *et seq.* Clearly Olivia Shakespear's "other lover" is not, as Clark suggests, her late husband. I take a simpler view of the poem than does Professor Clark. I assume that the poem does concern itself with the relationship between Yeats and Olivia Shakespear; that the "supreme theme of art and song" *is* love and that this has been the subject of their conversation. The "long silence" of this continuous friendship I take to refer to the fact that for many years they have not discussed their own sexual relationship: there are profound "silences" in continuous discourse. The evidence of these horoscopes is that they had a lot to discuss.
5. ALS, Lilly Library, Indiana, quoted in Harwood, loc. op. cit., p. 78.
6. See Harwood, op. cit., p. 92.
7. Richard Ellmann, *Yeats: the Man and the Masks* (London: Faber & Faber, 1961) p. 182.
8. WBY was in London in June 1910, at least from 10 June onwards. Another horoscope on blue deckle Coole Park paper and presumably also of this date, survives in the collection of Michael Butler Yeats. This third document is also headed "OS." and contains a series of calculations for the moon in her horoscope from June 1890 through until Jan. 1907. One significant date is April 1894, the month of their first meeting at the *Yellow Book* Inaugural Dinner. Then, her moon was in conjunction with Venus (radical). There is also a group of six conventional natal horoscopes from "OS", five of them in Yeats's hand, all of them on horoscope forms, and all datable c. 1910–1 (Coll. MBY). I am grateful to Professor Ronald Schuchard for details about Yeats's movements in the summer of 1910.
9. See A. Norman Jeffares, *A New Commentary on the Poems of W. B. Yeats* (London: Macmillan, 1984) pp. 123–4; Warwick Gould, "The Editor Takes Possession", *TLS*, 29 June 1984, 731–3 at 733, and subsequent correspondence from Mary FitzGerald (*TLS*, 20 July 1984, 811) and Warwick Gould (*TLS*, 10 Aug. 1984, 893).
10. The problem being that if lines 10–16 relate to Lady Gregory, then the poem refers to only two, and not "three" women, as Yeats states, since lines 4–9 also refer to Lady Gregory. A further draft of the poem is in the National Library of Ireland, MS 30,515. It is, however, unhelpful here, being a draft of the final, "Maud Gonne" section of the poem.

MSS in a Black Box: The Golden Dawn Papers of Dr William Wynn Westcott

R. A. Gilbert

A friend of mine who knew of my enthusiasm for the Golden Dawn and of my burrowing among its archives, read my description of the Order's archives[1] and asked me if I would like to see some regalia he had found that belonged with "Private Collection C". On examination the regalia proved not to have come from any of Waite's faction but to have been the property of Dr Westcott; nor were the wands and sceptres all: with them was a black japanned deed-box – *the* box about which Carnegie-Dickson had written to A. E. Waite in 1938. "You know, of course, that our old and mutual friend Dr. Wynn Westcott, left me most of his G.D. Order Documents and Papers, including his Diary of the founding of the G.D., and he also left a famous 'Black Box' containing the various *original* G.D. Documents addressed jointly to Dr. Felkin and myself, of which there was also an index in his 'Diary'. What happened to these forms another very interesting 'chapter' in G.D. History."[2]

That the box was locked and lacked a key was of little moment, for Victorian locks yield easily to large steel screwdrivers, and I had the dubious honour of being the first person in sixty years to examine the putative "*original* G.D. Documents". They do not, alas, include the crucial correspondence that passed between Mathers and Westcott in 1887, but they throw a flood of light into some of the dark corners of the Order's history. They also give rise to further questions. Why did Westcott keep a mummified hand among his papers?, Where *are* the Mathers letters? And what has become of Westcott's "Diary"? These questions I shall leave to the speculative and will confine myself to the papers and memorabilia that the box *did* contain.

On the basis of my suggested classification of Golden Dawn archives (*YA 5* 164–5), most of Westcott's papers are "historical", but it is virtually impossible to separate those concerning "origins" from other historical material. Much of his personal magical material has to be classed as "administrative and ritual", for some of the objects are the only known surviving examples: Westcott's set of Enochian chess pieces, his sashes for each of the grades to Adeptus Minor (5=6) and the original designs for the court cards of the Golden Dawn Tarot. In addition there are his own set of six Star Maps (relating the Tarot trumps to the constellations), his divinatory "Ring and Disk" and the original designs for the lamens and banners of the Outer Order. More important than these is a manuscript list of the "Flying Rolls", giving original and altered titles, dates of issue and the prices charged for providing copies. (This list is printed in the revised edition of Francis King's *Astral Projection, Magic and Alchemy: Golden Dawn Material by S. L. MacGregor Mathers and Others* (Wellingborough: Aquarian Press, 1987).

Manuscript drafts of Westcott's lectures on *The Practical Kabala* and on *Kabalistic Cosmogony* (both dated 1895) constitute a bridge between "ritual" and "historical" material. Other lectures by members of the Order are largely unofficial (e.g. T. H. Pattinson's clairvoyant vision of the Secret Chief in 1888, with an "improved" version by Mathers; and Oswald Murray's account of Mrs Pattinson's astral travelling, or *Spontaneous Exteriorisation*), but the *Addresses* are both official and minatory. The problems of Horus Temple and its fractious members are set out in Mathers's *Report on the state of Horus [Temple]* of March, 1893 and in Westcott's earlier *Address to Horus Temple*, delivered in November, 1892. Addresses to Isis-Urania Temple warn the members of the problems with the Bradford Temple.

Earlier papers concern the founding of the Osiris, Horus and Amen-Ra Temples. Westcott had retained the original charter of Osiris (virtually identical with that of Isis-Urania; it is illustrated in my *Golden Dawn Companion* (Aquarian Press, 1986), together with the Pledges of the Chiefs of each Temple to the Chiefs of the Second Order, the petition for the founding of Amen-Ra and a letter from Pattinson urging on Westcott the desirability of a Temple at Bradord: "I find 7 interested friends all ready to fall in with the idea of forming a G.D. here in Bradford, and the sooner this is done the better."[3]

The most informative document, however, is a small notebook that Westcott kept – as Registrar of the Order – listing every office-holder in each Temple from 1888 to 1897. From this it is possible to identify all the minor officers – who are mentioned nowhere else in the entire archives of the Golden Dawn. Yeats evidently took little part in the activities of the Outer Order, for he appears only once, as Stolistes of Isis-Urania from 22 March to 23 September 1892. In this capacity he would have been in charge of the robes, collars and insignia of the officers and was required "to watch over the cup of clear water, and to purify the Hall, the Fratres and Sorores, and the Candidate with water".

Westcott also kept a small number of Second Order documents: a series of annotated sketches by Mathers to illustrate the decoration of the sashes of the Adept grades, and two of the Order's *Annual Reports* for 1895 and 1896. The Reports raise a question about Yeats's activities in the Second Order. It is known from his own official record that Yeats had passed some of the earlier examinations in 1895,[4] and the Report for that year (read out on 13 June 1895) *may* refer to him: "Three Adepti have fully attained the Grade of Th[eoricus] A[deptus] M[inor] and two others have been named Theorici and have almost perfectly attained the Grade." It refers also to the "Institution of Four Theoric Officers" who have been identified by Ellic Howe[5] as Percy Bullock, Florence Farr, Dr Berridge and Annie Horniman. By the following June Westcott was able to report that "6 members have become Theorici making a total of ten. The new Theorici being V. H. Vigilate [Helen Rand], Volo [Mrs. Kennedy], A. P. S. [Anima Pura Sit=Dr H. Pullen Burry], Deo Date [Mrs. Hunter], Shemeber [Pamela Bullock], & Non Sine Numine [Col. Webber Smith]." If these six had all reached the grade during the year of the report, it would seem that one of the two who had "almost perfectly attained the grade" had fallen back. This one may have been Yeats but was more probably J. W. Brodie-Innes who was certainly a T. A. M. by November 1896,[6] from which it would appear that Yeats – for all his enthusiasm for examinations – was making very heavy weather of his magical studies. (He finally reached the Theoricus Adeptus Minor Grade in Felkin's Stella Matutina, on 10 July 1912.[7])

More entertaining than the Reports are the letters that Westcott carefully if unwisely preserved. These can be divided into official and unofficial correspondence, the former comprising letters relating to entry into the Second Order and the latter consisting of private letters from Brodie-Innes and correspondence concerning Mathers and Crowley.

The applications for admission to the Second Order were made by sixty-eight members between 1891 and 1896 (some of them wrote more than once – there are ninety-two letters in all). They range in tone from the deferential and obsequious to the casual approach of Dr Berridge: "I think next Wednesday will suit me, but I cannot be with you till 4 p.m.", and the quite lunatic letter of Frederick Johnson: "When the reaction comes upon him what wiser Teacher than the Good Angel in the disguise of Satan could he get? None!" Among them are letters from Yeats, Florence Farr, Annie Horniman and George Pollexfen, all of which are printed below.

Ten of the private letters from Brodie-Innes, dated between 1896 and 1900, concern his "Order of the Sun", while the remaining three – all of later date – relate to Aleister Crowley and to the Golden Dawn in its decline. There are five letters from Edward Maitland regretting the demise of the Hermetic Society but declining to join the newly formed Golden Dawn, Theresa O'Connell's long statement to Westcott about the founding of the Order,[8] and a startling letter of 1895 from Allan Bennett seeking a Charter for a new Temple in South London: "There are many of our Fratres and Sorores who are unable without great inconvenience to attend the Isis-Urania Temple: its meetings being so often held during the hours when we unlucky wights are bound by business ties and kept away." Accompanying this is Mathers's peremptory refusal.

More intriguing is the correspondence between Westcott, Crowley and others relating to Mathers's attempt to stop the publication of Golden Dawn rituals in Crowley's journal, *The Equinox*. Westcott saw the case as a golden opportunity to force Mathers to retract his damning revelation (or "slander" if one chooses to believe Westcott) about the forging of the Anna Sprengel letters. In March 1910 he drafted a long "retraction" for Mathers to copy and enclosed it in a letter to his friend A. Cadbury-Jones, who was then Secretary-General of the *Societas Rosicruciana in Anglia* and Westcott's right-hand man. Referring to Mathers's request for financial support he said: "If he wants a gift of money from me – he *must* write his withdrawal of the charge of forgery: – he ought to write *two* – one a private letter to me dated 1901 Dec. or early 1902 – and a confirmation referring to the present row – dated now. I send you copies of what I should require – I am not going to give him money for nothing." A second letter to Cadbury-Jones, of 27 March 1910, offered somewhat feeble evidence to rebut Mathers's charges and concluded with the words: "If he will do all I want, I will give him a five pound note: don't let it look like bribery." Evidently it did, the plan came to nothing and the papers came back to Westcott.

Such deviousness is, at best, embarrassing for those who choose still to believe in the "official" history of the founding of the Golden Dawn, and Westcott's papers do nothing for his good name, but their emergence from the "Black Box" is a delightful if unexpected gift to historians of the Order.

THE LETTERS

1. Florence Farr

123 Dalling Road,
Ravenscourt Park

Dear Dr. Westcott,

During the time I have been a Member of the G.D. Hermetic Society my whole life has assumed a new aspect. I cannot express the debt I feel I owe to the G.H. Chiefs of the order for putting me in the way of learning what I have. May I hope that by the favour of the G.H. Chiefs I may now be permitted to join the second order?

I am perfectly willing to accept the terms of the obligation I have received.[9]

Yours faithfully
Florence Emery

The letter is undated but was probably written in July, 1891; Florence Emery signed the Second Order Roll on 2 August 1891.

2. Annie Horniman

Surrey Mount,
Forest Hill,
Dec. 1st, /91

Care et G.H. Frater,

I have already passed through the Grades of the First Order & in addition there has been conferred on me the Grade of Lady of the Paths in the Portal of the

Vault of the Adepts. I now write to ask that I may be admitted to a full participation in the Mysteries of the Grade of Adeptus Minor.

I have received so much hope and satisfaction from the Knowledge which has been given me that I am most anxious to be allowed to go on, when it is considered fit for me. I hope to be able in the future to be of more service in the Society as well as to gain personally in Strength & Knowledge. Hoping that my sincere request may be granted.

Yours fraternally,

Soror "Fortiter et Recte" 5 = 6

3. W. B. Yeats

3 Blenheim Road,
Bedford Park,
Chiswick, W

Greatly honoured chiefs I am writing to seek your permission [to be examined: (*erased*)] to take the first examination preliminary to entering the second order. Soror SSDD can undertake my examination.

Yours faithfully

Demon est deus
inversus

Beneath the signature Westcott has added "Ap.5 Yes" Presumably this is 5 April 1892 (the letter is undated). Yeats signed the Second Order Roll on 20 January 1893.

4. George Pollexfen

(a)   27. Octr. 1894
                                                   Die Fr

Care & Very Honored Frater S.A.

I am gratified to learn that the Very Honord Chiefs have decided to permit me to enter the Second Order and I accept their invitation to do so.

And I shall feel obliged by your giving instruction to the Cancellarius to inform me as to what I have to prepare for the First Examination – as I would wish to be going on with my preparation for that examination with as little delay as possible, & am ever

Fraternally Yours
F.L

(b)   The Hotel Metropole
                                                        London. 21 Octr. 1895

Dr. Wynn Westcott.
Dear Sir & V.H. Frater,

   I have carefully read the addresses you kindly lent me I must say they cause
me much misgiving as to my fitness for admission to the Second Order. I feel that
I do not possess the strength of Health or the great Strength of Will and Energy
which some of the writers say are so necessary. But I had hoped notwithstanding
these grave limitations and notwithstanding the human frailties and worldly
blots attaching to me and of which I am fully sensible; that by working on to the
best of my capacities and in good faith in the Order I should perhaps sooner or
later find in that path much to strengthen me in those essential qualities
required; and to help me also to shed the material dross clinging to the higher
Self.

   I fully appreciate the teaching extended to me so far in the Outer.

   And if under the above circumstances I can be allowed to proceed further I
now apply (not by any means with a light heart) to be admitted to the Second
Order & am

                              Faithfully Yours
                              Geo. Pollexfen
P.S. And I shall present myself tomorrow Wednesday evening 7 p.m.

In fact it was two days later – he signed the Roll on 23 October, 1895.

                                    NOTES

1. R. A. Gilbert, "Magical Manuscripts, An Introduction to the Archives of Hermetic
   Order of the Golden Dawn" (*YA 5* [1987], 163–77). A summary account of the archives
   is contained in my *The Golden Dawn Companion: a Guide to the History, Structure, and
   Workings of the Hermetic Order of the Golden Dawn* (Wellingborough: Aquarian Press, 1987)
   pp. 176–9.
2. W. E. Carnegie-Dickson to A. E. Waite, 20 Nov. 1938. Collection of the present writer.
   The present location of the materials discussed in this paper is private.
3. T. H. Pattinson to W. Wynn Westcott, 27 Mar. 1888.
4. G. M. Harper, "From Zelator to Theoricus, Yeats's 'Link with the Invisible Degrees'",
   Yeats Studies, an International Journal, no. 1, eds R. O'Driscoll and Lorna Reynolds (1971)
   pp. 80–6.
5. E. Howe, *The Magicians of the Golden Dawn: a Documentary History of a Magical Order
   1887–1923* (London: Routledge & Kegan Paul, 1972) p. 115.
6. Howe, op. cit., p. 136.
7. Harper, op. cit., p. 83.
8. The statement was written at Westcott's request on 22 Aug. 1898. He evidently
   mistrusted Mathers already and was preparing his defence. The text of the statement
   appears in my *Golden Dawn Companion*, pp. 11–12.
9. The text of the "Obligation of an Adeptus Minor of the Order R.R. et A.C." is given in
   The Golden Dawn Companion, pp. 103–5.

Note

In my paper on the archives of the Order I stated that the Minute Book of Ahathoor
Temple contains no reference to Yeats (*YA 5*, 167–8). I was wrong: it does. Mr Roger
Parisious examined the manuscript and found a number of the leaves stuck together; on
separating them he found the entry for 24 February 1894, in which "V.H. Fra. Demon est
D.I." appears as Hegemon (i.e. the officer whose duty was to act "as the Guardian of the
Threshold of Entrance and the Preparer of the Way for the Enterer thereby") It was not a
happy occasion for Yeats, as among the apologies for absence was one from Soror Per
Ignem ad Lucem (i.e. Maud Gonne) "who was on the point of leaving Paris for a short
time" [R. A. G].

A Descriptive Catalog of W. B. Yeats's Library: Notes Supplementary

Wayne K. Chapman

[The notes below supplement and amend the 1985 first edition of *YL*, the format of which is largely followed and which should be consulted for the fullest description of each item listed.]

311. Burton, Robert. THE ANATOMY OF MELANCHOLY. Ed. by Rev. A. R. Shilleto. 3 vols. Bohn's Libraries. London: G. Bell, 1912.

Vol. 1 – since pp. 152–249 are cut, "206–11, 213–15; 218–19; 226–28" is a puzzling notation. Marginal strokes occur on pp. 170, 177, 206–11, 213–15, 218–19, 226–28, 232–33.

Vol. 2, pp. 40–83 cut. This is Part II. Sect. II. Mem. III – "Air rectified. With a digression of the Air."

Vol. 3, pp. 48–57, 96–107, 400–09 cut, as noted in *YL*, but also 511–22 (Index, CO–I), 527–30 (Index, Ls & Ms) and single odd leaves here and there. The first cut section is entitled "LOVE'S POWER AND EXTENT." In that section, on p. 52, is a significant occurrence of the word "crossway," noted in *YL*, within a passage standing beside Yeats's one-word annotation, "cross-roads"; there Venus frees a love-struck melancholic after he has consulted a "learned Magician" whose letter to Saturn invokes the "old fiend's" intercession. "Love," "magic" and "melancholy" are all in the cut sections of the Index.

369. Chapman, George. THE WORKS OF GEORGE CHAPMAN. Vol. 1: PLAYS, ed. by Richard Herne Shepherd. New ed. London: Chatto & Windus, 1889.

Unless otherwise noted, the following were missed in *YL*:

P. 175, long passage in BUSSY D'AMBOIS (V.i.) scored in columns a. & b. An "!" at one point in column a.

P. 176, an ink check mark in left margin.

P. 183, heavy scoring at bottom of column b. – I.i. of THE REVENGE OF BUSSY D'AMBOIS.

Pp. 196–97, scoring and underlining. As with p. 183, marked passages are spoken by Clermont.

P. 198, WBY's "largely undecipherable" comment reads: "All this moralysing in the day of this invention / would have meant as now, a tame second hand spirit – now, / only the violent & therefore never stated for never useful Bussy D'Amb[ois] / seems living." The following line is scored in IV.i.: "He turn'd wild lightning in the lackey's hands."

P. 200, scoring in b. margin beside "That in this one thing, all the discipline / Of manners and of manhood is contained; / A man to join himself with th'Universe / In his main sway, and make (in all things fit) / One with that All, and go on, round as it. . . ."

P. 202, two lines underscored: "Your noblest natures are most credulous. / Who gives no trust is apt to break. . . ."

P. 203, the passage referred to in *YL* is at first underlined and then scored in the margin for 17 lines; again, Clermont is speaking. Also underscored in a. column are the words "jesters, parasites, / Servile observers." The "partially undecipherable" marginal comment is perhaps "The[n?] what ever happen[s] of[? or "by"?] Fion / but not so passionate."

P. 204, marginal scoring and underlining.

P. 217, at variance with *YL*; in BYRON'S CONSPIRACY at l. 5ff, heavily scored beside the comment "Men in machine," written lengthwise in margin. Cf. the line: "The common scarecrows of all men's suits".

P. 219, some light scorings and underlinings in blue pencil.

P. 220, light strokes in a. margin.

Also marginal strokes on pp. 222–24, 231 & 233.

End of vol., the "long comment, only partially decipherable," reads as follows: "The Byron tragedy was popular – / note the intense subjectivity that / this implies in an audience – Did / not this subjectivity, by casting / the attention with logic & feeling / create ability? Were not all people / abler taken as individuals before / the rise of practical pre-occupations / & the government by opinion which / this implies. These lessen subjectivity / Compare not only the old / theatrical audiences but the / audience for oratory – They / were quicker in thought / as well as higher –"

453.   Cudworth, R[alph]. THE TRUE INTELLECTUAL SYSTEM OF
        THE UNIVERSE. The first part. . . . London: Richard Royston, 1678.

        "470 [should be 365]" is an error for "470 [should be 364]–365."

        If the "few pencil strokes in the unpaginated Preface" are Yeats's, they
        show his interest in the sections that argue against atheists in favour of a
        proof of the soul's immortality. The Preface served this work as an
        abstract, and there are a few strokes beyond the Preface, not far into the
        work proper. Scored are unnumbered pp. 3, 5, 6, 8, 13, 14 & 15. Of note
        is the scored passage on p. 8 on the "Pythagorick Doctrine *of the*
        Prae-Existence *of* Souls, . . . *founded upon the very same* Principle, *with the*
        Atomick Physiology".

        P. 3, underscoring of two Greek words and marginal note in pencil:
        "wooden necessity" (not in WBY'S hand.)

        Scorings also on pp. 5, 15 (from "Besides all this, no less Author than
        Plato affirms" to "and some with the Organs of another . . ."), and 18–19
        (6 evenly spaced strokes throughout XIX and for the first paragraph in
        Bk. I. Chap. I., "Incorporeal Substance asserted by the Ancients").

750.   Glanvil, Joseph. SADDUCISMUS TRIUMPHATUS. . . . Trans. with
        additions by Dr. Horneck. 4th ed. London: Printed for A. Bettesworth
        and J. Batley . . .; W. Mears, and J. Hooke, 1726.

        Marginal strokes also on pp. 9 of the letter from Heny More (separately
        numbered), on A2 of the Epistle Dedicatory, and a long scoring in ink on
        300 in "RELATION III. The Witchcraft of Elizabeth Style of Bayford,
        Widow".

878.   Herbert, Edward. THE AUTOBIOGRAPHY OF EDWARD, LORD
        HERBERT OF CHERBURY. With intro. [etc.] by Sidney Lee. 2nd ed.
        London: George Routledge, [1906].

        YL notes a column of numbers on back flyleaf ("88 / 107 / 143") but does
        not report passages marked on pp. 88 (a description of an inn-keeper's
        daughter in Lauguedoc province, France) and 107 (a passage about
        "ladies of much beauty and discretion, and particularly a sister of
        Bouteville, thought to be one of the chief perfections of the time . . .").

1033.   Jonson, Ben. THE WORKS OF BEN JONSON. Ed. by Lt. Col.
        Francis Cunningham. 3 vols. London: Chatto & Windus, [1910–12].

        Vol. 1, signed "Georgie Hyde Lees". Vol. 3 has more cut than

TIMBER. Most of UNDERWOODS and HORACE'S ART OF POETRY were cut, as was all of Vol. 1.

1180.   MacDonagh, Thomas. LITERATURE IN IRELAND. . . . Dublin: Talbot Press, 1916.

Marginal strokes appear on pp. 47 (an "x"), 52, 55, 60–61 (a "+"), 64–66, 68, 70 (double-scored at rt. and a "?" to left), 71–72, 78, 82, 88–89, 92–95, 97, 112, 127–28, 130, 133–34, 141, 149 & 151.

Inside back cover: "22" in *YL* should be "33". "138", "145", & "149" should be emended to "138–", "145#", and "149+". And "151–" should be added. These page refs. are not in Yeats's hand nor, it seems, are the textual markings.

1182.   ——. THOMAS CAMPION AND THE ART OF ENGLISH POETRY. Dublin: Hodges, Figgis, 1913.

As in 1180 (above), page refs. written inside back cover generally correspond to pages where stroking occurs in the text. The *YL* account of the list on the back cover should include "79" & "~~110~~ 100." Strokes occur on pp. 66, 69, 70 (foot), 71 (first 3 lines), 79 & 86. Strokes and notes do not appear to be Yeats's.

P. 39, beside "For that will still be free, / In spite of jealousy!", someone, perhaps Pound (see Thomas Parkinson's W. B. YEATS, THE LATER POETRY, p. 189), has pencilled: "But still will revel free / / But is by nature free / ordained free".

1377.   More, Dr. Henry. A COLLECTION OF SEVERAL PHILOSOPHICAL WRITINGS . . . 2nd ed. London: William Morden, 1662.

In "Immortality of the Soul", corners turned back are likely to be accidentals and in such state before Yeats came to own the book. Pages are brittle. Marginal strokes also on pp. 28, 103 (underscoring), 104 (double diagonal hatch-mark beside the page number).

In "Conjectura Cabalistica", p. 101, a passage on "Golden thighed Pythagoras" (Yeats's phrase) is *not* underlined as reported in *YL*. The page is devoid of marks of any kind, though a slip with "Golden Thigh" written on it was left at this point (according to ABY) by Roger Parisious – one of six markers that he left in the book.

P. 162, an "x" beside passage as reported in *YL*, made perhaps lightly in ink, probably not WBY's.

1380.   ——. THE THEOLOGICAL WORKS. London: Joseph Downing, 1708.

"Marginal markings, pencil, passim" – none of the marks or cyphers (?) appear to be Yeats's. *YL* notes frequent occurrence of no. "3" beside passages (none on p. 143 as reported). In fact, "3" occurs often in combination with other numbers (coincidentally, as part of p. refs.?), such as "143" at 3rd new paragraph of p. 144, where "3" stands left of paragraphs 1 & 2; on p. 321, last 7 lines of Bk. IX. Chap. 2.6 are scored and annotated "353"; on p. 345, at Bk. X. Chap. 2.1, the column of numbers "3/345/346/349". This suggests a marginal indexing or concordance system uncharacteristic of Yeats's use. Marginal comment ("–end"), beside passage on p. 155 about the Day of Judgment, does not appear to be in Yeats's hand. The *YL* comment that passages are about biblical symbols is pertinent to the selection cited as example. But passages are more often about righteousness (e.g., marked, numbered and underlined passage on p. 281) or the "Example of . . . Pastours" (p. 346, Chap. 2.4–5, long sections marked). Many marks in "Gospel-Precepts of Purity" and none in either "The main Principles of Astrology" or "The Pretended Art of Astrology".

1978.   Spenser, Edmund. THE WORKS OF EDMUND SPENSER. Ed. by J. Payne Collier. 5 vols. London: Bell and Daldy, 1862.

Vol. 2, corrections to the reading of annotations as follows:

II.3.29–31: "condense his description of her tres[s]"; cf. Spenser's "her yellow locks" etc.

P. 192, end of II.6: "the knights" should be "knights".

II.8.43, left: "?-x?/x"

P. 246, II.9.22, also stroking beside passage and diagram illustrating configuration of the House of Alma, single and triple strokes beside the long footnote; most heavily marked are the sentences "All parts of the ediface fitly joined together made 'a goodly Diapase,' or concord. The mystical interpretation of this verse by Kenelm Digby . . . and Upton, is, to say the least, quite unnecessary".

II.9.57: "memory not individual/is castle is an individual."

II.10.73, last line: "bridge of thunder".

II. end of 10: "quote . . . poetical" should be "give . . . a poetical".

II. end of 12: "quote all boo[k] Canto 12 It is most beautiful".

III.8.24: "old man in Waters of Wondrous Isles".

Vol. 4, corrections to reading of annotations as follows:

VI.10.4, last two lines: "x / Moricent".

P. 315, also a check-mark beside 1. 501.

P. 381, at "Prosopopoia": "making of shapes".

P. 453, at "Muiopotmos": "(Blind fate)".

2115.   Tennyson, Alfred. THE WORKS OF ALFRED TENNYSON. Cabinet Edition. Vol. 3: LOCKSLEY HALL and other poems. London: Henry S. King, 1874.

Facing half title p., a draft fragment of an early unpublished poem surviving in various lengths. *YL* is deceived by handwriting, speculating that this is "*not* an early poem as the style and edition would indicate". Contemporary drafts of the poem which this fragment rehearses are located in an album of juvenilia at the NLI (MS.12,161), where a number of loose leaves in pencil as well as fairer versions in ink survive. One of these is entitled, simply, "–Pan–." Among recent material acquired by the NLI from Senator Michael Yeats is perhaps a related fragment entitled "The Priest of Pan". The "brief biological notes" on the back flyleaf of LOCKSLEY HALL are complemented, in MS.12,161, by a schoolboy prank signed F. I. Gregg and Charles Johnston (watermark "1881").

2401.   Yeats, W[illiam] B[utler]. POEMS: SECOND SERIES. London: A. H. Bullen, 1909. *Wade* 83.

N.B.: a white label with "A" pasted on rebound grey boards. Cf. *YL* 2412a, RESPONSIBILITIES AND OTHER POEMS (1917, rev.), and *YL* 2444a, THE WILD SWANS AT COOLE (1920, rev.). The former bears a white label on the cover with: "B. Put/~~Print~~ first the section / called 'From the Green / Helmet & Other Poems' / (Page 85)". *YL* 2444a has a similar square of white paper pasted on cover with: "C." Together, "A," "B," and "C" vols., with a copy of MICHAEL ROBARTES AND THE DANCER (Cuala Press, 1920), provided the copytext for LATER POEMS (1922), *Wade* 134.

Dates have been entered beneath section titles as follows: "THE WIND AMONG THE REEDS / 1892–1899"; "THE OLD AGE OF QUEEN MAEVE / (1903.)"; "BAILE AND AILLINN / (1903)"; "IN THE SEVEN WOODS / (1899–1904)"; "THE SHADOWY WATERS / ~~1900~~ (1906)". Note continuity of dating as entered in *YL* 2412a and 2444a. Also note that it was this poetical version of THE SHADOWY

WATERS that went into LATER POEMS, while the "Acting version" from PLAYS FOR AN IRISH THEATRE (1911) went into PLAYS IN PROSE AND VERSE (1922; *Wade* 136).

P. 72, stanzaic break is closed between ll. 4 & 5 (rev.), as in *Wade* 134, LATER POEMS.

P. 78, l. 16 of "Adam's Curse" was *not* revised. And l. 18 was not cancelled although a revision of it appears at the foot of the page: "Chimed for an answer 'all we women know/~~know~~". This is *not* "working revision" but was copied from 2417, p. 158, for *Wade* 134.

Revisions at variance with *Wade* 134 in THE SHADOWY WATERS: p. 107, l. 30 (". . . eaten, and . . ."); p. 110, l. 74 (". . . seas again.") and l. 76 (". . . scale; kill Forgael").

2412.   ——. RESPONSIBILITIES AND OTHER POEMS. London: Macmillan, 1916. *Wade* 115.

Revisions and corrections in this copy were made to provide copytext for the 1917 revised edition, *not* "partial copytext for WADE 134". Neither *Wade* nor *VP* makes distinctions between the 1916 and 1917 printings of this book.

Lines in "The Grey Rock" and "The Two Kings" are numbered in pencil, left, usually at even lines.

P. 66, in ink, numeral "I" introduced by means of an arrow above "To a Child Dancing in the Wind," just as the new title "Two Years Later" is indicated beneath "II".

P. 90 ref. should be to p. 99.

P. 104, l. 4 of "To a Poet, who would have me Praise . . .": the article "a" seems included in the cancellation that is part of the revision, which then follows *Wade* 134 and agrees with *VP*.

2412a.   ——. RESPONSIBILITIES AND OTHER POEMS. London, 1917 revised.

This is *not* "another copy" of the 1916 first edition, as reported in *YL*, but a copy of the revised printing. Revisions here *did* provide partial copytext for *Wade* 134 (i.e., for the RESPONSIBILITIES and THE GREEN HELMET lyrics in LATER POEMS). But this volume was *not* used "in conjunction with 2412". It wouldn't need to be, for the revisions in 2412 were printed in this edition.

Both title p. and Contents have been excised. Cf. notes to *YL* 2401 (above) and 2444a (below).

Instructions on half title p. are circled and dates entered as follows: "(191 (1914) / 1912–1914."

P. xi: "Responsibilities / (19"

P. 28, l. 217 of "The Two Kings": period changed to comma; revision noted in *YL* is for l. 217a in *VP*.

P. 37, l. 17 of "To a Shade", rev. as per *Wade* 134 and as noted in *YL* but also bearing the cancelled revision: "one that had slandered you, an old foul mouth, has set. . .".

P. 40, l. 5 of "On those that hated 'The Playboy' . . ." "And" revised, in turn, as follows: "Even" > "And even" > "Even."

P. 43, ll. 43–53 in "The Three Beggars" rev. as per *Wade* 134.

P. 54, the unique variants cited for the paste-over copy of revisions in "The Hour Before Dawn" are close to *Wade* 134, differing by a word (in one case), by punctuation, by a contraction, or by obvious slips in spelling.

P. 56, beneath ll. 79 & 90, underscoring with "NP" beside, in each case, for stanziac breaks (first in *Wade* 134).

P. 83, title p. for "From the Green Helmet and Other Poems", the date "(1904–1912)" was originally "(1909–1912)": large "4" superimposed on "9." Cf. the dating on the same p. of the WSU copy of RESPONSIBILITIES, 1917 (see above p. 123).

2412b. ——. RESPONSIBILITIES AND OTHER POEMS. London, 1916.

Inside frt. cover, pencil notation: "Cover design" (not in WBY's hand). His only clean copy of the London first edition.

2412c. ——. RESPONSIBILITIES AND OTHER POEMS. London, 1917 (rev.).

Marks beside titles in Contents and strokes in text show that Yeats used this copy to survey the work of the volume and to mark the progress of its revision. It may have been put to use on two occasions: the first as early as Dec. 1, 1920; the second as late as his revision of THE HOUR-GLASS, about which his agent reported, on March 14, 1922, that Yeats had engaged a medieval Latin scholar to help with the Latin passages (B. L. Add. MS. 54898, f. 150). Poems marked were as follows: "Introductory Rhymes", "The Two Kings", "To a Wealthy Man", "Paudeen", "When Helen Lived", "The Three Beggars", "Beggar to Beggar Cried", "The Well and the Tree", "The Hour Before Dawn",

"The Player Queen", "The Realists", "The Witch", "The Mountain Tomb", "To a Child Dancing in the Wind", "To Years Later", "A Memory of Youth", "Fallen Majesty", "Friends", "A Coat", and "King and No King". – A matching ts. Contents exists, annotated (MBY 44, one of the as-yet-uncatalogued items from the Michael B. Yeats collection at the NLI), proving the importance of a complete disclosure of the marked titles, the scorings, and the annotations neglected in *YL*. All titles marked in Contents of 2412c were underscored in the ts. with "complete" beside (left) in pencil, except "The Witch". See pp. 6 & 7.

P. 6, below l. 72 in "The Grey Rock", at bot. of p., a long stroke around this passage. – Cf. the ts. Contents in which Yeats underlined the title of the poem but noted that his work with it was complete only "as far as 'foot after foot was giving way.'"

P. 7, top of the page: "Revising from here –/Dec 1 1920".

P. 14, in "The Two Kings", strokes marking off the passage ll. 38–44.

P. 18, single stroke, left, over speech beginning at l. 87; two strokes, rt., at the end of l. 91.

P. 19, two strokes, left, above speech beginning at end of l. 102.

P. 20, two strokes, rt., at end of l. 111; a curved stroke, left, from ll. 112 to 114; and two strokes, left, at l. 115.

P. 23, two strokes marking the passage ll. 147–53.

P. 24, two strokes, left, at l. 163.

P. 28, at the end of "The Two Kings", last 2 lines cancelled, followed by a 4-line revision (variant from printed texts): "And laughed aloud, & named this man & that/And welcomed all & praised their victory/ For he had heard that din on the horizon/And ridden towards it being ignorant". (Last line has been reinstated after its cancellation, above, save for punctuation).

P. 150 in THE HOUR-GLASS, ll. 334a–334e cancelled, in ink, and in margin: "Lati[n] –/A [circled]//Latin [in pencil beside cancelled l. 334e]." Passage clearly marked for replacement by insert – in effect, by the Latin translation provided for ll. 335–41 in *Wade* 136, PLAYS IN PROSE AND VERSE.

P. 151, ll. 345a–345e cancelled, entirely circumscribed, in ink, and attached to note: "Lati[n]/B [circled]//Latin [in pencil beside cancelled ll. 345d–e]". Passage replaced by Latin exchange in *Wade* 136, ll. 346–48.

P. 152, ll. 358–61, with revisions, circumscribed in ink with "C" (circled) beside; two other revisions for l. 361: "We are convinced of all you ha[ve] thou[ght]" and "Our bodies only were our mothers work" (or l. 345a, which was displaced by the Latin written for p. 151). This whole passage, marked for substitution as "A" and "B", is violently cancelled. Then 2nd half of l. 358 was revised: "Second Pupil/non iam pueri sumus" (also cancelled). Eventually, l. 358 is restored and WBY's Latin is given to First Pupil in l. 359. The "C" passage was replaced by the Latin exchange of ll. 359–62 in *Wade* 136.

2412d. Another copy. 1917 printing.

Clean except for dates by GY in Contents. Inserted letter and ms. have since been removed.

2413. ——. RESPONSIBILITIES AND OTHER POEMS. New York: Macmillan, 1916.

Revisions entered here bring the book into incomplete conformity with the London 1917 edition. However, the notations throughout "The Hour Before Dawn" mark where changes occurred in *Wade* 134, LATER POEMS.

P. 7 in "The Grey Rock", a pencil line between ll. 80 & 81. Stanza break never occurred at this location. This is 8 lines beyond the progress of revision marked in 2412c, above.

P. 52ff in "The Hour Before Dawn", lines "xed" stand for lines that are variant with *Wade* 134. Marking also designates new stanzas and, in one case, the place where stanzas were closed. Lines "xed" are 1, 3–4, 21–25, 27–28, 30, 33–37, 39–41, 44–48, 50–54, 56–57, 59–65, 67, 74, 91, 104, 116–21. These refs. are according to the numbering in this text, which is derived from *Wade* 134 (i.e., in the text of the revised and expanded poem); thus ll. 59 & 60 here are numbered "59" and "64". New stanzas per *Wade* 134 are indicated by "x" at the end of a line in margin, except one such break between ll. 106 & 107, which is closed in LATER POEMS. On p. 56, "time" is underscored with note in margin: "cf *line 74*". ("Time" is capitalized in l. 74).

P. 76, in "An Appointment," l. 8 has *not* been dropped in a substitution. "Nor heavy knitting of the brow" is the correct reading of the line *inserted after* l. 8, as per the revision made for RESPONSIBILITIES 1917. (See *YL* 2412 re p. 76, l. 9).

2413a. Another copy.

All but a few pages are cut.

2417.   ——. SELECTED POEMS. New York: Macmillan, 1921. *Wade* 128.

Flyleaf, WBY's signature and "4 Broad St./Oxford", fall beneath the cancelled inscription: "W S Nichol Service[?]/from W B Yeats/Nov 13 1921".

P. 137, l. 121 in "The Old Age of Queen Maeve," "terror strucken" to "terror stricken".

P. 145, l. 126ff of "Baile and Aillinn": ". . . he broke/then ran . . ." should be ". . . had broke/He ran. . . ." Revision follows *Wade* 134.

["The Old Age of Queen Maeve" and "Baile and Aillinn" were numbered in pencil at one time]'

P. 157, l. 17 of "Under the Moon", 2 versions entered in revision: the first is correct in *YL*; the second should be "Because of something told under the famished horn" (complete per *Wade* 134).

P. 158, ll. 14–17 in "Adam's Curse" rev. as per *Wade* 134; l. 18 variant as follows: "chimed for an answer 'all we women know . . .'" (essentially as noted in 2401, copytext for *Wade* 134).

2419.   ——. A SELECTION FROM THE POETRY OF W. B. YEATS. Leipzig: Bernhard Tauchnitz, 1913. *Wade* 103.

This was partial copytext for *Wade* 128, SELECTED POEMS (New York, 1921).

P. 7, in Contents, a note at top, in ink: "include all that is not marked 'omit'/WB Yeats". Poems marked "omit" on this page and notes for additions are accurate in *YL* except "also/note from/'Dramatic works.'"

P. 9, "The Ragged Wood" cancelled and marked "omit", in ink. "LYRICS (1904–1912)" revised to: ". . . (1904–1919)".

P. 10, before "NOTES," insertion of selected lyrics from remaining copytexts is indicated by an arrow from directions at bot., in ink: "add poems marked/in 'Responsibilities' & 'Wild Swans'/beginning with those in 'Responsibilities.'/WB Yeats".

Pp. 7–10 in Contents, numbers in pencil entered & circled in the margins, cancelled in ink; perhaps the original galley notations.

2444.   ——. THE WILD SWANS AT COOLE. London: Macmillan, 1919. *Wade* 124.

This is not the copy that joined 2419 and a marked copy of

RESPONSIBILITIES to make SELECTED POEMS (1921) nor the copytext for the 1920 revised printing of THE WILD SWANS AT COOLE. It did, however, contribute to one line in each, as noted in *YL*.

P. 29, l. 23 in "The Sad Shepherd" ["Shepherd and Goatherd"]: "pipes" > "pipe" (no printing follows).

P. 39 in "Lines Written in Dejection", slight changes in ll. 6 ("." > ";") and 7 (";" > ",") with ll. 8–9 cancelled and replaced, at foot, by:

> white in the white ~~bleached~~
> That ~~under the cold~~ moon beam shone   [no printing follows]
>   ^   ~~unconquered~~
> ~~That in the harsh moonlight shone,~~
> Banish my Mother^moon and vanished   [close to 1920 printing]

P. 39, l. 10: "And" rev. to "For" (cancelled) with "Ste[t].," left.

2444a. ——. THE WILD SWANS AT COOLE. London, 1920 (revised).

Revisions here provided partial copytext for *Wade* 134 (see notes above for 2401 and 2412a). This is not "another copy" of the 1919 first edition.

P. 1, "Wild Swans at Coole" marked: "C1".

P. 27, "The Sad Shepherd" marked: "C2".

P. 56, end of l. 30 in "His Phoenix," period added; revisions noted in *YL*, all per *Wade* 134 (save "out" in rev. of l. 26).

P. 72 marked: "C4".

2444b. ——. THE WILD SWANS AT COOLE. London, 1919.
&
2444c.

Descriptions confirmed.

REVIEWS

YEATS IN HIS LETTERS: A REVIEW ESSAY

John Kelly (ed.) and Eric Domville (assoc. ed.), *The Collected Letters of W. B. Yeats, Volume I: 1865-1895* (Oxford: Clarendon Press, 1986) pp. xlii + 548.

Reviewed by Phillip L. Marcus

This long-awaited first volume of the collected edition of Yeats's correspondence is an outstanding achievement. That the editorial task has taken so long is really not surprising, given the voluminous amount of material and the daunting process of locating, deciphering, dating and annotating that material. Archives and private collections on five continents have been searched, with results far beyond those anticipated. When complete, the *Collected Letters* is expected to run to at least twelve volumes and to contain nearly 7000 letters, eight times the number included in Allan Wade's edition of 1954. Letters are still coming to light, as witnessed by the two that turned up too late for inclusion in the text of this first volume and had to be relegated to the end of the book.

Volume I contains some 350 letters, nearly half of which are printed for the first time, and the editors indicate that the proportion of new material will increase in every subsequent volume. The advance over Wade is particularly dramatic for the year 1893, for which he included only three letters. The new edition offers twenty-four letters previously unpublished, as well as one that had previously appeared in a journal, and relocates three others that Wade had assigned to the preceding year. Dating is an exceptionally difficult task, as Yeats himself was so casual about it – there are twenty-two letters from 18, Woburn Buildings dated only "Tuesday", and even one headed "Feb. 30th" (x1,446). Here the editors of the collected edition have a distinct advantage over their predecessors: having so many *more* letters makes it easier for them to discover the clues that indicate sequence, and thus their judgment is to be preferred to Wade's. A valuable byproduct of their efforts is the detailed fourteen-page Chronology.

Insofar as possible, all previously published letters have been retranscribed from the originals. Given Yeats's notoriously difficult hand, which Brendan Kennelly has likened to "the havoc of an orgy of spiders on a plate full of ink", this scrupulousness is essential. For instance, although in general Wade did quite a good job, he has Yeats writing to AE in 1891, "I forgot *Tired*, I wish you would sent it me" (*L* 182; *CL11* 266). What Yeats actually wrote was "Tireil" – i.e., *Tiriel*. He had been studying it for the edition on which he was currently at work, and indeed in the same letter adds "I am now getting on with Blake & hope to get the book done before long." Anyone who has worked with Yeats's manuscripts will be quick to forgive such errors, though in this case the questionable existence of any plausibly relevant text entitled *Tired* should have been disquieting and in combination with the Blakean reference in the following paragraph might have pointed to the correct reading. Similarly, either Wade or the printer omitted "Oisin" from the list of works Yeats told his father would be included in Unwin's collection *Poems* (*L* 237; *CL1* 408, letter of 5 November 1894). In these and the other limited opportunities I have had to check the transcriptional accuracy of the editors of the *Collected Letters* they have earned my full confidence. The only fairly certain error in transcription I have found occurs in an 1895 letter to Standish James O'Grady (p. 472), where one of Yeats's carelessly placed crosses of a "t" looks enough like the dot of an "i" so that an interrogative "Is it . . ." has been transcribed as "It is . . ."; and even in this instance the initial word is so ill-formed that only the fact that the sense of the passage seems to demand a question provides sufficient incentive for the act of faith needed to read as "Is" what actually *looks like* "so".

Yeats was well aware of his poor handwriting, and also of his erratic spelling and idiosyncratic punctuation practices; more than once he expressed the desire that his letters should be amended before publication. Wade shared this feeling, and regularised those appearing in his edition. The editors of the *Collected Letters*, fearing that regularisation would have eliminated "much of the immediacy and personality" of Yeats's correspondence, have opted to "reproduce the physiognomy of his letters, orthographic warts and all" (xxvi). Their fidelity to the originals, while far greater than Wade's, has its limits. The reader is provided with discreet editorial assistance in the form of occasional silently inserted full stops, brackets, and inverted commas, as well as bracketed "intended readings" and queries of uncertain readings. I only noticed one instance in which such assistance seems necessary and has not been provided: in a letter apologising to Unwin for delayed and perhaps too extensive proof corrections, Yeats wrote "These few pages should not add appreciably to the expense & will not add at all to the necessary delay as it is would have in any case to see a second revise of the preface" (p. 466). Presumably Yeats through haste or because of the potentially delicate subject accidentally omitted an "I" between "is" and "would".

The editors' general practice has been to include "significant cancelled passages". It is possible to argue, of course, that almost any cancellation *could* be significant, even if only as an indicator of the writer's degree of concentration or involvement, and that preserving them all would be in keeping with the aim of fidelity to the characteristic flavour of Yeats's correspondence. Carrying the principle to such an extreme, however, would probably make reading through the resulting, cluttered text almost as laborious as reading the originals. And typography can only indicate up to a certain point the features of holograph material. Scholars will still sometimes need to work with the original documents, to examine the papers and inks used (which offer possible clues to biographical information and even to the dating of concurrently written literary texts), to check the transcription of crucial readings, and even to scan the author's hand for features that betray emotional states or a mind grappling with complicated ideas or the feelings of his correspondents. To facilitate this, the editors have identified (as Wade did not) the location of each letter except those in private hands. The overall effect of the transcription principles and procedures is to make the volume more valuable to scholars than its predecessor without significantly lessening its potential appeal to other readers.

Some readers, scholarly and general alike, may object to the extraordinary fullness of the annotation, and especially the amount of detail the notes contain about persons other than Yeats. The editors' justification of their practice is that "chronologically the letters interweave to give the close texture of a full and creative life. Such a texture makes itself felt in the wealth of allusions and names with which the letters abound as he attempts to 'hammer' into unity apparently disparate but earnestly pursued interests. For this reason, it was . . . obvious that the edition must be amply annotated. For a writer who saw Unity of Being as a central goal it seems appropriate that passing references should not only be satisfactorily explained but also located in the wider context of his life and work" (xlii). This relationship of notes to text is well exemplified by a letter of 1888 in which Yeats tells Katharine Tynan "I am going to Lady Wildes reception this afternoon. She was not visable – being not yet up needing as the servent put it 'a great deel of rest' when I called last Sunday afternoon. I wonder if I shall find her as delightful as her book – as delightful as she is certainly unconventional" (p. 87). Wade did not footnote the passage. Kelly and Domville gloss it with a reference to a diary kept by Lily Yeats, who sometimes accompanied her brother on visits there, and "marvelled at the many cameo brooches worn by their hostess, greeting her guests at the door of the reception room. Red-paper-covered lamps gave 'a kind of lowering twilight', and tea was handed round by two elderly Irish maids who knew everyone, Lady Wilde having an antipathy to smart English servants". This note nicely captures the atmosphere Yeats would encounter in the salon of the venerable Young Ireland poet and even reveals the point of his quotation from the servant, whose Irishness and familiarity he had been subtly alluding to. Taken together, the notes to the volume help build up a vivid picture of Yeats's world – especially his London – in the 'eighties and 'nineties. Moreover, because the editors have so diligently explored the immense archive of Yeats family papers and other sources such as the papers of Katharine Tynan and various publishers' records, the annotations constitute a valuable reference source for other scholars wishing to pursue questions further than the notes themselves can.

The degree of accuracy in the notes is very high, and I noted only the barest handful of slips: the date of Ferguson's *Lays of the Western Gael* is given as 1864 on page 13 and (correctly) as 1865 on page 52; the letter on page 129 appears only on page 103 (not pages 102–3) in Wade; on pages 347 and 391, the comma after *Homeward* in the title of AE's volume should be deleted; in note 2 on page 371; "Grattan" is misspelled in its second occurrence; on page 375, "this letter to

WBY" should presumably read "this letter from WBY"; the letter dated "Feb 20th" on p. 77 is said on p. xi to be dated "Feb 31". Note 4 on page 400 is correct, but would be strengthened by addition of the information that Maud Gonne translated de Jubainville's French for Yeats (Samuel Levenson, *Maud Gonne* [New York: Reader's Digest Press, 1976], p. 392).

To reduce the need for particularly bulky notes on figures and organisations of major importance in Yeats's early life, the editors have added forty pages of capsule sketches in a "Biographical and Historical Appendix" that, like the Chronology, is valuable for its own sake as a rich and accurate repository of information.

The legitimacy of such interests for literary critics is frequently challenged these days, of course. Much contemporary academic attention has been directed towards problems of the indeterminacy of language and consequently towards literary "theory" itself and away from texts and their authors. But those who have not abandoned the human perspective, who continue to believe that the "life" and "work" constitute an interdependent whole and that the judicious critic can effect the complex transaction of describing the relationship, will probably make extensive use of letters – verbal constructs that exist in a space somewhere between the bundle of accident and incoherence that sits down to the breakfast table and the author's formal *oeuvre*. The appeal is especially great with correspondence such as Yeats's, which provides also a rich and full record of the growth of his literary ideas as well as his own running commentary on his intentions and practice as a writer. The way in which letters might figure in the process of effecting such transactions is illustrated graphically by the fascinating letter to "Mary Cronin", now demoted from first to third in the order of the surviving correspondence but still the earliest in which Yeats writes *consciously* as a poet:

> I send you the verses you asked for I have very few poem under a great many hundred lines but of those that I have this is the shortest and most most intelligible. its subject was suggested by <my last visit to the Monday evening> my last two visits to Kilrock. I am afraid you will not much care for it – not being used to my peculearitys which will never be done justice to and until they have become classics and are set for examinations.

> Yours truly
> W B Yeats

PS as you will see my great aim is directness and extreme simplicity.

> A flower has blossomed, the world heart core
> The petels and leves were a mo[o]n white flame
> A gathred the flower, the <soul> colourless lore
> The aboundant meadow of fate and fame
> Many men gathers and few may use
> T[he] secret oil and the sacret cruse

> (pp. 5, 7)

The editors in their excellent "General Introduction" seem to take the postscript at face value (p. xxxvi). It is true that there may be an element of prophetic seriousness of vocation in the reference to the poems becoming classics and being set for examinations, but in any case the archness of the reference shows that he felt he could expect his correspondent to appreciate a joke. He had said of the poem enclosed that it was not only his shortest lyric but also his "most intelligible" and that it contained "peculearitys" that might keep Mrs Cronin from appreciating it; thus there is already a discrepancy between letter and postscript. The editors speculate that the poem, which was written on the verso of the draft letter, may not have been the one actually sent. On the other hand, it does share some of the key concerns of the letter: fame ("classics"), and a sacred rite kept apart from the great mass of men – to whom consequently it must seem obscure and "peculiar". (Was *this* poem perhaps written as a *further response* to thoughts the letter had raised in his mind?) Even allowing for obscurities arising from editorial difficulties in transcription (there are six variants from Wade, who gave this one text *literatim*), this poem could scarcely have been offered as an exemplification of "directness and extreme simplicity". If it was the poem he sent, the postscript surely has to be taken ironically, as the internal contradiction noted above may in any case require. Yeats, then, was able to see a humorous side to the difficulties his work presented.

And yet we know that at times in his early years (as well as later) Yeats did yearn to write a simple, easily intelligible poetry. Is it *possible*, then, to see the postscript as sincere? To do so requires what may well be an overelaborate hypothetical reconstruction of events. We must posit that after writing the draft letter, intended to accompany an obscure poem (the one now on the verso, or another) and thus having no postscript, he was led by reflection on the problem of unintelligibility to an effort to reach the larger audience of which his correspondent was typical and wrote a *new* poem, unlike his previous lyrics in reflecting "directness and extreme simplicity" so successfully that Mary Cronin *would* see that this had been his aim. The postscript would then have been added to the original draft letter, though not in fact reconcilable with it, and he would have produced and sent a revised letter consistent with the accompanying poem. In that case, the surviving draft would suggest not irony but Yeats's famously antithetical imagination moving in a new direction. And if the lines inscribed on the verso of the draft letter were a further response to the contrast between his other lyrics and the suppositious new one, then "A flower has blossomed . . ." dramatises the pendulum's swing to the other extreme and may represent a (temporary) conscious choice of the esoteric course even though it meant inevitable obscurity.

For purposes of analysing Yeats's thought and charting its development, we obviously have to have the most complete record possible. Although William of Ockham would make short work of the hypothesis of sincerity involving the postscript, some private collection or overlooked archive could at any time yield up a currently unknown document that would support it. Wade's edition includes a letter Yeats wrote to his sister Lily on 20 January 1895, beginning "I have read Miss Hopper & like her" (*L* 244–6; *CL1* 426–9). Working nearly two decades ago on the Yeats–Nora Hopper relationship I came across in the Houghton Library at Harvard a second, then-unpublished letter of the same date, this one to Katharine Tynan. Because in this one he began with and seemed more troubled by Miss Hopper's apparent plagiarisms from her work and his, I concluded that he had written it first. But even in it he showed himself genuinely attracted by her work and determined for the purpose of adding another to his recruits for the "Irish literary movement" to see it in the best possible light (*CL1* 425–6); and by the time he wrote to Lily he had grown so positive that he declared himself anxious to find a place in which to review the book.

A letter of 27 January 1895, published for the first time in the new edition, adds some crucial information to the story of their relationship. Moved by a combination of his own admiration and insinuations of plagiarism in a *Daily Express* review of *Ballads in Prose*, Yeats now wrote directly to Miss Hopper, whom he had apparently never met:

> Our Irish literature is yet so small, & what work of sublety & style it possesses is so inconsiderable, that I cannot resist the pleasure of writing to tell you of the great pleasure your exquizite book has given me. It is the most finished, the most distinguished volume we have had out of Ireland this decade. It has given me great pleasure to find by stray words & sentences that my own little collections of Irish folk lore have been of use to you. I put them to gether, for no other purpose what ever than to help what I beleive to be a growing school of legendary literature, to fling off the rhetoric of '48' & put on the humility & wisdom of the ancient world. I say this because I am told that one of the Dublin papers, while admitting your literary power, has said something about your 'copying' or 'plagiarising' from some thing of mine; & I want you therefore to know how much I admire your book. I shall take every oppertunity . . . to introduce your book to Irish journalists & readers. (*CL1* 432)

The anonymous reviewer's position was essentially the same as Yeats's had been in the letters of the 20 January. The repeated "pleasures" may seem to protest too much, and Yeats's wording adroitly sidesteps a *denial* of the charge; but it is hard not to feel that he had genuinely convinced himself of its injustice. *Writing directly to Miss Hopper* was in effect an act of identification with her against such criticisms; and he lived up to his promise by propagandising on her behalf for the rest of the century.

There is a further interesting contrast with the Tynan letter, in which, enmeshed as he currently was in arguing with Dowden that the best contemporary Irish literature had eschewed the stylistic weaknesses of Young Ireland propagandistic verse, he referred to Miss Hopper's use of the folklore anthologies he had compiled "that they might influence Irish literature & help lift it out of rhetoric". The comparable sentence in the letter to Miss Hopper herself significantly adds the phrase about putting on "the humility & wisdom of the ancient world". That a modern literature based on the early Irish legends and the folk tradition stemming from them could help the fallen world recover the values of a prelapsarian Golden Age was an ideal Yeats had suggested in his first published essay:

> Sir Samuel Ferguson's special claim to our attention is that he went back to the Irish cycle [of legends], finding it, in truth, a fountain that, in the passage of centuries, was overgrown with weeds and grass, so that the very way to it was forgotten of the poets; but now that his feet have worn the pathway, many others will follow, and bring thence living waters for the healing of our nation, helping us to live the larger life of the Spirit, and lifting our souls away from their selfish joys and sorrows to be the companions of those who lived greatly among the woods and hills when the world was young. ("The Poetry of Sir Samuel Ferguson," *Irish Fireside*, 9 Oct. 1886, p. 220; *UP1*, 82)

He had been exploring this ideal ever since, and would continue to do so until the very end of his life, when it informed "The Statues" and *The Death of Cuchulain*. He may have been silent about it in the earlier letter out of deference to Miss Tynan's devout Catholicism; Miss Hopper, by contrast, he apparently felt he could count on to contribute to the process of restoration.

Yet another unpublished letter, written to Yeats's father a few days later, reveals that Miss Hopper wrote back a warm acknowledgment of Yeats's praise at the same time he had received a letter from George Sigerson repeating the assertions of plagiarism:

> Sigerson writes to me to say that her verse is an exact imitation of my own & of Mrs Hinkson's. Curiously enough I can see the resemblance to Mrs Hinkson, & in one place to Hyde, but not to my self. I suppose however one cannot recognise ones own manner. I do see however that she has taken a good many names & allusions from my folklore books, & that two or three of her plots are suggested by my things. (*CL1* 436)

Having previously come to grips with his feelings, he dismissed the new criticism with almost comic ease. But the closeness he now so readily accepted had other ramifications as well. In the same letter he went on to speak of his discouragement over the slow progress of his own work, including *The Shadowy Waters*. A letter of three months earlier reveals the sort of difficulties he was experiencing with that play: "In my struggle to keep it concrete I fear I shall so over load it with legendary detail that it will be unfit for any theatrical purpose . . ." (*CL1* 407). As early as the letter to Katharine Tynan he had noted about Miss Hopper that "her great lack is solidity & lucidity" and later in 1895 he offered as his sole reservation about her work that "here and there there is too much of filmy vagueness, as in visions in the wizard's glass, before the mystical sweeper has swept the clouds away with his broom" ("Irish National Literature. Contemporary Prose Writers," *Bookman*, Aug. 1895, p. 140; *UP1* 370). As a working writer, therefore, he must, despite all his sincere praise, have found Miss Hopper's work (in which the legends had failed to provide adequate concreteness) an incarnation of one of his own negative impulses and thus an example to be avoided. The juxtaposition in this letter was almost certainly accidental rather than subliminal, but reminds us nevertheless how complex at any given time was the interplay among the various elements in Yeats's imagination.

The process by which he developed his own thought and vision through encounters with the work of others is further dramatized by the 1895 letter to O'Grady, whose retellings of the story of Cú Chulainn had not only helped Yeats discover the virtues of the legendary material but had also made him aware of the importance of the Irish "bardic order" in creating that literature and bringing the ideals embodied in it to bear upon their society and thereby influencing its development. (This was an image of the poet destined to appeal to him far more than the posthumous scholasticism envisioned in the early letter to Mary Cronin). In an 1895 article Yeats, though praising O'Grady as the best of modern Irish prose writers, had detected elements of nationalist feeling at a period in Irish history when the Unionist O'Grady had seen only the clash of an old order with a new, the Irish petty chieftains of the sixteenth century warring with each other rather than presenting a united front to the Elizabethan invaders. When O'Grady charged Yeats with anachronism, Yeats defended his view with an argument O'Grady's own early work had helped him to formulate. He cited the Gaelic poem "O'Byrne's Bard to the Clans of Wicklow" partly because with its reference to "Erin's foes" it seemed to embody a "national" or (as Yeats was willing to rephrase himself) "racial" hatred; but partly also because, set in the later sixteenth century, it represented the discordant clans of Wicklow exhorted to unity by O'Byrne's bard himself. Thus the poem was offered as evidence to support Yeats's queried hypothesis that "while the racial unity of England expressed itself in a method of government, the racial unity of Ireland expressed it self in things like the bardic order & in popular instincts & prejudices. That while the English nobles therefore expressed English racial purpose at its best, the Irish nobles, warped by their little princedoms & their precarious dynasties were more for themselves & less for Ireland, than the bards, & harpers & the masses of the people?" (*CL1* 471–3.) By this point in his career Yeats had encountered powerful opposition from his Nationalist allies over his role in the controversy with Gavan Duffy and criticisms he made during and after that affair of Young Ireland literature. His own patriotism thus impugned, Yeats found an increasing attractiveness in the view that the bardic order had itself been the key force behind the emergence of Irish national or racial feeling and that he more than the Young Irelanders (who in general made little use of legendary and folk materials) was their legitimate heir. The need for such a belief was to grow in him as the number and vehemence of his enemies increased. The letter to O'Grady could almost be said to constitute an embryonic scenario for *The King's Threshold* (written in 1903), in which the poets assert their rightful predominance over the nobles and through their songs filled with Edenic images usher in "the great race that is to come". One of his immediate sources for the play, Edwin Ellis's *Sancan the Bard*, he had recommended to Katharine Tynan earlier in the same year as the letter to O'Grady, in the very letter in which he had asked her to lend him Nora Hopper's *Ballads in Prose*. In the light of his exchange with O'Grady, Hopper's use of the Irish legends, and his own, can thus be seen to have another level of significance, a link with the bardic order. The letter to O'Grady went on to praise O'Grady's version of the story of Cú Chulainn's death as "not less than any epic tale in the world". Yeats's own version of that story, in his last play, ended with the image of the artist, a last inheritor of the bardic tradition, recreating the legend once again in order to restore that "most ancient race":

> No body like his body
> Has modern woman borne,
> But an old man looking back on life
> Imagines it in scorn[.]

The process of accretion exemplified in the instances I have explored here will grow more richly textured with every succeeding volume of the *Collected Letters*. Splendidly begun, the edition must inevitably come to be recognised as a fitting record of one of the greatest, most fascinating creative minds in history, one of those few, in Eliot's words, "whose history is the history of their own time, who are a part of the consciousness of an age which cannot be understood without them". We await, with even more anticipation, volume II.

Sandra F. Siegel (ed.), *'Purgatory': Manuscript Materials Including the Author's Final Text by W. B. Yeats* The Cornell Yeats (Ithaca and London: Cornell University Press, 1986) pp. xi + 222.

Reviewed by Richard Allen Cave

A first glance might suggest we possess a peculiarly full array of materials from which to reconstruct the creative process that went to the shaping of *Purgatory*: scenarios; a sketch for a possible stage-setting; two verse drafts; four typescripts with holograph revisions; page-proofs corrected by Yeats of the ill-fated Longford edition of *On The Boiler* in which the play was designed to appear first but which was abandoned and, with the exception of a handful of copies, destroyed at Mrs Yeats's request after the poet's death; the Alex. Thom edition of *On The Boiler*; and the Cuala *Last Poems and Two Plays* of 1939. However, the complex and messy publishing history of the play and the absence of two crucial and related items complicate matters considerably. Composition of *Purgatory* as with *The Death of Cuchulain* was remarkably intense. The scenarios create with surprising fullness the plot-line of the play which underwent little change as the initial idea was realised as a dramatic text; amplification and revision were directed at character-delineation primarily; the quality of the handwriting suggests composition in energetic bursts. The manuscript materials intimate an acute imaginative engagement on Yeats's part – an excitement growing out of sustained reverie. Soon after the play's conception Yeats sensed its relation to the pattern of ideas that had gone into the writing of *On The Boiler*, which he was completing alongside the drafting of the drama between March and May of 1938. A decision to stage *Purgatory* at the Abbey with a revival of *On Baile's Strand* in that August seems to have clarified in Yeats's mind the decision to publish the play and essay together to coincide with the performances so that audiences might read *Purgatory* as well as see it and above all else set the play in the intellectual continuum in which it was conceived. Haste was clearly essential if that objective was to be realised, but at this point Yeats gave a copy of the manuscript to F. R. Higgins to arrange the printing; Higgins failed to appreciate the urgency of the situation and offered the material to Longford, a printer who had little experience of publications of this kind. Sandra Siegel dates this as occuring at the end of June. From here the confusions begin.

The play was staged as planned to largely adverse critical reaction, which the availability of a text might have checked; but the edition was not ready. More performances were prepared for early December and again possibly in the New Year and Yeats repeated through the autumn and winter to Higgins his wish that the edition be ready for publication to coincide with these revivals. Yeats received and corrected galleys and a first set of page proofs at uncertain dates (he was of course wintering abroad); but his hopes were still not realised. What is interesting in all this is Yeats's insistence regarding the Abbey's revivals of the production: "I want *Purgatory* played from 'On The Boiler' *version* (my italics)." Sandra Siegel quotes this hitherto unpublished letter from Yeats to Higgins dated 24 December 1938 which is now in the possession of the Humanities Research Center at Austin, Texas; but she does not explore its possible implications regarding the extant material.

Four typescripts survive, here labelled TS4, TS5, TS6 and TS7 to reflect the catalogue-references in the National Library of Ireland. Professor Siegel convincingly argues that their chronological ordering should be TS6, TS4, TS5 and TS7; only the last two are reproduced in this volume, TS5 being considered the best version in relation to the subsequent printing history of the play. By piecing together bits of information which Professor Siegel records but does not comment on, it seems clear that TS4 has potentially an unusual and distinctive status. Compared with the other typescripts it has, we are told, been much folded – "in half once horizontally and then folded once again. It also bears a crease mark from having been folded vertically in half". Later in a section headed "Notes on Textual Problems in TSS 5, 6, and 4" we learn that TS4 has throughout a number of stage directions written in pencil, "possibly in Yeats's hand" which "suggest that this typescript might have been used as a rehearsal text". If so, this would have to have been for the first production at the Abbey in August 1938, as Yeats was out the country during subsequent stagings by the company in his lifetime. That this supposition is more than likely is strengthened by the nature of the directions themselves which are quite different from the stage directions ultimately printed in the play or for that matter in any other play by Yeats in its published format, in that they are couched in the standard abbreviations used by actors and directors in rehearsal: "X to LC", for example, meaning "Crosses to Left Centre-Stage"; "X to boy"; "X to R". Whether or not the hand is Yeats's as seems likely, this copy of the typescript has clearly been used during rehearsals. The much-creased condition of the pages would further support this supposition.

Professor Siegel dates TS5 as later than TS4; it shows holograph cancellations in ink of lines which are deleted apparently in TS4 in *pencil*, the medium in which the directions are written. TS5 contains the latest substantial holograph revisions to the text; they are few but in dramatic terms they are crucial and immensely powerful in effect; they almost all relate to the characterisation of the Boy. Throughout the scenarios and the manuscript verse drafts Yeats concentrates on clarifying his perception of the Old Man's mind; and the Boy with his questions seems to exist as a convenient vehicle to stimulate his father to further musing. This rather colourless account of the Boy's character (if he is anything, he is fearful and morose) survives into the *unrevised* TS5. The revisions are small but they transform the Boy into a lively, quick-witted youth. The correction of the third line of his opening speech from "Holding up this old pack" to "Hill or hollow, shouldering this pack" has greater actuality of physical effort, while "Hill or hollow" in echoing the pattern established by "Half door, hall door / Hither and thither, day and night" enforces the sense of the Boy's resistence to the seemingly endless drudgery of their life together. Having succinctly established this state of mind, Yeats then revises the flat, disinterested question that formed his next speech – "What do you know about this place?" – which half-heartedly responds to the Old Man's observations about the ruins they find themselves among, into a question tense with expectation showing the Boy has a sharp mind: "So you have come this path before?" He suddenly apprehends their wandering may not be as aimless as he has supposed. This establishes the Boy's independence and anticipates an uncertainty which will be a source of much of the play's tension: is the Old Man acting throughout on impulse? or following through a previously determined plan or ritual? Further revisions firstly tighten up the Old Man's imagined account of the night of his conception by removing circumstantial details about the situation of the various rooms in the mansion which formerly slackened the tension; and then strengthen the Boy's growing awareness that some weird patterning of events involving a logic of parallel situations is being worked out (he catches up his father's reference to being sixteen when the first murder was accomplished and his original line – "And that's my age" – is extended to "But that's my age, sixteen years old / At the Puck Fair"). The next change is a substantial addition to the events leading up to the second murder: as the two men struggle with the bag and spill the money, the Boy now threatens his father and in terms that, though impulsively uttered, commit him to the determining cycles of fate that obsess the Old Man – "What if I killed you? You killed my granddad / Because you were young & he was old. / Now I am young & you are old". This gives greater dramatic point and momentum to the Boy's sudden seeing of the ghost ("A dead living murdered buried man") he has believed a figment of his father's crazed imagination. The terror implicit in the addition is rooted in metaphysical apprehensions and by a further addition Yeats renders with even greater immediacy the psychological shock the youth is experiencing in seeing manifested before him a figure "That was a bundle of old bones / Before I was born". In the unrevised typescript the Boy simply sees the lighted window and the ghost while the two men squabble over the pack and in terrified silence meets his death; in these revisions his sudden awareness of the inexorable and determining pattern of events as his true "inheritance" from the ruined house and his ancestors culminates in his great cry of "Horrible! Horrible!". The revisions make for a dynamic climax by giving the role of the Boy greater psychological interest and development that enhances the growing irony and pathos of the conclusion.

Now: the holograph revisions to TS5 on Professor Siegel's dating are later than TS4, which in all likelihood was used as a rehearsal script. What was the text played at the first production at the Abbey? Was the text of TS4 used? If so, were the revisions made on TS5 a consequence of the play going into production? Or were the changes made during the rehearsal period? There is ample evidence relating to earlier plays that Yeats regularly effected changes in response to his experience of the texts in rehearsal and/or performance, sharpening the dramatic impact. Did Yeats give an *unrevised* typescript to Higgins (which was then passed to Longford and set); then revise the play in the light of his experience of *Purgatory* in performance on TS5 and TS7 and enter the changes on the galley-proofs when he received them sometime late in September? This would account for his reiterated anxiety that subsequent revivals be played from the "On The Boiler" *version*. Professor Siegel just assumes that TS5 was revised before the first production and that TS5 was a copy of the text set by Longford; but she does not offer us the reasoning behind this assumption. Moreover this leaves wholly unexplained many interesting facets about the extant material, particularly concerning TS4, which she chooses, sadly, not to present in facsimile and transcription. While the typescripts can be set in order, they cannot be precisely dated, of course; and the really crucial document in the history of the play's publication is the one that is missing: Yeats's corrected galley-proofs, which would establish which specific text (also missing) was given by Higgins to the printers and when precisely the all-important final revisions were made. Professor Siegel handles the intricate history of *Purgatory* well, but I would argue the evolution of the play as we know it is *potentially* more intricate and exciting than her own interpretation of her splendid editorial work suggests.

The transcriptions and bibliographical details are as meticulously done here as in Professor Marcus's exemplary edition of *The Death of Cuchulain*, its predecessor in The Cornell Yeats. Impressive too is Professor Siegel's introductory account of the relationship between *Purgatory* and the ideas explored in *On The Boiler*, especially of the way the play opens up for discussion much of the argument in the essay about Sophocles' Oedipus plays, which, after the staging of Yeats's versions at the Abbey, seem to have been a powerful inspirational force in the last decade of his career. Like Professor Marcus, Professor Siegel chooses sensitively to intimate ways in which the reader may interpret the growth and revising of the text rather than attempt a detailed exposition. This nicely matches Yeats's way with the play which is to rework the material so that it affects the audience as a process of discovery through imaginative engagement with the two characters. At first the scenarios and drafts warn the audience that all the characters are evil and the Old Man sits relentlessly in judgement on himself as polluted. Revision enhanced instead the patterning of events, namely that the Old Man is reiterating his own "transgression" in murdering a second time even as he imagines his parents are renewing their guilt and that he is adding to the burden of consequence following on from his mother's ill-judged marriage, not redeeming the past as he hopes. The patterning achieved particular force and a suitably grim tragic decorum once Yeats had decided on stabbing rather than strangulation for the murders: "My father and my son on the same jack knife". This gives the idea of the cycles of inherited corruption a more hideous because physical immediacy than lines originally conceived like "Father and son evil after evil and I my self / Evil upon evil pollution of her blood". Another major and decisive change relates to tone. In the scenario and initial drafting the Old Man is impassioned, excitable, impulsive, his nerves at full stretch. Not only would this make for too unrelieved an intensity in performance, difficult for an actor to sustain, it also implied too soon the Old Man's deranged condition which would incline an audience to assume a detached, critical stance from the first. The revisions slowly lower the tone, suppressing the intensity of feeling; the Old Man's manner becomes reasoning, thoughtful, so that only gradually is his logic perceived to be the lethal force it proves in time. The murder of his father as recounted by him has none of the spontaneity of the actual event; through the passage of time and the workings of memory and conscience the Old Man has found a way of justifying the crime to himself by investing it with the status of ritual. Only one carefully selected verb – "I *stuck* him with a knife" – and the grotesque detail – "That knife that cuts my dinner now" – conveys any sense of the bloody reality. The horror and the pathos of the play as finally realised lie in our perception of the dangerous divorce that exists in the Old Man's mind between thought and feeling, which the Boy, who at first to our surprise is inclined laughingly to dismiss his father's talk as mad, understands only when it is too late to save himself from the consequences. The brilliance of the play in performance lies in the way Yeats controls his audiences' responses such that, like the Boy, they perceive where the Old Man's ritualising habit of mind and his obsession with consequences is all tending, just seconds before his knife strikes out again. The Old Man's logic is a mask covering with an air of plausibility an all-consuming madness. What is remarkable about the composition of *Purgatory* is that Yeats clearly knew from the first that the play had to be compressed, succinctly achieved, for the maximum effectiveness: at no point, not even in the first scenario, did he set out past events as in any way distinct from present developments; the enveloping net of consequence enmeshing past, present and future in its treacherous coils was always his subject. He did not work through revision to achieve a compression; the subject presented itself to his imagination in its full intricacy. (One recalls "Those masterful images [that] because complete / Grew in pure mind" of "The Circus Animals' Desertion".) Yeats's objective in shaping his initial inspiration towards realisation on the stage was clearly to engross the spectator's imagination and make the play performed, like a reading of the edition he planned for *On The Boiler*, a voyage of discovery about individual perception and the shaping pressures of time which we call destiny.

Peter Sacks, *The English Elegy: Studies in the Genre from Spenser to Yeats*. (Baltimore: Johns Hopkins University Press, 1985) 328pp + notes + index.

Reviewed by Roy J. Booth

"Studies" might give a misleading idea of Peter Sacks's impressive book, which is really a unified study of the genre, consistent in its approach to the poems considered. It is not a survey of "elegy", but an attempt to interpret the conventions of the genre, to approach the "core of loss". The elegies selected are subjected to an investigation that is psychologically based; intended to reveal patterns, instinctual rather than formal, of resumed song, anger in bereavement, assimilated grief and consolation. Sacks's book is made interesting by his willingness to try his approach on less obvious poems – elegy in the form of epigram (Jonson), or lyric (Hardy), alongside the full scale monodies.

It is a long book: for instance, the author likes if possible to quote, stanza by stanza, or section by section, whole poems ("Lycidas"; "Ave atque Vale"; "In memory of Major Robert Gregory"). The argument, depending upon psychological process, allows no anticipations or ransacking. Measured progress is made through the poems.

Sacks essentially sees elegies as recapitulations of an original loss. The work of mourning is referred to the infant's voluntary relinquishment of the primary object of desire, the mother, in the admission of the power of another authority, the father (associated with time, death, even with the recourse to language). Finding a substitute for the mother, and taking on a separate identity from her are other elements of the "core of loss" Sacks sees recapitulated in elegy. In elegies, the mourner controls again a grief like the first grief, discovers a later target for anger, comes through another phase when the outward-going emotions, having nowhere to attach, become limited to the self. Sacks extends his discussion into vegetation myth: the treatment of the deceased in elegy parallels the way in which ritual has figured its related instances of loss, retribution and consolation. The vegetation god, "the predecessor of almost every elegised subject", springs from, and returns to regeneration in the mother-matrix.

An elegy then reaches back to the infant's cry of abandonment when the mother accedes to the infant's renunciation of its own desire; it is the veil of words which first hid the primary forbidden desire, and now hides the dead who regress to that re-unified state.

The author of another recent book on this subject, G. W. Pigman III (*Grief and English Renaissance Elegy*) is a "practicing psychoanalytic counselor". Sacks has at least the manner of a psychotherapist leading a patient back, gently but persistently. In a single paragraph (p. 28) our hand is held and we are drawn on with a sequence of sentences starting with or turning around such phrases as these: "From either perspective then. . . . To put it simply. . . . Now however . . . it is worth noting. . . . Indeed, as we shall see. . . . But whether. . . . Perhaps needless to add." This is extreme, but characteristic. Inevitably, everyone will have a point where they want to resist ("The totem thus became the symbolic tool for societal reproduction"). But even when Sack's pattern has become predictable, his insight is startlingly persuasive in application – the transition from section 54 of 'In Memoriam' ("what am I? / An infant crying in the night . . . with no language but a cry") to the denunciation of (mother) nature red in tooth and claw in section 56; the transition in "Lycidas" from female to male addressees (all of them fictions that "make up or evoke a presence where there is none"); Hardy "conjuring and banishing" his wife in *Poems 1912–13*, related here to Freud's observation of his grandson's "fort-da" game played to master maternal absences, or "travelling the immense distance from 'Woman' to 'the woman' in 'The Voice.' " In their context, these readings do suggest no random search, but the posited pattern turning up in the investigations of the man who knows where to look.

Among the characteristics of elegy Sacks considers is the apparent use of elegy for displays of artistic virtuosity, as an opportunity to surpass: Milton exhausting a genre in "Lycidas", Shelley seeing in "Adonais" something "better in point of composition than anything I have written", Yeats with his "long poem in memory of Robert Gregory, which is among my best works". For Sacks, consolation in the elegy depends upon celebration of the power of the father, and assimilation of it in motifs of ingestion, absorption or inheritance of a dead man's power. He traces the relation of elegy to eclogue, the singing match or contest. From Colin Clout's faltering claim to be the true heir to the poetic legacy of Chaucer, to Swinburne ostentatiously emulating the synaesthesia of Baudelaire, and Hardy in his turn absorbing the power of Swinburne (in "A Singer Asleep"), Sacks stresses the way that "few elegies can be fully read without an appreciation of their frequently combative struggles for inheritance".

Perhaps the most interesting account of a poet confronting the illustrious dead is chapter 10, on Yeats's "In Memory of Major Robert Gregory". Yeats's first poem was "Shepherd and Goatherd", "like that Spenser wrote for Sir Philip Sidney". After this "chilly impersonation", as Sacks calls it, Yeats looked for a non-pastoral Renaissance model for elegiac emulation. As O. B. Hardison has pointed out, the elegy for the Renaissance was often a poem of praise, as much of grief. Indeed there are poems that might be called *aretological*, discoursing of *arete*, excellence, and this was the theme and effect Yeats wanted. In this context of the

consummate abilities of the deceased, and the attempted assimilation of it by the
mourner, Sacks defends the *rightness* of the stanza Yeats added to the poem at the
request of Robert Gregory's wife:

> The stanza (8) . . . begins the work of recuperating and amalgamating, in the
> figure of Gregory, the different virtues of the other three dead men. The pacing
> of the lines is superb and further stresses Yeats's aesthetic imitation of
> Gregory's headlong drive, his recklessness and mastery. . . . After the painful
> "falling", "dying", "much travelling" and "having grown sluggish", these
> lines soar with an apparent release of pent-up energy. They refer, after all, to
> uncurbing, leaping, racing without a bit – all images of unchecked desire.

The rest of Sacks's discussion relates the stanza to the "primitive origins and
functions of the genre"; the reverence due to a deity whose energies release the
desire inhibited in the mourner. In these lines and throughout, the *ménage* of the
long stanza, copied, as Frank Kermode pointed out in his *Romantic Image*, from
Cowley's poem "On the death of Mr. William Hervey", is Yeats's double
emulation, of Gregory's controlling skill, and that of the predecessor poet.

   In the discussion of poets and their predecessors, as critics too have their
anxieties of influence, Harold Bloom is allowed no closer than a series of
footnotes. Occasionally, Sacks seems to have chosen the poetic influences upon
his poets narrowly. Surely Shakespearean lamentations for the drowned impinge
more formatively upon "Lycidas" than "The Shepheardes Calender"? Tying
Yeats's elegy to Cowley's is perhaps another case. Cowley's poem is uneven.
Beside the splendour of its varied refrain line, it is also a youthfully sentimental
poem on the loss of a "sweet companion", stressing the pious virtues of its
scholar-subject, who dies pathetically, "Infectious Death" forbidding the
Mourners a farewell kiss. Simultaneously, Cowley's is a poem like Cleveland's
upon Edward King, written in the tradition of witty elegy, a university poem
working hyperbolical conceits upon its subject's learning ("We have lost in him
Arts that not yet are *found*") and precosity ("Thou *Ripe*, and yet thy *Life* but
Green!").

   Sacks says that Fulke Greville's elegy for Sidney (*Spenser*, ed. de Selincourt
p. 559, l. 8) contributed the phrase "a world's delight" to Yeats's poem (St 9).
Perhaps Yeats appreciated that he was repeating a repetition, for Greville was
seconding the Countess of Pembroke's phrase (*Spenser*, p. 549, l. 49,) in the
"Doleful Lay of Clorinda". It does suggest that Yeats was "casting about among
the personal elegies of the Renaissance" (as Frank Kermode put it) to elegise
"*Our* Sidney and our perfect man". But rather than settling upon Cowley's poem
as a non pastoral Renaissance elegy, didn't Yeats go to *the* poem in which an
older man describes the excellence possible in the intensely lived short life, *the*
display of artistically mature virtuosity: Ben Jonson's Cary-Morison Ode? Here
we find the quality by which Sacks distinguishes Yeats's poems from Cowley's,
the "driving through stanzas with an extraordinary momentum", and a pivoting
from long-lived lethargy to the soldier and virtuous son: "all offices were done by

him. . . . Nothing perfect done / But as a Cary, or a Morison", like Gregory's "all he did done perfectly" after "old George Pollexfen". Yeats's 11th stanza must imitate the effect of epigram-within-elegy of Jonson's famous "It is not growing like a tree" stanza.

Both T. McAlindon (*PMLA*, 82, 1967, pp. 168–9) and Daniel Harris (in his *Yeats Coole Park and Ballylee*, 1974) have mentioned the possibility of a connection between the poems. But Sacks had decided to omit the Jonson poem from consideration (Note on p. 344 to his Ben Jonson section, despite the tempting appropriateness to his theme of Jonson's opening conceit of the child returning to the womb "Ere thou wert half got out", having been confronted by a prodigious paternal Hannibal razing the town, not exchanging the womb for "the horror of that sack").

But to the horror of this Sacks? For Sacks is for preference an accomplished describer of the shape of clouds. Jonson's obstetrics are hardly the kind of archetype he likes to bring swimmingly into half-view. There is, after all, something Nephelidiac about a critical work that accommodates such (the phrase suggests itself) an unhealthy lashing of Swinburne, even reading into "Ave atque Vale" qualities of "unusual emphasis and condensation" (not the moist kind), of "exploration" and "clear consolidation".

In his footnotes (fully documented, in the American way, probably omitting only Peter Levi's discussion and practice of elegy), a different critic emerges, less fastidiously indistinct. There is a splendid footnote on Victorian coffins, another on Yeats at tea with, but not apparently going on a much-elegised picnic with, Hardy. The book would have been better for more of such colour. His collaborators at the press relax too: it is only in the footnotes that there is any smallest sign of a misprint. On this typographical note, I think there must be a symbolic quality to deduce from the book's tiny full stops (while commas and semi-colons, which imply continuation, feature a bold slash). Hung up about coming to an end, eh?

Balachandra Rajan, *The Form of the Unfinished, English Poetics from Spenser to Pound* (Princeton University Press, 1985) 312 pp.

Reviewed by Roy J. Booth

The Renaissance writer was often challenged by another writer's incomplete work. The story of Orlando in love passed from Boiardo to Ariosto. Spenser, not taking Chaucer's point, continued both of the *Canterbury Tales* that were deliberately incomplete, and left his own challenge to Ralph Knevett, who did a continuation of the over-assimilative *Faerie Queene*. Milton regretted, and his father's acquaintance John Lane attended to, the imagined incompleteness of *The Squire's Tale*. Original and major as Chapman, or irredeemably minor as Petowe, the finishing school was large, workers of artistic piety in a short-lived age. The "magnificent knight" who finished Martorell's *Tirant lo Blanc* modestly hopes the only just literary critic (in Hopkin's phrase) will reward his labours with the glory of Paradise.

Balachandra Rajan offers in *The Form of the Unfinished* what he hopes will be continued by other critics and so develop rewardingly into an "independent aesthetic" for the unfinished poem. Unfinished poems make up "a strand in the literary heritage" that he doesn't necessarily see as discontinuous; because one feature of the unfinished is the invitation to "successor poems", provoked in more subtle ways than the simple desire to finish an incomplete telling, poems that may in their turn be unfinished. Rather resisting going as far as Shelley's "macro-poem of ongoing human consciousness", his symbol is a gathering of the scattered limbs of Osiris, "continuous progress to a deferred conclusion".

Unfinishedness is an area to which it is inevitably difficult to give hard-edged definition. To obviously unfinished poems like *The Faerie Queene* and "inconclusive" poems like *The Triumph of Life*, are added poems of generic contestation (*Paradise Lost*), "unclosed poems" (Marvell), works that contribute individually to a "macro-poem" (*The Waste Land* and Eliot's total *oeuvre*). Rajan's suppleness of mind is evident. So many tactics threaten, but never in fact become the game without rules. A "do it yourself" poetry of "continuation", either "summoned into existence" by the "vehement closure" of a prior poem, or provoked by a poem inconclusive on the page and "incomplete in the mind of the reader" is envisaged, as for instance by feminists who say they are more interested in the response of the Coy Mistress than the lover who importures her with such fine feeling for the pleasures of delay.

Yeats, whom Rajan studied in his *W. B. Yeats: a Critical Introduction* (1965), and who still suffuses his mind, is used a provisional boundary, often in company with Donne (but not Landor) as an exemplar of a "poetry of stances": "the decisive closure a stance invites may have to be placed in relationship to other stances elsewhere in the oeuvre" (p. 302). Rajan might have illustrated this point by discussing such "vehement finalities . . . summoning into existence another poem with a contrary field" as "Sailing to Byzantium", which may be considered an antecedent text to the "Dialogue between Self and Soul" with its "choice of rebirth rather than deliverance from birth" (as Yeats told Olivia Shakespear). In fact he discusses only one Yeats poem in any detail, "Byzantium", which "in repudiating the world of generation . . . unavoidably recreates what it scorns". This is a different sort of unfinishedness, "the questioning of closure by forces within the poem". Interestingly, Yeats's reaction to Marvell's "Horation Ode", a prime instance (for this study) of a poem incomplete in the mind of its reader, turns it into a poem of unequivocal closure: "It had been easier to fight, to die even, for Charles' house with Marvell's poem in the memory" (in "Poetry and Tradition").

There are of course exclusions in a book that repeatedly regrets the limitation to particular discussions enforced by its scope. Rajan's line of unfinishedness passes exclusively from renaissance to romantic to modernist. Rajan takes pains to "filiate" poem to successor poem, generally by notable allusions such as "The world was all before them" and its derivatives, occasionally tenuously: in the rather baffled chapter on *Don Juan*, where the discussion is largely turned over to other critics, an imagined resemblance of Jerome McGann's comment on Byron to some phrases in Milton serves as one of the links between the poets. It would have been interesting to see Rajan try his point of view on Browning's repeatedly complete *Ring and the Book*, or Tennyson's *Morte d'Arthur*, mysteriously the 11th book of "some twelve" by his mouthpiece poet Everard Hall, but the last of his own *Idylls*.

Thomas McFarland's *Romanticism and the forms of Ruin* seems to have kept Rajan from more than cloudy stuff on Wordsworth and Coleridge. "Christabel" seems a particularly hasty exclusion from this study. Neil Fraistat's *The Poem and the Book*, with its insights into the organisation of Keats's volumes would be an interesting supplement to Rajan's absorbing discussion of the twice unfinished "Hyperion".

This is a book in which different readers will find different good things – best perhaps where the subject poem offers most to the discussion. The chapters on Spenser and Keats are agile and continuously interesting. And in such chapters the book reads more easily. Rajan's accommodations of his discussion to poetry of such different ages and effects can at times suggest the flow of the uninterruptable.

Dealing with the unfinished, this book has nevertheless an aspect of summing-up, drawing together the kind of poems Rajan has dealt with previously. He leaves it to them to be "self-effacing". The index entry on B. Rajan is by no means complete – there is an element of dispersed self-bibliography. The Eliot chapter goes a lap of honour where Rajan clearly considers himself to have run victoriously. A flutter of footnotes waves congratulation. Rajan is careful in his Milton chapter not to fall over his own laurels as a "principal advocate" of historically situated readings. We are often invited in the course of reading to re-examine paragraphs for which Rajan retrospectively proposes augmented meaning. The book ends with a translation of *Rig Veda* X 129. The connection of such teachings to English poetry brings to mind how Lodovick Briskett depicts his friend Spenser putting forward the view of "the Brachmani men of so great fame in India" that self-knowledge was a pre-requisite, not a consequence, of being a scholar.

Rajan's book justly claims the attention of scholars of renaissance, romantic and modern poetry, especially those with a penchant for theory. Vulgar biographical accidentals, like Shelley drowning before being able to go on with *The Triumph of Life* are austerely treated. The main contribution this book makes stems from the insight his theme has given him into the long poem, the "self-revisionary" impulse in poems that must remain "true to their beginnings", the long poem finally being seen as "fundamentally dialogic". Balachandra Rajan in fact tries Yeats as subject rather than boundary in *Yeats: an Annual of Critical and Textual Studies* III (1985). The essay, entitled " 'Its Own Executioner': Yeats and the Fragment" (pp. 72–87), is not however the missing piece of a jigsaw, with Rajan having wittily sent an incomplete book on unfinishedness to the press. The little that is said in discussion of *poems* by Yeats is in the book, with the same formulation of Yeats's "poetry of stances".

Rajan here sets Yeats against the modernism of Pound and Eliot, "the new poetic dominated by a technique of methodical fragmentation". In a characteristic sequence of proposition-floating and self-revision, the image of Yeats re-building the tower, (not *à la tour abolie*), dissolves into a "countertruth": "Yeats writes only in fragments", is fundamentally more indeterminate than Pound and Eliot. Yeats, the "poet of contraries" achieves firm closures through "stylizations of experience", but plays between opposites that deny closure. Rajan then performs a piece of mental yoga that can only seem unexpected to readers of the essay alone, in looking in the opposite direction, to Byron, to surmise what Yeats inherited from this romantic poet of stances, referring to the present book for a full context. Rajan does not suffer from second thoughts that disable speculation. Propositions ramify, rather than explanations: he collaborates with a poem to attach it to all that is outside it, and make it endless. Those medieval and renaissance finishers-off seem a long way away!

Joseph M. Hassett, *Yeats and the Poetics of Hate* (Dublin: Gill and Macmillan; New York: St. Martin's Press, 1986).

Steven Putzel, *Reconstructing Yeats: 'The Secret Rose' and 'The Wind Among the Reeds'* (Dublin: Gill and Macmillan; Totowa, New Jersey: Barnes & Noble, 1986).

Reviewed by Barton R. Friedman

Steven Putzel's *Reconstructing Yeats: 'The Secret Rose' and 'The Wind Among the Reeds'* and Joseph M. Hassett's *Yeats and the Poetics of Hate* both address the poet's absorption in the war between the spiritual and natural orders. Putzel, as his subtitle indicates, focuses on Yeats in the nineties. Hassett, while touching on his early work, focuses on the twentieth-century Yeats, from *Per Amica Silentia Lunae* to *Last Poems*. Each is interested, moreover, in how Yeats's intellectual encounters shape his attitudes and his art: Putzel in his encounters with the occult and Irish folklore; Hassett in his encounters not only with the occult but negatively with his father and Locke, positively with his Anglo-Irish forebears – Berkeley, Burke, Goldsmith, and especially Swift.

Putzel proposes that, to grasp the significance of *The Secret Rose* and *The Wind Among the Reeds*, we must strip away the barriers revision has set between ourselves and their author, reconstructing the Yeats of 1897 and 1899. Hassett proposes that, to understand the work emanating from Yeats's poetic maturity, we must acknowledge the source of its energy in hate. Putzel argues that *The Secret Rose* bears essentially the same relation to *The Wind Among the Reeds* as *A Vision* to the great work of the late twenties and thirties. Hassett argues that the great work of the late twenties and thirties is rooted in the same struggle with

Bacon, Newton, and primarily Locke, to which Yeats had been called first perhaps by Blake, and which encroached on his life through the tension between himself as a young man seeking spiritual truth and his aggressively agnostic father.

If most of this sounds familiar, it should. Neither Putzel nor Hassett takes a radically new stance toward Yeats's career. The strength of their books lies in some of the readings of specific texts that their conceptual frameworks enable them to build. Hassett thus establishes the presence of Porphyry behind the image of Swift's "blood-sodden breast" in "Blood and the Moon". Because blood comprises at least part of the moisture of life into which souls sink at generation, and because the souls of the dead are raised into communion with the living by inhaling blood, the "Odour of blood on the ancestral stair" of Yeats's tower can summon Swift. "Blood and the Moon" becomes an act of mediumship, enabling the poet to share in that "wisdom [which] is the property of the dead".

Hassett's treatment of "Blood and the Moon" reflects the superiority of his critical method to Putzel's. Where he not only tracks Yeats's sources but shows how Yeats appropriates them, absorbs them into the substance of his work, Putzel too often tends merely to list them; and since what he lists – alchemy, hermeticism, Gnosticism, Neoplatonism, Irish myth and folklore, Blake, the Pre-Raphaelites, Pater, the French symbolists – reproduces Yeats's standard intellectual store, as scholars have inventoried it over the years, one wonders how much it adds to the contribution his book makes.

Putzel is also, for a student of *The Secret Rose* and *The Wind Among the Reeds*, curiously intolerant of Yeats's occultism. Commenting on "The Book of the Great Dhoul and Hanrahan the Red", he reports:

> After wading through pages and pages of notebooks in which Yeats scribbled down a record of his invocations with all the fervour and seriousness of a devoted occultist, I find it refreshing to read Yeats's light-hearted treatment of Hanrahan's bumbling attempt to follow "a receipt for making spirits appear". Just as Hanrahan reads that he will need a bat, sure enough, "a bat fluttered in through the half-closed door . . .". Hanrahan flails about with the handle of a hoe until the beast is subdued. Unlike Yeats in his invocations, Hanrahan doesn't have a clue what to ask Cleena when, to his surprise, she actually appears.

This sort of thing tells us more about Putzel than about "The Book of the Great Dhoul and Hanrahan the Red" – and it misreads the story. Though Yeats renders Hanrahan a comic figure, he means, neither by the bat's convenient appearance nor by Hanrahan's confusion at Cleena's, to trivialise the power of magic. The bat's appearance manifests the Sidhe starting to draw Hanrahan into their orbit; Hanrahan's inarticulateness before Cleena manifests his suspension between the state of material being in which he is caught and the state of spiritual being for which he has unconsciously begun to yearn.

The irony that Cleena has, for love of Hanrahan, entered the world Hanrahan would escape determines the story's tone. That Hanrahan's intensifying desire for a world accessible to him only through death was more suited to tragic than to comic handling partly accounts for the thorough revision to which Yeats subjected the entire sequence between 1897 and 1908. Putzel's apparent failure to recognise that he could use the later versions of Hanrahan's wanderings to illuminate the earlier seems to me among the limitations of his approach.

He nonetheless offers some penetrating insights into the Hanrahan stories, as well as into other stories from *The Secret Rose* and poems from *The Wind Among the Reeds*. Exploring the crucial metaphor of fishing in *The Wind Among the Reeds*, he observes that the fishers, the fish they catch, and their means of catching them coalesce. While Aengus in "The Song of Wandering Aengus" goes "out to the hazel wood", he believes, to seek his dinner, the fire in his head driving him to the stream has been lit by the "glimmering girl" into which his catch turns. Aengus, not she, nor the silver trout from which she metamorphoses, is the real quarry.

Putzel finds a comparable irony in "Rosa Alchemica". Brought by Michael Robartes to the Temple of the Alchemical Rose, the anonymous narrator is asked to study a book suggestive of *The Secret Rose* itself, thereby engaging us in a "multi-layered fiction in which the narrator, a character in the book we are reading, is reading a book that closely resembles the book that we are reading". Yeats manoeuvres us into identifying with his ultimately hollow protagonist.

What Putzel does not stress is that Yeats manoeuvres us, induces us to share the protagonist's consciousness, by rendering him anonymous and by allowing him to tell his own story: in effect drawing us into becoming the narrator as we read. This failure to pursue his insights fully, and thereby to develop more than very partial perspectives on the works he addresses, constitutes one of the frustrations of Putzel's book. Though he notes, I think properly, that Yeats's revised opening to "Rosa Alchemica" echoes Poe's "Ligeia", the important questions – why Yeats may have borrowed a rhetorical strategy from Poe, what that strategy may reveal about Yeats's designs – go unexplored. Though he argues, I think cogently, that "The Vision of Hanrahan the Red" makes a kind of "prose *aisling*", ultimately about the epiphanal process from which poems evolve, what this crucial episode says about Hanrahan inexorably declining toward death, how it blends into the episode recounting his death, are questions merely brushed over.

Indeed, Putzel discovers significance in "The Death of Hanrahan the Red" chiefly in the irony that the curse Hanrahan had earlier uttered against eagle, pike, yew, and all old men now recoils on him. That death may promise transcendence of the world in which men grow old apparently strikes Putzel – if not Yeats – as without import. While the triumph inherent in death – Hanrahan having no longer to seek love on the breast of mortal women – is effectively rendered a major theme in the sequence, especially its closing story, only through revision, Putzel's indifference to it seems more a function of his effort to impose a historical schema on *The Secret Rose*, comparable to the historical schema of *A Vision*, than of its absence from the narrative, even in 1897. If every age represented in *The Secret Rose* incorporates a historical cycle at the end of which things fall apart, its heroes are necessarily caught at the moment of defeat. Each is, as Putzel describes Proud Costello, "the last of a dying breed".

The trouble with this argument lies not in its accuracy but in its abstraction. The word to which Putzel returns again and again in treating the symbology of *The Secret Rose* is "system" – as if he were reading not a volume of tales, even if with a unifying structure, but *A Vision* itself, with all its elaborate diagrams and metaphysical arcana. I doubt that any reader outside what Putzel calls the "Yeats industry" reads the book, or that Yeats meant to have it read, this way. The implications of so reading it are nicely encapsulated by Putzel characterizing the epiphanal moment, recurrently the focus of *The Secret Rose*, as an intersection of diachronic and synchronic time – which does no more than recast the Wordsworthian concept of "spots of time" (appropriated by Yeats for "The Vision of Hanrahan the Red") into the currently fashionable language of critical theory; and obscures Yeats's central concern with capturing individual and psychic, as well as historical and cosmic, experience.

Hassett's terms for describing the same phenomenon bring us nearer Yeats's art. Addressing "Ego Dominus Tuus" in its context as epigraph to *Per Amica Silentia Lunae*, he suggests that the poem, and the remarkable exploration of the creative process it introduces, posit an overmastering spirit, a daimon, who calls the timid poet out of himself, at least briefly merging his mind with the Great Mind, thus making poetry possible. This dynamic, or its absence, seems at work even in *The Secret Rose*. The sterility of the narrator in "Rosa Alchemica" is manifest in his flight from initiation into Robartes's Order back into the aesthetic retreat of his Dublin rooms. The victory Hanrahan wins at death is manifest (as revised anyway) in the courage he finds to ask the question he had failed to ask on Slieve Echtge.

Hassett discovers an epitomising statement of this experience as a stimulus to poetry in *My Soul's* utterance in "A Dialogue of Self and Soul":

> Such fullness in that quarter overflows
> And falls into the basin of the mind
> That man is stricken deaf and dumb and blind,
> For intellect no longer knows
> *Is* from the *Ought*, or *Knower* from the *Known* –

The Neoplatonic image of fullness overflowing into the mind's basin promises – "If but imagination scorn the earth / And intellect its wandering" – union of the poet's mind with the *anima mundi*. And, as Hassett stresses, Locke's whole epistemology collapses before this union: the man is deaf, dumb, and blind, incapable of sense perception; he can no longer distinguish "is" from "ought", "knower" from "known".

His progress toward union of the individual and collective minds starts, that is, with rejection of the Lockean separation of "is" from "ought", "knower" from "known." As Hassett reads "Ego Dominus Tuus", to be a poet is to embrace hatred of alien ideas, rather than the "deliberate happiness" embodied in Keats. For it is only by embracing hate that one transcends hate: "That is to say", in the pronouncement of *My Soul*, "ascends to Heaven . . .".

Hate, Hassett argues, is for Yeats the source of creative energy. Much of his book is devoted to redeeming the poet from the charge that his hates led him into Fascism, as much of Putzel's is devoted to redeeming him from the charge that his early work is insignificant. Yeats's anger, Hassett insists, is – like Swift's – directed at abstractions, not individuals: "I hate and detest that animal called man; although I heartily love John, Peter, Thomas, and so forth". And Hassett tries (with, he admits, imperfect success) to shore up his defence of Yeats by proposing the blood lust in even that most enigmatic poem, "Hound Voice", be read as the struggle of imagination to realize the One against the divisive force of a profane world:

> The case for a metaphorical reading of the blood is that the poet and the kindred "women that I picked" share a terrible vision as they sleep, a vision that could be vanquished by those who learned from Hermes [Trismegistus] that unquiet dreams in sleeping blood can be overcome by a powerfully imagined hound. Perhaps, however, the raging man of *On the Boiler* insists too strongly on a real massacre to permit ungrudging acceptance of the blood of the contemporaneous "Hound Voice" as pure metaphor.

Hassett might better have cited the apology Yeats in April 1936 made to Ethel Mannin for refusing to join Ernst Toller in recommending Carl von Ossietsky, then dying in a Nazi concentration camp, for the Nobel Prize:

> I am not callous, every nerve trembles with horror at what is happening in Europe, "the ceremony of innocence is drowned".

And moved, one supposes by his horror, he rewrote the songs he had written for O'Duffy's Blue Shirts, so they could be sung by nobody.

Rendering them singable by nobody proclaims Yeats's conviction that the breakdown in western civilization of which Fascism was a symptom lay beyond the capacity of politics to fix. As Hassett asserts, and as I think Putzel would agree, the dynamic inherent in Yeats's theory of history is not political but religious – apocalyptic. Putzel observes of *The Secret Rose* that, throughout, the "pre-apocalyptic moment" seems indefinitely extended, "the spiritial history of Ireland appears as perpetual crisis". Or, as Yeats himself confronts the crisis, in summing up his own memories at the end of *Reveries over Childhood and Youth*, "When I think of all the books I have read, and of the wise words I have heard spoken, and of the anxiety I have given to parents and grandparents, and of the hopes that I have had, all life weighed in the scales of my own life seems to me a preparation for something that never happens." We can, finally, do no more than prepare ourselves for it to happen.

D. E. S. Maxwell, *A Critical History of Modern Irish Drama 1891–1980*, (Cambridge University Press, 1984) pp. xvii + 250.
William J. Feeney, *Drama in Hardwicke Street: a History of the Irish Theatre Company* (Farleigh Dickinson University Press, 1984) pp. 319.

Reviewed by Richard Allen Cave

The writing of literary histories is notoriously difficult; writing a history of dramatic literature that also attempts to cover over ninety years of theatre history too is to work against almost impossible odds. The chief problem is determining the potential reader for such a book: the informed scholar with a wealth of reading in the field behind him; the layman, prompted by a genuine curiosity; or the student anxious for guidance on how to enter a complex area of research. Overly long expositions of the plots of plays will weary readers in the first category, but are necessary information for the other two types of reader if they are to appreciate any critical debate about authors chosen for comment. Experienced readers may legitimately expect some discussion of the body of critical opinion on a major playwright, where it exists, though too subtly detailed or combative an account may well lose the attention of readers with a less developed knowledge. Gauging a proper balance between exposition and debate is crucial.

Professor Maxwell hits the mark exactly in the last two chapters of his *Critical History of Modern Irish Drama* where his subject is playwriting since 1956 with special reference to the work of Beckett and Friel, since he has ample room to find an original perspective. There is little published criticism of most of the writers discussed and, while there is a massive corpus of published work on Beckett's drama, no one has attempted to assess its influence on the younger generation of Irish dramatists. Both chapters are a good stimulus to further reading and theatregoing; their excellence leaves one pondering why Professor Maxwell did not expand his material and devote his entire book to the theatrical contexts that have shaped the work of Brian Friel and his contemporaries. Apparently out of a concern for "continuities", Professor Maxwell has chosen to recount yet again the story of the founding of the Abbey, the Dublin Drama League, the Gate and review the roll-call of dramatists who created a specifically *Irish* drama. Here the balance is repeatedly misjudged. Too much that requires discussion is given summary treatment out of concern, presumably, for the exigencies of space and in a manner that is either cavalier or waspish. Too often a pithy judgement is left undemonstrated (the epigrammatic wit may delight the informed reader but leave the layman bemused), such as the observation of T. C. Murray's tragedies that "the place possessed narrowly possesses" or the comment that Denis Johnston's dramatic method is to set "rhetorics against one another as a means of enquiry into the sentiments that they are used to express". More troubling where a tradition of critical argument exists is the tendency to present only that side of the debate that reflects Professor Maxwell's own opinion and with an authority that suggests to the unwary that this is the consensus view. He introduces Lady Gregory's plays by quoting without questioning Malone's dislike of what he senses is her "patronage and unconscious snobbery", allows this to colour a brief account of *Twenty-Five* and *Spreading the News*, then generalises about her flawed achievement on the basis of two of her earliest works. This ignores her long creative career, the range of styles Lady Gregory perfected, her nationalism, the enduring popularity in the theatre of many plays not even mentioned, and the work of a number of critics whose approach is more enthusiastic than Maxwell's own. The critical method here is dishonest; it is so, yet more extensively and damagingly, when applied to O'Casey.

When reaching for discriminations to prove his sense of continuities or, more usually, to disprove the continuities sensed by rival critics, Professor Maxwell can be misleading and insensitive. Setting out, for example, to question the "modish invocation of Beckett as Yeats's heir", he argues that Yeats's ironies depend on a quality of "once-upon-a-time", of lost worlds of heroic ideals and an expansiveness celebrated in the fictions of saga and legend while "Beckett's derelicts, talking to keep their void intact, have no such memories". In a superficial way this is accurate: Beckett's characters possess no race-memory, have no sense of themselves as caught up in cycles of history that give them an indisputably Irish identity. Yet memory, the pressure of a sense of the past that is deemed to be crucial because different from present circumstance, is a central preoccupation of Beckett's: it informs the impulse that compels Didi and Gogo to wait for Godot; all four characters in *Endgame* remember and the quality of their remembering does much to distinguish them as individuals; Winnie has her "that time", her recall of a former state, as does Krapp with his tapes and the Mouth in *Not I*. This past is not heroic in dimension but certainly expansive compared with the characters' known present: a time of carefree, unthinking, unquestioning innocence when one could simply *be*, untroubled by metaphysical apprehensions. Yeats's characters measure themselves against the expectations of myth, Beckett's against stories about themselves of their own devising: an element of "once-upon-a-time" is present in both dramatists' plays and in both this is a source of pathos and of complex ironies.

The sections on Yeats are in fact the ones most seriously at fault. He is honoured as founder and guiding spirit of the dramatic movement but his plays are relentlessly criticised as failures though few of them are given detailed treatment. Generalisations flourish which give wrong impressions: "Yeats had found a form [the Noh] adaptable to his vision and for the rest of his drama adhered to it", we are informed after a discussion of *At the Hawk's Well*; yet this hardly accounts for the variety of the *Four Plays for Dancers* let alone subsequent works. How can *The Words Upon the Window Pane*, *The Herne's Egg*, *Purgatory* and *The Death of Cuchulain* be said to share a common form? Later comes the assertion that the verse of the plays, for all the aesthetic "borrowings from Irish legend and European and Japanese drama", "remained intractable. It is the unmistakable, single voice of the lyric poet, imposed on all the characters, withdrawn, neglectful of the inhabited, waiting stage". One may be forgiven for wondering whether Professor Maxwell possesses an ear at all for spoken verse if he cannot detect how rhythm and syntax are used with great flexibility to define character in the plays, to distinguish Fergus, Naisi, Deirdre and Conchubar as complex sentient individuals in the early tragedy and to render too the various transformations, unconscious and willed, that Deirdre undergoes before she accepts and achieves death as her fitting end. Different styles of verse characterise the King as distinct from the Stroller in *The King of the Great Clock Tower*, or the Old Man from the Boy in *Purgatory*. To argue that Yeats imposes a single voice on all his characters is to view him as deficient in one of the central creative gifts necessary to a dramatist: an imaginative engagement with the inner dimensions of each of his created personae. On the strength of merely the three plays mentioned above, the deficiency in perception would seem to be Professor Maxwell's, not Yeats's. Much space is devoted to arguing that Yeats's drama asserts "the sovereignty of words"; despite his preoccupation with Noh drama, we are told, he stopped short of a theatre "in which speech defers to acts without words". And yet in the last third of *The King of the Great Clock Tower* words fail and *meaning* is conveyed through mime, song and dance; a dance that moves from a frenzy of hatred to a tense stillness shapes one of the climaxes of *The Death of Cuchulain*. Admittedly Yeats never devised (as Beckett was to do) scenarios for mimes, but he increasingly stylised movement so that it would enhance an audience's perception of the symbolic implications of his themes. Movement in many of the plays has the status of metaphor. In flat contradiction of himself Professor Maxwell argues just this point in describing the dramatic function of movement, the patterns of disintegrating triangles that make a "sustained visual motif" throughout *At the Hawk's Well*, another play in which dance affords the climax and defines the lure of the alien, the fascination of the unknown, which determines Cuchulain's final choice: "although the play cannot be discussed wholly in terms of a balletic structure, that is indispensably part of its unity". This is accurate; but it intimates a dramatic form in which words are not sovereign but work with the other arts of the theatre – dance, music, song, mime, scenic design – to create a play that is total symbol. Much recent criticism of the plays has defined their excellence through a study of their sophistication of poetic effect in performance, but Professor Maxwell asserts that they do not seem to him "to warrant this enthusiastic discipleship"; they are rather "sketches for a verse drama that never attained full being". Having stated that opinion, he never defends it by open and detailed confrontation with the opposed view: that is either tersely dismissed as modish or relegated to brief mention in the footnotes.

It is not only in the generalisations about Yeats as dramatist that Professor Maxwell is found wanting; many of his readings of the few plays he studies in detail seem wayward, framed to coerce the reader into acquiescing to his larger estimate of the poet. *The Hour Glass*, for example, is criticised for a "repetitiveness in the Wise Man's search for a believer"; but this is to miss the point that the Magus's rationality would reduce humankind to a patterned mundane uniformity. The wife and the students are the product of a world-view that denies any value in faith or in imagination. If this is not established in the early scenes of the play then the pathos of the students' failure to appreciate the urgency and genuine desperation of the Wise Man in his quest for a believer would lose its power: his anguish cannot be perceived by them as anything but *comic* acting; his innermost fears are the object of their ridicule; yet their perceptions have been shaped by his teaching; the scene realises a vision of hell which is entirely of the Wise Man's creating. He experiences what it is to be nothing and that motivates his final trust in God's mercy. The conception of the parable is meticulously thought through in terms of its theatrical realisation.

Of *On Baile's Strand* Professor Maxwell questions: "What is Cuchulain's nemesis, witchcraft or political ineptitude? The play does not ask that question: the fracture between its two worlds insists on it". Is that *fracture* genuinely a part of the play or of the critic's devising? Maxwell sees Cuchulain while arguing of politics with Conchubar as "also a subject of the country of the Sidhe". Throughout the cycle of Cuchulain plays, the hero is tempted by that other world but invariably at the last resists its attraction; he is never its subject; even when reaching through the coils of Fand's hair to kiss her mouth and know oblivion, thoughts of his bridal night with Emer intrude drawing him back to the world of mire, endeavour and potential jealousies (*The Only Jealousy of Emer*). The witchcraft in *On Baile's Strand* is not a part of Cuchulain's consciousness, the *idea* of its being so is a political ploy on Conchubar's part to make the hero doubt his intuitions about the Young Stranger. Conchubar works throughout the play to stabilise his power by taming Cuchulain to his will; he will brook no denial or challenge. Cuchulain would prefer to live in and for the moment which he finds exciting for being ever unpredictable; it is because he sees no value in taking thought for the morrow that he can be so readily trapped by the High King's statecraft. His courage makes him despise Conchubar's caution and so fail to perceive the threat to him that it embodies; it is the essence of his character (here and throughout the cycle) that he knows no sense of danger. By binding him to an oath of fealty and then compelling him to act on it, Conchubar is making Cuchulain fight against his own nature; and the play works out the terrible ironies of this in psychological, emotional and familial terms. Nemesis in the play has little to do with magic or political ineptitude; it is bound up in the strengths and limitations of Cuchulain's fundamental being as it defines itself through what Yeats, seeing the play in old age, described as "creative joy separated from fear". Cuchulain's nemesis is his intrinsic passion for a vigorous life. Again Yeats's sense of character and his artistry are much richer than Professor Maxwell would have us believe. What is troubling about this *History* is that its method does not encourage the uninformed reader to approach Yeats's plays with any degree of sympathy; nor the theatre director or actor. At one point the theatre is actually berated: "The very fact that there is a dispute over the dramatic merits of Yeats's plays is in itself evidence enough that the Abbey should have been keeping them alive". But Professor Maxwell does not present either the dispute or the plays in a lively fashion likely to stimulate the interest, let alone the creativity, of a performer.

William Feeney's *Drama in Hardwicke Street* is theatre history of an altogether different calibre. This is a lovingly researched study of a theatre group whose importance could easily be overlooked and indirectly a dispassionate, honest and caring biography of Edward Martyn in the role of impresario. The Irish Theatre Company throve in the wake of the defunct Theatre of Ireland between 1914 and 1920; its policy was to introduce the best of new continental drama (Ibsen, Strindberg, Chekov) to Dublin and to promote an Irish theatre of ideas to offset what the group considered the Abbey's special domain, the peasant play. It numbered amongst its directors and actors a considerable number of men and women directly involved in the Easter Rising; its recovery after the tragic deaths or imprisonment of many of its personnel in 1916 and its survival for four more years despite the continuing harrassment of some of the members is in itself a remarkable chapter of social and political history. What is surprising is to discover how little if at all the chosen repertoire of the Irish Theatre Company reflected the Nationalist sympathies of the directors (Plunkett, Thomas MacDonagh and Martyn) and the casts. Few of its social and "problem" plays dealt with specifically Irish issues and at no time did the theatre become a propagandist platform. The image it sought to promote was of an Ireland of urbane and cosmopolitan sympathies, open-minded, fond of debate, aesthetically aware. Ironically these were the values that a decade earlier Yeats and the Fays had hoped to promote through the work of the Abbey but had been prevented from pursuing by the force of critical opinion and the counter-arguments of Yeats's fellow directors, Lady Gregory and Synge. A further irony is that though Martyn hoped to foster a school of dramatists, the ethos and house-style of the Irish Theatre Company were so rigidly adhered to that new playwrights could be sure of a much more welcoming and constructive reception at the Abbey than at Hardwicke Street.

The eventual demise of the Irish Theatre Company was brought about by the defection of John MacDonagh to the world of films, by Martyn's failing health and, most fascinating of reasons, by virtue of the very principles that had all long been the theatre's *raison d'être*: the Hardwicke Street Theatre was an uncomfortable, ill-equipped venue; there was scant effort at advertising; Martyn wished the group to play for a fit audience that was decisively few and these were somehow to divine the presence of a Nationalist theatre and to attend and accept the rigours of the environment as part of a kind of pilgrimage for an aesthetic and political cause – much as Martyn attended Bayreuth, to judge by Moore's account in *Hail and Farewell*. There were rarely proper settings as such; the plays were performed within groups of curtains usually designed by the Dun Emer Guild who shared the Hardwicke Street premises. It is interesting that, in the very years when Yeats under the inspiration of the Noh was writing for a bare stage plays to be realised by the audience "in the eye of mind", Martyn's company were discarding the superficial trappings of realism and naturalism to present even Ibsen-inspired drama in a pared-down style as essentially *mental* theatre. In both instances, the actor is as a consequence left very vulnerable and a performance stands or falls by his skill. Since many of the actors in the Irish Theatre Company were amateurs, enthusiastic but not always gifted, this was taking a considerable risk. Lady Gregory and Yeats worked hard to instil professional disciplines in Abbey actors and had anticipated that the Theatre of Ireland would be the victim of its amateurishness; and till 1916 the same might have been expected of Martyn's new group (the front curtain regularly stuck, the lights failed, the order of plays in a programme was changed to allow performers to go off to dances or parties). Pulling through together after Easter 1916 seems to have instilled a new rigour and sense of decorum.

Professor Feeney's method is to piece together an account of each of the productions from reviews, diaries (usually Joseph Holloway's), personal reminiscences, letters and from this he conveys a remarkably exact sense of what the day-by-day working life of the company was like, its methods of rehearsal and staging, the internal debates and disputes about an appropriate repertoire, style, casting, revivals. This is immensely valuable on two counts. Firstly it enables one to perceive the extent to which the Irish Theatre Company laid the foundations for the work of the Dublin Drama League at the Abbey and of the Gate Theatre (MacLiammoir painted one of the few full-scale settings used by Martyn's company and the Reddin family had a strong commitment to all three ventures so there were distinct lines of connection and continuities of aim and achievement). Secondly and more by implication than by direct statement, the study conveys to the Yeats scholar a profound sense of his entrepreneurial skills in keeping the Abbey open as a repertory theatre; even with plays that were not to his personal taste he could envisage proper standards for performance and promote them. Martyn was never more than a dilettante who had the money to realise a private vision, which he was willing to share with others if they were prepared to share it on his terms. Yeats may have carped about the exigencies of "theatre business", but the Abbey is a testimony to an imagination that could vigorously embrace the practicalities of the stage and the disciplines of professionalism. James Flannery recently examined the early history of the Abbey to demonstrate the extent to which Yeats was truly a "man of the theatre". Professor Feeney offers a different but complementary perspective that fully endorses that judgement.

Calvary and *The Resurrection* at the Peacock Theatre, Dublin: First Performance 15 September 1986.

Reviewed by Katharine Worth

The double bill of *Calvary* and *The Resurrection* at the Peacock Theatre in September must count as one of the high experimental moments in the stage history of Yeats's plays. Remarkably, *Calvary* had not been played in Dublin before; an odd fact that added to the excitement of seeing these new productions by Raymond Yeates, a director already known for his inventive approach to Yeats's drama.

Those who knew the plays must have wondered how well these two very different pieces would fit together. In one way, of course, they make a natural double bill, with *The Resurrection* providing the astonishing sequel to the story that appeared to end in *Calvary*. Stylistically it is another matter. A play so firmly fixed in the dance convention as *Calvary* might well have combined awkwardly with the more-or-less naturalistic *The Resurrection*.

It was a particular triumph for the director that no such awkwardness was felt. He drew *The Resurrection* into the ambience of *Calvary* by his imaginative treatment of the Musicians, in both plays a group of three women; strange, half-Japanese, half-Beckettian figures in long, rope-like wigs, wearing bleached layers of grey-white cloth with voluminous sleeves. In *Calvary* these were subtly suggestive of birds' wings. It soon became clear that the Japanese designer's hints at the alien theatre convention of Nō in the Musicians' costumes were part of an imaginative directorial strategy for conjuring up in both plays the alien world lying outside the reach of Christ. The Musicians did not just tell of this world; they seemed of it. Their not-quite-human appearance in their stylised make-up and streaming, coarse-haired wigs, related them equally to the bird images of *Calvary* and the equivocal transvestites performing their Dionysiac rites in *The Resurrection*. It was a thrilling moment of theatre when the three women standing at the edge of the rostrum representing the room where the Christians awaited the risen Christ, began to raise their feet in a strange, high dance step, as if acting out the ritual of their more savage god. Such wordless additions infused the Greek's long narrative – which is the nearest we get to seeing the Dionysiac rituals in Yeats's text – with tremendous energy, making them seem a more seductive as well as threatening alternative to the newly-forming religion inside the Christians' room.

In *Calvary* too the Musicians drew from the text some wonderfully fresh and unexpected moments, as when they made a fugue out of the brief lyric, "Take but his love away"; one voice coming in after the other on contralto or soprano note, building up the sound like a burst of bird song, till the last line, "And the moon at the full", was dropped by a single voice into a bird-haunted silence.

This was all music of the speaking voice. The Musicians lost the instrumental role Yeats had envisaged for them to the percussionist-composer, Noel Eccles. His music must surely be among the most delectable and compelling ever composed for Yeats's plays. An astonishing range of sounds emerged from the music centre where he was clearly visible to the audience, with his array of exotic instruments: vibraphone and congas, Eastern gongs, talking drums, tom toms, the shaker that announced with an ominous hiss the entry of Judas. Unearthly effects from the electronic sound track were artfully woven with live sound to create an ambience in which everything that happened seemed both amazing and natural. Music was an actor in the piece; from the wailing boom, like a ghostly bittern, that prepared for the opening refrain of Calvary, "God has not died for the white heron" to the Rio carnival style of syncopation, full of dangerous energy, that conjured up the Dionysiac street theatre of *The Resurrection* or the great clap of sound proclaiming the entry of the risen Christ.

In the discussions that followed each preview one or two members of the audience (evidently less used than most of us to "in the round" techniques) confessed to being disconcerted by the visibility of the percussionist and even to the entry of the actors through the spectators: they hankered after a more distant proscenium view, especially for *The Resurrection* which they found the easier play to like. One wondered if this was subconsciously a wish to get further away from the pressing and uncomfortable reality the miraculous story acquired when it was brought so close. Disturbance was the very effect Yeats aimed at, of course, though he was also rather nervous about it. (He was relieved at the strike which prevented publication of religious as well as political newspapers and reviews at the time *The Resurrection* had its first performance at the Abbey Theatre in 1934). *Calvary* was written with studio or drawing-room performance in mind from the start and though Yeats first planned *The Ressurection* for a proscenium stage, he thought later that it might be done at the Peacock, with the Musicians on the steps in front of the proscenium, one of his various devices for breaking down the conventional separation of actors and audience.

The audience at the Peacock sat in two raked blocks, looking down at the simple rostrum stage in the centre of the acting space; a decorative screen shielded some exits and suggested the possibility of off-stage spaces such as the invisible room in the second play where the "Eleven" sit waiting. The three masked actors who made their way down the rostra steps to the stage of *Calvary* created some powerful physical groupings. Christ in blank white mask and blue robe faced Lazarus in skull mask and ragged pink, across the full distance of the stage, while Judas, in darker bronze colours, fell into the position of Christ's shadow as he reluctantly followed the direction written into the script: "He has been chosen to hold up the cross".

This cross was a remarkable property. "Property" was the word in more than one sense, for Christ held and used it as if he did indeed own it, was somehow in love with it (such was the director's thought). Made of perspex, it had the lightness and transparency of an object that was both there and not there; a realisation, in fact, of the First Musician's description: "The cross that but exists because He dreams it / Shortens His breath and wears away His strength". This was a true "dreaming back", a re-run in which Christ too could play with his role, as he did on his first entry, lying on the ground holding his cross above him; or later when he raised it in the air as a symbol of the power which has brought Lazarus back from death against his will. Christ's confrontations with the two who resist their pre-ordained role in his story acquired real physical force in this production. Those who knew nothing of Yeats's complex thoughts on objective and subjective phases or on the cyclical nature of mystical philosophies could still appreciate the action as a desperate existentialist struggle between proud personalities, each seeking to will its own way of life – and death. The high stylisation, the masks, the insidious choral reminders of the bird world that mysteriously extends the thought of Lazarus and Judas; none of this prevented the development of human feeling. A sudden awkward gesture of Judas, poking his head down, as in a spasm of self-hatred; the exit of Lazarus, with "deathly face" but energetic on a crutch "like a young foal", to the sound of a desolate wind; Christ lying *on* his cross for the final performance, calling in pain "My

Father, why has Thou forsaken Me?"', these were moments of poignant humanity.

At the point where Christ cries to his Father, Raymond Yeates introduced the most unexpected and startling of all his innovations. Before the dance had gone beyond its opening phase, it ended: Christ picked up his cross and left the stage, as did the Roman soldiers (played by the three women Musicians, with helmets and spears over their flowing kirtles, like Valkyries). Then everything began again. Again the women sang of the white heron for whom Christ had not died, again Christ made his entry with the perspex cross and Lazarus limped energetically to his place. But now all places were on the opposite side; if we had first seen Christ at a distance across the acting space and Lazarus had brushed past us, this time it was the other way round; a hypnotic mirror image of the first run.

This brilliantly simple idea had some profound repercussions. There were interesting practical advantages. It was good, for one thing, to see the stage picture complete, an experience "in the round" staging does not usually allow. *Calvary* is a very short play (as a member of the audience had said, somewhat accusingly!) but it is exceedingly dense. So it was also good to have the chance to grasp again at its complex allusions and imagery. Most subtly, the repetition created a dizzy Beckettian sense of endless replay, just the experience promised by the play's emphasis on "dreaming through" and on the round of the dance. When this dance was reached for a second time, taken through whirling revolutions to a great crescendo and then returned to the close we had already witnessed, Christ picking up his cross and departing, the effect was, as in Beckett's *Play*, of an experience that could not end. Always Christ would win his Pyrrhic victory; always the lonely triumph of the "objective" mind would yield its place on the wheel to the other loneliness the Musicians remind us of at the close:

> The ger-eagle has chosen his part
> In blue deep of the upper air
> Where one-eyed day can meet his stare;
> He is content with his savage heart.

The theatrical power of *Calvary* provided a fine launching pad for *The Resurrection*. After the high flights of the first play, there was contrast and dramatic relief in the down-to-earth prose conversation between the Greek and Hebrew. With realistic anxiety they discussed the likely fate of their Christian sect, the true nature of Christ, or the rising tide of Dionysiac worship. Through this more mundane dialogue the director wove a colourful thread of theatre poetry, picking up Yeats's bare directions for drum beats or music, and giving Vincent O'Neill, the movement director, scope for some wonderfully inventive gestural drama. The three women of the chorus were a real presence; sitting on camp stools at three points of the rostrum, intently watching the men in the imaginary room; or moving nearer the still centre with snaky movements of the hips, to the erotic and ominous syncopation of the carnival music. It was an episode of extraordinary intensity when they fell silent with great suddenness after their cries of "God has arisen". The tension of the Christians in the room, waiting for the risen Christ the Syrian has promised them, and the tension of the Dionysiac ritual awaited release in the same climax. To the sound of a mounting heartbeat percussion, the Christ of *Calvary*, in his white mask, made his way through the audience, into the room. We, the audience, like the actors, had seen him crucified, an added element in the palpable tension and shock of the moment when the Greek stretches out his hand to touch the phantom (as he believes it), and feels the heartbeat. His shriek, "The heart of a phantom is beating!" expressed a terror the performance had made completely real for the audience.

In its achievement of so much feeling through such intense stylisation, the double bill proved itself a great gift from director and company both to lovers of Yeats and to those who hardly know the plays. It is to be hoped that Raymond Yeates and the Abbey Theatre will give us many more opportunities for tasting these pleasures.

C. K. Stead, *Pound, Yeats, Eliot and the Modernist Movement* (London: Macmillan; New Brunswick, New Jersey: Rutgers University Press, 1986) 396 pp.

Reviewed by Hugh Witemeyer

This book revises the account of Anglo-American Modernist poetry presented in C. K. Stead's *The New Poetic* (1964). Stead still regards Modernism as "the principal tidal movement of poetry in English in the twentieth century", with strong "roots in Romanticism" and momentous implications for contemporary writing (pp. 4–5, 75). Stead's definition of Modernism has changed, though, and with it his pantheon of poets. He now views Modernism in terms of an ideology of open forms. He therefore demotes from a central position in the movement all poets who write in closed forms and traditional metres. "Modernism . . . (as I now see it) included Pound and Eliot but not Yeats" and not Hardy or Auden either (p. 3). In Stead's hands this restrictive argument takes a moralistic turn that may antagonise more readers than it wins over.

Stead correctly emphasises "the continuity of Romantic, Symbolist and Modernist modes" in poetry (p. 122). But his oversimplified view of Romanticism produces an impoverished account of that continuity. Romanticism for Stead originates in an existential confrontation of the self with the world and in a revolt against an Augustan tradition of discursive statement, closure, and logical limitations of meaning. "Discourse can give us a gloss on experience," but only poetry "can give us *the experience itself*," Stead naively declares (p. 339). "Thinking" is "more effectively communicated in prose, while poetry reserves for itself those elusive reaches of fact and feeling prior to thought and beyond it" (p. 150). "The whole movement of literary history since the

REVIEW COPY FROM

Houndmills Basingstoke Hampshire RG21 2XS
Telephone: Basingstoke (0256) 29242

AUTHOR Edited by Warwick Gould

TITLE YEATS ANNUAL NO 6

PUBLICATION DATE 15TH DECEMBER 1988

PRICE £45.00

The publishers have much pleasure in sending you this work for review.
They would appreciate receiving 2 copies of any notice which you may
publish, but request that it does not appear before the publication
date given. Please send reviews addressed to the Academic Publicity
Department.

Romantics" has been toward a poetry of experience rather than ideas and of organic rather than mechanical forms (p. 340). This teleology leads toward a poetry "not fixed in meaning" or "closed off by hard and fast readings" (p. 310).

> The well-made poem, the formal artefact with a beginning[,] a middle and an end, its final rhyme clanging shut like a gate on the reader's imagination, was replaced by the open-ended piece in which a nicely judged incompleteness might invite the reader into participation in the linguistic action. (p. 327)

Only open forms can "follow the natural organic movement of the poetic imagination" and "preserve a close sense of the actuality of experience by not allowing established stanza and metrical patterns to appropriate the subject or occasion of the poem" (pp. 96, 158).

By defining Modernism in prescriptive terms of open forms, Stead reduces the history of twentieth-century poetry in English to a war between good neo-Romantics and bad neo-Augustans. The former include Pound, early Eliot, William Carlos Williams, the Imagists, "the Beat poets (Ginsberg, Ferlinghetti, Corso), the Black Mountain Group (Olson, Creeley, Dorn), the San Francisco poets (Duncan, Snyder, Spicer), the New York school (O'Hara, Ashberry [sic], Koch)" and others (p. 327). The latter include Hardy, middle and later Yeats, Eliot after 1930, Wilfred Owen and the other war poets, the Georgian realists, the entire Auden generation, and The Movement. The politicised and idea-governed poetry of the 1930s is a retreat from Modernism and thus "from poetry itself" (p. 353). Moreover, a refusal to write in open forms indicates either a constitutional flaw or a moral failure in the modern poet. For example, it is "a failure of the heart in Hardy that keeps him always laced up inside his metrical forms" (p. 146). And this weakness in Hardy has "produced meanness, modesty and limitation in his heirs" (p. 349).

Yeats, too, exhibits both stylistic and human limitations. "Hag-ridden by formal metrics," he "would not understand or be able to work in open forms" (pp. 22, 24). Although Pound helped him to modernise his diction, he "could not go all the way with Pound" to free-verse forms (p. 30). Adhering to "the well-made poem, the isolated self-enclosed unit," Yeats "thinks his poems out as statements and as rhetorical structures, until there is no room for form to discover and to create meaning – only to contain it" (pp. 21, 82). Thus Yeats "seems often the most Augustan and artificial of modern poets" rather than the last Romantic he claimed to be (p. 154). Like neo-classical personifications, his symbols are often "mere abstractions in fancy dress, a form of decorative writing" (p. 154).

These "bad rhetorical habits" reflect Yeats's "very large and aspiring ego," according to Stead (pp. 145, 142). The poet's attitude toward nature is appropriative and histrionic: "'Another emblem there!' Yeats cries as a swan flies over, and this absurdity, the symbolist as game-hunter, becomes a touchstone for authorial egotism" (p. 342). This grotesque caricature of Yeats teeters uncertainly upon a slender base of specific analysis; the best-known of the few poems discussed in detail by Stead is "In Memory of Major Robert Gregory".

Stead's Eliot is an emotional and Romantic poet whose "neo-classicism was skin-deep" (p. 120). In "The Love Song of J. Alfred Prufrock" he created "the first fully-fledged Modernist poem in English" and in *The Waste Land*, with Pound's help, "one of the great poems of the English language" (pp. 51, 123). But neither is "a conscious construct" or "a work of planned symbolism" (p. 1). "There never was any plan" for *The Waste Land*, and Eliot's notes to the poem "were a smokescreen" (pp. 125, 356). Nor does his anti-Romantic literary criticism illuminate the true nature of his early achievement.

After Eliot's conversion his poetry begins, in Stead's view, to decline. *Four Quartets* are "drab and sombre, lack-lustre, abstract, short on verbal energy" and "only half alive" (pp. 195, 229). Their "dessication, aridity, poverty of spirit" make them "a poem from which there are only negative lessons to be learned" (p. 234). Again, poetic deficiencies are for Stead inseparable from personal deficiencies. The "dark treadmill verse of much of *Four Quartets*" indicates that "the negative aspects of Eliot's personality" are uppermost (pp. 212, 198). He has "little capacity left for an open receiving of the phenomenal world, little trust in his fellow creatures or willingness to give and receive love" (p. 229). His religious politics were "the product of a disordered mind," and aligned him "with Hitler" during the 1930s (pp. 208, 219).

Pound is the hero of Stead's argument. *The Cantos* is the open-form poem par excellence. Canto 47 is "surely one of the great poems in English of the twentieth century," and the *Pisan Cantos* is one of the two consummate masterpieces of Modernism, "nearer than any poetry of consequence I can think of to the feel of life as we know it subjectively, hour by hour, even minute by minute" (pp. 270, 321, 293). Pound's presentative method, which minimises "ego-assertion" on the part of the author, makes "even the most turgid passages of the Cantos in some sense 'pure'" (pp. 318, 236–7).

As this last claim suggests, the terms in which Stead lionizes Pound may not always persuade an unconverted reader. To take another example, Stead argues that obscurity is not a problem in *The Cantos* because "the reader's primary and abiding experience is of ear, eye and imagination rather than of conscious intellect" (p. 293). Since "there is no precise relation between comprehension and depth of response", the reader is advised to take a "'big gulps' approach" to the poem rather than an "'*Annotated Index*' approach" (pp. 262, 260, 256). To look up an allusion spoils its effect, Stead believes; Eliot's quotation of Wagner in "The Burial of the Dead," for instance, "may be said to work more purely the less that is known about it" (p. 96). Apparently the "big gulps" approach swallows Modernist poetry without digesting much of it.

The biggest gulps of all will be taken by readers who find Pound spared the moral indictments handed out to Yeats, Hardy, and Eliot. Stead's welcome affirmation of "the basic *sanity* of Pound the poet, whatever kind of crank or madman he might have been in his lesser roles" would be more palatable if the critic had been more forgiving to Pound's peers (p. 311). One may praise

Reviews 285

Pound's "magnanimity" without denigrating "the 'histrionic' Yeats and the cucumber cool Eliot" (p. 341). Having conceded that Pound's "Fascism and anti-semitism [were] much more explicit and virulent than anything to be found in Eliot," Stead nevertheless asserts that "there are surely Blakean precepts to support a sneaking preference for this unholy terror, scourge of Jews and Christians, over the seemly Eliot whose poison (as in *After Strange Gods*, for example) was so carefully measured and administered" (pp. 251, 280). On Blakean grounds of "innocent energy" Stead also defends Pound's use of the word *chink* as "one of the bizarre splendours" of the Chinese history cantos (p. 276). Far from winning new admiration for Pound, this kind of reasoning seems likelier to create a backlash of feeling against him.

Stead's final chapter clarifies the argument of his book by revealing the nature of his involvement with the issues he has been discussing. This chapter surveys the impact of Modernism upon British and American poetry since 1950, concentrating upon the American post-Modernists, upon The Movement, and upon Donald Davie's changing assessments of Pound. As Stead recalls the oppressive New Zealand poetry scene of the 1950s and vents his unabated animosity toward The Movement, he contests anew the open-form wars of the early and middle 1960s. His book comes into focus as a polemical version of literary history constructed by a practising poet to justify the most passionate commitments of his formative years.

To see the book in this light helps to account for its methodology, a dated fusion of Black-Mountain ideology with Leavisite moralism. It also helps to explain the exemption Stead grants himself from conventional scholarly obligations of thoroughness, accuracy, and fairness. As a poet's polemic, the book need not mention the extensive critical debate over the relationship of Romanticism to Modernism that has gone on since the publication of Frank Kermode's *Romantic Image*. The correction of typographical errors on pp. 12, 28, 60, 202, 219, 243, 322, 327, and 351 is likewise a matter of low priority. Disinterestedness, evenhandedness, and objectivity belong to a world of genteel academic discourse to which Stead's manifesto makes no pretensions.

Speaking of objectivity, one wonders how far Stead would take his subjectivist rationale of open forms in poetry. Many recent defences of open form and of *The Waste Land* and *The Cantos* adopt a post-Structuralist line of which Stead seems unaware. Given his beliefs in linguistic referentiality, mimesis, and determinacy (pp. 357, 333, 215) one suspects that Stead's sympathy with the latest version of the ideology of open forms might be limited. How would this vigorous controversialist attack some of the issues that his current account of Modernism leaves unaddressed?

Patricia Clements *Baudelaire and the English Tradition* (Princeton University Press, 1985) pp. 442.
Anca Vlasopolos *The Symbolic Method of Coleridge, Baudelaire, and Yeats* (Detroit: Wayne State University Press, 1983) pp. 218.

Reviewed by Pamela Bickley

Clements and Vlasopolos offer different interpretations of nineteenth- and
twentieth-century literary relations: the former bases her discussion on the
nature of Baudelaire's influence and uncovers a "history of relations among
generations of English poets" (p. 9); the latter attempts to establish a
methodological tradition stemming from Coleridge's process of
"symbolization".

Patricia Clements's book is concerned with Baudelaire's "mythic status as the
originator of the modern" (p. 4) – an idea already considered in Michael
Hamburger's *The Truth of Poetry: Tensions in Modern Poetry from Baudelaire to the
1960's* (1969). Clements gives a detailed and scholarly account of Baudelaire's
"protean presence" in modern English literature and deals impressively with the
many ambivalent transformations of this mythology – from Swinburne's
adoption of Baudelaire as "Frater" to Eliot's canonisation of Baudelaire as "Poet
and Saint". The unfolding tradition is a complex one with many of its illuminati
rejecting the faith of their predecessors to discover their own Baudelaire. Pater
carefully conceals his debt to Baudelaire; Huxley caricatures and murders
Baudelaire in the figure of Spandrell; Eliot ignores the anglicised apostolic
succession and places Baudelaire in a tradition "From Poe to Valéry". In her
assertion that Baudelaire is a progenitor of modernism, Clements is perhaps
guilty of protesting overmuch: there is a dichotomy between the work's thesis
and its achievement. The Introduction lists a haphazard collection of works
apparently influenced by Baudelaire but such an indiscriminate compilation
begs many questions which are not satisfactorily answered. Here, also,
Clements's style fails. "Baudelaire glitters at the surface of *Sons and Lovers* . . .
animates the argumentative texture of *Women in Love* . . . and, with Conrad, he
supplies the underlying shape of *Mrs Dalloway* . . ." (p. 6). This is misleading.
Further, it suggests that Baudelaire's relationship with the central tradition of
modernism is to be examined and this is not the case.

Clements might have considered how far Baudelaire's "presence" can be
detected in poetic echoes. Baudelaire's "La Beauté" is a figure – "comme un rêve
de pierre" – enthroned "dans l'azur comme un sphinx incompris". The subject
differs substantially from Yeats's "Lapis Lazuli" yet the impression of the
poems' conclusions is strikingly similar: "Mes yeux, mes larges yeux aux clartés
éternelles!"; "their eyes, / Their ancient, glittering eyes, are gay".

Vlasopolos acknowledges that the basis for her tradition is tenuous and
indirect. Baudelaire knew of Coleridge only as far as Poe knew Coleridge; Yeats
is considerably less influenced by Coleridge than by Blake or Shelley. But she is
too cautious in supposing that Yeats had only a "second-hand, fragmentary
knowledge of *Les Fleurs du Mal*" (p. 138). Yeats frequently visited Paris during
the 1890's and knew the work of the French Symbolist writers influenced by
Baudelaire. Yeats's friendship with Symons, particularly the time in Fountain
Court, coincided with Symons's reading for *The Symbolist Movement*. Such direct
influences are not, admittedly, of pre-eminent importance to Vlasopolos as her

concern is with the nature of "symbolic method" in two "commonly agreed-upon genre(s)" (p. 140) – the "Greater Romantic Lyric" and "Romantic Quest". She examines the "pursuit of psychic integrity" (p. 24) – a nebulous concept which causes a good deal of imprecision – yoking this with a "humanist aim" (p. 138) which muddies the waters still further. The over-dependence upon Abrams's nomenclature becomes wearisome; frequent repetition can render such terms meaningless. "(Yeats's) great poems of symbolisation whether traditional Greater Romantic Lyrics or not, revolve around the illumination of Coleridge's best known Conversation Poems . . ." (pp. 137–8). Any possible insight is submerged beneath the terminology.

The nineteenth-century tradition – Swinburne, Pater, Wilde, Symons – is discussed by Clements with clarity although, again, there is a tendency to impel her material too impatiently into the twentieth century and insist too far that aspects of this writing tend to the proto-modernist. At the same time, Clements's elucidation of this material is often refreshing. She cuts incisively through "careless retrospective" views of Swinburne and reveals that Swinburne's interpretation of Baudelaire is a complex one with far more significance than a legacy of algolagnic lyrics might suggest. In *Ave Atque Vale* Swinburne creates a lyric tradition completely removed from "Tennyson and Cie.", drawing upon Baudelaire and Gautier. In his speech to The Royal Literary Fund, 1886, he champions an international brotherhood of artists, protests the right of poets to deal with unorthodox subject matter and announces that the language of criticism stands in need of revision.

Clements establishes that Wilde, too, is more than a "cliché of decadence" largely created by Huysmans; he unites nineteenth-century aestheticism by proclaiming Swinburne, Pater and Baudelaire "perfect" as a "disturbing and disintegrating force" (quoted p. 144). Wilde not only responds to the artifice of Baudelaire's "Eloge du Maquillage" (*Le Peintre de la Vie Moderne*) but he also adopts the philosophical pessimism of Baudelaire's conclusion. Clements establishes Wilde's identification with the self-torturer of "L'Héautontimorouménos" – "Ne suis-je pas un faux accord / Dans la divine symphonie, / Grâce à la vorace Ironie / Qui me secoue et qui me mord?" This duality proves a compelling means of examining Wilde's writing which might have been pursued further by considering the implication of Baudelaire's "Hymne à la Beauté: "Viens-tu du ciel profond ou sors tu de l'abîme, / Ô Beauté? ton regard, infernal et divin, / Verse confusément le bienfait et le crime." It seems unnecessary to claim that Wilde's irony connects him with "the uncertain epistemology of much current writing . . . Stoppard and Gray, for instance . . ." (p. 151). An examination of Wilde's poetry would have been interesting in this context.

D. M. Hill has already established that Pater's *anders-streben* is derived from Baudelaire and Clements pursues further Pater's concealed debt to Baudelaire through *Gaston de Latour*, discovering that Gaston's conflict between old and new is answered by Baudelaire's definition of "La Modernité" (*Le Peintre de la Vie Moderne*) – "C'est le transitoire, le fugitif, le contigent, la moitié de l'art dont

l'autre moitié est l'éternel et l'immuable." (*Oeuvres Complètes*, II, p. 695 –
afterwards *O.C.*). It is Baudelaire who emerges as the hero and modernist of the
work despite Pater's "conscious displacement of allegory" (p. 93).

Clements rightly sees Symons as "a figure of the transition" (p. 216). *The
Symbolist Movement* is a work which begins to move beyond nineteenth century
preoccupations with its enquiry into the nature of modernity in verse. When
Symons speaks of ". . . an attempt to spiritualise literature, to evade the old
bondage of rhetoric, the old bondage of exteriority" his sentiments could,
equally, be those of Baudelaire or Yeats. Some avenues are left unexplored here –
Clements might have considered the existing Pre-Raphaelite tradition of
reciprocity between the arts and, say, the symbolism of Rossetti's sonnets. The
association between Rossetti and Baudelaire is one which Symons makes.
Certainly, more attention could be devoted to the collaboration between Symons
and Yeats. After all, Yeats is the "one perfectly sympathetic reader . . ." of *The
Symbolist Movement* and "chief representative of that movement in our country".
The mysticism of Symons's definition of Symbolism dervies from Yeats's
occultism. Yeats's understanding of the Symbolist tradition and his
incorporation of it into his occult thought can be seen in "Rosa Alchemica", as
published in the *Savoy*, 1896: "I remembered, as I read, that mood which Edgar
Poe found in a wine-cup, and how it passed into France and took possession of
Baudelaire, and from Baudelaire passed to England and the Pre-Raphaelites,
and then again returned to France, and still wanders the world, enlarging its
power as it goes, awaiting the time when it shall be, perhaps alone, or, with other
moods, master over a great new religion . . ." (*VSR* 143–4, l. 481v.)

Clements chooses to move from Symons to a consideration of a host of minor
figures – the Imagists, Sitwell, John Middleton Murry, with their own respective
satellites. The discussion of Sitwell herself is persuasive and interesting: it would
be worth remembering Yeats's comments on Sitwell in his Introduction to *The
Oxford Book of Modern Verse* and in "Modern Poetry: A Broadcast". Yeats praises
those aspects of her verse which are distinctly Baudelairean – both her language
and a quality of "terror" which cannot be allayed by civilisation. But there
needed to be a finer discrimination here; *Point Counter Point* surely does not merit
such detailed comment and J. C. Squire does not deserve more than a glance.
Murry is ultimately a dispiriting figure among the canon of "modernists" as we
are reminded of his judgement that Proust and Joyce were "essentially nothing".

Clements identifies Baudelaire's "correspondances" as the basis of symbolism
and conducive to modernism: "The germ of the mythic method as it appears in
the elaborate explanatory *Vision* of Yeats, the great chart of *Ulysses* or even the
notes to *The Waste Land* – lies here" (p. 136). Such references to Yeats and Joyce
are left unexplored. Too often there is an inclination to fall back on "Le Voyage"
with its revelation of "une oasis d'horreur dans un désert d' ennui" as the basis of
all interior journeys in modern literature. Equally, there is a ready assumption
that Baudelaire's poetry is "modernist" because it deals uncompromisingly with
the "Fourmillante Cité". The connection between Baudelaire and Conrad is not
confined to "Le Voyage" and *Heart of Darkness* but is apparent also in *The Mirror*

of the Sea: "La mer est ton miroir; tu contemples ton âme / Dans le déroulement
infini de sa lame, / Et ton esprit n'est pas un gouffre moins amer" ("L'Homme et
la Mer"). And the echo of Baudelaire's "La Modernité" is surely present in
Woolf's *Modern Fiction*: "Is it not the task of the novelist to convey this varying,
this unknown and uncircumscribed spirit, whatever aberration or complexity it
may display . . .?" Both Clements and Vlasopolos do refer to Baudelaire's place
in *A Vision* but needed to examine the implications of the spiritual and sexual as
"opposed yet parallel existences" (*L* 715). When Yeats wrote to Oliva
Shakespear in 1926 that his own poetry "becomes love poetry before I am
finished with it" (*ibid.*) he was reading Baudelaire and Plotinus. Vlasopolos
stresses "[t]he primacy Yeats places on passion" (p. 150) but might consider
Baudelaire's concern with passion and modernity in art, expressed in his
comments on those artists who are most representative of their age. Wagner is
"le représentant le plus vrai de la nature moderne" because of "l'énergie
passionnée de son expression . . ." (*O.C.*, II, p. 806). Delacroix is seen as
"passionnément amoureux de la passion et froidement déterminé a chercher les
moyens d'exprimer la passion . . ." (*O.C.*, II, p. 746) – reminiscent of Yeats's
desire to write a poem "as cold and passionate as the dawn". Vlasopolos
misjudges this badly. She claims that "Coleridge and Baudelaire show little
patience with cold-bloodedness in the creative process . . ." (p. 150). In fact
Baudelaire praises Poe – "l'un des hommes les plus inspirés que je connaisse"
(*O.C.*, II, p. 335) – "à cacher la spontanéité, à simuler le sang-froid et la
délibération." (*ibid.*) Baudelaire quotes Poe's assertion that "qu'aucun point de
ma composition n'a été abandonné au hasard, et que l'oeuvre entière a marché
pas à pas vers son but avec la précision et la logique rigoureuse d'un problème
mathématique." (*ibid.*) Yeats, too, regarded Poe as "so certainly the greatest of
American poets, and always and for all lands a great lyric poet" (Letter
published in *The Book of the Poe Centenary etc.*, ed. C. W. Kent and J. S. Patton,
[Charlottesville: University of Virginia, 1909], p. 207). Vlasopolos's discussion
of Yeats's "correspondances" does little to compensate for Clements's neglect.
Vlasopolos makes the curious statement that Yeats "Armed against nature by
his study of Blake . . . dispense(s) with correspondances." (l. 136). This reveals a
lack of understanding of all the writers under discussion.

It is Baudelaire who could be said to be "against nature" when, for instance,
writing to Fernand Desnoyers about his ability to write nature poetry: "J'ai
même toujours pensé qu'il y avait dans la nature, florissante et rajeunie, quelque
chose d'impudent et d'affligeant" (*Correspondance*, I, p. 248). In *Le Peintre de la Vie
Moderne* he writes that "C'est cette infaillable nature qui a créé la parricide et
l'anthropophagie, et mille autres abominations que la pudeur et la délicatesse
nous empêchent de nommer" (*O.C.*, II, p. 715). Equally, Yeats does not
dispense with "correspondances"; his symbolism derives from "one great
memory, the memory of Nature herself." As Vlasopolos's book is a study of
"symbolic method", it might have been helpful to consider to what extent the
symbolism of Yeats and Baudelaire is influenced by Swedenborg. Baudelaire's
theory of "corespondances" moves much further than the synaesthesia of his

sonnet: "*L'imagination* est la plus *scientifique* des facultés, parce que seule elle comprend *l'analogie universelle*, ou ce qu'une religion mystique appelle la *correspondance*" (*Correspondance*, I, p. 336). The association here between science and mysticism is one which Yeats would have understood and would have been disturbed by.

Vlasopolos's argument is often weakened by a limiting dependence upon *Les Fleurs du Mal*: while she is aware that Yeatsian reverie represents a "startling parallelism" with Baudelaire, her amazement derives from her hypothesis that Yeats knew only, and sketchily, *Les Fleurs du Mal*. Baudelaire's influence always stemmed from his prose as well as his verse and Yeats might well have known Baudelaire's comment on Delacroix: "C'est l'infini dans le fini. C'est le rêve! et je n'entends pas par ce mot le capharnaüms de la nuit, mais la vision produite par une intense méditation . . ." (*O.C.*, II, pp. 636–7). Unlike Clements, Vlasopolos does not detect a movement towards modernism. Baudelaire and Yeats "in turn rediscover and expand upon Coleridge's symbolic method" but "To Yeats there was no heroism of modern life, no modern beauty, no modern act worth all his admiration" (p. 189). This is, at the very least, a vast over-simplification.

Clements's thesis reaches its conclusion with her discussion of Eliot. She deals with Baudelaire's pervasive influence upon Eliot's poetry as well as Eliot's critical writing. Here, Baudelaire becomes the moral critic "aware of what most mattered: the problem of good and evil" (quoted p. 336). He is eventually mythologised as ". . . alone in the solitude which is only known to great Saints" (quoted p. 368). To Eliot "*notre* Baudelaire" is sharply distinct from "the Swinburnian violet-coloured fog of the nineties" (quoted p. 384). and Eliot seeks to reclaim Baudelaire from any taint of association with fin-de-siècle poetics. Despite this intention, Eliot's judgements of Baudelaire are not always a clean break with the past and Clements gives an excellent analysis of the extent to which Eliot's attitudes can, at times, resemble precisely those he wished to disavow. Clements reveals a complex web of influence; her book is well-documented throughout; it is a judicious and scholarly work which is to be recommended. Despite individual insights in Vlasopolos's work, I did not feel that a persuasive thesis emerges. Her style is clumsy and her translations of Baudelaire infelicitous. "Ennui" is a pathological condition, it is not simply "Boredom"; "Spleen et Idéal" is self-explanatory and should not be rendered as "Bile and the Ideal"; the vocabulary of "tel le vieux Vagabond" is equally obvious and "like the old bum" is a reading which jars. This is, after all, the poetry of "(le) roi des poètes, *un vrai dieu* . . .".

Marie Roberts, *British Poets and Secret Societies* (London & Sydney: Croom Helm, 1986) pp. xv + 181.

Reviewed by R. A. Gilbert

The stated aim of this book is to explore "the influence of the secret societies" upon the work of five British poets – Smart, Burns, Shelley, Kipling and Yeats – all of whom were either members, alleged members or admirers of "one or other secret society": for the author believes that "artistic inspiration may be derived from participation in a secret creative underworld" and that "a survey of the relationship between poets and clandestine brotherhoods will open up this neglected area of literary history and criticism". So it may, and so it might, but such a thesis demands rigorous standards of accuracy, objectivity and consistency if it is to be maintained – standards that Dr Roberts consistently fails to apply to her own work, preferring instead to say with Humpty Dumpty, "When *I* use a word it means just what I choose it to mean".

Not that she is alone in this, for enthusiastic amateurs of "secret societies" – and especially of freemasonry – have long been in the habit of building fantastic cloud castles upon their reveries. Dr Roberts, moreover, appears to have the benefit of a greater understanding of "The Hidden Mysteries of Nature and Science" than is given to the average freemason, and she thus finds meanings in the poems she examines undreamed of by their authors.

The first to suffer from this inspired misinterpretation is Christopher Smart, whose earnest, Christocentric personal religion is banished from his poetry to be replaced by a masonic deism that Dr Roberts elsewhere describes as "paganism" and "a Gnostic heresy". But then, she is convinced that "It has been universally accepted by scholars that Christopher Smart was a Freemason" – a somewhat rash conviction given the flimsy nature of the supporting evidence. It also seems not to have occurred to her that the symbolism of Smart's poetry and that of masonic ritual might have a common, but independent, Biblical origin.

With Burns and Kipling she is on firmer ground, for both were certainly freemasons and both wrote specifically masonic poems. But while they utilised masonic terminology and symbolism in their work, neither their lives nor their poetry were moulded by freemasonry. Nor would either poet have recognised freemasonry as a "secret society": something it neither was then nor is now. And here it should be emphasised that Dr Roberts is surprisingly ill-informed on the whole subject of masonry: surprisingly, for it is central to her thesis and she has evidently read widely upon it, albeit with little success in understanding what she has read. This has led her to make such unwarranted claims as that God "was known in Masonic circles as the Master. The leader of the lodge, called by the same name, was, therefore, a representative of the deity" (p. 114) and to perpetuate such historical falsehoods as that "Elias Ashmole was instrumental in turning the fraternity into a speculative organisation which 'accepted' members" (p. 6).

Freemasonry is not, however, Dr Roberts's only "secret society". Shelley was concerned with "the Illuminati, the Assassins, and the Rosicrucians" although it was no more than "an imaginative identification since he never actually belonged to any of these organisations" (p. 88). Indeed, why she considers him at all in a book on British *poets* is not entirely clear, for it is only his prose works that are examined. Perhaps he was introduced for the sake of *St. Irvyne*, his quite dreadful "Rosicrucian" novel, and thus to act as a sprat for her real Rosicrucian mackerel: W. B. Yeats.

Where Yeats is concerned, Rosicrucianism means the Golden Dawn – that fatal Will o' the Wisp which has led so many commentators into the swamp of unreason. Dr Roberts, alas, is no exception. Her errors of fact are legion and a complete catalogue of them would render this a most unwieldy review. Some of them, however, should be noticed.

The Golden Dawn was not "founded by William R. Woodman, William Wynn Westcott and the Reverend A. F. A. Woodford" (p. 133), nor was it – as she immediately afterwards claims – "largely Mathers's own creation" (p. 134). The Order was invented by Westcott and brought into being with the help of his colleagues, Mathers and Dr Woodman. And while it is true that Mathers became effective head of the Order in 1897, he did not alienate the members "by elevating himself to the position of Supreme Magus, a grade considered to be beyond the reach of any mortal being" (p. 134), if for no other reason than that this was not a grade of the Golden Dawn but the highest rank in the *Societas Rosicruciana in Anglia*, a position held, successively, by Woodman and Westcott until their respective deaths (neither of them being immortal). Mathers *did* provoke the "rebellion" of 1900, but it is odd to claim that he then "took refuge in Paris" when he had been living there since 1892.

Dr Roberts is equally unreliable over numbers and names. By 1900 the Golden Dawn had something in excess of three hundred members, not "approximately a hundred", but it had not "succeeded in recruiting" either George Russell (AE) or Herbert Burrows. True, J. W. Brodie-Innes *was* a member, but he was a lawyer and not "the Astronomer Royal of Scotland" (nor, for that matter, was William Peck, with whom Dr Roberts has evidently confused him: *he* was merely City Astronomer for Edinburgh). She is on safer ground in affirming that Maud Gonne was suspicious of Golden Dawn initiations at "Mark Masons' Hall on Euston Road": a fully justified suspicion seeing that the Hall was in Great Queen Street.

Nor is this mangling of the history of the Golden Dawn enough for Dr Roberts, she must also mangle Yeats's role within it. When "The Body of Father Christian Rosencrux" was written in the Summer of 1895 it was not "shortly after his initiation into the degree of Adeptus Minor" (p. 145) for Yeats had entered the Second Order, the R.R. et A.C., in January of 1893, and while he may have derived his quotation beginning "The wind bloweth where it listeth" from the Second Order's *Ritual U*, he more probably took it from its New Testament source in St. John's Gospel (3:8). Dr Roberts is not, it seems, familiar with the text of the Authorised Version. And if, as she bizarrely implies, the text of "The Adoration of the Magi", "reflected Yeats's own rejection of the Rosicrucianism inherent in the Golden Dawn and then finally of the Order itself" (p. 149), it is difficult to see why he remained within the wholly Rosicrucian Second Order for a further twenty-five years.

She does make an attempt to illustrate this "rejection" of the Order by dwelling on the Celtic Mysteries, but without, apparently, realising that insofar as these rituals were worked at all it was among Golden Dawn members with whom Yeats continued to work long after the Celtic Mysteries had ceased to be. There were, unquestionably, aspects of the Golden Dawn that Yeats did not like, and *Is the Order of R.R. and A.C. to remain a Magical Order?* was written to counteract the influence of the "Groups" of which he so strongly disapproved: but it was far from being the attack upon the Order itself that Dr Roberts takes it to be.

It is, of course, true to say that Yeats's work *was* influenced by his membership of the Golden Dawn, as it was by his other esoteric interests, but this influence was not necessarily felt in the ways in which Dr Roberts suggests. If "The Two Trees" does derive from the Golden Dawn rather than from Blake, then the trees are those of the Sephiroth (Life) and the Qlipoth (Evil), and not the two pillars of Mercy and Severity. But then, Dr Roberts is continually seeking masonic parallels; for her the title of *The Winding Stair* is taken "from masonic symbolism" and not, as Yeats himself declared, from "the Winding Stair of Ballylee". This approach is scarcely surprising, for her reading is nothing if not selective. She quotes Curtis Bradford's remark that Yeats's occultism is "the price we had to pay for his poetry" but she omits to point out that he actually wrote "my work had forced me to discard as untenable the widely accepted notion that Yeats's esoteric interests were, so to speak, the price we had to pay for his poetry" (Quoted by William O'Donnell, in *Yeats as Adept and Artist*, [*YO* 55]). Given the longer quotation it is surely less than just to term Bradford's remark "cynical".

Presumably unable or unwilling to seek primary source material, Dr Roberts has delved too deeply into the secondary sources for the Golden Dawn. Referring to the cipher manuscripts she states that Westcott "alleged that he had passed the manuscripts on to Mathers to decipher the outer rituals many of which were written out in bat's blood" (p. 134). Her source for this nonsense is not given but it is, in fact, a wilful distortion of a passing reference, not to the cipher scripts but to magical rituals in general, in William O'Donnell's essay *Yeats as Adept and Artist* (*YO* 56). O'Donnell's source, which *is* given, is more instructive: in Mathers's translation of *The Greater Key of Solomon* bat's blood is recommended for use as ink when writing the ritual words for "Operations of mockery, invisibility and deceit". Which, if any, of these is most appropriate to *British Poets and Secret Societies* is for the individual reader to determine should he be so unwise as to purchase the book and to compound his folly by reading it.

Masaru Sekine, *Ze-Ami and His Theories of Noh Drama* (Gerrards Cross: Colin Smythe, 1985) pp. 184.

Reviewed by Richard Taylor

The single reference to Yeats in Sekine's absorbing study occurs in a discussion of the inherent spirituality of Ze-Ami's art which is grounded in the Zen concept of negating selfhood, the ego becoming at one with the universe. The author suggests that it is precisely this feature of *Noh* which explains why the Western mind (exemplified by Yeats) has been so intrigued by such a highly abstract and symbolic form. As a generalisation, the statement is unexceptionable, but I much prefer Sekine's striking formulation of a typical *Noh* protagonist's predicament.

> *The shite* is a heroic creature caught like a fly in amber by an obsessive interest in a highly wrought emotional movement [*sic.*] from an earthly past, a crisis such as sudden death, unplacated vengeance or distressed love. This moment, or crucial phase, is evoked as being externally in the mind of the *shite* preventing his or her soul's evolution or dissolution into grace. (p. 106)

Yeats did not insist that the greater share of his heroes and heroines act out ghostly recollection in disquietude, but otherwise, the analysis is amazingly relevant to his concept of ritual drama. However attractive the abstract metaphysics of *Zen*, Yeats was, perhaps, more deeply interested in an individual and personal working out of such notions.

Zeami and His Theories of Noh Drama is indeed a work that anyone interested in Yeats and his experimental drama should read, in that it provides an authorative reference point by which to gauge and understand just how original Yeats's contribution to modernist theatre, in fact, was. Although he had very little real knowledge of *Noh*, it does become clear on reading Sekine, that Yeats also had a very intuitive appreciation for the calculated illusion of psychological reality which is its aim, as well as for some of the ways in which its effects are achieved. Characteristically, Sekine finds the perfect trope: "The impact of most *Noh* plays has a cumulative effect, like a frequently experienced dream, and depends more on the depth of feeling portrayed than the nature of the (often internal) conflict revealed" (p. 107).

However different in both nature and intention, *Noh* does provide a convenient scheme of *concepts* against which to contrast Yeats's experiments in ritual drama. Perhaps the most interesting notions concern acting theory and here, Sekine's discussion is really illuminating. Surely it is one of the most authoritative accounts that we have in English and could only have been written by a trained and sensitive actor. The exactly prescribed movements and sounds of tradition and training are only a vehicle through which an actor conveys his "own original feeling for a part, or a song, for a moment of crisis or comment on human love or anguish." (p. 145). Spontaneity rather than standardisation is the goal; tradition must be mastered and then transcended. A creative force generated by the actor himself should inform the purely physical effort, and Sekine is an excellent explicator of Zeami's often vague and metaphysical contradictions.

He is particularly good on the theory of contrasts which underlies the effectiveness of *Noh* and even manages to reconcile the paradox of an actor's total identification with the role while remaining conscious of the effect he is making by watching his every moment as though from outside his own body. "An actor who [fuses] his critical and intuitive qualities correctly is really working on a subconscious level [which] takes over the conscious creative efforts" (p. 97). Best of all, I liked the elucidation of Ze-Ami's strictures on recognising an actor's ability by his physical efforts, but find that it applies equally well to the way in which *Noh* acting suggests the intensity of feeling and psychological reality of a particular character: "One can see the stream and the formation of a river bed by looking at the waves on its surface" (p. 127).

Anyone not even vaguely familiar with classical Japanese theatre and especially those who have never experienced a *Noh* performance will have difficulty in puzzling out references to *kata* postures and dance movements. The photographs do help but could have been more closely related to the text with explicit description, and one sorely regrets the exclusion of Ze-Ami's nude drawings illustrating particular acting techniques. The chapters on various genres of *Noh* and the composition of a play are well done, as is that on *Hana*, an aesthetic of delicacy, refinement and restraint which delights in natural contradictions and ambiguities such as the exquisiteness of a "flower of sadness" or the desolate beauty of a withered, flowerless tree.

The least rewarding discussion is on the History of *Noh* with which the book begins. The culture and history of Japan are indeed complex, in any case, and for anyone who isn't already in the know, this account will be rather mystifying as it is of necessity highly abbreviated and allusive. Otherwise, the work is very successful in achieving its stated intention of arranging Ze-Ami's ideas in a rationalised format with commentary and explication. There is a glossary as well as a Select Bibliography and the volume is handsomely produced as well as being well-edited.

BIBLIOGRAPHICAL
AND RESEARCH
MATERIALS

A Recent Yeats Bibliography, 1985–86

Warwick Gould

Our fourth bibliography contains recent published work, including reviews, and information upon recent dissertations compiled from *Dissertation Abstracts International* and the *Aslib Index to Theses*. It also includes items from earlier periods not cited elsewhere but recently rediscovered. The arrangement is simply alphabetical, as the list is short enough to be read without undue discomfort. Only the occasional annotation seemed necessary. It has not been possible to view every item and exceptionally one or two items are incomplete. These are signalled (*i*) at the end of the entry: they have been included because the missing information does not preclude relatively easy recovery of the item in question, and it has been thought important enough to justify such inclusion.

Many scholars have once again assisted me. Japanese items signalled by the symbol (J) after the entry have been supplied and their titles translated by Tetsuro Sano. Hungarian items (H) have been provided and their titles translated by Maria Kurdi. In all such cases the symbol indicates the language in which the item is written. The symbol (*tt*) after some other entries, usually of Russian origin, indicates a translated title. Maureen Murphy provided an unpublished checklist, and Yvette Sencer, William J. Feeney and K. P. S. Jochum provided published listings. Angela Carter and David Ward of the library of Royal Holloway and Bedford New College, University of London undertook computer searches of several data bases. Others who provided useful listings include James Lovic Allen, Wayne K. Chapman, Robert Fraser, R. A. Gilbert, John Harwood, A. Norman Jeffares, K. P. S. Jochum, Richard Londraville, Colin McDowell, Phillip L. Marcus, Bruce Morris, Ann Saddlemyer, Ronald Schuchard, Henry Segerström, Colin Smythe, Charlotte Stoudt, Deirdre Toomey. I am especially indebted to Christina See for her typing. Remaining errors are my own responsibility.

I should be pleased to receive more information from all quarters, as well as off-prints and review copies, and especially information relating to the period prior to 1940.

Abbott, Craig S., "The Case of Scharmel Iris", *Papers of the Bibliographical Society of America* 77:1 (First Quarter 1983) 15–34. Doubts attribution of *Wade* 288A.

Adams, Hazard, "Byron, Yeats, and Joyce: Heroism and Technic", *Studies in Romanticism* 24:3 (Autumn 1985) 399–412.

Adams, Hazard, "Constituting Yeats's Poems as a Book", *YAACTS* 4, 1–16.

Allen, James Lovic, "What Rough Beast?: Yeats's 'The Second Coming' and *A Vision*" *REAL: The Yearbook of Research in English and American Literature* 3 (1985) 223–3.

Allen, James Lovic, "The Yeats Tapes", *ILS* 2:2 (Oct. 1983) 17, 19.

Allen, Woody, *Without Feathers* (London: Elm Tree Books, 1976; Sphere Books 1978) Contains "The Irish Genius", pp. 177–22. A Commentary on "*The Annotated Poems of Sean O'Shawn*, the great Irish poet, considered by many to be the most incomprehensible and hence the finest poet of his time".

Allott, Miriam, "Attitudes to Shelley: the Vagaries of a Critical Reputation" in Allott (ed.) *Essays on Shelley* (Liverpool University Press, 1982) pp. 1–38.

Altieri, Charles, "Abstraction as Art: Modernist Poetry in Relation to Painting", *Dada/Surrealism*, 10–11 (1982) 106–34.

[Anon], "Fifty Years on: *The Winding Stair*" *TLS*, 7 Oct. 1983, 1087 (reprint of original review).

[Anon ed.], *Ireland's Field Day: Field Day Theatre Company* (London: Hutchinson, 1985). Contains essays by Seamus Deane, Seamus Heaney, Richard Kearney, Declan Kiberd, Tom Paulin and Denis Donoghue ("The man to beat is Yeats" p. 120).

[Anon], "Microfilmed Yeats [sic] works reproduced on acid-free paper" *Library Journal*, 15 June 1986, 23.

[Anon], "Visit of Mr. W. B. Yeats" *The Aberdeen Daily Journal* 24 Jan. 1907, 4. (Reprints "When you are old" and anticipates WBY's lecture to the Franco-Scottish Society on 25 Jan., presided over by H. J. Grierson, with whom WBY stayed.)

[Anon], "The Yeats Summer School", *ILS* 5:1 (spring 1986) 13.

Arkins, Brian, "Yeats and the Prophecy of Eunapius" *N & Q* 32:3 (1985) 378–9.

Armstrong, T. D., "The Poetry of Winter: the Idea and Nature of the Late Career in the Works of Hardy, Yeats and Stevens". Ph.D. University of London, 1986.

Armstrong-Jensen, Alison, Review of *Yeats Annual No 4*, *ILS* 5:2 (Autumn 1986) 23.

Baker, Carlos, "The Poet as Janus: Originality and Imitation in Modern Poetry" *Proceedings of the American Philosophical Society Held at Philadelphia for Promoting Useful Knowledge* 128: 2 (June 1984), 167–72.

Barber, Charles, *Poetry in English: An Introduction* (London: Macmillan, 1983). On WBY: 63–9, 98–101.

Baron, Michael, "Yeats, Wordsworth and the Communal Sense: the Case of 'If I were Four-and-Twenty'", *YA* 5 (1987) 63–82.

Barrow, Craig Wallace, Review of Bernard Krimm *W. B. Yeats and the Emergence of the Irish Free State*, *Éire-Ireland*, 18:3 (Autumn 1983) 147–9.

Barrow, Craig Wallace, Review of *Yeats Annual No 1*, *Éire-Ireland*, 20:2, (Summer, 1985) 147–9.

Beckett, Samuel, *Disjecta: Miscellaneous Writings and a Dramatic Fragment*, ed. Ruby Cohn, (London: Calder & Boyars, 1983). See "Recent Irish Poetry", 70–6.

Bensko, John Richard, "Narrative in the Modern Short Poem", Ph.D. 1985, The Florida State University, Order No. AAD85–22740. *DAI* 46: 08, 2297–A.

Berlin, Isaiah, *Vico and Herder: Two Studies in the History of Ideas* (London: The Hogarth Press, 1976). Yeats cited, p. 95.

Bogoeva, Ljiljana, "Traženje smisla i puta: 'Putovanje u Vizant' Vilijama Batlera Jejtsa", *Gradina*, 18:3 (Mar. 1983) 90–7.

Bonaccorso, Richard, Review of *William Butler Yeats* by Richard F. Peterson, *Éire-Ireland*, XIX:2 (summer 1984) 159–60.

Bornstein, George, "Yeats's Romantic Dante" in his *Dante among the Moderns* (Chapel Hill: University of North Carolina Press, 1985) pp. 11–38.

Bornstein, George, and Finneran, Richard J., *Yeats: an Annual of Critical and Textual Studies*, III – 1985: (Ithaca and London: Cornell University Press, 1985). A Special Issue on Yeats and Modern

Poetry. Contains, in addition to contents cited elsewhere under author: Deborah Martin Gonzales, "Dissertation Abstracts, 1984"; Mary FitzGerald, "*Passim*: Brief Notices"; and reviews of Hazard Adams's *Philosophy of the Literary Symbolic* by Edward Engelberg; 4 Yeats Plays at the Peacock Theatre, 1984 and Karen Dorn's *Players and Painted Stage etc.* by David Krause; A. Norman Jeffares's *A New Commentary on the Poems of W. B. Yeats* by James Olney; Alan Himber's edition of *The Letters of John Quinn to William Butler Yeats* by William M. Murphy; Augustine Martin's *W. B. Yeats* by Terence Diggory; Rama Nand Rai's *W. B. Yeats: Poetic Theory and Practice* and Ramesh Chandra Shah's *Yeats and Eliot: Perspectives on India* by E. P. Bollier; Michael Steinman's *Yeats's Heroic Figures etc.* by Douglas Archibald; Geoffrey Thurley's *The Turbulent Dream etc.* by K. P. S. Jochum; Anca Vlasopolos's *The Symbolic Method of Coleridge, Baudelaire and Yeats* by Michael André Bernstein; Richard J. Finneran's edition of W. B. Yeats: *The Poems: A New Edition* and *Editing Yeats's Poems* by Seamus Heaney, reprinted from the *New York Times Book Review* (18 Mar. 1984).

Bradbrook, Muriel C., *Aspects of Dramatic Form in the English and the Irish Renaissance* (Brighton: Harvester Press; Totowa: Barnes & Noble Books, 1983). (Collected Papers of M. C. B., vol. III). Contains "Yeats and the Elizabethans", 131–45; "Yeats and the Noh Drama of Japan", 160–72.

Brady, Anne M. & Cleeve, Brian, *A Biographical Dictionary of Irish Writers* (N.Y.: St Martin's Press, 1985). Reviewed in *ILS* 5:1 (spring 1986) by Robert G. Lowery ("To Be Used With Care"), 19, in *TLS* 1 Nov 1985 by Declan Kiberd ("Unrevised verdicts"), 1240.

Buckley, Vincent, *Memory Ireland: Insights into the Contemporary Irish Condition* (New York: Viking Penguin, 1985). Reviewed in *ILS* by Lucy McDiarmid ("Cantankerous Silliness"), 5:1 (spring 1986) 21.

Bulletin of the Yeats Society of Japan, Oct. 1985, contains: Ohno, Mitsuko, "The Woman in the Mirror: Yeats's Idea of Woman"; Nakao, Masami, "The People, the Land,

and the Art: On 'In Memory of Major Robert Gregory'"; Symposium on "The Man and the Echo"; Mizuta, Iwao, "On 'The Man and the Echo'"; Matsumura, Ken'ichi, "A Soundscape of 'The Man and the Echo'"; Suzuki, Mark S., "'The Man and the Echo': Overtones and Reverberation"; Shimizu, Hiroshi, "*Un Sauvage* Reads "The Man and the Echo'"; Saddlemyer, Ann, "Yeats's Voices in the Theatre: *The Words upon the Window-Pane*". (J)

Burrow, Craig Wallace, Review of *YA* 1, *Éire-Ireland*, XX:2 (summer 1985) 147–9.

Bush, Ronald, "Yeats, Spooks, Nursery Rhymes, and the Vicissitudes of Late Modernism", *YAACTS* III (1985) 17–33.

Byars, John A., "W. B. Yeats and Wise Blood", *Flannery O'Connor Bulletin* 14 (1985) 88–93.

Calahan, James M., *Great Hatred, Little Room: the Irish Historical Novel.* (Syracuse University Press, 1983). Refs.

Callan, Edward, *Auden: a Carnival of Intellect* (New York: Oxford University Press, 1983) contains "Disenchantment with Yeats: From Singing-Master to Ogre", pp. 143–62.

Canary, Robert H., *T. S. Eliot: the Poet and his Critics* (Chicago: American Library Association, 1982). Scattered refs.

Cardullo, Bert, "Notes towards a Production of W. B. Yeats's *The Countess Cathleen*", *Canadian Journal of Irish Studies*, 11:2 (Dec. 1985) 49–67.

Carlson, Marvin, *Theories of the Theatre: a Historical and Critical Survey*, from the *Greeks to the Present* (Ithaca and London: 1984). Scattered refs. indexed.

Cavanaugh, Catherine, "Love and Forgiveness in Yeats's Poetry", Ph.D. 1984, State University of New York at Binghamton. Order No. AAD84–16787. *DAI* 45: 04 1120–A.

——, *Love and Forgiveness in Yeats's Poetry* (Ann Arbor: UMI Research Press, 1986).

Ceci, Louis L., "The Case for Syntactic Imagery", *College English* (1984) 45:5/ 431–49.

Christie's New York: Modern Literature from the Library of James Gilvarry, Friday 7 Feb. 1986. Yeats items lots 463–565: Books, letters, MSS, photographs, association items. See also Reif, Rita, "Auctions: Legacy of a Bibliomane", *New York Times*, 135 (1 Feb. 1986) p. 14 (N).

Christie's Valuable Autograph Letters & Historical Documents, Sale 20 July 1983 (London: Christie's, 1983). WBY items in lots 366, 396, 397. See also Geraldine Norman, "£18,360 for Yeats's Mail to a Lady" *The Times*, 21 July 1983, 2 and Sarah Bradford, "Sales of Books and MSS" *TLS*, 5 Aug. 1983, 843–4.

Citati, Pietro, "Restare in Irlanda a vivere le fiabe", *Corriere della sera* (26 Sept. 1982) 3. Review of Italian translation (by Dario Calimani) of *John Sherman & Dhoya*.

——, "Come vivere allegri insieme ai folletti" (Review of *Fiabe irlandesi*, Italian translation of *Fairy and Folk Tales of Ireland*, 1973), *Corriere della Sera* (10 Mar. 1982) 3.

Clark, Rosalind Elizabeth, "Goddess, Fairy Mistress, and Sovereignty: Women of the Irish Supernatural", Ph.D. 1985, University of Massachusetts. Order No. AAD85–0(533. *DAI* 46:03 704–A.

Clements, Patricia, *Baudelaire and the English Tradition* (Princeton University Press, 1985).

Coe, Richard N., *When the Grass was Taller: Autobiography and the Experience of Childhood* (New Haven and London: Yale University Press 1984) Yeats, pp. 284–5. Reviewed by Rosemary Dinnage in *TLS*, 2 Aug. 1985, 844.

Coombes, Harry, "Yeats and Synge, Sligo and the H-Block", *Haltwhistle Quarterly*, 10 (spring 1983) 7–16.

Courtney, Richard, *Outline History of British Drama* (Totowa: Barnes & Noble Books, 1983), WBY 196–9.

Crawford, Alan, *C. R. Ashbee: Architect, Designer and Romantic Socialist* (London & New Haven: Yale University Press, 1985) Mentions of and comparisons with WBY *passim* e.g. 231. Reviewed *The Times*, 7 Nov. 1985 by Fiona MacCarthy "Ideas man of Arts and Crafts".

Daalder, Joost, "Dogs and Foxes in D. H. Lawrence and W. H. Auden" *Zeitschrift für Anglistik und Amerikanistik* 32:4 (1984) 330–4. (On "In Memory of W. B. Yeats".)

Dalsimer, Adele, "Plays and Place: Lady Gregory and Coole Park". Review of

Mary FitzGerald (ed.) *Selected Plays of Lady Gregory*, and Colin Smythe, *A Guide to Coole Park, Co. Galway*, *ILS*, 4:1 (spring, 1985) 39.

Dancy, Eric Burton, "A Great Poet Speaks for Ireland" (Interview with WBY), *Daily Express* (London), 7 July 1932, 8. Includes photograph. (See above, pp. 86f.

d'Arch Smith, Timothy, *The Books of the Beast* Essays on Aleister Crawley, Montague Summers, Francis Barrett, and Others (Wellingborough: Aquarian Crucible Books, 1987). Contains "'Pregnant with Mandrakes' Florence Farr" – reprinted from the same author's edition of Florence Farr's *Egyptian Magic* (Wellingborough: Aquarian Press, 1982).

d'Arch Smith, Timothy, (ed.), *Egyptian Magic* by Florence Farr (Wellingborough: Aquarian Press, 1982) first published as one of W. Wynn Westcott's Collectanea Hermetica' (1896) by "S.S.D.D.". Now with an introductory essay by T. d'Arch Smith.

Daruwala, Maneck Homi, "Good Intentions: the Romantic Aesthetics of Oscar Wilde's Criticism", *Victorian Institute Journal*, 12 (1984) 105–32.

Dasenbrock, Reed Way, *The Literary Vorticism of Ezra Pound and Wyndham Lewis: Towards the Condition of Painting* (Baltimore and London: Johns Hopkins University Press, 1985). Several WBY refs.

Davie, Donald, "Attending to Landor", *Ironwood*, 12:2 (autumn 1984) 103–11.

Davie, Donald, Letter to the Editor, *Paideuma* (3:3, 151–2. Reply to Colin McDowell (*Paideuma*, 13:2) on Pound, Yeats, and the Perennial Philosophy.

Dawe, Gerald, and Longley, Edna, *Across a Roaring Hill: the Protestant Imagination in Modern Ireland*. Essays in honour of John Hewitt. (Belfast: Blackstaff Press, 1985). Contains *inter alia* John Kelly, "Choosing and Inventing: Yeats and Ireland", 1–24. Reviewed by Maureen Murphy in *ILS* 5:1 (spring 1986) 1, 13, by Patricia Craig in *TLS* ("Elusive allegiances"), 1 Nov. 1985, 1238, illustrated.

Deane, Seamus, "Joyce and Nationalism" in Colin McCabe (ed.), *James Joyce: New*

Perspectives (Brighton: Harvester Press, 1982).

Diggory, Terence, "American Poets' Responses to Yeats's Prose: Marianne Moore and Allen Ginsberg", *YAACTS* III (1985) 34–59.

Dolan, Bricriu, Review of A. S. Knowland, *W. B. Yeats: Dramatist of Vision*, Richard Taylor, *A Reader's Guide to the Plays of W. B. Yeats*; Karen Dorn, *Players and Painted Stage etc. Journal of Irish Literature*, 14: 2 (May 1985) 76–7.

Donoghue, Denis, "A myth and its unmasking", *TLS*, 1 Nov. 1985, 1239–40. Reviews Seamus Deane's *Celtic Revivals* and W. J. McCormack's *Ascendancy and Tradition in Anglo-Irish Literature*.

Donoghue, Denis, "Poets in their Places", Review of Lucy McDiarmid, *Saving Civilization etc.*, *New Republic* (7 Dec. 1985) 38–40.

Dorn, Karen, (ed.), "W. B. Yeats's Unpublished Talk on His Vision of *King Oedipus* Broadcast from the BBC Belfast Studio on 8 Sept. 1931, with an Introductory Note" *YA* 5 (1987) 195–9.

Eagleton, Terry, "Poetry, Pleasure, and Politics", in *Formations of Politics* (London: Routledge & Kegan Paul, 1983) 58–65. Discusses "Easter 1916".

Eagleton, Terry, "Politics and Sexuality in W. B. Yeats", *Crane Bag*, 9:2 (1985) 138–42.

Earle, Ralph Harding, "Yeats's Passionate Syntax", Ph.D., The University of North Carolina at Chapel Hill, 1985, Order No. DA8605590, *DAI* 47: 02 (Aug. 1986) 535–A.

Ellmann, Richard, *Samuel Beckett Nayman of Noland*: In celebration of Samuel Beckett's 80th birthday 13 Apr. 1986. A lecture delivered at the Library of Congress on 16 Apr. 1985, (Washington: Library of Congress, 1986). Comparisons with Yeats, *passim*.

Ellmann, Richard, "Yeats and Vico", *ILS* 2:2 (Oct. 1983) 1, 19.

Engler, Balz, *Reading and Listening: the Modes of Communicating Poetry and their influence on the texts* (Berne: Francke, 1982) see pp. 29–31.

Ewart, Gavin, Review of Jon Stallworthy, *Out of Bounds London Magazine* 3:11 (Feb. 1964) 94–6 ("Yeats, for us, is the great singing siren whose rock is covered with poets' bones").

Fallon, Brian, "The Old Man in the New World". Review of J. B. Yeats, *Letters to his Son W. B. Yeats and Others, (1869–1922) Irish Times*, 28 May 1983, 14.

Farag, Fahmy, Review of Cairns Craig, *Yeats Eliot Pound and the Politics of Poetry etc.*, and Lucy McDiarmid, *Saving Civilization etc.* in *Canadian Journal of Irish Studies*, 11: 2 (Dec. 1984) 87–8.

Farag, Fahmy, "Forcing Reading and Writing on Those who want Neither: W. B. Yeats and the Irish Oral Tradition", *Canadian Journal of Irish Studies*, 12:2 (Dec. 1985) 7–15.

Fielder, Mari Kathleen, Review of Karen Dorn, *Players and Painted Stage etc.*, Robert Hogan and Richard Burnham. *The Art of the Amateur etc.*, *Theatre Journal*, 37: 3 (Oct. 1985) 394–5.

Finkelstein, Norman M., "Jack Spicer's Ghosts and the Gnosis of History", *Boundary* 2 9:2 (winter 1981) 47–56.

Finneran, Richard J. (ed.), *Critical Essays on W. B. Yeats* (Boston: G. K. Hall & Co., 1986). Contains: Editor's 8 pp. introduction; self-selected reprints of the following pieces: Hazard Adams, "Some Yeatsian Versions of Comedy" (1965); George Bornstein "Yeats and the Greater Romantic Lyric" (1977); David R. Clark, "*Deirdre*: the Rigour of Logic" (1965); Richard Ellmann; "Ez and Old Billyum" (1967); Edward Engelberg, "'He too was in Arcadia': Yeats and the Paradox of the Fortunate Fall' (1965); George Mills Harper, "'Intellectual Hatred' and 'Intellectual Nationalism'; the Paradox of Passionate Politics" (1971); Daniel A. Harris, "Tragic War" (1974); James Olney, "Sex and the Dead: *Daimones* of Yeats and Jung" (1981); Thomas Parkinson, "The Passionate Syntax" (1964); M. L. Rosenthal and Sally M. Gall, "The Evolution of William Butler Yeats's Sequences II (1929–38)" (1983); Jon Stallworthy, "The Dynastic Theme" (1969); Donald T. Torchiana, "'Among School Children' and the Education of the Irish Spirit" (1965); Thomas R. Whitaker, On "Meditations in Time of Civil War" (1964).

Finneran, Richard J., "W. B. Yeats: A

Commentary on the *New Commentary*". Review of A. Norman Jeffares, *A New Commentary etc.*, in *Review*, 7 (1985) 163–89.

Finneran, Richard J., *Yeats: an Annual of Critical and Textual Studies, Volume IV, 1986* (Ann Arbor: UMI Research Press, 1986). Contains in addition to items cited elsewhere under author: "Dissertation Abstracts, 1985" compiled by Deborah Martin Gonzales; *"Passim:* Brief Notices" by Mary FitzGerald and reviews of Carlos Baker, *The Echoing Green* by Hugh Witemeyer; Birgit Bramsbäck *Folklore and W. B. Yeats*, by Mary Helen Thuente; Carol T. Christ, *Victorian and Modern Poetics* by Daniel A. Harris; Graham Hough, *The Mystery Religion of W. B. Yeats*; Ian Jack, *The Poet and His Audience* by Andrew Carpenter; Bettina L. Knapp, *A Jungian Approach to Literature* by Barbara J. Frieling; Okifumi Komesu, *The Double Perspective of Yeats's Aesthetic* by Hazard Adams; D. E. S. Maxwell, *A Critical History of Modern Irish Drama* by James F. Kilroy; Michael North, *The Final Sculpture: Public Monuments and Modern Poets* by Terence Diggory; Edward O'Shea, *A Descriptive Catalog of W. B. Yeats's Library* by George Bornstein.

Finneran, Richard J., "Yeats's Politics", *Review*, 5 (1983) 59–68. Review of Bernard Krimm, *W. B. Yeats and the Emergence of the Irish Free State etc.*; Grattan Freyer, *W. B. Yeats and the Anti-Democratic Tradition*. E. Cullingford, *Yeats, Ireland and Fascism*.

Finney, Brian, "W. B. Yeats: Reveries over Childhood and Youth" in *The Inner I: British Literary Autobiography of the Twentieth Century* (New York: Oxford University Press, 1985) pp. 150–7.

Fite, David, "Yeats and the Spectre of Modernism" in *Harold Bloom: the Rhetoric of Romantic Vision* (Amherst: University of Massachusetts Press, 1985) pp. 35–54.

Fitzgerald, David, "Off Centre" Review of Grattan Freyer, *W. B. Yeats and the Anti-Democratic Tradition Irish Press*, 25 Feb. 1982, 6.

Fitzgerald, Jennifer, Review of Tom Paulin, *Ireland and the English Crisis, ILS* 4:1 (spring 1985).

Fitzmaurice, Gabriel, "A Student's View" (of the Yeats Summer School) *ILS* 5:1 (spring 1986) 13.

Flannery, James W., Review of Saddlemyer (ed.), *Theatre Business, Theatre Survey* 24: 1–2 (May–Nov. 1983) 141–5.

Fleming, Deborah Diane, "The Irish Peasant in the Work of W. B. Yeats and J. M. Synge" Ph.D. 1985, The Ohio State University. Order No. AAD86–02994. *DAI* 46: 12 3724–A.

Foley, Brian, "Yeats's 'King Goll': Sources, Revision, and Revisions" *YAACTS*, 4, 17–32.

Foreman, Lewis, *Bax: a Composer and his Times* (London: Scolar Press, 1983).

Foster, John Wilson, "Apocalypse then and now". Review of W. I. Thompson *The Imagination of an Insurrection, Canadian Journal of Irish Studies*, 9:2 (Dec. 1983) 87–91.

Foster, John Wilson, "Yeats and the Easter Rising", *Canadian Journal of Irish Studies*, 11:1 (June 1984) 21–34.

Foster, Roy, "Companionabilities". Review of JBY *Letters to his Son etc.*, *TLS*, 1 July 1983, 691.

Frayne, John P., Review of David R. Clark, *Yeats at Songs and Choruses JEGP* 84:2 (Apr. 1985) 284–6.

Frazier, Adrian, "John Montague's Language of the Tribe", *Canadian Journal of Irish Studies*, 9:2 (Dec. 1983) 57–75.

French, William, "For 'Gentle Graceful Dorothy', a Tardy Obit", *Paideuma*, 12:1 (spring 1983) 89–112.

Frye, Northrop, "In the earth, or in the air?". Review of Paul De Man, *The Rhetoric of Romanticism, TLS* 17 Jan. 1986, 51–2.

Gallagher, Philip, "Teaching and Publishing: the Yolk, the White, the One Shell", *Massachusetts Studies in English*, 9:2 (1983) 13–23.

Gardner, Joann, "The Rhymers' Club Reviews and Yeats's Myth of Failure", *YAACTS* 4, 33–54.

Garratt, Robert F., *Modern Irish Poetry: Tradition and Continuity from Yeats to Heaney* (Berkeley, Los Angeles & London: University of California Press, 1986).

Garver, Joseph C., "Die Macht der Phantasie: Die 'heredity of influence' als literarisches Thema" *Saeculum*, 33:3–4 (1982) 287–311.

Genet, Jacqueline, "W. B. Yeats: La

Poetique du visible et de l'invisible" in Sylvere Monod, *De William Shakespeare à William Golding: melanges dèdies à la memoire de Jean-Paul Vernier* (Rouen: Universitaire de Rouen, 1984).

Geniusiene, I., "The Key Symbols of Yeats's Poetry", *Transactions of the Tartu University* (Tartu), (1984) 44–51. (*tt*).

Giannotti, Thomas John, "A Language of Silence: Writing the Self in Yeats and Synge, Joyce and Beckett" Ph.D. 1985, The University of California at Riverside. Order No. AAD–04129. *DAI* 46:12, 3725–A.

Gilbert, R. A., *The Golden Dawn Companion A Guide to the History, Structure, and Workings of the Hermetic Order of the Golden Dawn* (Wellingborough: Aquarian Press, 1986).

——, "Magical Manuscripts: an Introduction to the Archives of the Hermetic Order of the Golden Dawn" *YA* 5 (1987) 163–77.

Gilham, D. G., Review of Vinod Sena, *W. B. Yeats: the Poet as Critic, UCT Studies in English*, 13 (Nov. 1983) 72–4.

Glyn, Andy, "Literary Giants Crowded her Girlhood Life" *Camden New Journal*, 21 Aug. 1986, 10 (Moira Gaster's memories of WBY at the home of her father, Robert Lynd).

[Goethe Institute, Dublin], *German Studies in Anglo-Irish Literature 1972–1982*, An exhibition. With checklist by Heinz Kosok. (Dublin: Goethe Institute, 1983.)

Goggin, Edward William, "Blest: Cohesion and Ironic Deflation in Six Short Poem Sequences of W. B. Yeats" Ph.D., Fordham University, 1985. Order No. DA 8612857, *DAI* 47: 03 (Sept. 1986) 910–A.

Goldring, Maurice, *Faith of our Fathers: the Formation of Irish Nationalist Ideology, 1890–1920*, translated by Frances de Burgh-Whyte (Dublin: Repsol, 1982).

Good, Maeve, "W. B. Yeats and the Creation of a Tragic Universe", Ph.D. TCD, 1984. *DAI* 46 (spring 1985) Series C, 4126 C.

——, *W. B. Yeats and the Creation of a Tragic Universe* (London: Macmillan, 1987).

Goodman, Ann, "Phonological Aspects of Metaphor in Anglo-American Poetry" *Sigma*, 6 (1981) 109–21.

Gould Warwick, "The 'myth [in] . . . reply to a myth' – Yeats, Balzac, and Joachim of Fiore", *YA* 5 (1987) 238–51.

——, "A Recent Yeats Bibliography, 1984–85", *YA* 5 (1987) 320–40.

——, "'What is the explanation of it all?': Yeats's 'little poem about nothing'", *YA* 5 (1987) 212–13.

Gould, Warwick (ed.), *Yeats Annual No 4*, reviewed in *The Boston Irish News*, May 1986, 11.

——, *Yeats Annual No 5* (London: The Macmillan Press; Atlantic Highlands: Humanities Press, 1987). As well as articles cited separately under author, this number contains: Reviews of Mary Lou Kohfeldt's *Lady Gregory etc* by James Pethica; Joseph Adams's *Yeats and the Masks of Syntax* by Kathleen Wales; Seamus Deane's *Celtic Revivals etc.*, and Mary C. King's *The Drama of J. M. Synge* by Declan Kiberd; Tom Paulin's *Ireland and the English Crisis* and Lucy McDiarmid's *Saving Civilization etc.* by Andrew Gibson; Eric Binnie's *The Theatrical Designs of Charles Ricketts* by J. G. P. Delaney; Ellic Howe's *The Alchemist of the Golden Dawn: the Letters of the Revd W. A. Ayton etc.* by Warwick Gould; "A Biographical Miscellany: Some Recent Biographies, Biographical Studies, Memoirs and Letters" (reviews of 8 titles) by Genevieve Brennan; "Publications Received".

Gramm, Christie Diane, "The Development of Prophecy in the Poetry of W. B. Yeats", Ph.D. 1985, University of Oregon. NBG85–20714. *DAI* 46: 07, 1948–A.

Grennan, Eamon, "Leaving Cert Poetry: Yeats", *Irish Times* (10 Dec. 1984) 14.

Grigson, Geoffrey, *The Faber Book of Reflective Verse* (London: Faber & Faber, 1984). Reprints 3 poems.

Grubb, H. T. Hunt, "Yeats as an Occultist", *The Occult Review*, LXVII:4 (Oct. 1940) 191–5.

Gubernatis, Raphaël de, "Irish Saké", *Nouvel observateur*, 11–17 Nov. 1983, 11. Reviews *Au puits de l'épervier*, directed by Hideyuki Yano.

Gurney, Ivor, *War Letters*, ed. R. K. R. Thornton (Manchester: Mid-Northumberland Arts Group/Carcanet New Press, 1983) refs.

Gutierrez, Donald, "Yeats and the Noh

Theatre" in *The Maze in the Mind of the World: Labyrinths in Modern Literature* (Troy, N.Y.: Whitston Publishing Co., 1985) pp. 38–54.

Hagemann, E. R., "Incoming Correspondence to Dorothy and Ezra Pound at the Lilly Library", *Paideuma*, 12:1 (spring 1983) 131–56.

Hamilton, David, *The Monkey Gland Affair* (London: Chatto & Windus, 1986), The Steinach operation and WBY, pp. 137, 150.

Harkness, Marguerite, *The Aesthetics of Dedalus and Bloom* (Lewisburg: Bucknell University Press; London and Toronto: Associated University Press, 1984). Yeats cited *passim*.

Harper, George Mills, *The Making of Yeats's 'A Vision': a Study of the Automatic Script*, 2 vols (London: Macmillan 1987).

—— and Sprayberry, Sandra L., "Notes on 'Another Song of a Fool' and 'Towards Break of Day'", *YAACTS* 4, 69–86.

Harris, John Robert, "A Critical Prologue to the Epic Genre: Homer, Vergil, and the Ulster Cycle", Ph.D. 1984, The University of Texas at Austin, NBG 84–21717, *DAI* 45: 07, 2092–A.

Hartman, Charles, "At the Border", *Ohio Review*, 28, 1982, 81–92. Includes note on "The Old Men Admiring Themselves . . .".

Hartman, Charles O., "Verse and Voice", *Ironwood*, 12:2 (autumn 1984) 25–33.

Hartnoll, Phyllis (ed.), *The Oxford Companion to the Theatre* (Oxford University Press, 1983) *passim*.

Hasan, Massodul, "Yeats's Theory of Drama", *Indian Journal of English Studies*, 24 (1984) 43–52.

Hasegawa, Toshimitsu, "The Structure of *The Only Jealousy of Emer*", *Review of English Literature* (Kyoto University) 50, Mar. 1985, (J).

Hassett, Joseph M., "Yeats and the Chief Consolation of Genius" *YAACTS* 4, 55–68.

Hassett, Joseph M., *Yeats and the Poetics of Hate* (Dublin: Gill & Macmillan; New York: St. Martin's Press, 1986). Reviewed in *ILS*, 5:2 (autumn 1986) 24–5, by Sean Dunne, "A Healthy Hate".

Heaney, Seamus (intro.), *Poems in their Place* (BBC: 1981) Video cassette re Coole Park and Thoor Ballylee, photographed by Russ Walker, produced by John Ormond.

Heaney, Seamus and Hughes, Ted (eds), *The Rattle Bag: an Anthology of Poetry* (London: Faber & Faber, 1982) 11 poems, selections, and lyrics (from plays by WBY).

Hepburn, James, "Leda and the Dumbledore" in *Critic into Anti-Critic* (Columbia: S.C.: Camden House, 1984) pp. 115–24.

Hirata, Yasushi, "The Modernity of *The Dreaming of the Bones*", *Bulletin of Tachibana Women's University*, 12, Dec. 1985, (J).

Hugo, Leon, Review of A. E. Dyson, *Yeats, Eliot and R. S. Thomas etc.*, *UNISA English Studies*, 21:2 (Sept. 1983) 55–6.

Hyde, H. Montgomery, "Yeats and Gogarty" (Memories) *YA* 5 (1987) 154–60.

Hyde Lees, George, "Horoscopes Wanted", *The Occult Review*, XXIV:1, July 1916, 51–2. Letter addressed from 16 Montpelier Sq., S.W.

Imlah, Mick, "Unprepared to be Shot", *TLS*, 15 July 1983, 753. Reviews *Cathleen ni Houlihan* at the Lyric Studio, Hammersmith.

Jack, Ian, *The Poet and his Audience* (Cambridge University Press, 1984). "Yeats: Always an Irish Writer", 144–68.

Jackson, Thomas H., "Herder, Pound, and the Concept of Expression" *MLQ* 44:4 (Dec. 1984) 374–93.

Jacobs, Margaret Elizabeth Guernsey, "Swordsman, Saint or Prophet . . . 'Is That, perhaps, the Sole Theme?' Yeats's Shaping of Autobiography into Prophecy through Creation of a Personal Myth", Ph.D. Emory University, 1985. Order No. DA 8516570, *DAI*, 46:06 (Dec. 1985) 1634–A.

Jaffe, Grace M., "Vignettes" (Memories of George Yeats), *YA* 5 (1987) 139–53.

James, Clive, *Unreliable Memoirs* (London: Jonathan Cape, 1980). Ch. 15, Yeats v. Pound.

Jay, Gregory S., *T. S. Eliot and the Poetics of Literary History* (Baton Rouge: Louisiana State University Press, 1983) WBY in "Little Gidding", 235–41.

Jeffares, A. Norman, *Parameters of Irish Literature in English*: A lecture given at the Princess Grace Irish Library on Friday 25

April at 8.00 pm. The Princess Grace Irish Library Lectures: 1 (Gerrards Cross: Colin Smythe, 1986).

Jeffares, A. Norman, "Yeats" in Simon Trussler (ed.), *20th Century Drama* (London: Macmillan, 1983) and in Stan Smith (ed.), *20th Century Poetry* (London: Macmillan, 1983).

Jochum, K. P. S., "A Yeats Bibliography for 1983", *YAACTS* III, 1985, 175–205.

Jochum, K. P. S., "A Yeats Bibliography for 1984", *YAACTS* IV, 143–76.

John, Brian, Review of Saddlemyer (ed.), *Theatre Business, University of Toronto Quarterly*, 52:4 (summer 1983) 434–5.

Johnson, Anthony L., "A Glance at Yeats, Eliot and Pound" in *A Vitalist Seminar: Studies in the Poetry of Peter Russell, Anthony L. Johnson and William Oxley* (Salzburg: Inst. für Anglistik und Amerikanistik, University of Salzburg, 1984).

Johnson, Wendy Stacy, "Sons and Fathers: Yeats, Joyce, and Faulkner" in *Sons and Fathers: the Generation Link in Literature 1780–1980* (New York: Peter Lang, 1985) pp. 153–202.

Jordan, Carmel Patricia, "A Terrible Beauty: the Mask of Cuchulain in 'Easter 1916'" Ph.D. Fordham University, 1984 Order No. DA8506336, *DAI* 46: 04 (Oct. 1985) 989–A.

Kalina de Piszk, Rosa, "La paradoja como elemento unificador en El tigre luminoso de Alfonso Chase", *Kanina: Revista de Artes y Letras de la Universidad de Costa Rica* 7:2 (July–Dec. 1983) 39–42.

Kavanagh, Peter, *The Story of the Abbey Theatre* (Orono: National Poetry Foundation, 1984) rpt. of 1950 edn.

Keane, Patrick J., "Yeats's Counter-Enlightenment", *Salmagundi*, 68–9 (autumn 1985) 125–45.

Kearney, Richard (ed.), *The Irish Mind: Exploring Intellectual Traditions* (Dublin: Wolfhound Press, 1985). Contains *inter alia* "Shaw, Wilde, Synge and Yeats: Ideas, Epigrams, Blackberries and Chassis" (John Jordan) and "The Unknown Thought of W. B. Yeats" (Elizabeth Cullingford) pp. 209–25; 226–43. Reviewed in *ILS* 4:1 (spring 1985) by Michael D. Higgins: by Conor Cruise O'Brien, "The Nationalist Trend", *TLS* 1 Nov. 1985, 1230–1; in *IUR* 15:1 (spring 1985) 101 *et seq.* (i)

Kemp, Peter, "High and Low Talk", *TLS*, 1 July 1983, 699. Reviews "Makers: Joyce, Yeats, and Wilde", a BBC TV programme with Richard Ellmann and Seamus Heaney.

Kenner, Hugh, "A Possible Source in Coleridge for 'The Phases of the Moon'", *YAACTS* III, 1985, 173–4.

Khorolsky, V., "Alexander Block and William Butler Yeats – The Ways of Symbolism" in *A. Block's Poetry and Folkloristic Literary Tradition* (Omsk: 1984) pp. 118–125 (*tt*).

Khorolsky, V., "Symbolism of Alexander Block and William Butler Yeats: Some Problems of Typology of European Symbolism" in *Problems of Russian Literature* (L'vov: 1985) 45:1, 90–6 (*tt*).

Kiberd, Declan, "W. B. Yeats: Robartes's Quarrel with the Dancer" in his *Men and Feminism* (London: The Macmillan Press; New York: St. Martin's Press, 1985) pp. 103–35. Reviewed by Mary Cullen in *ILS*, 5:1 (spring 1986) 19.

Kinsella, Thomas (ed.), *The New Oxford Book of Irish Verse* (Oxford University Press, 1986). Contains poems by WBY. Reviewed in *ILS*, 5: 2 (autumn 1986) 25 by Kevin Barry, "The Kinsella Book of Irish Verse".

Kirby, Sheelah, *The Yeats Country* (Mountrath; Dolmen, 1985) rpt.

Knapp, Bettina L., *Archetype, Dance, and the Writer* (Troy: Bethel Publishing, 1983), contains "Yeats: the Archetypal *Vagina Dentata* Dances", pp. 111–27.

Knapp, Bettina L., *A Jungian Approach to Literature* (University of Southern Illinois Press, 1984). Contains "Yeats (1865–1939): '*At the Hawk's Well*': an unintegrated '*anima*' shapes a hero's destiny" (pp. 227–64).

Koebner, Thomas (ed.), *Zwischen den Weltkriegen* (Wiesbaden: Adakdemische Verlagsgesellschaft Athenaion, 1983) contains Franz Norgert Mennemeier "Das neue Drama", pp. 79–110, and Heinz Kosok, "Die britische und anglo-irische Literatur", 417–54.

Komesu, Okifumi, "*At the Hawk's Well* and *Take No Izumi* in a 'Creative circle'", *YA* 5 (1987) 103–13.

Korab, Karl, *Irland* Mit 102 Farbabbildungen nach Photographien und 20 Reproduktionen nach

Zeichnungen von Karl Korab. Gedichte von W. B. Yeats (Vienna: Brandstätter, 1982).

Kuch, Peter, "'Laying the Ghosts'? – W. B. Yeats's Lecture on Ghosts and Dreams" *YA* 5 (1987) 114–35.

Kuch, Peter, *Yeats and A. E. "the antagonism that unites dear friends"* (Gerrards Cross: Colin Smythe; Totowa, New Jersey: Barnes & Noble Books, 1986) 291 pp + 16 pp plates. Reviewed by Monk Gobbon in *Hibernia*, July/Aug. 1986 (i).

Kuch, Peter, "Yeats and the Occult", *Prudentia*, Supplementary Number, 1985: *The Concept of Spirit*, 199–218.

Laity, Cassandra, "W. B. Yeats and Florence Farr: the Influence of the 'New Woman' Actress on Yeats's Changing Images of Women", *Modern Drama*, 28:4 (Dec. 1985) 620–37.

Lang, Andrew, *The Disentanglers* (London: Longmans, Green & Co., 1902) (c. 1901). A collection of tales. In "Adventure of the Canadian Heiress", one finds Mr. Blake who like "other modern Celtic poets . . . was entirely ignorant of the melodious language of his ancestors, though it had often been stated in the literary papers that he was 'going to begin' to take lessons" (p. 334). The bard then recites from Kuno Meyer's "The Voyage of Bran".

Larkin, Philip, *Required Writing Miscellaneous Pieces 1955–82* (London: Faber & Faber, 1983). WBY mentioned e.g. pp. 29, 136–7.

Lavelle, Tom, "William Butler Yeats and the Dishes", *Gorey Detail* 6 (summer 1982) 29. Poem.

Lee, Sang-Kyong, *Nô und europäisches Theater: Eine Untersuchung der Auswirkungen des No auf Gestaltung und Inszenierung des zeitgenössischen europäischen Dramas* (Frankfurt: Lang, 1983) – see pp. 161–87.

Leaman, Warren, "Yeats: Skeptic on Stage", *Éire-Ireland*, XXI:I (spring 1986) 129–35.

Lense, Edward, "Pynchon's V" *Explicator*, 43:1 (autumn 1984) 60–1. Allusions to WBY.

Le Gallienne, Richard, *Young Lives* (Bristol: John Arrowsmith; London: Simpkin, Marshall, Hamilton, Kent & Co., 1898). Novel, into which WBY and Lionel Johnson come anonymously, the former as "a young Irish poet who, in the intervals of his raising the devil, writes very beautiful lyrics that he may well have learned from the fairies. It is his method to seem mad on magic and such things" (pp. 308–9).

Leonard, Nicholas, "Yeats Postscript on the 'Island of Sinners'". Review of JBY *Letters to his son etc.*, *Irish Independent*, 4 June 1983, 5.

Levenson, Leah, *With Wooden Sword: a Portrait of Francis Sheehy-Skeffington, Militant Pacifist* (Dublin: Gill & Macmillan, 1983).

Lewis, Roselle M., "William Butler Yeats: With his Medium Under a Spell in America's Cult Country", *Los Angeles Times*, 17 Jan. 1982, Book Review Section, 3.

Lindsay, Jack, (ed.), *Loving Mad Tom Bedlamite Verses of the XVI & VXII Centuries with five illustrations by Robert Graves. . . . Musical transcriptions by Peter Warlock* (London: Fanfrolico, 1927). Cites *A Vision* as a modern "book of moons" (p. 84).

Logan, John, "At Drumcliff Churchyard, County Sligo", *Threshold*, 34 (winter 1983/4) 54–5. Poem.

Londraville, Richard, "W. B. Yeats's Anti-Theatre and Its Analogs in Chinese Drama: The Staging of the Cuchulain Cycle", *Asian Culture Quarterly*, XI:3 (autumn 1983) 23–31. Illustrated in colour.

Longenbach, James, "The Order of the Brothers Minor: Pound and Yeats at Stone Cottage, 1913–1916" *Paideuma*, 14:2–3 (autumn–winter 1985) 395–403.

Longenbach, James Burton, "A Sense of the Past: Pound, Eliot, and Modernist Poetics of History", Ph.D. Princeton University, 1985, AAD85–14065; *DAI* 46: 05, 1277–A.

Longley, Edna, "Criticism wanted", *TLS*, 1 Nov. 1985, 1233–4 (Viewpoint article on Irish literature and criticism).

Lucy, Sean, tr. Joris Duytschaever, "Wat is typisch in de poezie van Yeats?" *De Vlaamse Gids* (Belgium), 68:3 (May–June 1984) 7–15.

Lundkvist, Artur, "Engelsk lyrik". Reviews *inter alia The Oxford Book of Modern Verse Bonniers litterära magasin*

(Sweden) 6 (May 1937) 373–5. Illustrated with a reproduction of a drawing of WBY by Betsy Graves.

Lynch, M. Kelly, "The Smiling Public Man: Joseph O'Neill and His Works", *Journal of Irish Literature*, 12:2 (May 1983) 3–72.

McCord, J., "John Butler Yeats, the Brotherhood, and William Blake" *Bulletin of Research in the Humanities*, 86: I (spring 1983) 10–32.

McCormack, W. J., *Ascendancy and Tradition in Anglo-Irish Literature* (Oxford University Press, 1985).

——, "Goldsmith, Biography and the Phenomenology of Anglo-Irish Literature", in Andrew Swarbrick, (ed.), *The Art of Oliver Goldsmith* (London: Vision; Totowa, Barnes & Noble Books, 1984).

Macdonald, Andrew Paul, "Flame under Flame" (Original composition, symphony in three movements) Mus. D. 1985, The University of Michigan. Order No. AAD85–20845 *DAI* 46:07, 1774–A.

McDowell, Colin, "The Opening of the Tinctures in Yeats's *A Vision*", *Éire-Ireland*, 20:3 (autumn 1985) 71–92.

——, "The Six Discarnate States of *A Vision* (1937)", *YAACTS* 4, 87–98.

——, "W. B. Yeats's *A Vision*: a Study of its Meaning", M.A., Monash, 1982.

—— and Materer, Timothy, "Gyre and Vortex: W. B. Yeats and Ezra Pound", *Twentieth Century Literature*, 31:4 (winter 1985). (*i*)

McDowell, Edwin, "A New Yorker's link with literary figures (Jeanne R. Foster)" *New York Times*, 133 (3 Sept. 1984) p. 15 (N), p. 12 (L).

McGowan, Moray, "Pale Mother, Pale Daughter? Some Reflections on Böll's Leni Gruyten and Katharina Blum" *German Life and Letters*, 37:3 (Apr. 1984) 218–28.

McGuinness, Nora Mahoney, "The Creative Universe of Jack B. Yeats" Ph.D., The University of California at Davis, 1984. Order No. DA8507315. *DAI* 46:02 (Aug. 1985) 421–A.

McMahan, Noreen Dee, "Tragedy as Eternal Return: Yeats's and Nietzsche's Reversal of Aristotle" Ph.D., The University of Texas at Austin, 1984.

Order No. DA.8513262. *DAI* 46: 04 (Oct. 1985) 990–A.

McVeigh, P. J., "Mirror and Mask: a Study of the major autobiographical prose of William Butler Yeats", Ph.D. 1984. TCD. *DAI* 46 (spring 1985), Series C. 4130c.

Malhotra, R. K., "W. B. Yeats: Contrast as a Structural Device in His Poetry" *Panjab University Research Bulletin*, 14:2 (Oct. 1983) 157–65.

Marcus, Phillip L., "Lawrence, Yeats, and the Resurrection of the Body", in his edited collection, *D. H. Lawrence: a Centenary Consideration* (Ithaca & London: Cornell University Press, 1985) pp. 210–36.

——, "Yeats's 'Last Poems': a Reconsideration", *YA* 5 (1987) 3–14.

Markgraf, Carl, "At the Abbey Theatre". Review of Saddlemyer [ed.], *Theatre Business*, *ELT*, 26:4 (1983) 324–6.

Martin, Stoddard, *Art, Messianism and Crime: a Study of Antinomianism in Modern Literature and Lives* (London: Macmillan, 1986).

Materer, Timothy, *The Correspondence of Ezra Pound Pound/Lewis: The Letters of Ezra Pound and Wyndham Lewis* (London: Faber & Faber, 1985) Scattered refs. Reviewed by Julian Symons in TLS, 6 Nov. 1985, 1259, "Kicking up devilment".

Matthews, James H., *Voices: a Life of Frank O'Connor* (New York: Atheneum, 1983). Refs.

Meihuizen, N. C. T., "W. B. Yeats – Poet of Regeneration", M.A., University of Natal, 1984.

Meir, Colin, "Yeats's Minstrel Voice", *Gaeliana*, 5 (1983) 81–98.

Melmoth, John, "Promoting passion". Review of Francis Stuart's *Faillandia*, *TLS*, 17 Jan. 1986, 57. WBY mentioned.

Mercier, Vivian, "Gael and Gaul: Irish–French Literary Relations, 1870–1970", *Scripsi*, 3 (*i*).

Meyer, Bill, "Yeats's Last Eyes; Yeats Jogs on the Cliff Paths", *Gorey Detail*, 7 (1983) 28. Two poems.

Miller, Liam, "The Eye of the Mind: Yeats and the Theatre of the Imagination", *Temenos*, 7, 1986, pp. 29–69, with illustrations taken from the same author's *The Noble Drama of W. B. Yeats*

(1977) and one drawing by Leonard Baskin from *A Tower of Polished Black Stones* (1971).

Miller, Susan Fisher, "Hopes and Fears for the Tower: William Morris's influence at Yeats's Ballylee", *Éire-Ireland*, XXI:2 (summer 1986) 43–57.

Moriguchi, Saburo, "Repulsion and Attraction: Yeats's Criticism on Bernard Shaw", *The Bulletin of the Faculty of Law and Literature* (Ehime University) 18 Nov. 1985. (J)

Morris, Bruce (ed.), "Arthur Symons's Letters to W. B. Yeats: 1892–1902" *YA 5* (1987) 46–61.

Morris, Bruce, "Elaborate Form: Symons, Yeats, and Mallarmé, *YAACTS* 4, 99–120.

Murray, Patrick J. (ed.), *The Deer's Cry: a Treasury of Irish Religious Verse* (Dublin: Four Courts Press, 1986). Contains poems by WBY. Reviewed by Coilin Owens in *ILS*, 5: 2 (autumn 1986) 26 ("Irish Devotional Verse").

Nash, Paul, *Outline: an Autobiography and Other Writings* with a preface by Herbert Read. (London: Faber & Faber, 1949). See pp. 84, 88 on *The Wind Among the Reeds* and Nash's meeting with Yeats to discuss illustrating it.

Nichols, Brooks Ashton, "The Poetics of Epiphany: Nineteenth Century Origins of the Modern Literary 'Moment'" Ph.D. 1984, The University of Virginia, NBG85–15502, *DAI*, 46: 07, 1051–A.

Nims, John Frederick, "Yeats and the Careless Muse" in his *Local Habitations: Essays on Poetry* (Ann Arbor: University of Michigan Press, 1985) pp. 176–88.

North, Michael, *The Final Sculpture: Public Monuments and Modern Poetry* (Ithaca and London: Cornell University Press, 1985). "W. B. Yeats", pp. 41–99.

Nye, Robert, "The Fruits of Ancestor Worship". Review of *JBY Letters to his son etc.*, *Scotsman*, 4 June 1983, *Weekend Scotsman*, 5.

Oakes, Randy W., "W. B. Yeats and Walker Percy's *The Second Coming*" *Notes on Contemporary Literature*, 14: 1 (Jan. 1984) 9–10.

Oates, Joyce Carol, *The Profane Art: Essays and Reviews* (New York; Dutton, 1983) contains "At least I have made a Woman of Her': Images of Women in Yeats,

Lawrence, Faulkner", 35–62, reprinted from *Georgia Review*, 37:1 (spring 1983) 7–30.

"O'Brien, Desmond", [i.e. Richard Ashe King]. Review of *The Secret Rose* in 'Letter on Books', *Truth* (15 Apr. 1897) 945.

Ó Broin, León, *Protestant Nationalists in Revolutionary Ireland: the Stopford Connection* (Dublin: Gill and Macmillan; Totowa: Barnes & Noble Books, 1985).

O'Connell, Maurice R., Review of Elizabeth Cullingford's *Yeats, Ireland, and Fascism*, in *Clio*, 13:3 (spring 1984) 303–5.

O'Donnell, William H., *The Poetry of William Butler Yeats: an Introduction* (New York: Ungar, 1986) 186 pp.

Ohno, Mitsuko, "Yeats and Feminism: on 'Michael Robartes and the Dancer'" *Evergreen* (Aichi Shukutoku University) 7 Mar. 1985. (J)

Christopher Okigbo, *Collected Poems*, with a preface by Paul Theroux and an Introduction by Adewale Maja-Pearce (London: Heinemann, 1986). Contains "Lament of the Masks" (For W. B. Yeats) pp. 79–82.

Old, W. R., Review of the Ellis & Yeats edition of Blake's *Works*, *The Theosophist* (1893) 697–9.

Omidsalar, Mahmound, "W. B. Yeats's 'Cuchulain's Fight with the Sea'" in *American Imago*, 42:3 (autumn 1985) 315–33.

O'Neill, Charles, Review of *Yeats Annual No 3*, *ILS* 5:2 (autumn 1986) 23.

Opitz, Michael J., "Poetry as Appropriate Epistology: Gregory Bateson and W. B. Yeats", Ph.D. 1985, The University of Minnesota, NBG85–28829, *DAI*, 46:10, 3042–A.

Orr, Leonard, "Yeats's Theories of Fiction", *Éire-Ireland*, XXI:2 (summer 1986) 152–8.

O'Shea, Edward, "'An Old Bullet Imbedded in the Flesh': the Migration of Yeats's 'Three Songs to the Same Tune'", *YAACTS* 4, 121–42.

Oura, Yukio, "Regarding the Yeats Society of Japan", *YA 5* (1987) 252–3.

Oura, Yukio, "Women around Yeats (6)", *Shujitu English Studies* (Shujitu Women's University), Mar. 1985 (J).

Pack, Robert, "Yeats as Spectator to Death" in *Affirming Limits Essays on Mortality, Choice, and Poetic Form*

(Amherst: University of Massachusetts Press, 1985) pp. 151–73; also in *Denver Quarterly*, 19:4 (spring 1985) 93–110.

Page, Tim, "Music: Antheil and Yeats", *New York Times*, 12 July 1983, C11. Review of a production of *Fighting the Waves* by the Castle Hill Theater Co.

Parkinson, Thomas, "Yeats and the Limits of Modernity", *YAACTS* III, 1985, 60–71.

Pasles, Chris. Review of *Letters to His Son W. B. Yeats and Others, Los Angeles Times* 103, 15 July 1984, Section B, 8.

Paulin, Tom, "The Case for Geoffrey Hill", (Review of Peter Robinson (ed.), *Geoffrey Hill: Essays on his Work, LRB*, 4 Apr. 1985, 13–14. Paulin's comparison of a line of Hill's to "Soul clap its hands, and sing" led to a controversy on the source of that line. See Martin Dodsworth and also E. E. Duncan-Jones (*LRB*, 23 May, p. 4); Tom Paulin (*LRB*, 6 June, 4); Craig Raine (*LRB*, 20 June, 4); Martin Dodsworth (*LRB*, 18 July 4); Tom Paulin (*LRB*, 1 Aug. 4); Martin Dodsworth (*LRB*, 5 Sept. 4); John Lucas (*LRB*, 3 Oct., 4).

Paulin, Tom, *The Faber Book of Political Verse* (London: Faber & Faber, 1986). See also intro., pp. 19–21, 41–4. Reprints 8 poems. Reviewed by George Steiner, *TLS*, 23 May 1986, 547–8 in "Criticisms of life, voices of protest"; by John Devitt in *ILS*, 5:2 (autumn 1986) 27.

Petersen, Robert C., "Yeats the Autobiographer: a Dialogue of Self and Soul", *ELT* 26:2 (1983) 143–4.

Peterson, C. Review of James Olney, *The Rhizome and the Flower, Journal of Analytical Psychology*, 27:4 (1982) 391–2.

Phillips, C. L., "The Writing and Performance of *The Hour-Glass*", *YA* 5 (1987) 83–102.

Phillips, Peter, Review of Watkins, *Yeats & Owen, Poetry Wales*, 18:3 (1983) 56–7.

Poger, Sidney, Review of Douglas Archibald, *Yeats Éire-Ireland*, XIX:2 (summer 1984) 152–4.

Poger, Sidney, Review of Lucy McDiarmid, *Saving Civilisation etc.*, *Éire-Ireland*, 20:3 (autumn 1985) 150–2.

Poger, Sidney. Review of *YAACTS* 2, *Éire-Ireland* XX1:1 (spring 1986) 151–2.

Ponnuswamy, Krishna, "Yeats and Tagore: a Comparative Study of their

Plays", Ph.D. Madurai Kamaraj University, 1984, NBG85–18890, *DAI* 46: 07, 1933–A.

Prokosch, Frederic, *Voices: a Memoir* (London & Boston: Faber & Faber, 1983). Scattered refs.

Pruitt, Virginia D., "W. B. Yeats: Rage, Order, and the Mask" *Éire-Ireland*, XX1:2 (summer 1986) 141–5.

Putzel, Steven, *Reconstructing Yeats: 'The Secret Rose' and 'The Wind among the Reeds'* (Dublin: Gill & Macmillan; Totowa: Barnes & Noble Books, 1986). Reviewed in *ILS* 5: 2 (autumn 1986) 23, by Terence Brown ("A Book Hard to Warm To").

Quinn, Bob, *Atlantean: Ireland's North African and Maritime Heritage* (London & New York: Quartet Books, 1986). On *Deirdre* and exotic references to Arab culture, 35–7.

Radcliffe, Evan, "Yeats and the Quest for Unity: 'Among School Children' and 'Unity of Being'", *Colby Library Quarterly*, 21:3, Sept. 1985) 109–21.

Rader, Ralph W., "Notes on some structural varieties and variations in dramatic 'I' poems and their theoretical implications", *Victorian Poetry*, 22:2 (summer 1984) 103–20.

Raine, Kathleen, *Yeats the Initiate: Essays on certain themes in the writings of W. B. Yeats* (Mountrath: The Dolmen Press; London: Allen & Unwin Limited, 1986). Contains reprinted, updated and new essays as follows: "Hades wrapped in Cloud" (1976); "Fairy and Folk Tales of Ireland, an Introduction to Yeats's Selection" (1973); "Ben Bulben Sets the Scene" (published in French, 1981); "AE" (1975); "Yeats's debt to Blake" (revised from 1966 version); "From Blake to *A Vision*" (1979); "Yeats, The Tarot and the Golden Dawn" (1972); "Death-in-Life and Life-in-Death" (1974); "Blake, Yeats and Pythagoras" (1982); "Yeats and Kabir" (1984); "Purgatory" (1986); "Yeats and the Creed of Saint Patrick" (1986); "Giraldus" (1986); "Yeats's Singing School: A personal acknowledgment" (1980). Profusely illustrated.

Rajan, Balachandra, "Its own Executioner: Yeats and the Fragment" *YAACTS* III (1985) 72–87.

Ramratnam, Malati, *W. B. Yeats and the*

Craft of Verse (Lanham: University Press of America, 1985).

Remnick, David, "Playhouse of the Western World. Revivals and Classics in the Dublin Theater" *Washington Post*, 107, 12 Aug. 1984, p. H 1.

Reeves, Marjorie, and Gould, Warwick, *Joachim of Fiore and the Myth of the Eternal Evangel in the Nineteenth Century* (Oxford: Clarendon Press, 1987). See Ch. IX "W. B. Yeats: A Noble Antinomianism", pp. 202–78 and *passim*.

Reising, Russell J., "Yeats, the Rhymers' Club, and Pound's Hugh Selwyn Mauberley", *Journal of Modern Literature*, 12:1 (Mar. 1985) 179–82.

Ricks, Christopher, *The Force of Poetry* (Oxford: Clarendon Press, 1984). Scattered Refs.

Ricks, Christopher, "Speaking Well", *London Review of Books*, 18–31 Aug. 1983, 3, 5–6.

Roberts, Marie, *British Poets and Secret Societies* (London & Sydney: Croom Helm, 1986).

Robertson, Jillian, "Yeats mystery unearthed" *The Times*, 19 Aug. 1986, 8. "Where is the great Irish poet buried?"

Robertson, P. J. M., "Criticism and Creativity IV: Blake and Yeats" *Queen's Quarterly*, 91:4 (winter 1984) 941–53.

Rodway, Allan, Review of Cairns Craig, *Yeats, Eliot, Pound etc.*, *Notes & Queries* 228/30:6 (Dec. 1983) 558–9.

Rogers, William Elford, *The Three Genres and the Interpretation of Lyric* (Princeton University Press, 1983), see pp. 86–94; 107–9.

Rolleston, T. W. *Myths and Legends of the Celtic Race* (1911) reprinted, (London: Constable, 1985): noticed *TLS*, 1 Nov. 1985, 1240.

Ronsley, Joseph, Review of Terence Diggory, *Yeats and American Poetry*, *Queen's Quarterly* 92:1 (spring 1985) 173–5.

Rosenfeld, Ray, "Yeats Plays at Lyric, Belfast" *Irish Times*, 1 July 1983, 10. On McCready's production of *Purgatory*, *Calvary*, and *The Resurrection*.

Rückert, Ingrid, *The Touch of Sympathy: Philip Larkin and Thom Gunn Zwei Beiträge zur englischen Gegenwartsdichtung* (Heidelberg: winter 1982) Anglistische Forschungen 162). Refs.

Ryan, R., Review of Michael Steinman,

Yeats's Heroic Figures etc., *UNISA English Studies*, 22:2 (1984) 51–2.

Ryapolova, Vera, "W. B. Yeats and Irish Artistic Culture, 1890–1930" (Moscow: 1985) (*i*, *tt*).

Sacks, Peter, *The English Elegy Studies in the Genre from Spenser to Yeats* (Baltimore: Johns Hopkins University Press, 1985). See also "Phi Beta Kappa Award (to three authors for outstanding books published in the United States)" *New York Times*, 135, 7 Dec. 1985, p. 12 (N), p. 17 (L).

Salinger, Helmut, *William Butler Yeats: Seine Gedichte und Gedanken* (Bern: Francke, 1983).

Sano, Tetsuro, "An Elegy for Parnell: Yeats and 1848", *Review of English Literature* (Kyoto University) 50, Mar. 1985. (J)

Sargeant-Quittanson, Regine, "Arthur Symons et les mouvements décadents des années 1890", Doctorat, Rheims, 1981.

Schirmer, Gregory Alan, *The Poetry of Austin Clarke* (University of Notre Dame Press; Mountrath: Dolmen, 1983); refs.

Schirmer, Walter Franz, *Geschichte der englischen und amerikanischen Literatur: Von den Anfangen bis zur Gegenwart*, ed. Arno Esch, (Tübingen: Niemeyer, 1983) 2 v. contains (by Esch) "W. B. Yeats und die keltische Renaissance", 2, 855–59; "Das Irische Drama", 2: 907–14.

Schneider, Joseph L., "Yeats and the Common Man", *Studies: an Irish Quarterly Review* 73:289 (spring 1984) 37–46.

Schuchard, Ronald, "Yeats, Arnold, and the Morbidity of Modernism" *YAACTS* III, 1985, 88–106.

Schultz, Robert, "A Detailed Chronology of Ezra Pound's London Years 1908–1920" *Paideuma*, 11:3 (winter 1982) 456–72; 12:2–3 (autumn–winter 1983) 357–73.

Sekine, Masaru, *The Irish Writer and the Theatre* (Gerrards Cross: Colin Smythe; Totowa: Barnes & Noble Books, 1986). Contains: Masaru Sekine's "Yeats and the Noh", 151–66; Sumiku Sugiyama, "What is *The Player Queen* all about?"; Robert Welch, "The Emergence of modern Anglo-Irish Drama", 208–17; Katharine Worth, "Scenic Imagery in the Plays of Yeats and Beckett", 218–32;

Richard Allen Cave, "Dramatising the Life of Swift", 17–32. Indexed, Yeats, *passim*.

——, *Ze-Ami and His Theories of Noh Drama* (Gerrards Cross: Colin Smythe, 1985). Reviewed by Peter van de Kamp in *ILS* 5:1 (spring 1986) 16 ("Yeats's Noh-Noh Drama").

Shimazu, Akira, "Haughtiness and Solitude in W. B. Yeats", *The Bulletin of the Faculty of Commerce* (Meiji University) 67:2–7, Feb. 1985. (J)

——, *W. B. Yeats and Occultism* (Tokyo, 1985). (J)

Sidnell, Michael J., "'Tara Uprooted': Yeats's *In the Seven Woods* in Relation to Modernism", *YAACTS* III, 1985, 107–20.

Siegmund-Schultze, Dorothea (ed.), *Irland: Gesellschaft und Kultur III* (Halle: Martin-Luther-Universität Halle-Wittenberg, 1982). (Wissenschaftliche Beiträge, 1982/8 [F35].) Containing D. Siegmund-Schultze: "St. Patrick of Ireland – an Inquiry into a National Symbol", 19–31; Alla Saruchanian: "The Irish Literary Revival – Some Aspects", 115–24; Maurice Goldring: "Intellectual Response to the Dublin Lockout and Strike, 1913–1914", 164–78; Wolfgang Wicht: "Yeats and Joyce: Some General Remarks", 204–12.

Silver, Jeremy (ed.), "George Barnes's 'W. B. Yeats and Broadcasting', 1940", *YA* 5 (1987) 189–94.

Silver Jeremy, "W. B. Yeats and the BBC: a Reassessment" *YA* 5 (1987) 181–5.

——, "Yeats Material in the Radio Telefís Eireann Archives", *YA* 5 (1987) 186–8.

Simmons, James, *Sean O'Casey* (London: Macmillan, 1983).

Smith, Stan, "Porphyry's Cup: Yeats, Forgetfulness and the Narrative Order" *YA* 5 (1987) 15–45.

Sotheby's Sale of English Literature and History: Printed Books and Manuscripts, 10/11 July 1986. "Yeats items", lots 243–276, including MS of "The Lake Isle of Innisfree"; Proofs of *"The King's Threshold"*; numerous letters; inscribed copies, rare first editions, volumes from the library of Frederic Prokosch; annotated copies etc., from the library of the late James F. Gallagher (1912–79).

Spivak, Gayatri Chakravorty, "Finding

Feminine Readings: Dante – Yeats" in Ira Konigsberg (ed.), *American Criticism in the Poststructuralist Age* (Ann Abor: University of Michigan, 1981) 42–65.

Stanford, Donald E., *British Poets 1880–1914* (Detroit: Gale, 1983) (Dictionary of Literary Biography, 19). Contains B. L. Reid, "William Butler Yeats", 399–452.

Stapleton, Michael, *The Cambridge Guide to English Literature* (Cambridge University Press, 1983).

Stead, C. K., *Pound, Yeats, Eliot and the Modernist Movement* (London: The Macmillan Press; New Brunswick, N.J.: Rutgers University Press, 1986).

Stephens, James, *The Charwoman's Daughter* (London: Macmillan, 1912). Contains a portrait of WBY, pp. 34–5. (See above p. 175.)

——, *Uncollected Prose of James Stephens*, ed. Patricia A. McFate (London: Macmillan, 1983, 2 vols). Contains refs and "W. B. Yeats: a Tribute" 2:248–50.

Stonyk, Margaret, *Nineteenth Century English Literature* (London: Macmillan, 1983) refs.

Sugiyama, Sumiko, *Yeats: Fatherland and Song* (Kyoto, 1985). (J)

Suzuki, Hiroshi, "The Raging Wind in *The Wind Among the Reeds*", *Journal of Liberal Arts* (Waseda University) 77, Jan. 1985. (J)

Sutton, David C., "Location Register of Twentieth-Century English Literary Manuscripts and Letters: a Cumulative Yeats Listing (to autumn 1985)", *YA* 5 (1987) 289–319.

[Symons, Arthur], Review of *Ideas of Good and Evil* (1903) *The Athenaeum*: 3948, 27 June (1903) 807–8.

Tate, Allen, *The Poetry Reviews of Allen Tate 1924–44*, ed. Ashley Brown and Frances Neel Cheney (Baton Rouge: Louisiana State University Press, 1983). See "Yeats's Last Friendship", 195–6.

Taylor, Richard, "Die mystisch-okkulte Renaissance: Rituelle Magie und symbolistische Dichtung" in Manfred Pfister and Bernd Schulte-Middelich (eds), *Die'Nineties: Das englische Fin de siècle zwischen Dekadenz und Socialkritik* (Munich: Francke, 1983) 100–14.

Thallinger, Renate, "William Butler Yeats's 'Crossways' and 'The Rose'" in Haslauer, Wilfried, *A Salzburg*

Miscellany: English and American Studies 1964–1984 (Salzburg: Inst. für Anglistik und Amerikanistik, 1984).

Thiesmeyer, Lynn, "Meditations Against Chaos: Yeats's War of Irish Independence", *Perspectives on Contemporary Literature*, 10 (1984) 23–32.

Thornbury, Charles, "John Berryman and the 'Majestic Shade' of W. B. Yeats", *YAACTS* III (1985) 121–72.

Tierce, Michael Thomas, "Eggs, Small Beer, and Hardy: The Poetry and Prose of Philip Larkin", Ph.D. 1985, The University of Tennessee. Order no. AAD85–11406. *DAI* 46:03 700–A.

Tippett, Brian, Review of Grattan Freyer, *W. B. Yeats and the Anti-Democratic Tradition* and Elizabeth Cullingford, *Yeats Ireland and Fascism, Literature and History*, 9:1 (spring 1983) 127–8.

Tishunina, N. V., "Zhanrovoe svoeobrazie 'teatra masok' U. B. Ìetsa" in *Problemy zhanra literatur stran Zapannoi Evropy i SZhA* (XIX-pervaîa polovina XX vv) Mezhvuzovskii sbornik nauchnykh trudov (Leningrad: Leningradskiĭ ordena Trudovogo Krasnogo Znameni gosudarstvennyĭ pedagogicheskiĭ institut imeni A. I. Gertsena 1983) 39–56.

Tolley, A. T., "Philip Larkin's Unpublished Book: in the Grip of Light", *Agenda*, 22:2 (summer 1984) 76–87. Comparisons with WBY.

Toomey, Deirdre, (ed.), "Bards of the Gael and Gall: an Uncollected Review by Yeats in *The Illustrated London News*", *YA* 5 (1987) 203–11.

Torchiana, Donald T., *Backgrounds for Joyce's Dubliners* (Boston, London, Sydney: Allen & Unwin, 1986). Y mentioned *passim*.

Totten, Charles F., Review of *Yeats, Sligo and Ireland*, *Éire-Ireland*, XIX:1 (spring 1984) 153–6.

Tracy, Robert, "Energy, Ecstasy, Elegy: Yeats and the Death of Robert Gregory", *Éire-Ireland*, XIX:1 (spring 1984) 26–47.

Usandizaga, Aranzazu, *Teatro y politica: el movimiento dramatico irlandes* (Bellaterra: Universidad autonoma de Barcelona, 1985).

Vajda, Miklos, *Klasszikus angol koltök* (Budapest: Európa Könykiadó, 1986) 2 vols. This Hungarian selection of

"Classical English Poets contains translations of 24 poems by WBY, by László Kardos, Géza Képes, Sándor Weöres, Gábor Garai, Ágnes Gergely, László Kálnoky, Gyula Tellér, Gyözö Ferencz, Zsuzsa Rakovsky, Zoltán Jékely, László Benjamin, Gábor Görgey, Dezsö Tandori, Gyula Illyés, István Vas. (H)

Vickery, John B., *Myths and Texts: Strategies of Incorporation and Displacement* (Baton Rouge: Louisiana State University Press, 1983).

Wade, Allan, *Memories of the London Theatre 1900–1914*, edited by Alan Andrews (London: Society for Theatre Research, 1983) – indexed.

Wall, Richard, "A Note on Yeats and the Folk Tradition", *Canadian Journal of Irish Studies*, 11:2 (Dec. 1985) 47–8.

Wallace, Martin, *100 Irish Lives* (Newton Abbot: David & Charles; Totowa: Barnes & Noble Books, 1983), see pp. 139–40.

Walsh, Caroline, *The Homes of Irish Writers* (Dublin: Anvil Books, 1982).

Ward, Margaret, *Unmanageable Revolutionaries: Women and Irish Nationalism* (Dingle: Brandon; London: Pluto Press, 1983).

Ward, Robert E., Review of Mary Lou Kohfeldt, *Lady Gregory etc.*, *Éire-Ireland*, XX1:1 (spring 1986) 155–8.

Weaver, Jack W., "Celebrating IASAIL-Japan", a Review of Masaru Sekine's edited collection, *Irish Writers and Society at Large*, *ILS* 5:2 (autumn 1986) 13.

Weissman, Judith, "'Somewhere in Ear-Shot': Yeats's Admonitory Gods", *Western American Literature*, 19:2 (summer 1984) 16–31.

Welch, Robert (ed.), *The Way Back: George Moore's 'The Untilled Field' and 'The Lake'* (Dublin: Wolfhound, 1982) *passim*.

Woolf, Virginia, *The Diary of Virginia Woolf*, 4, 1931–1935, ed. Anne Oliver Bell (London: Hogarth, 1982). References *passim*.

West, Trevor, *Horace Plunkett, Co-Operation and Politics An Irish Biography* (Gerrards Cross: Colin Smythe; Baltimore: The Catholic University of America Press, 1986).

Wicht, Wolfgang, "William Butler Yeats und das widerspruchsvolle Gegenbild der Kunst" in *Englische und Amerikanische Lyrik des 20. Jahrhunderts im Weltliterarischen Kontext* Beiträge der Arbeitsberatung vom 28 bis 30 Apr. 1980 in Ahrenshoop zur Bestimmung von Ziel und Methode des Forschungsprojekts. (Rostok: Wilhelm-Pieck-Universität Sektion Sprach-und Literaturwissenschaft, 1981) 46–56.

Wood, A., "Yeats and Measurement: the Important of Order and Form in Art", *South Atlantic Review*, 50:4 (Nov. 1985) 65–80.

Wootton, Carol, *Selective Affinities: Comparative Essays from Goethe to Arden* (New York: Lang, 1983). "Goethe and Yeats within the Context of European Romanticism", 11–32; "The Courtly Tradition: an Aspect of the Life and Works of Goethe and W. B. Yeats", 33–59; "Goethe, Yeats and the Problem of Old Age: The Final Phase", 153–68.

Worth, Katharine, review of A. N. Jeffares (ed.), *Poems of W. B. Yeats A New Selection*, *RES* NS XXXVII: 146 (May 1986) 287–8.

Woudhuysen, H. R., "Sale of Books and MSS" *TLS*, 14 Feb. 1986, 175. On the Gilvarry sale at Christie's N.Y.

Wright, David, "Not for Publication: the Correspondence of Yeats and Joyce", *Canadian Journal of Irish Studies*, 10:1 (June 1984) 113–26.

Wright, David G., "Yeats as a Novelist", *Journal of Modern Literature*, 12:2 (July 1985) 261–76.

Yamasaki, Hiroyoki, "Yeats and Allegory", *Hiroshima Studies in English Language and Literature* (Hiroshima University) 29: Special Number, Feb. 1985. (J)

Yeats, Michael, "The Abortion Referendum", *Irish Times*, 5 May 1983, 11; Letter *re* breach of copyright in respect of "The Second Coming".

[Yeats, W. B.], Kent, Charles William, and Patton, John Shelton (eds), *The Book of the Poe Centenary: a Record of the Exercises at the University of Virginia January 16–19, 1909, in Commemoration of the One Hundredth Birthday of Edgar Allen Poe* (Charlottesville: University of Virginia, 1909). WBY contributed a letter in praise of "one who is so certainly the greatest of American poets, and always and for all lands a great lyric poet" (p. 207).

Yeats, W. B., Kelly, John, and Domville, Eric (eds), *The Collected Letters of W. B. Yeats, Vol. I: 1865–1895* (Oxford: Clarendon Press, 1986). Reviewed in: *The Guardian*, "Full of mysticism and magic" by John Montague, 30 Jan. 1986, 20; in *ILS* 5:2 (autumn, 1986), 24 by Julian Moynahan; in *The Sunday Times* by John Carey ("Every last scrawl", 9 Feb. 1986, 43); by James Fenton in *The Times* ("Irish bard head and mumbo-jumbo"), 6 Feb. 1986, 11; David Holloway in *The Daily Telegraph* ("Yeats on the way up", 7 Feb. 1986, 16); Seamus Heaney, *The Observer*, 23 Feb. 1986, 28, ("Genius on stilts"); by Richard Ellmann in *New Republic*, 194, 12 May 1986, 33; by John Gross in *New York Times*, 135, 22 Apr. 1986, p. 23 (N), p. C20 (L); by Auberon Waugh in *The Sunday Telegraph* (*ii*), 12 ("Voice from Innisfree"); by Terence de Vere White in *The Irish Times*, 1 Feb. 1986, Weekend 4, ("Yeats in his Letters"); by Roy Fuller in *The London Magazine*, Apr./May 1986, 145–8, ("Log-Rolling"); by Elspeth Cameron in *The Globe and Mail*; 13 Sept. 1986 F 23, ("Enigma in yellow"); by Denis Donoghue in *The New York Review of Books*, 14 Aug. 1986, 14–16 ("The Young Yeats"); by Tom Paulin in the *London Review of Books*, 3 Apr. 1986, 9–10 ("Dreadful Sentiments"); by Conor Cruise O'Brien in *The Listener*, 20 Mar. 1986, 24–5 ("'Was Irish national feeling not noble and enlightened by definition, then?'"); by Seamus Deane in *TLS*, 7 Mar. 1986, 235–6 ("The Poet's dream of an audience"); discussed by Denis Donoghue and Paul Vaughan on *Kaleidoscope*, BBC Radio 4, 13 & 14 Feb. 1986.

Yeats, W. B., Contributions, mostly from *The Celtic Twilight, Ideas of Good and Evil*, to *A Calendar of Philosophy edited by Florence Farr from the Works of Great Writers* (London: Frank Palmer, 1910) with page and cover designs by W. S. Lear. Yeats's contributions can be found for 16 Jan., 10, 16, 21, 22 Feb., 22 Mar., 5, 19 Apr., 15 May, 26 July, 12 Aug., 26 Oct., 15, 25 Nov., 1, 4 Dec.

——, *El Crepúscula Celta* (Spanish

translation by Tavier Marias), (Madrid: Alfaguara S.A., 1985).

——, *Geef nooit het hele hart.* Dutch translation by A. Roland Holst and Jan Eijkelboom (Vianen: Kwadraat, 1982), Poems.

——, *Ierse elfenverhalen en andere volksvertellingen uit Ierland.* Samengesteld en ingeleid door W. B. Yeats translated by Hilde Lichtendahl (Den Haag: Sirius en Siderius, 1981) Dutch translation of *Fairy and Folk Tales of Ireland,* 1973.

——, "Memorandum Prepared for the Synge Estate by W. B. Yeats" *Long Room,* 24–5 (spring–autumn, 1982) 39–40.

——, *A Poet to his Beloved: the Early Love Poems of W. B. Yeats,* intro. by Richard Eberhart (New York: St. Martin's Press, 1985).

——, *The Poems: A New Edition,* ed. Richard J. Finneran. Reviewed in *Library Journal,* 109, p. 97 (1), (Jan. 1984); by Gary MacEoin in *National Catholic Reporter,* 20 (20 July 1984), 20; by Merle Rubin in *Christian Science Monitor* 76 (19 Apr. 1984) 22.

——, *Purgatórium* Hungarian translation of Purgatory by Gábor Garai in Tamás Ungvári (selector and ed.), *XX. századi angol drámák Twentieth Century English Plays* (Budapest: Europa Könyvkiadó, 1985). (H)

——, *Purgatory Manuscript Materials including the Author's Final Text by W. B. Yeats,* edited by Sandra F. Siegel (The Cornell Yeats, Ithaca and London: Cornell University Press, 1986).

——, "Ujdhesa në ligenin Iniseri, Ardhja e dytë. Lundrimi për Bizant" Albanian translations of "The Lake Isle of Innisfree", "The Second Coming" and "Sailing to Byzantium" by Hamdi Daci, *Rilindja,* 3 Feb. 1983, 12.

——, *W. B. Yeats*: Where There is Nothing & *W. B. Yeats and Lady Gregory*: The Unicorn from the Stars (Washington: Catholic University of America Press; Gerrards Cross: Colin Smythe, 1987), ed. Katharine Worth.

Yeremina, Irina, "The Irish Poets of the 1916 Rising and W. B. Yeats" *Problems of Realism in Foreign Literature of the 19th and 20th Centuries* (Moscow; 1983) pp. 128–39. (*i, tt*)

Yoshino, Masaaki, "Yeats's Logic of Death: the Fairy Poems and the Gregory Poems", *Studies in English Literature* (The English Literary Society of Japan) Mar. 1985. (J)

ANNOUNCED FOR PUBLICATION

Alderson-Smith, Peter, *W. B. Yeats and the Tribes of Danu: Three Views of Ireland's Fairies* (Gerrards Cross: Colin Smythe; Totowa, N.J.: Barnes & Noble Books, 1987).

Clark, David R., *Visible Array: Yeats's Theatre of Dream and Reality* (Mountrath: Dolmen Press, 1987).

Fletcher, Ian, *W. B. Yeats and his Contemporaries* (New York: St. Martin's Press, 1987).

Gregory, Lady Isabella Augusta, *Lady Gregory's Journals Volume Two Books Thirty to Forty-Four,* ed. Daniel J. Murphy, with an afterword by Colin Smythe (Gerrards Cross: Colin Smythe, 1987). Includes WBY's "The Death of Lady Gregory", vol. 15 of *The Coole Edition of the Works of Lady Gregory.*

Martin, Heather Carmen, *W. B. Yeats:* *Metaphysician as Dramatist* (Waterloo, Ontario: Wilfred Laurier University Press; Gerrards Cross: Colin Smythe, 1987).

Prentki, Tim and Bushrui, Suheil, *The International Companion to the Poetry of W. B. Yeats* (Gerrards Cross: Colin Smythe, 1987).

Saddlemyer, Anne and Smythe, Colin (eds), *Lady Gregory Fifty Years After* (Gerrards Cross: Colin Smythe; Totowa: Barnes & Noble Books, 1987).

Yeats, W. B., *Prefaces and Introductions,* ed. William H. O'Donnell (London: The Macmillan Press, 1987). A volume in *The Collected Edition of the Works of W. B. Yeats.*

——, *Sailing from Avalon: W. B. Yeats's First Play, "Vivien and Time",* transcribed from the Manuscripts and edited with a Commentary by David R. Clark and

Rosalind E. Clark (Northampton, Mass.: Pennyroyal, 1987). Illustrated by Barry Moser.

——, *Yeats's Writing of "Sophocles' King Oedipus"*: The Manuscripts transcribed and edited with a Commentary by David R. Clark and James B. McGuire (Philadelphia and Gerrards Cross:

Published for the American Philosophical Society by Colin Smythe, 1987).

Zach, Wolfgang and Kosok, Heinz, *Literary Interrelations: Ireland, England, and the World* Proceedings of the Graz Conference of IASAIL, 1985 (Tübingen, 1986, 3 vols).

Publications Received

Copies of the following were kindly sent to *Yeats Annual*, but we were unable to review them in this number. We hope to do so in the next. Further details of them, including full descriptions of the contents of volumes of essays, will be found in our current bibliography. Ed.

[Anon. ed.], *Ireland's Field Day: Field Day Theatre Company* (London: Hutchinson, 1985).

Ellmann, Richard, *Samuel Beckett, Nayman of Noland* (Washington: Library of Congress, 1986).

Finneran, Richard J. (ed.), *Critical Essays on W. B. Yeats* (Boston: G. K. Hall & Co., 1986).

Jenkins, Brian, *Sir William Gregory of Coole: the biography of an Anglo-Irishman* (Gerrards Cross: Colin Smythe, 1986).

Kearney, Richard, *The Irish Mind: Exploring Intellectual Traditions* (Dublin: Wolfhound Press, 1985).

Kinsella, Thomas (ed.), *The New Oxford Book of Irish Verse* (Oxford University Press, 1986).

Kuch, Peter, *Yeats and A.E. "the antagonism that unites dear friends"* (Gerrards Cross: Colin Smythe; Totowa, N.J.: Barnes & Noble Books, 1986).

O'Donnell, William H., *The Poetry of William Butler Yeats: an Introduction* (New York: Ungar, 1986).

Perloff, Marjorie, *The Dance of the Intellect* (Cambridge University Press, 1986).

Raine, Kathleen (ed.), *Temenos: a Review devoted to the Arts of the Imagination*, no. 7, 1986.

Raine, Kathleen, *Yeats the Initiate: Essays on certain themes in the writings of W. B. Yeats* (Mountrath: Dolmen Press; London: Allen & Unwin, 1986).

West, Trevor, *Horace Plunkett, Co-Operation and Politics: an Irish Biography* (Gerrards Cross: Colin Smythe, 1986).